AMERICANS FROM AFRICA
■ ■
OLD MEMORIES, NEW MOODS

CONTRIBUTORS

Raymond and Alice Bauer
Lerone Bennett, Jr.
Robert Blauner
Stokely Carmichael
Erik H. Erikson
Eugene D. Genovese
Lewis M. Killian
Martin Luther King, Jr.
Joyce Ladner
Christopher Lasch
C. Eric Lincoln
Gary T. Marx
Tom Mboya
August Meier
Richard B. Moore
Gerald W. Mullin
George Plimpton
Alvin F. Poussaint
Elliott Rudwick
Mike Thelwell
Nat Turner
Aaron Wildavsky
Nathan Wright, Jr.
Aristide and Vera Zolberg

THE EDITOR

Peter I. Rose received his A.B. from Syracuse University and his M.A. and Ph.D. from Cornell University. At present he is Chairman of the Department of Sociology and Anthropology at Smith College, a member of the graduate faculty of the University of Massachusetts, and Visiting Professor at Yale University. He has also taught at Goucher College, Wesleyan University, the University of Colorado, and the University of Leicester in England, where he was a Fulbright Lecturer in 1964–1965.

Professor Rose has written numerous scholarly articles and reviews and has been editor of *The Research Bulletin in Intergroup Relations*. He is the author of *They and We: Racial and Ethnic Relations in the United States* (1964) and *The Subject Is Race: Traditional Ideologies and the Teaching of Race Relations* (1968) and the editor of *The Study of Society* (1967) and *The Ghetto and Beyond* (1969).

ATHERTON PRESS, INC. · New York · 1970

AMERICANS FROM AFRICA

■ ■

OLD MEMORIES, NEW MOODS

Edited by Peter I. Rose

ACKNOWLEDGMENTS

August Meier and Elliott Rudwick, Gerald W. Mullin, and Mina Davis Caulfield prepared original essays for these volumes. They have added much to the assessment of the black experience. Their contributions are gratefully acknowledged. So, of course, are those of the other authors whose work is edited and reprinted in the pages below.

My thanks are also due to many people behind the scenes, especially my friends Ely Chinoy and David Riesman, my assistant Deborah Keehn Black, and many students and faculty members at Smith, Wesleyan, Colorado, and UCLA who gave advice and counsel on various aspects of the project.

Finally, I wish to thank Charles D. Lieber, Marlene Mandel, and the Atherton staff for their many helpful suggestions and constant support in the preparation of this book of controversies.

PETER I. ROSE

ACKNOWLEDGEMENTS

CONTENTS
OLD MEMORIES, NEW MOODS

■

BLACK PROTEST

Who Was Nat Turner?

Freedom Now!

▌▌

IN QUEST OF COMMUNITY

Whither Black Power?

"Negroes" Nevermore

CONTENTS

SLAVERY AND ITS AFTERMATH

I

THE AFRICAN AS SLAVE

Africa and the New Americans

The Legacy of Slavery

▌▌ THIS SIDE OF JORDAN

Down Home and Up North

Community, Class, and Family Life

CONTRIBUTORS

RAYMOND BAUER is Professor of Business Administration at Harvard University. He is the author of *Second Order Consequences* and the co-author of *Studies in the Negro Market* and *Advertising in America: The Consumer View.*

LERONE BENNETT, JR., is Senior Editor of *Ebony.* His many books include *Confrontation: Black and White; The Negro Mood; What Manner of Man: A Biography of Martin Luther King, Jr.; Before the Mayflower: A History of the Negro in America, 1619–1964;* and *Black Power, U.S.A.*

ROBERT BLAUNER teaches sociology at the University of California, Berkeley. He is the author of *Alienation and Freedom* and "Whitewash Over Watts," which appeared in *Transaction.* He has recently completed a new book, *The Unique Americans.*

STOKELY CARMICHAEL is the former head of the Student Non-Violent Coordinating Committee. With Charles V. Hamilton he wrote *Black Power: The Politics of Liberation in America.*

ERIK H. ERIKSON, Professor of Psychiatry at the Harvard Medical School, is the author of *Childhood and Society, Identity and the Life Cycle,* and *Insight and Responsibility.* He has also published psychoanalytic studies of the lives of Luther and Gandhi.

EUGENE D. GENOVESE, author of *The Political Economy of Slavery,* is Chairman of the Department of History at the University of Rochester.

LEWIS M. KILLIAN is Professor of Sociology at the University of Massachusetts, Amherst. He is the author of *The Impossible Revolution?: Black Power and the American Dream* and *White Southerners* and is co-author of *The Racial Crisis in America.*

MARTIN LUTHER KING, JR., received the Noble Peace Prize in 1964. The leader of the Southern Christian Leadership Conference, the late Dr. King wrote several books on the subject of nonviolent direct action, including *Stride Toward Freedom* and *Where Do We Go From Here?: Chaos or Community.*

JOYCE LADNER is Assistant Professor of Sociology at the University of Southern Illinois and is also affiliated with the Institute of the Black World, The Martin Luther King, Jr., Memorial Center, in Atlanta, Georgia.

CHRISTOPHER LASCH is Professor of History at Northwestern University. He is the author of *The American Liberal and the Russian Revolution, The New Radicalism in America, The Social Thought of Jane Addams,* and *The Agony of the American Left.*

C. ERIC LINCOLN is Professor of Sociology at the Union Theological Seminary. His many books include *The Black Muslims in the United States* and *My Face is Black.*

GARY T. MARX teaches sociology at Harvard University. He is the author of *Protest and Prejudice.*

TOM MBOYA, author of *Freedom and After,* was Minister of Economic Development and Planning in his native land of Kenya at the time of his assassination in the spring of 1969.

AUGUST MEIER is University Professor of History at Kent State University. He is author of *Negro Thought in America, 1880–1915* and co-author, with Elliott Rudwick, of *From Plantation to Ghetto.* Meier and Rudwick also edited *The Making of Black America.*

RICHARD B. MOORE is the owner and manager of the Frederick Douglass Book Store in New York and is the founder of "The Committee to Present the Truth about the Negro."

GERALD W. MULLIN teaches history at Smith College. The author of *Slavery in Colonial Virginia,* he is completing a study of the relationship between religion, acculturation, and American Negro slave rebellions.

GEORGE PLIMPTON is editor of *The Paris Review* and author of *Out of My League, Paper Lion,* and *Bogey Man.*

ALVIN F. POUSSAINT teaches psychiatry at the Tufts University Medical School. His articles have appeared in *The New York Times Magazine, Ebony,* and other publications.

ELLIOTT RUDWICK is Professor of Sociology at Kent State University. He is the author of *W. E. B. DuBois* and *Race Riot at East St. Louis,* and, with August Meier, co-author of *From Plantation to Ghetto* and co-editor of *The Making of Black America.*

MIKE THELWELL, a teacher and free-lance writer, is head of the Black Studies Program at the University of Massachusetts, Amherst. "Back with the Wind: Mr. Styron and the Reverend

Turner" was published in *William Styron's Nat Turner: Ten Black Writers Respond*. Other articles have appeared in the *Massachusetts Review, Freedomways*, and other publications.

NAT TURNER, a slave, led one of the most famous of all revolts in 1831 in Southampton, Virginia.

AARON WILDAVSKY, Chairman of the Department of Political Science at the University of California, Berkeley, is the author of *The Politics of Budgetary Process* and *Leadership in a Small-Town* and co-author of *Presidential Elections*.

NATHAN WRIGHT, JR., was Plans Committee Chairman of the 1967 Conference on Black Power. He lectures on urban sociology at New York City Community College and is the author of *One Bread, One Body* and *Black Power and Urban Unrest*.

ARISTIDE ZOLBERG is Chairman of the Political Science Department at the University of Chicago. He is also Director of the Center for the Comparative Study of Political Development. His books include *One-Party Government in the Ivory Coast* and *Creating Political Disorders*. VERA ZOLBERG has taught at the University of Wisconsin and St. Xavier College, Chicago.

INTRODUCTION

THE PAST, THE PRESENT, AND THE FUTURE

Young black militants are, as one said recently, "a new breed of cat." They see themselves as the vanguard of a movement to erase once and forever the stigma imposed by white slave masters and perpetuated by segregationists over the last hundred years. They want everyone—parents and peers, white liberals and conservatives—to know that times have changed and that they are black *men*, not black *boys*. Often using the future as a guide to the past, they have called for a new view of the black experience, one in which "the real truth about black people will finally be known." Having long sought equality, they are now seeking "equal time" as well.

In response to mounting pressure, colleges and universities (and some public schools) have introduced Afro-American programs and curricular innovations geared to the special needs of black students. From among the welter of proposals and pronouncements requesting (or, more often, demanding) such programs, one message has come across loud and clear: "We will be *Negroes* no more."

This mood, its strategy and its rhetorical style, has signaled the end of an old era and the beginning of a new phase in black–white relations in the United States. In many ways, with the benefit of hindsight, one can say it was inevitable that such a shift in character and focus and leadership should come to pass.

The new ideology is a culmination of years of struggle and crisis during which black people were trying to come to grips with their unique problems and their constantly thwarted desires to become full-fledged Americans.

Among the various techniques of protest, two types of action were most prevalent from the time of emancipation to its centennial. One centered on Negroes themselves and was concerned with "uplift": the learning of useful skills and such Puritan virtues as thrift and practicality, and the instilling of pride in self and neighbor. The other focused on integration and the attainment of civil rights. In the first instance, the underlying notion seemed to be that black people would show the white man that they were responsible, upright, and talented citizens and that, in time, they would be ready to take their place beside anyone. In the latter, the argument was that the problem was not the Negro's but the white man's and *he* should be made to change. Thus the seeds were sown.

Booker T. Washington was the best-known advocate of the uplift philosophy. At Tuskegee Institute, which he founded, he put into practice his bootstrap operation. A generation later a West Indian, Marcus Garvey, was to turn Washington's accommodationism into strident black nationalism. But with all the fervor and pageantry, Garvey, like Washington, exhorted his followers to prove to the world that black men were truly respectable. In time those who were to lead the many mosques of the Temple of Islam were to go even beyond Garvey, claiming black supremacy and rejecting Christianity. Yet, even the Black Muslims could not and did not reject the Puritan values. On the contrary, they built them into a basic credo for everyday life.

The reaction against Washington's accommodationist plans was publicly voiced by but few Negro leaders. Two who did speak out were Monroe Trotter and W. E. B. DuBois. DuBois was one of the founders of the integrated and, for its time, militant National Association for the Advancement of Colored People. (DuBois, of course, was to become a black nationalist in later years.) In time, other alphabetical labels were to be added to that of the NAACP: CORE, SCLC, SNCC, each one more militant, more "engaged" than the one before. Still, until 1964, most of those who followed the banner of Integration were possessed with a sense of mission that would ultimately culminate in that grand day, the Golden Jubilee, when color would not matter any longer, when the Dream of the Reverend Dr. Martin Luther King and a thousand other Negro preachers would no longer have to be deferred. "Free at last," they would cry out, "Free at last. Lord, God Almighty, we're free at last."

BLACK POWER

By the time of the centennial of Emancipation (and, for some, before), it was quite evident to many outside observers and to many of the field workers that neither apolitical blackwardness nor soulless militance could turn the tide of racism, so deep did it flow. Since there was little likelihood that they could really go it alone and even less that they could (or would) ever "turn white," those called Ne-

groes were going to have to learn (or to relearn) sooner or later
that to make it, they had to take pride in themselves *and* become
politicized. They had to hearken to what Frederick Douglass had prescribed a hundred years before the Student Non-Violent Coordinating Committee was born. Said Douglass,

> Those who profess to favor freedom yet deprecate agitation are
> men who want crops without plowing up the ground; they want rain
> without thunder and lightning. They want the ocean without the awful
> roar of its many waters. . . . Power concedes nothing without de-
> mand. It never did and it never will. Find out just what any people
> will quietly submit to and you have found out the exact measure of in-
> justice and wrong which will be imposed upon them, and these will
> continue till they are resisted with either words or blows, or with both.
> The limits of tyrants are prescribed by the endurance of those whom
> they oppress.

And Black Power did, in fact, begin as a movement of words, im-
passioned words exhorting poor sharecroppers to get out and exercise
their franchise. But this was not enough. Intimidation and threats
raised the ire of the civil rights workers and turned many black
pacifists into soldiers while turning away many white allies. The code
of Thoreau and Gandhi was being replaced by the law of Ham-
murabi—much as Frederick Douglass had suggested.

For years, Negro leaders and their white allies had counseled
patience and fortitude. Until quite recently their authority went unchallenged, for it was widely felt that the liberal integrationists
(black and white) were on the right path. Civil rights campaigns in
the late 1950s and the early 1960s, and the bills passed by Congress
in their wake, seemed, to some at least, positive proof of the efficacy
of nonviolent direct action. But as many of the victories proved
Pyrrhic, as tensions mounted between black field-workers who saw
radical pacifism as a tactic and whites for whom it was a way of life,
as the Vietnam war siphoned off funds that (it was said) would have
been earmarked for ghetto reconstruction, and, most of all, as the
relative deprivation of black people became more apparent, the climate shifted. The movement went sour and the old coalitions began
to break apart.

Unquestionably, the urban riots were also an exacerbating factor.
Many whites who had begun to feel some sense of sympathy with
the embattled civil rights workers, or, at least, were talking of "giving
Negroes their due," grew increasingly fearful—and hostile—as they
saw the flames of Rochester and Watts and Detroit on their television
sets or, in some cases, from their upstairs windows. Charges and
countercharges, cries of duplicity on the one hand and corruption on

the other, shouts of "burn, baby, burn" and "get the honkies" mixed with "send them back to Africa." Frontlash. Backlash. A cacophony of sounds, a montage of color, and a litany of curses filled the air—and the airwaves.

Given the disillusionment and the fear, the persistence of institutionalized segregation and, especially, the fact that little was being done to satisfy those poorest blacks whose expectations had suddenly begun to rise, it is little wonder that the hymn "We Shall Overcome" was replaced—literally and figuratively—with "Black Power."

The new mood began to reach out and envelop the unorganized masses of Negroes, particularly in the northern ghettos where few meaningful communal institutions existed around which people could rally and where even the oratory of the Reverend Martin Luther King could not arouse. The focus began to shift, too, away from integration and toward the more basic matter of "getting it together."

In the early 1920s E. Franklin Frazier said, "if the masses of Negroes can save their self-respect and remain free of hate, so much the better. But . . . I believe, it would be better for the Negro's soul to be seared with hate than dwarfed by self-abasement. . . ." Again it was being argued that there is a psychosocial need for black people to call the "Man" to task rather than accepting and internalizing second-class status and all it means. As William H. Grier and Price Cobbs have recently shown, there has long been (and remains) an almost desperate need to find a sense of positive selfhood and of meaningful peoplehood, too.

To accomplish this has meant that the leadership would have to change as well. And it did. Whites had to be eased or pushed out of positions of dominance to make room for those who could more easily identify with, and be identified with, the black masses. And the new leaders had to prove to their followers that black was the symbol of "light" at the end of their tunnel.

As Black Panthers gained a certain amount of notoriety, those in the "traditional organizations" changed too. SNCC became more militant. CORE turned away from its original stance of integration in favor of black consciousness. The Urban League and the NAACP sounded more militant even while trying to assuage the anxiety of white liberals who did not understand what was happening. The Southern Christian Leadership Conference continued fighting its battles for jobs and freedom but also began forming uneasy coalitions with other embattled minority groups. Despite many differences in symbol (the clenched fist or the double bar of "equality"), in slogan, and in style, pride and protest were joined and, for many, it had become a time to be black.

THE SECOND RECONSTRUCTION

The real question that remains is whether the new turn of events will facilitate the growth of genuine and relevant organizations with power to effect both psychological and political changes in the black communities and to make the need of those communities apparent to the rest of society, or whether the "Second Reconstruction" will end in tragic failure like the first. Those who take the former position are quick to invoke the model offered by other minority groups. They say that, in essence, Black Power is not an attempt to destroy society but to provide a basis for pride and representation to those lacking it; the same kind of pride and recognition that the English, the Italians, the Irish, the Jews, and others have had in themselves, using, among other things, the same sort of "creative distortion" of history. It is also seen as the basis for the formation of institutions that can implement organized actions to aid in the ascent up the ladder. Those who believe this to be the case suggest that the "ethnicity" *already* existing among Negroes must be strengthened and embellished, and that *once again* ethnic power must become a factor to reckon with. They say that this is really nothing new—it is as American as apple pie.

But there are others who argue that the zeal to have everybody listen to the rage boiling up from inside may well be self-defeating, for few black leaders will be able to translate their language of estrangement into a meaningful remedy that will cure the disease of racism without killing the patient. No easy way out of the present dilemma is to be seen. Old techniques have failed because they never reached those who needed help most. New techniques (as advocated by the black militants and others) will fail, it is said, because they will inevitably alienate the very people who are most needed in abetting the transition, those concerned liberal people in the school-room and universities, on planning boards and in the government. Simon Lazarus goes so far as to suggest that many well-meaning liberals, ignoring the innuendoes of a genuine separatist rebellion, often tend to give Black Power a familiar, pluralistic face and, believing their own propaganda, have begun to offer Black Power (or their version of Black Power) "both to whites on their right and to blacks on their left." He goes on to say that "convinced that black leaders *should* not adopt systematic violence as a tactic, liberals have assumed they *will* not adopt it." The point is well taken, especially

given what is now known about the tensions extant in American society, on the campuses, and particularly in the ghetto areas. But it
should not be exaggerated either. The majority of black Americans,
including many in the slums, still want to join the society, not turn
it upside down. And, for many, Black Power (read "bloc power") is
still seen as a way to get in. How long they will feel that way is highly
speculative.

It is becoming more and more difficult to predict what will happen on the racial front in the coming years than it was a few years
ago. Then the past was used as a fairly accurate guide to the future
and the predictions made were based on a critical assessment of data
available to anyone bothering to sift through them. Among the evidence was a pretty clear picture that few white people were about
to support any efforts to effect changes unless they were pressured
into it. In celebrating the passage of the Civil Rights Acts of 1960,
1964, 1965, and even of 1968, it is easy to forget that these victories
were the results of protest marches, boycotts, demonstrations, and
threats of disruption. Such activities, it seems, did more to bring
about changes in the status quo than all the pious platitudes from
segregated pulpits or the admonitions of the specialists in urban
affairs and poverty.

The federal government, dedicated to opening New Frontiers and
making a Great Society and dedicated to waging war on poverty, got
itself so bogged down in Vietnam that it could offer only monumental
legislation and modest programs for implementation—programs offered to show good faith but construed by many as being proof
of continued tokenism and contributing to the over-all "minus-sum
game," as Aaron Wildavsky has called it.

Minus-sum games are those, he says, in which every player leaves
the contest worse off than when he entered. "Promise a lot; deliver
a little. . . . Lead people to believe they will be much better off,
but let there be no dramatic improvement. . . . Have middle class
civil servants hire upper class student radicals to use lower class
Negroes as a battering ram against the existing political systems; then
complain that people are going around disrupting things and chastise
local politicians for not cooperating with those out to do them in.
. . . Feel guilty about what has happened to black people; tell them
you are surprised they have not revolted before; express shock and
dismay when they follow your advice." And so forth.

Those who warned about the dangers of such "games" were often
told that the problem was being exaggerated or that they were ner-
vous nellies inadvertently disrupting the cause of civil rights by trying to keep everybody's expectations within certain realistic bounds.

And now many other voices have been added to those who decry the sociologists and the behaviorally oriented political scientists for their reluctance to take more radical stands.

The entry of large numbers of such critics—mounting the stumps from Harlem to Watts and the campus stages from Boston to Berkeley, and writing in old Negro papers and the new black ones—has brought about many changes in the black mood and the black movement. The crystal balls are far cloudier ("Whitey doesn't know what we're going to do next"—and he doesn't) and the emanations from the computers are consequently less reliable. Given what was known before, the Black Power movement was an almost inevitable next stage for those who were called "darker brethren" and treated like hired hands by most Americans.

PERSPECTIVES ON BLACK PROTEST AND THE QUEST FOR COMMUNITY

Now that many black Americans themselves have begun to question the way their past has been handled, and now that some have begun to claim that no white man can ever speak *for* them, it is increasingly difficult for anyone, black or white, to separate fancy from fact. Still, lest rhetoric become a substitute for scholarship and politics a substitute for social science, attempts must be made. This book is such an attempt. Concerned with the roots, the patterns, the consequences, and the meaning of black protest, this volume offers varied assessments as seen through the eyes of twenty-five black and white historians, journalists, psychiatrists, and social scientists.

Few topics are more timely, or more controversial, than that brought out by the publication of William Styron's historical novel *The Confessions of Nat Turner*. It seemed fitting that the first "controversy" considered here is the question "Who *Was* Nat Turner?"

Volume II thus begins with a view of day-to-day resistance to slavery as presented in a famous article by Raymond and Alice Bauer and a commentary on the whole issue by the economic historian Eugene D. Genovese. These essays are followed by Gerald W. Mullin's fascinating documentation and assessment of "Gabriel's Insurrection."

Rather than excerpting sections from Styron's book, the original *Confessions* (which the slave Nat told to Thomas R. Gray in 1831) are reprinted. But Styron is to be heard from as well. The day his book was published, George Plimpton interviewed the author. That interview, which originally appeared in *The New York Times Book Review,* is reprinted. It is followed by a critique of Styron and other white writers who use historical episodes (in which black men are involved) as the basis for their "nonfiction fiction." The author, an instructor in English and a literary critic, is West Indian–born Mike Thelwell. His essay is called "The White Nat Turner."

The chorus of "We Shall Overcome" already has a remote quality. To some it echoes a more hopeful time, a time of promise. It brings back memories of early champions of civil rights and the moving oratory of the late Martin Luther King. It intones the spirit of what was once called the "Awakening." This period is described in an original essay, "Radicals and Conservatives," by August Meier and Elliott Rudwick. The reader will find that even their assessment is filled with contradiction and conflicts and an undercurrent of militancy that is further explained in Gary T. Marx's report. Nathan Wright, Jr., one of the leading intellectual leaders of various conferences on Black Power, describes the crisis that led many to turn away from traditional avenues toward more radical ones. Aristide and Vera Zolberg see a specter haunting the newest phase in the movement, the tendency to Americanize the works of Frantz Fanon and other vehement anticolonial writers. Lewis M. Killian sees it too. He raises some troubling questions about certain "revolutionary myths" and describes the strains toward and problems inherent in a revolutionary movement of black Americans.

Then there is the last issue: Black Power itself. In the third section, Stokely Carmichael "speaks" first and sets forth his demands and those of the Student Non-Violent Coordinating Committee, circa 1966. Joyce Ladner, a sociologist who was there, explains what Black Power means to Negroes in Mississippi. Aaron Wildavsky, a political scientist with an interest in urban politics, is concerned about what he sees as the negative consequences of advocacy by black (and white) radicals out to change the system but unable to control those whose cause is theirs. Christopher Lasch sees other problems with Black Power, particularly as described by Carmichael. But, as if to counter, the late Martin Luther King claims that the concept Black Power itself can mean many things and, perhaps, it is a harbinger of better times, times when black men can walk with pride and in security.

The volume ends with a collection of essays grouped under the title " 'Negroes' Nevermore." The first of these were written by two psychiatrists, Erik H. Erikson and Alvin Poussaint, who offer their assessments of the *concept* of identity in race relations and the *problem* of racial identity.

The reader will want to peruse the remaining articles in the order presented: C. Eric Lincoln discusses the notion of "negritude" while Lerone Bennett, Jr., asks "What's in a Name?" Why should black people be called Negroes? And why should Negro people be called black? Some answers to these and other queries are given in the next two pieces: Richard B. Moore's "Africa Conscious Harlem," which is followed by the late Tom Mboya's view that "The American Negro Cannot Look to Africa for an Escape." Points and counterpoints.

The section, and the volume, ends with a provocative commentary by the sociologist Robert Blauner, who asks a rather all-encompassing question: Is black culture a myth or a reality?

In Volume I of this two-part collection, most articles dealt with how black Africans became "Negroes"—and what this has meant. Here, in Volume II, the tables are turned: The basic issue in the pages to follow is centered on the problems of "getting it together" and the assertion of black pride.

BLACK PROTEST

Who Was Nat Turner?

I saluted them on coming up, and asked Will how came he there, he answered, his life was worth no more than others, and his liberty as dear to him. I asked him if he thought to obtain it? He said he would, or lose his life. This was enough to put him in full confidence. . . . it was quickly agreed we should commence at home on that night, and until we had armed and equipped ourselves, and gathered sufficient force, neither age nor sex was to be spared. . . .

NAT TURNER

Melville J. Herskovits was one of the first social scientists to document the character of African "survivals" in the New World. Raymond and Alice Bauer, who worked under the noted anthropologist, were among the first to describe the day to day resistance to slavery that occurred on plantations throughout the American South.

Their essay, originally published in 1942, helped to dispel the myth of docility offered by both proslavery and abolitionist factions. It also served to explain why indirect methods of retaliation—including the destruction of property, malingering, feigning disability, and even infanticide—were more prevalent than outright revolts.

1

Raymond Bauer

Alice Bauer

DAY TO DAY RESISTANCE TO SLAVERY [1]

The tradition that has grown up about Negro slavery is that the
slaves were docile, well adapted to slavery, and reasonably content
with their lot. A standard work on the Negro problem in the United
States says:

> The Negroes brought into the New World situation and presently
> reduced to a perpetual servitude became very rapidly accommodated
> to the environment and status. The explanation of the comparative
> ease with which this was brought about doubtless lies in the peculiar
> racial traits of the Negro peoples themselves. They are strong and
> robust in physique and so everywhere sought after as laborers. In dis-
> position they are cheerful, kindly and sociable: in character they are
> characteristically extrovert, so readily obedient and easily contented.
> More than most other social groups they are patiently tolerant under
> abuse and oppression and little inclined to struggle against difficulties.
> These facts of racial temperament and disposition make the Negroes

From *Journal of Negro History*, 27 (October 1942), 388–419, published by the
Association for the Study of Negro Life and History, Inc.

more amenable to the condition of slavery than perhaps any other racial group.[2]

This concept is gradually being changed as the study of slave revolts, and of the social tension caused by the constant threat of revolt progresses.[3] In answer to the question, " 'Are the masters afraid of insurrection?' (a slave) says, 'They live in constant fear upon this subject. The least unusual noise at night alarms them greatly. They cry out, 'What is that?' 'Are the boys all in?' " [4]

The purpose of this paper is to study a less spectacular aspect of slavery—the day to day resistance to slavery, since it is felt that such a study will throw some further light on the nature of the Negro's reaction to slavery. Our investigation has made it apparent that the Negroes not only were very discontented, but that they developed effective protest techniques in the form of indirect retaliation for their enslavement. Since this conclusion differs sharply from commonly accepted belief, it would perhaps be of value if a brief preliminary statement were made of how belief so at variance with the available documentary materials could gain such acceptance.

The picture of the docile, contented Negro slave grew out of two lines of argument used in ante-bellum times. The pro-slavery faction contended that the slaves came of an inferior race, and that they were happy and contented in their subordinate position, and that the dancing and singing Negro exemplified their assumption. Abolitionists, on the other hand, tended to depict the Negro slave as a passive instrument, a good and faithful worker exploited and beaten by a cruel master. As one reads the controversial literature on the slavery question, it soon becomes apparent that both sides presented the Negro as a docile creature; one side because it wished to prove that he was contented, the other because it wished to prove that he was grossly mistreated. Both conceptions have persisted to the present time. Writers who romanticize the "Old South" idealize the condition of the slaves, and make of them happy, willing servitors, while those who are concerned with furthering the interests of the Negroes are careful to avoid mention of any aggressive tendencies which might be used as a pretext for further suppressing the Negroes.

Many travelers in the South have accepted the overt behavior of the slaves at its face value. The "yas suh, Cap'n," the smiling, bowing, and scraping of the Negroes have been taken as tokens of contentment. Redpath's conversations with slaves indicated how deep seated this behavior was.[5] This point of view, however, neglects the fact that the whites have always insisted on certain forms of behavior as a token of acceptance of inferior status by the Negro. The following quotation from Dollard is pertinent:

An informant already cited has referred to the Negro as a "Dr. Jekyll and Mr. Hyde." He was making an observation that is well understood among Negroes—that he has a kind of dual personality, two rôles, one that he is forced to play with white people and one the "real Negro" as he appears in his dealings with his own people. What the white southern people see who "know their Negroes" is the rôle that they have forced the Negro to accept, his caste role.[6]

The conceptual framework within which this paper is written is that the Negro slaves were forced into certain outward forms of compliance to slavery; that, except for the few who were able to escape to the North, the Negroes had to accept the institution of slavery and make their adjustments to that institution. The patterns of adjustment which we have found operative are: slowing up of work, destruction of property, malingering and self-mutilation.

The sources of our material are: (1) general works on slavery, labor, and the Negro; (2) the journals and the travel accounts of southerners and of visitors to the slave territory; and (3) the biographies and autobiographies of slaves. Most of the secondary sources take some cognizance of the fact that slaves slowed up their work, feigned illness, and the like, but this behavior is regarded as a curiosity. There has been no attempt by those writers who set down such facts to understand their social and economic significance. The journals and travel-books vary greatly in the amount of information they contain. This, of course, is due to the authors' variations in interest and acuteness. Olmsted's *Seaboard Slave States*, for instance, abounds in anecdotes, and in expressions of opinion as to the extent of loafing and malingering. Susan Smedes' *Memorials of a Southern Planter*, on the other hand, contains just one foot-noted reference to any such behavior. Life stories of ex-slaves emphasize running away, forms of punishment, and other aspects of slavery that would make interesting reading. Yet while references to slowing up work, or feigning illness, are thus few in number, where they are made they are stated in such a way that they leave no doubt that there was a persistent pattern of such behavior.

> Slaveholders ever underate the intelligence with which they have to grapple. I really understood the old man's mutterings, attitudes and gestures, about as well as he did himself. But slaveholders never encourage that kind of communication, with the slaves, by which they might learn to measure the depths of his knowledge. Ignorance is a high virtue in a human chattel; and as the master studies to keep the slave ignorant, the slave is cunning enough to make the master think he succeeds. The slave fully appreciates the saying, "where ignorance is bliss 'tis folly to be wise." [7]

We have felt it wise to quote extensively. Much of the meaning of incidents and interpretations lies in the phrasing of the author—in sensing his own emphasis on what he says. Methodologically, in attempting to analyze an existing stereotype, as we are trying to do here, it would seem wisest to present the picture as it appeared to contemporaries, and thus as given in their own words.

II

The Negroes were well aware that the work they did benefited only the master. "The slaves work and the planter gets the benefit of it." [8] "The conversation among the slaves was that they worked hard and got no benefit, that the masters got it all." [9] It is thus not surprising that one finds many recurring comments that a slave did not do half a good day's work in a day. A northerner whom Lyell met in the South said:

> Half the population of the south is employed in seeing that the other half do their work, and they who do work, accomplish half what they might do under a better system. [10]

An English visitor with a very strong pro-slavery bias corroborates this:

> The amount of work expected of the field hand will not be more than one half of what would be demanded of a white man; and even that will not be properly done unless he be constantly overlooked. [11]

Statements of other writers are to the same effect:

> It is a common remark of those persons acquainted with slave-labour, that their proportion is as one to two. This is not too great an estimate in favour of the free-labourer; and the circumstances of their situation produce a still greater disparity. [12]
>
> A capitalist was having a building erected in Petersburg, and his slaves were employed in carrying up the brick and mortar for the masons on their heads: a Northerner, standing near, remarked to him that they moved so indolently that it seemed as if they were trying to see how long they could be in mounting the ladder without actually stopping. The builder started to reprove them, but after moving a step turned back and said: "It would only make them move more slowly still when I am not looking at them, if I should hurry now. *And what motive have they to do better?* It's no concern of theirs how long the masons wait. I am sure if I was in their place, I shouldn't move as fast as they do." [13]

A well-informed capitalist and slave-holder remarked,

> In working niggers, we always calculate that they will not labor at all except to avoid punishment, and they will never do more than just

enough to save themselves from being punished, and no amount of punishment will prevent their working carelessly or indifferently. It always seems on the plantations as if they took pains to break all the tools and spoil all the cattle that they possibly can, even when they know they'll be directly punished for it.[14]

Just how much of this was due to indifference and how much due to deliberate slowing up is hard to determine. Both factors most probably entered. A worker who had to devote himself to a dull task from which he can hope to gain nothing by exercising initiative soon slips into such a frame of mind that he does nothing more than go through the motions. His chief concern is to escape from the realities of his task and put it in the back of his mind as much as possible.

There is, indeed, a strong possibility that this behavior was a form of indirect aggression. While such an hypothesis cannot be demonstrated on the basis of the available contemporary data, it is supported by Dollard's interpretation of similar behavior which he found in Southern towns.

If the reader has ever seen Stepin Fetchit in the movies, he can picture this type of character. Fetchit always plays the part of a well-accommodated lower-class Negro, whining, vacillating, shambling, stupid, and moved by very simple cravings. There is probably an element of resistance to white society in the shambling, sullenly slow pace of the Negro; it is the gesture of a man who is forced to work for ends not his own and who expresses his reluctance to perform under these circumstances.[15]

Certainly description after description emphasizes the mechanical plodding of the slave workers:

John Lamar wrote, "My man Ned the carpenter is idle or nearly so at the plantation. He is fixing gates and, like the idle groom in Pickwick, trying to fool himself into the belief that he is doing something—He is an eye servant." [16]

Those I saw at work appeared to me to move very slowly and awkwardly, as did those engaged in the stables. These also were very stupid and dilatory in executing any orders given them, so that Mr. C. would frequently take the duty off their hands into his own, rather than wait for them, or make them correct their blunders; they were much, in these respects, what our farmers call *dumb Paddees*—that is, Irishmen who do not readily understand the English language, and who are still weak and stiff from the effects of the emigrating voyage. At the entrance gate was a porter's lodge, and, as I approached I saw a black face peeping at me from it, but both when I entered and left, I was obliged to dismount and open the gate myself.

Altogether, it struck me—slaves coming here as they naturally did in comparison with free laborers, as commonly employed on my own and my neighbors' farms, in exactly similar duties—that they must have been difficult to direct efficiently, and that it must be irksome and trying to one's patience, to have to superintend their labor.[17]

To what extent this reluctant labor was the rule may be appreciated when it is pointed out that a southern doctor classified it under the name *Dysaethesia Aethiopica* as a mental disease peculiar to Negroes. Olmsted quotes this Dr. Cartwright as follows:

From the careless movements of the individual affected with this complaint, they are apt to do much mischief, which appears as if intentional, but it is mostly owing to the stupidity of mind and insensibility of the nerves induced by the disease. Thus, they break, waste, and destroy everything they handle—abuse horses and cattle—tear, burn, or rend their own clothing, and, paying no attention to the rights of property, steal others to replace what they have destroyed. They wander about at night, and keep in a half nodding state by day. They slight their work—cut up corn, cotton and tobacco, when hoeing it, as if for pure mischief. They raise disturbances with their overseers, and among their fellow servants, without cause or motive, and seem to be insensible to pain when subjected to punishment.

The term "rascality" given to this disease by overseers, is founded on an erroneous hypothesis, and leads to an incorrect empirical treatment, which seldom or never cures it.[18]

There are only two possible intepretations of the doctor's statement. Either the slaves were so extraordinarily lazy that they gave the appearance of being mentally diseased, or the doctor was decribing cases of hebephrenic schizophrenia. Either situation is startling. The phenomenon was obviously widespread, and if it was actually a mental disease it certainly would indicate that Negroes did not become "easily adjusted to slavery."

Whatever the case, it is certain that the slaves consciously saved their energy. Olmsted, who always had his eye open for such incidents, reported:

The overseer rode among them, on a horse, carrying in his hand a raw-hide whip, constantly directing and encouraging them; but, as my companion and I, both, several times noticed, as often as he visited one line of the operations, the hands at the other end would discontinue their labor, until he turned to ride toward them again.[19]

The few statements on this point we have by ex-slaves seem to indicate that the slaves as a group made a general policy of not letting the master get the upper hand.

I had become large and strong; and had begun to take pride in the fact that I could do as much hard work as some of the older men. There is much rivalry among slaves, at times, as to which can do the most work, and masters generally seek to promote such rivalry. But some of us were too wise to race with each other very long. Such racing, we had the sagacity to see, was not likely to pay. We had times out for measuring each other's strength, but we knew too much to keep up the competition so long as to produce an extraordinary day's work. We knew that if, by extraordinary exertion, a large quantity of work was done in one day, the fact, becoming known to the master, might lead him to require the same amount every day. This thought was enough to bring us to a dead halt whenever so much excited for the race.[20]

Writer after writer, describing incidents in which slaves were compelled to assist in punishing other slaves, states that they did so with the greatest of reluctance.

The hands stood still;—they knew Randall—and they knew him also take a powerful man, and were afraid to grapple with him. As soon as Cook had ordered the men to seize him, Randall turned to them, and said—"Boys, you all know me; you know that I can handle any three of you, and the man that lays hands on me shall die. This white man can't whip me himself, and therefore he has called you to help him." The overseer was unable to prevail upon them to seize and secure Randall, and finally ordered them all to go to their work together.[21]

In some cases it was noted that the slave resisting punishment took pains not to treat his fellows with any more than the absolute minimum of violence.

With such demonstrations of solidarity among the slaves it is not surprising to find a slave telling of how he and his fellows "captured" the institution of the driver. The slave Solomon Northrup was such a driver. His task was to whip the other slaves in order to make them work.

"Practice makes perfect," truly; and during eight years' experience as a driver I learned to handle the whip with marvelous dexterity and precision, throwing the lash within a hair's breadth of the back, the ear, the nose without, however, touching either of them. If Epps was observed at a distance, or we had reason to apprehend he was sneaking somewhere in the vicinity, I would commence plying the lash vigorously, when, according to arrangement, they would squirm and screech as if in agony, although not one of them had in fact been grazed. Patsey would take occasion, if he made his appearance presently, to mumble in his hearing some complaints that Platt was whipping them the whole time, and Uncle Abram, with an appearance of honesty peculiar to himself would declare roundly I had just whipped them worse than General Jackson whipped the enemy at New Orleans.[22]

Williams, another slave whose task was to drive his fellows, said:

He was at these periods terribly severe to his hands, and would order me to use up the cracker of my whip every day upon the poor creatures who were toiling in the field; and in order to satisfy him, I used to tear it off when returning home at night. He would then praise me for a good fellow and invite me to drink with him.[23]

The amount of slowing up of labor by the slaves must, in the aggregate, have caused a tremendous financial loss to plantation owners. The only way we have of estimating it quantitatively is through comparison of the work done in different plantations and under different systems of labor. The statement is frequently made that production on a plantation varied more than 100% from time to time. Comparison in the output of slaves in different parts of the South also showed variations of over 100%. Most significant is the improvement in output obtained under the task, whereby the slaves were given a specific task to fulfill for their day's work, any time left over being their own. Olmsted gives us our best information on this point:

> These tasks certainly would not be considered excessively hard by a northern laborer; and, in point of fact, the more industrious and active hands finished them often by two o'clock. I saw one or two leaving the field soon after one o'clock, several about two; and between three and four, I met a dozen women and several men coming home to their cabins, having finished their day's work.
>
> Under this "Organization of Labor" most of the slaves work rapidly and well. In nearly all ordinary work, custom has settled the extent of the task, and it is difficult to increase it. The driver who marks it out, has to remain on the ground until it is finished, and has no interest in overmeasuring it; and if it should be systematically increased very much, there is danger of a general stampede to the swamp, a danger the slave can always hold before his master's cupidity.[24]
>
> It is the custom of tobacco manufacturers to hire slaves and free negroes at a certain rate of wages each year. A task of 45 pounds per day is given them to work up, and all they choose to do more than this, they are paid for—payment being made once a fortnight; and invariably this over-wages is used by the slave for himself, and is usually spent in drinking, licentiousness, and gambling. The man was grumbling that he had saved but $20 to spend at the holidays. One of the manufacturers offered to show me by his books, that nearly all gained by over-work $5 a month, many $20 and some as much as $28.[25]
>
> He (the speaker) was executor of an estate in which, among other negroes, there was one very smart man, who, he knew perfectly well, ought to be earning for the estate $150 a year, and who could if he chose, yet whose wages for a year being let out by the day or job, had amounted to but $18, while he had paid for medical attendance upon him $45.[26]

The executor of the estate finally arranged for this man to work out his freedom, which he readily accomplished.

A quantitative estimate can be made from another situation which Olmsted observed. Rain during a previous day had made certain parts of the work more difficult than others. The slaves were therefore put on day work, since it would not be possible to lay out equitable tasks.

Ordinarily it is done by tasks—a certain number of the small divisions of the field being given to each hand to burn in a day; but owing to a more than usual amount of rain having fallen lately, and some other causes, making the work harder in some places than in others, the women were now working by the day, under the direction of a "driver," a negro man, who walked about among them, taking care they had left nothing unburned. Mr. X inspected the ground they had gone over, to see whether the driver had done his duty. It had been sufficiently well burned, but not more than a quarter as much ground had been gone over, he said, as was usually burned in tasked work,—and he thought they had been very lazy, and reprimanded them for it.[27]

Most revealing of all is this statement:

"Well, now, old man," said I, "you go and cut me two cords today!" "Oh, massa! two cords! Nobody could do dat. Oh! massa, dat is too hard! Neber heard o' nobody's cuttin' more 'n a cord o' wood in a day, round heah. No nigger couldn't do it." "Well, old man, you have two cords of wood cut to-night or to-morrow morning you shall get two hundred lashes—that's all there is about it. So look sharp." And he did it and ever since no negro ever cut less than two cords a day for me, though my neighbors never get but one cord. It was just so with a great many other things—mauling rails—I always have two hundred rails mauled in a day; just twice what it is the custom of the country to expect of a negro, and just twice as many as my negroes had been made to do before I managed them myself.

These estimates, let it be recollected in conclusion, are all deliberately and carefully made by gentlemen of liberal education, who have had unusual facilities of observing both at the North and the South.[28]

The slaves were well aware of their economic value, and used it to good advantage. The skilled laborers among the slaves knew their worth, and frequently rebelled against unsatisfactory work situations. Slaves who were hired out would run away from the masters who had hired them, and then either return home, or remain in hiding until they felt like returning to work.

The slave, if he is indisposed to work, and especially if he is not treated well, or does not like the master who has hired him, will sham sickness—even make himself sick or lame—that he need not work. But a more serious loss frequently arises, when the slave, thinking he is worked too hard, or being angered by punishment or unkind treatment, "getting the sulks," takes to "the swamp," and comes back when he has a mind to. Often this will not be till the year is up for which he is engaged, when he will return to his owner, who, glad to find his property safe, and that it has not died in the swamp, or gone to Canada, forgets to punish him, and immediately sends him for another year to a new master.

"But, meanwhile, how does the negro support life in the swamp?" I asked.

"Oh, he gets sheep and pigs and calves, and fowls and turkey; sometimes they will kill a small cow. We have often seen the fires, where they were cooking them, through the woods in the swamp yonder. If it is cold, he will crawl under a fodder stack, or go into the cabins with some of the other negroes, and in the same way, you see, he can get all the corn, or almost anything else he wants."

"He steals them from his master?"

"From anyone: frequently from me. I have had many a sheep taken by them." [29]

"It is a common thing, then?"

"Certainly it is, very common, and the loss is sometimes exceedingly provoking. One of my neighbors here was going to build, and hired two mechanics for a year. Just as he was ready to put his house up, the two men, taking offense at something, both ran away, and did not come back at all, till their year was out, and then their owner immediately hired them out again to another man." [30]

One plantation overseer wrote to the plantation owner concerning a carpenter he had hired out to one G. Moore:

Not long before Jim run away G More (sic.) wanted him to make some gates and I sent him theireselves (sic.) and he run away from him and cum home and then he left me withow (sic.) a cause.[31]

Even the threat of a whipping did not deter such slaves from running off for a time when they were displeased. The quotation from Olmsted below is typical of a constantly recurring pattern of statements:

The manager told me that the people often ran away after they have been whipped or something else had happened to make them angry. They hide in the swamp and come into the cabins at night to get food. They seldom remain away more than a fortnight and when they come in they are whipped.[32]

Some of the resistance took on the aspects of organized strikes:

Occasionally, however, a squad would strike in a body as a protest against severities. An episode of this sort was recounted in a letter of a Georgia overseer to his absent employer: "Sir: I write you a few lines in order to let you know that six of your hands has left the plantation —every man but Jack. They displeased me with their work and I give some of them a few lashes, Tom with the rest. On Wednesday morning they were missing. I think they are lying out until they can see you or your Uncle Jack." The slaves could not negotiate directly at such a

time, but while they lay in the woods they might make overtures to
the overseer through slaves on a neighboring plantation as to terms
upon which they would return to work, or they might await their
master's posthaste arrival and appeal to him for a redress of grievances.
Humble as their demeanor might be, their power of renewing the pressure by repeating their act could not be ignored.[33]

John Holmes, an escaped slave, told how he ran off and hid in
the swamp after an overseer attempted to whip him.

> At last they told all the neighbors if I would come home, they wouldn't
> whip me. I was a great hand to work and made a great deal of money
> for our folks.[34]

The same overseer had further trouble with the slaves.

> She (a slave) was better with her fists, and beat him, but he was better
> at wrestling and threw her down. He then called the men to help him,
> but all hid from him in the brush where we were working. . . . Then
> (later) the calculation was to whip us every one, because we did not
> help the overseer. . . . That night every one of us went away into the
> woods. . . . We went back, but after a while (the overseer) came
> back too, and stayed the year out. He whipped the women but he did
> not whip the men, of fear they would run away.[35]

III

The indifference of the slaves to the welfare of the masters extended
itself to a complete contempt for property values. The slaves were so
careless with tools that they were equipped with special tools, and
more clumsy than ordinary ones:

> The *"nigger hoe"* was first introduced into Virginia as a substitute for
> the plow, in breaking up the soil. The law fixes its weight at four
> pounds,—as heavy as the woodman's axe. It is still used, not only in
> Virginia, but in Georgia and the Carolinas. The planters tell us, as
> the reason for its use, that the negroes would break a Yankee hoe in
> pieces on the first root, or stone that might be in their way. An instruc-
> tive commentary on the difference between free and slave labor! [36]
>
> The absence of motive, and the consequent want of mental energy
> to give vigor to the arm of the slave is the source of another great
> drawback upon the usefulness of his labour. His implements or tools
> are at least one-third (in some instances more than twofold) heavier
> and stronger than the northern man's to counteract his want of skill
> and interest in his work. A Negro hoe or scythe would be a curiosity
> to a New England farmer.[37]

Not only tools but livestock suffered from the mistreatment by
the slaves. Olmsted found not only the "nigger hoe" but even dis-

covered that mules were substituted for horses because horses could not stand up under the treatment of the slaves.

> I am shown tools that no man in his senses, with us, would allow a laborer, to whom he was paying wages, to be encumbered with; and the excessive weight and clumsiness of which, I would judge, would make work at least ten per cent greater than those ordinarily used with us. And I am assured that, in the careless and clumsy way they must be used by the slaves, anything lighter or less crude could not be furnished them with good economy, and that such tools as we constantly give our laborers and find profit in giving them, would not last out a day in a Virginia corn-field—much lighter and more free from stones though it be than ours.
>
> So, too, when I ask why mules are so universally substituted for horses on the farm, the first reason given, and confessedly the most conclusive one, is, that horses cannnot bear the treatment they always must get from negroes; horses are always soon foundered or crippled by them but mules will bear cudgeling, and lose a meal or two now and then, and not be materially injured, and they do not take cold or get sick if neglected or overworked. But I do not need to go further than to the window of the room in which I am writing, to see, at almost any time, treatment of cattle that would insure the immediate discharge of the driver, by almost any farmer owning them in the North.[38]

Redpath verifies Olmsted's statement—by telling how he saw slaves treat stock. It is important to note that Redpath was a strong abolitionist and most sympathetic toward the slaves.

> He rode the near horse, and held a heavy cowhide in his hand, with which from time to time he lashed the leaders, as barbarous drivers lash oxen when at work. Whenever we came to a hill, especially if it was very steep, he dismounted, lashed the horses with all his strength, varying his performances by picking up stones, none of them smaller than half a brick, and throwing them with all his force, at the horses' legs. He seldom missed.
>
> The wagon was laden with two tons of plaster in sacks.
>
> This is a fair specimen of the style in which Negroes treat stock.[39]

The indifference to live-stock is well illustrated by an incident which Olmsted recounts:

> I came, one afternoon, upon a herd of uncommonly fine cattle as they were being turned out of a field by a negro woman. She had given herself the trouble to let down but two of the seven bars of the fence, and they were obliged to leap over a barrier at least four feet high. Last of all came, very unwillingly, a handsome heifer, heavy with calf; the woman urged her with a cudgel and she jumped, but lodging on her belly, as I came up she lay bent, and, as it seemed, helplessly hung upon the top bar. . . . The woman struck her severely and with a painful effort she boggled over.[40]

In the Sea Islands off the coast of Georgia, Kemble reported that the slaves started immense fires, destroying large sections of woods through carelessness or maliciousness.

> The "field hands" make fires to cook their midday food wherever they happen to be working, and sometimes through their careless neglect, but sometimes, too, undoubtedly on purpose, the woods are set fire to by these means. One benefit they consider . . . is the destruction of the dreaded rattlesnakes.[41]

The slaves on Lewis' West Indies plantation let cattle get into one of his best cane-pieces because they neglected to guard them, being more interested in a dance which was going on. They were fully aware that the cattle were ruining the sugar cane, but kept right on singing and dancing. Lewis was able to get only a handful of house servants to drive the cattle out of the cane, and that not until the cane-piece was ruined.[42]

One tobacco planter complained that his slaves would cut the young plants indiscriminately unless they were watched. When it became late in the season and there was need of haste to avoid frost they would work only the thickest leaving the sparser ones untouched.[43] Another planter said that he could cultivate only the poorer grades of tobacco because the slaves would not give necessary attention to the finer sort of plants.[44] An English visitor said:

> The kitchens and out-offices are always at the distance of several yards from the principal dwelling. This is done as well to guard against the house-Negroes through carelessness setting the houses on fire, for they generally sit over it half the night, as to keep out their noise. (sic.) [45]

The full import of these practices strikes home fully only when they are read in the words of the original observers. Olmsted's comments, and the ease with which he found incidents to illustrate them, are most valuable. So important is his testimony that we must once more quote him at some length.

> Incidents, trifling in themselves, constantly betray to a stranger the bad economy of using enslaved servants. The catastrophe of one such occurred since I began to write this letter. I ordered a fire to be made in my room, as I was going out this morning. On my return, I found a grand fire—the room door having been closed and locked upon it "out of order." Just now, while I was writing, down tumbled upon the floor, and rolled away close to the valance of the bed, half a hod-full of ignited coal, which had been so piled upon the diminutive grate, and left without a fender or any guard, that this result was almost inevitable. If I had not returned at the time I did, the house would have been fired.[46]
>
>   On the rice plantation which I have particularly described, the slaves were, I judge, treated with at least as much discretion and

judicious consideration of economy, consistently with humane regard to their health, comfort, and morals, as on any other in all the Slave States; yet I could not avoid observing—and I certainly took no pains to do so, nor were any special facilities offered me for it—repeated instances of that waste and misapplication of labor which it can never be possible to guard against, when the agents of industry are slaves. Many such evidences of waste it would not be easy to specify; and others, which remain in my memory after some weeks, do not adequately account for the general impression that all I saw gave me; but there were, for instance, under my observation gates left open and bars left down, against standing orders; rails removed from fences by the negroes (as was conjectured) to kindle their fires with, mules lamed, and implements broken, by careless usage; a flat boat, carelessly secured, going adrift on the river; men ordered to cart rails for a new fence depositing them so that a double expense of labor would be required to lay them, more than would have needed if they had been placed, as they might have almost as easily been, by a slight exercise of forethought . . . making statements which their owner was obliged to receive as sufficient excuse, though, he told me, he felt assured they were false—all going to show habitual carelessness, indolence, and mere eye-service.[47]

But not only did the Negro slaves refuse to work, and not only did they destroy property, but they even made it impossible for planters to introduce new work techniques by feigning clumsiness. They prevented the introduction of the plow in this way on many plantations.[48] Olmsted here cites many instances. Lewis, quoted in *Plantation Documents*, found the same thing true in Jamaica.

It appears to me that nothing could afford so much relief to the negroes, under the existing system of Jamaica, as the substituting of labor of animals for that of slaves in agriculture wherever such a measure is practicable. On leaving the island, I impressed this wish of mine upon the mind of my agents with all my power; but the only result has been the creating of a very considerable expense in the purchase of ploughs, oxen and farming implements; the awkwardness and still more the obstinacy of the few negroes, whose services were indispensable, was not to be overcome: they broke plough after plough, and ruined beast after beast, till the attempt was abandoned in despair.[49]

IV

Malingering was a well-known phenomenon throughout the slave states.[50] The purpose of feigning illness was generally to avoid work, although occasionally a slave who was being sold would feign a disability either to avoid being sold to an undesirable master, or to lower his purchase price so as to obtain revenge on a former master.

The women occasionally pretended to be pregnant, because pregnant women were given lighter work assignments and were allowed extra rations of food.

In a situation such as this in which physical disability was an advantage, one would expect much malingering. One might also expect to find functional mental disorders, hysterical disorders which would get one out of work. There is some evidence that many had such functional disorders.

There are many complaints described in Dr. Cartwright's treatise, to which the Negroes, in slavery, seem to be peculiarly subject.

Negro-consumption, a disease almost unknown to medical men of the Northern States and of Europe, is also sometimes fearfully prevalent among the slaves. "It is of importance," says the Doctor, "to know the pathognomic signs in its early stages, not only in regard to its treatment but to detect impositions, as negroes, afflicted with this complaint are often for sale; the acceleration of the pulse, on exercise, incapacitates them for labor, as they quickly give out, and have to leave their work. This induces their owners to sell them, although they may not know the cause of their inability to labor. Many of the negroes brought South, for sale, are in the incipient stages of this disease; they are found to be inefficient laborers, and sold in consequence thereof. The effect of superstition—a firm belief that he is poisoned or conjured— upon the patient's mind, already in a morbid state (dyaesthesia), and his health affected from hard usage, overtasking or exposure, want of wholesome food, good clothing, warm, comfortable lodging, with the distressing idea (sometimes) that he is an object of hatred or dislike, both to his master or fellow-servants, and has no one to befriend him, tends directly to generate that erythism of mind which is the essential cause of negro consumption. . . . Remedies should be assisted by removing the *original cause* [51] of the dissatisfaction or trouble of mind, and by using every means to make the patient comfortable, satisfied and happy." [52]

Of course it is impossible to determine the extent of these disorders. Assuming that Dr. Cartwright's assumption was correct, very few observers would be qualified to make an adequate diagnosis, and a very small proportion of these would be inclined to accept his interpretation. After all, functional disorders are in many cases almost impossible to tell from real disorders or from feigning, and since the behavior which Cartwright describes could very easily be interpreted on another, and easier, level by a less acute observer.

Of the extent to which illness was feigned there can, however, be little doubt. Some of the feigning was quite obvious, and one might wonder why such flagrant abuses were tolerated. The important thing to remember is that a slave was an important economic investment. Most slave owners sooner or later found out that it was more

profitable to give the slave the benefit of the doubt. A sick slave
driven to work might very well die.

> But the same gentleman admitted that he had sometimes been mistaken
> and had made men go to work when they afterwards proved to be
> really ill; therefore, when one of his people told him he was not able
> to work, he usually thought, "very likely he'll be all the better for a
> day's rest, whether he's really ill or not," and would let him off with-
> out being very particular in his examination. Lately he had been getting
> a new overseer, and when he was engaging him he told him that this
> was his way. The observer replied, "It's my way too, now; it didn't
> used to be, but I had a lesson. There was a nigger one day at Mr.
> ——'s who was sulky and complaining; he said he couldn't work. I
> looked at his tongue, and it was right clean, and I thought it was
> nothing but damned sulkiness so I paddled him, and made him go to
> work; but, two days after, he was under ground. He was a good eight
> hundred dollar nigger, and it was a lesson to me about taming pos-
> sums, that I ain't going to forget in a hurry." [53]

So one might find situations like this:

> At one, which was evidently the "sick house" or hospital, there were
> several negroes, of both sexes, wrapped in blankets, and reclining on
> the door steps or on the ground, basking in sunshine. Some of them
> looked ill, but all were chatting and laughing as I rode up to make in-
> quiry.[54]

The situation turned in on itself. The masters were always suspicious of the sick slaves, so that slaves who were moderately sick
accentuated their symptoms in order to make out a convincing case.

> It is said to be nearly as difficult to form a satisfactory diagnosis of
> negroes' disorders, as it is of infants', because their imagination of
> symptoms is so vivid, and because not the smallest reliance is to be
> placed on their accounts of what they have felt or done. If a man is
> really ill, he fears lest he should be thought to be simulating, and there-
> fore exaggerates all his pains, and locates them in whatever he sup-
> poses to be the most vital parts of his system.
>
> Frequently the invalid slaves will neglect or refuse to use the
> remedies prescribed for their recovery. They will conceal pills, for
> instance, under their tongue, and declare they have swallowed them,
> when, from their producing no effect, it will be afterwards evident that
> they have not. This general custom I heard ascribed to habit acquired
> when they were not very disagreeably ill and were loth to be made
> quite well enough to have to go to work again.[55]

Fortunately in this field we have some quantitative estimates
which enable us to appreciate fully the extent of these practices.
Sydnor has digested the records of sickness on various plantations.
From the Wheeles plantation records he found that of 1,429 working

days 179 were lost on account of sickness, a ratio of almost one to seven. On the Bowles' plantation, in one year 159½ days were missed on account of sickness but only five days were on Sundays. This is a recurrent pattern, everybody sick on Saturday, and scarcely anybody sick on Sunday. On the Leigh plantation, where thirty persons were working there were 398 days of sickness. In examining this record Sydnor discovered that the rate of sickness was greatest at the times of the year when there was the most work to be done.[56] Olmsted says that he never visited a plantation on which twenty Negroes were employed where he did not find one or more not at work on some trivial pretext.[57]

Lewis' anecdote is typical:

> On Saturday morning there were no fewer than forty-five persons (not including children) in the hospital; which makes nearly a fifth of my whole gang. Of these the medical people assured me that not above seven had anything whatever the matter with them. . . . And sure enough on Sunday morning they all walked away from the hospital to amuse themselves, except about seven or eight.[58]

Sometimes the feigning did not work, as is shown by two incidents that Olmsted relates:

> A Mr. X asked if there were any sick people.
> "Nobody, oney dat boy Sam, sar."
> "What Sam is that?"
> "Dat little Sam, sar; Tom's Sue's Sam, sar."
> "What's the matter with him?"
> "Don' spec der's nothing much de matter wid him nof, sar. He came in Sa'dy, complaining he had de stomach-ache, an' I give him some ile, sar, 'spec he mus' be well dis time, but he din go out dis mornin'."
> "Well, I see to him."
> Mr. X went to Tom's Sue's cabin, looked at the boy and concluded that he was well, though he lay abed, and pretended to cry with pain, ordered him to go out to work.[59]
> A planter asked the nurse if anyone else was sick.
> "Oney dat woman Caroline."
> "What do you think is the matter with her?"
> "Well, I don't think there is anything de matter wid her, masser; I mus answer you for true, I don't tink anything de matter wid her, oney she's a little sore from dat whipping she got."
> The manager found the woman groaning on a dirty bed and after examining her, scolded her and sent her to work.[60]

The prevalence of malingering may be better appreciated when one realizes that despite the fact that Olmsted refers to it throughout four volumes of his works, in one place he has five whole pages of anecdotes concerning it.[61]

Pretending to be pregnant was a type of escape in a class by itself, since the fraud must inevitably have been discovered. This in itself may give us some insight into the Negroes' attitude toward the relative advantages of escaping work and of escaping punishment. Just as the slave who ran off into the woods for a temporary relief from work, the pseudo-pregnant woman must have realized in advance that she would inevitably be punished.

I will tell you of a most comical account Mr. —— has given me of the prolonged and still protracted pseudo-pregnancy of a woman called Markie, who for many more months than are generally required for the process of continuing the human species, pretended to be what the Germans pathetically and poetically call "in good hope" and continued to reap increased rations as the reward of her expectation, till she finally had to disappoint the estate and receive a flogging.[62]

One woman sought to escape from the consequences of her fraud. The results were quite tragic:

A young slave woman, Becky by name, had given pregnancy as the reason for a continued slackness in her work. Her master became skeptical and gave notice that she was to be examined and might expect the whip in case her excuse were not substantiated. Two days afterwards a Negro midwife announced that Becky's baby had been born; but at the same time a neighboring planter began search for a child nine months old which was missing from his quarter. This child was found in Becky's cabin, with its two teeth pulled and the tip of its navel cut off. It died; and Becky was convicted only of manslaughter.[63]

An outstanding example of malingering is given by Smedes, a writer who insisted so emphatically on the devotion of the slaves to their masters.

The cook's husband, who for years had looked on himself as nearly blind, and therefore unable to do more than work about her, and put her wood on the fire, sometimes cutting a stick or two, made no less than eighteen good crops for himself when the war was over. He was one of the best farmers in the country.[64]

The most effective means of retaliation against an unpopular master which the slave had at his command was by feigning disability on the auction block. How often this was done we do not know, but Phillips accepts it as a recognized pattern.

Those on the block often times praised their own strength and talents, for it was a matter of pride to fetch high prices. On the other hand if a slave should bear a grudge against his seller, or should hope to be bought only by someone who would expect but light service he might pretend a disability though he had it not.[65]

Coleman offers the same opinion:

Similar actions were not unknown in slave sales. Frequently on such occasions there is a strong indisposition in such creatures to be sold, and that by stratagem to avoid sale, they may frequently feign sickness, or magnify any particular complaint with which they are affected.[66]

As was customary at a public auction of slaves, the auctioner announced that Mr. Anderson, the master, would give a bill of sale for his slave with the usual guarantee—"sound of mind and body and a slave for life." While there began a lively bidding among the Negro traders, George suddenly assumed a strange appearance—his head was thrown back, his eyes rolled wildly, his body and limbs began to twitch and jerk in an unheard of manner.

"What's the matter with your boy, Mr. Anderson?" one of the traders asked the owner, who, astonished and puzzled, drew nearer the block. But Mr. Anderson did not answer the question. George was now foaming at the mouth, and the violent twitching and jerking increased precipitously.

"What's the matter with you, boy?" gruffly demanded the trader. "O, I 'es fits I has!" exclaimed George, whereupon his body doubled up and rolled off the block.

Of course the auction was hastily terminated. George was hustled off to jail, and a doctor sent for, but, after a careful examination, the medical man was somewhat mystified as to the slave's actual condition. He advised the master to leave George in the jailer's custody for a while, promising to look in on him the next morning. Under his master's instruction, the wily slave was put to bed in the debtor's room, where he soon sank, apparently, into a sound sleep.

Next morning when the jailer brought in breakfast, he found the bed empty. George was gone, and nothing was heard of him again until word came, several weeks later, that he was safe in Canada.[67]

Or, again, we read:

A young girl, of twenty years or thereabouts, was the next commodity put up. Her right hand was entirely useless—"dead," as she aptly called it. One finger had been cut off by a doctor, and the auctioneer stated that she herself chopped off the other finger—her forefinger—because it hurt her, and she thought that to cut it off would cure it.

"Didn't you cut your finger off?" asked a man, " 'kase you was mad?"

She looked at him quietly, but with a glance of contempt, and said:

"No, you see it was a sort o' sore, and I thought it would be better to cut it off than be plagued with it."

Several persons around me expressed the opinion that she had done it willfully, to spite her master or mistress, or to keep her from being sold down South.[68]

Another instance is described as follows:

As I came up, a second-rate plantation hand of the name of Noah, but whom the crier persisted in calling "Noey," was being offered, it being an administrator's sale. Noey, on mounting the steps, had assumed a most drooping aspect, hanging his head and affecting the feebleness of old age. He had probably hoped to have avoided sale by a dodge, which is very common in such cases. But the first bid—$1,000— startled him, and he looked eagerly to the quarter whence it proceeded. "Never mind who he is, he has got the money. Now, gentlemen, just go on; who will say fifty." And so the crier proceeds with his monotonous calling. "I ain't worth all that, mass'r; I ain't much count no how," cried Noey energetically to the first bidder. "Yes you are, Noey— ah, $1,000, thank you, sir," replies the crier." [69]

The strength of Negro resistance to slavery becomes apparent in the extent to which the slaves mutilated themselves in their efforts to escape work. A girl on Lewis' plantation who had been injured tied pack thread around her wounds when they started to heal and then rubbed dirt in them. In her anxiety to avoid work she gave herself a very serious infection.[70] But this action was mild compared to that of others.

General Leslie Coombs, of Lexington, owned a man named Ennis, a house carpenter. He had bargained with a slave-trader to take him and carry him down the river. Ennis was determined not to go. He took a broadaxe and cut one hand off; then contrived to lift the axe, with his arm pressing it to his body, and let it fall upon the other, cutting off the ends of the fingers.[71]

"But some on 'em would rather be shot then be took, sir," he added simply.

A farmer living near a swamp confirmed this account, and said he knew of three or four being shot on one day.[72]

Planters had much trouble with slaves fresh from Africa, the new slaves committing suicide in great numbers. Ebo landing in the Sea Islands was the site of the mass suicide of Ebo slaves who simply walked in a body into the ocean and drowned themselves. A planter writing on the handling of slaves mentions the difficulty of adjusting the Africans to slavery. He advocates mixing them in with seasoned slaves.

It too often happens that poor masters, who have no other slaves or are too greedy, require hard labor of these fresh negroes, exhaust them quickly, lose them by sickness and more often by grief. Often they hasten their own death; some wound themselves, others stifle themselves by drawing in the tongue so as to close the breathing passage, others take poison, or flee and perish of misery and hunger.[73]

The one problem of Negro resistance to slavery which is most enticing is that of the attitude of slave mothers toward their children. There are frequent references in the literature to Negro women who boasted about the number of "niggers they hade for the massah," but breeding was probably quite secondary to sex activity. It would be interesting to discover the motives behind this apparent pleasure in presenting babies to the master. Some of the women may have been sincere in their pride. What makes this problem peculiarly important is the presence of much indirect evidence that, the Negro mothers either had no affection for their children, or did not want them to be raised as slaves.

We know quite well that African Negroes are (at least reasonably) able to take care of their children, and that the slave women efficiently tended the children of the plantation mistress. Yet one runs across comment after comment that the Negro mothers were ignorant, and careless, and did not know how to care for their own offspring. Typical of such statements is this:

> The Negro mothers are often so ignorant and indolent, that they cannot be trusted to keep awake and administer medicine to their own children; so that the mistress has often to sit up all night with a sick Negro child.[74]

Guion Johnson states that plantation owners in the Sea Islands offered the mothers rewards to take good care of their children. They were paid for those who survived the first year! This at least would indicate that there was something to be desired in their attitude toward their children.

Occasionally one runs across a reference to a slave mother killing her child, but the statements are almost invariably incomplete. For instance, Catterall [75] has a record of a trial, the details of which are: "The prisoner was indicted for murder of her own child," no more. Or a plantation overseer writes, "Elizabeth's child died last night. She smothered it somehow." [76] There is no indication as to whether or not the smothering was deliberate.

Several cases, where it was certain that parents killed their children to keep them from slavery, have been described. They are important enough to be given in detail.

> Of all the cases of slave rendition, the saddest and probably the most circulated at the time was that of Margaret Garner. Winter was the best time for flight across the Ohio River, for when it was frozen over the difficulties of crossing were fewer. Simeon Garner, with his wife Margaret and two children, fled from slavery in Kentucky during the cold winter of 1856 and, after crossing the frozen stream at night, made their ways to the house of a free Negro in Cincinnati.

Quickly tracing the fugitive Negroes to their hideout in Cincinnati, the armed pursuers, after some resistance, broke down the door and entered the house. There they found Margaret, the mother, who, preferring death to slavery for her children, had striven to take their lives, and one child lay dead on the floor. The case was immediately brought into court, where despite the efforts made by sympathetic whites, rendition was ordered. On their return to slavery, Margaret in despair attempted to drown herself and child by jumping into the river but even the deliverance of death was denied her, for she was recovered and soon thereafter sold to a trader who took her to the cotton fields of the Far South.[77]

Not only were slaves known to take the lives of their masters or overseers, but they were now and then charged with the murder of their own children, sometimes to prevent them from growing up in bondage. In Covington a father and mother, shut up in a slave baracoon and doomed to the southern market, "when there was no eye to pity them and no arm to save," did by mutual agreement "send the souls of their children to Heaven rather than have them descend to the hell of slavery," and then both parents committed suicide.[78]

"Take off your shoes, Sylva," said Mrs. A., "and let this gentleman see your feet."

"I don't want to," said Sylva.

"But I want you to," said her mistress.

"I don't care if you do," replied Sylva sullenly.

"You must," said the mistress firmly.

The fear of punishment impelled her to remove the shoes. Four toes on one foot, and two on the other were wanting! "There!" said the mistress, "my husband, who learned the blacksmith's trade for the purpose of teaching it to the slaves, to increase their market value, has, with his own hands, pounded off and wrung off all those toes, when insane with passion. And it was only last week that he thought Sylva was saucy to me, and he gave her thirty lashes with the horse whip. She was so old that I could not bear to see it, and I left the house.

"Sylva says," Mrs. A. continued, "that she has been the mother of thirteen children, every one of whom she has destroyed with her own hands, in their infancy, rather than have them suffer slavery!" [79]

V

The patterns of resistance to slavery studied in this paper are: (1) deliberate slowing up of work; (2) destruction of property, and indifferent work; (3) feigning illness and pregnancy; (4) injuring one's self; (5) suicide; (6) a possibility that a significant number of slave mothers killed their children.

The motivation behind these acts was undoubtedly complex. The most obvious of the motives was a desire to avoid work. It has been demonstrated that the slaves were acutely conscious of the fact that they had nothing to gain by hard work except in those instances where they were working under the task system. The destruction of property and the poor quality of the slaves' work was mainly due to their indifference to their tasks. There is enough evidence that they could, and did, work hard and well when sufficiently motivated to refute any contention that the Negro slaves were congenitally poor workers.

Many of the slaves reacted to the institution of slavery in a far more drastic fashion than could be manifested by a mere desire to avoid work. Some of these slaves committed suicide; others killed members of their families, usually their children, in order that they might not grow up as slaves.

Possibly the most significant aspect of these patterns of resistance is the aggression against the white masters they imply. Unfortunately, however, though this aspect may be the most significant, it is the least subject to proof. On the plane of logic, there is every reason to believe that a people held in bondage would devise techniques such as have been described above as an indirect means of retaliation. The statement of Dollard, previously quoted,[30] indicates that such techniques (slowness, inefficiency, etc.) are used at the present time as a means of indirect aggression.

The material presented here suggests the need for a reconsideration of the concept of the Negro's easy adjustment to slavery. He was not a cheerful, efficient worker, as has been assumed. Rather, he was frequently rebellious, and almost always sullen, as any person faced with a disagreeable situation from which he cannot escape will normally be. Nor, can the belief that racial inferiority is responsible for inefficient workmanship on his part be supported. For such deficiencies of his workmanship as he manifested, or, indeed, may still be manifested, are seen to be explainable in terms that are in no sense to be couched in the conventional mold of inherent racial differences.

NOTES

1 We wish to express our appreciation to Professor M. J. Herskovits, under whose direction this research has been carried on.
2 Reuter, E. B., *The American Race Problem,* New York, 1927, p. 7.
3 Cf. Aptheker, Herbert, "American Negro Slave Revolts," *Science and Society,* 1:512–538, 1937; Wish, Harvey, "American Slave Insurrections before 1861," *Journal of Negro History,* 23:435–450, 1928; Wish, Harvey, "The Slave Insurrection Panic of 1856," *Journal of Southern History,* 5:206–222, 1939; see also Herskovits, M. J., *The Myth of the Negro Past,* pp. 99–105.

4 Clarke, Lewis, *Narratives of the Sufferings of Lewis and Milton Clarke,* Boston, 1846, p. 123.
5 Redpath, James, *The Roving Editor: or, Talks with Slaves in the Southern States,* New York, 1859.
6 Dollard, John, *Caste and Class in a Southern Town,* New Haven, 1937, pp. 255, 256.
7 Douglass, Frederick, *Life and Times of Frederick Douglass,* p. 8.
8 William Brown, an escaped slave; in Benjamin Drew, *The Refugee,* Boston, 1856, p. 281.
9 Thomas Hedgebeth, a free Negro, in Benjamin Drew, *The Refugee,* Boston, 1856, p. 276.
10 Lyell, Sir Charles, *A Second Visit to the United States of America,* New York, 1849, II, 72.
11 Ozanne, T. D., *The South as It Is,* London, 1863, pp. 165, 166.
12 Anon., *An Inquiry Into the Condition and Prospects of the African Race,* Philadelphia, 1839, p. 83.
13 Olmsted, F. L., *A Journey in the Seaboard Slave States,* New York, 1863, p. 210.
14 *Ibid.,* p. 104.
15 Dollard, *op. cit.,* p. 257.
16 Phillips, U. B., *American Negro Slavery,* New York, 1918, p. 192.
17 Olmsted, *op. cit.,* p. 11.
18 Olmsted, *op. cit.,* pp. 192, 193.
19 *Ibid.,* p. 388.
20 Douglass, *op. cit.,* p. 261.
21 Brown, W. W., *Life of Williams Welles Brown, A Fugitive Slave,* Boston, 1848, p. 18. See also Williams, James, *Narratives of James Williams,* Boston, 1838, pp. 56, 62, 65.
22 Northup, Solomon, *Twelve Years a Slave,* 1853, pp. 226, 227.
23 Williams, James, *Narratives of James Williams,* Boston, 1838, p. 43.
24 Olmsted, *op. cit.,* pp. 435, 436.
25 *Ibid.,* p. 103.
26 *Ibid.,* p. 103.
27 *Ibid.,* p. 430.
28 *Ibid.,* p. 207.
29 The speaker had freed his slaves.
30 Olmsted, *op. cit.,* pp. 100, 101.
31 Bassett, J. S., *The Southern Plantation Overseer as Revealed in His Letters,* Northampton, Mass., 1925, p. 66.
32 Olmsted, F. L., *A Journey in the Back Country,* New York, 1863, p. 79.
33 Phillips, U. B., *American Negro Slavery,* pp. 303, 304.
34 Drew, B., *The Refugee,* p. 164.
35 *Ibid.,* p. 167.
36 Parson, C. G., *Inside View of Slavery,* Boston, 1853, p. 94.
37 Anon. *An Inquiry Into the Condition and Prospects of the African Race,* Philadelphia, 1839, p. 83.
38 Olmsted, F. L., *A Journey in the Seaboard Slave States,* pp. 46, 47.
39 Redpath, *op. cit.,* p. 241.
40 Olmsted, F. L., *A Journey in the Back Country,* p. 227.
41 Kemble, F. A., *Journal of a Residence on a Georgian Plantation in 1838–1839,* New York, 1863, p. 242.
42 Lewis, M. G., *Journal of a West Indian Proprietor, 1815–1817,* London, 1929, p. 267.
43 Phillips, U. B., *Plantation and Frontier Documents, 1649–1863,* Cleveland, 1909, p. 34.
44 Olmsted, F. L., *A Journey in the Seaboard Slave States,* p. 91.
45 Hanson, C. W., *The Stranger in America,* London, 1807, p. 357.

46 Olmsted, F. L., *A Journey in the Seaboard Slave States*, p. 145.
47 *Ibid.*, p. 480.
48 *Ibid.*, pp. 481–484.
49 Phillips, U. B., *Plantation and Frontier Documents, 1694–1863*, p. 137.
50 Since this paper was written a significant contribution has appeared which throws a new light on the subject of slave illness. (Felice Swados, "Negro Health on the Ante Bellum Plantations," *Bulletin of the History of Medicine,* vol. x, no. 3, October, 1941.) Though Swados demonstrated that the rate of actual sickness among the Negroes was very high, she leaves some doubt as to what proportion of sickness was feigned. For instance, in a footnote (p. 472) she refers to Sydnor's compilations of the records of sickness on several plantations as indications of the extent of actual sickness, even going so far as to note that on one plantation most of the sickness occurred during the picking season. Sydnor, himself, indicates that he believes that these records demonstrate that a great deal of the sickness was feigned.
51 Cartwright's italics.
52 Olmsted, F. L., *A Journey in the Seaboard Slave States*, p. 193.
53 *Ibid.*, p. 189.
54 *Ibid.*, pp. 416, 417.
55 *Ibid.*, p. 187.
56 Sydnor, C. S., *Slavery in Mississippi*, New York, 1933, pp. 45ff.
57 Olmsted, F. L., *A Journey in the Seaboard Slave States*, p. 187.
58 Lewis, M. G., *Journal of a West Indian Proprietor, 1815–1817*, London, 1929, p. 168.
59 Olmsted, F. L., *A Journey in the Seaboard Slave States*, pp. 423, 424.
60 Olmsted, F. L., *A Journey in the Back Country*, p. 77.
61 Olmsted, F. L., *A Journey in the Seaboard Slave States*, pp. 187–191.
62 Kemble, F. A., *op. cit.*, p. 235.
63 Phillips, U. B., *American Negro Slavery*, p. 436.
64 Smedes, S., *Memorials of a Southern Planter*, Baltimore, 1887, p. 80.
65 Phillips, U. B., *American Negro Slavery*, p. 199.
66 Coleman, J. W., *Slavery Times in Kentucky*, Chapel Hill, N.C., 1940, p. 130.
67 *Ibid.*, pp. 129–130.
68 Redpath, *op. cit.*, pp. 253–254.
69 Pollard, E. A., *The Southern Spy*, Washington, 1859, pp. 13–14.
70 Lewis, *op. cit.*, p. 168.
71 Clarke, *op. cit.*, p. 125.
72 Olmsted, F. L., *A Journey in the Seaboard Slave States*, p. 160.
73 Phillips, U. B., *Plantation and Frontier Documents*, II, p. 31.
74 Lyell, *op. cit.*, p. 264.
75 Catterall, H. H. (ed.), *Judicial Cases Concerning American Slavery and the Negro*, Washington, D.C., 1926–1937, Vol. II, p. 59.
76 Bassett, *op. cit.*, p. 59.
77 Coleman, J. W., *op. cit.*, p. 208.
78 *Ibid.*, p. 269.
79 Parson, C. G., *op. cit.*, p. 212.
80 See above, p. 9.

Eugene D. Genovese says that the "principal task of radical historians . . . has too often been to provide the masses with historical heroes, to make them aware of their glorious tradition of resistance to oppression, and to portray them as implacably hostile to the social order in which they have been held." He goes on to say that the evidence often belies the claims made—and that this is particularly true of the search for black revolutionaries in ante-bellum America.

Genovese offers several reasons for the extremely weak revolutionary tradition among North American slaves in contrast to that in Latin America. He does not deny that there was resistance, but he does entertain the possibility that the play acting, stealing, and malingering might have had quite a different effect on both master and slave than that suggested by many writers (such as the Bauers).

Genovese attributes the failure of early black protest to a lack of political consciousness rather than to "docility" or "infantilization." He notes that then, as in recent times, black nationalism offered the best hope for change.

Many black critics reject Genovese's view of the past. Few, however, disagree with his thoughts on what to do about the future.

2

Eugene D. Genovese

THE ROOTS OF BLACK NATIONALISM

American radicals have long been imprisoned by the pernicious
notion that the masses are necessarily both good and revolutionary,
and by the even more pernicious notion that, if they are not, they
should be. The principal task of radical historians therefore has too
often been to provide the masses with historical heroes, to make them
aware of their glorious tradition of resistance to oppression, and to
portray them as having been implacably hostile to the social order in
which they have been held. This viewpoint now dominates the black
liberation movement, which has been fed for decades by white radical
historians who in this one respect have set the ideological pace for
their liberal colleagues. It has become virtually sacrilege—or at least
white chauvinism—to suggest that slavery was a social system within
which whites and blacks lived in harmony as well as antagonism, that
there is little evidence of massive, organized opposition to the regime,
that the blacks did not establish a revolutionary tradition of much

From Eugene D. Genovese, "The Legacy of Slavery and the Roots of Black
Nationalism," *Studies on the Left*, 6 (November–December 1966), 3–26.

significance, and that our main problem is to discover the reasons for
the widespread accommodation and, perhaps more important, the
long-term effects both of the accommodation and of that resistance
which did occur.

In 1831 Nat Turner led a slave revolt on which has hung most of
the legend of armed black resistance to slavery. Of the 250 or so
revolts chronicled and analyzed in Herbert Aptheker's *American
Negro Slave Revolts*,[1] Turner's has pride of place and was described
by Aptheker as a "cataclysm." Yet, when we look closely, this revolt,
like the total history of such revolts, recedes in importance and magnitude. As many of Aptheker's critics have pointed out, most of the 250
revolts probably never happened, being the imagination of hysterical
or self-serving whites, insignificant plots that never matured, or mere
local disturbances of a questionable nature. Of the three major revolts, one, Denmark Vesey's, was crushed before it came to fruition;
only Gabriel Prosser's in 1800 and Turner's reached impressive proportions. Even so painstaking and thorough a scholar as Aptheker has
been unable to discover firm evidence of a major revolt between 1831
and 1865. As for Turner's, less than one hundred slaves joined. A
revolt of this size would rate little more than a page or two in a
comprehensive work on slave revolts in Brazil. To cite only two outstanding examples, runaway slaves in the Brazilian Northeast organized their own colony, Palmares, and waged a 65-year struggle for
autonomy with as many as 20,000 people.[2] During the first four
decades of the nineteenth century there were a series of violent and
extensive risings in Bahia, culminating in the great Muslim-led holy
war of 1835.[3] We need not dwell on Haiti,[4] as the record of Jamaica,
Cuba and other countries is also impressive. Even if, as Aptheker
suggests, news of many smaller risings was suppressed, the effect
would have been to prevent the accumulation of a tradition to encourage and sustain revolt-prone slaves. On balance, we find the
absence or extreme weakness of such a tradition.

There were many reasons for this extreme weakness. First, we
need to consider the kind of Africans brought here. It has long been
falsely assumed that, since slave traders mixed their cargoes, all parts
of the hemisphere received similarly mixed bags. But Brazil, for example, received large numbers of Angolans and Congolese, whose military, religious and cultural traditions made them especially difficult
to control.[5] Brazil also received a large number of Muslim slaves from
Upper Guinea who proved intractable everywhere in the hemisphere.
The United States, on the other hand, largely drew its slaves from
those portions of Lower Guinea which had a population previously
disciplined to servitude and domination. Ironically, these Africans

were, in some respects, among the most advanced in technical culture.

Second, the slave trade to the United States came to an end in 1808, although illegal importations continued to trickle in; in contrast, the trade to Cuba and Brazil continued well into the nineteenth century. The presence of large numbers of newly imported Africans can generally be correlated with incidence of revolt. In the United States the great majority of slaves during the antebellum period had been born and raised on Southern plantations. Their ranks received little reinforcement from newly enslaved and aggressive Africans.

Third, a review of the history of Brazil and the Caribbean suggests that an important ingredient in the development of revolts out of local disturbances was the division of the whites into warring factions and the general weakness of the state apparatus. Together with these conditions went the general influence of geography in relation to state power. Where suitable terrain was combined with a weak state, runaway slaves could and did found maroon colonies, which directly fomented revolts and kept alive a tradition of armed resistance. With minor qualifications, these conditions did not exist in the United States.

Fourth, a substantial revolt presupposed the formation of ideology and leadership. In Brazil and the Caribbean two circumstances combined to encourage both: the cultivation of sugar led to the establishment of plantations averaging perhaps 200 slaves or more, and the size of the white population was small. As a result the blacks could keep alive much of their African culture or could develop a syncretized Afro-Brazilian or Afro-Cuba culture, which militated against the loss of identity and which could, under proper conditions, nurture resistance movements. Apart from Islam, non-Christian religious cults, generally of a syncretized type, played a great role in hemispheric slave revolts. In the United States an imposed Protestantism, when effective, generally kept the slaves docile.

Half the slaves in the United States lived on units of twenty or less; most of the others lived on plantations of fifty or less. Although blacks heavily outnumbered whites in large areas of the South, they were, in general, floating in a white sea. The white planters were residents, not absentees; the non-slaveholders were loyal, armed and disciplined; the country immediately beyond the plantation areas was inhabited by armed whites completely hostile to the blacks. Death, not refuge, lay beyond the plantation. For this reason, among others, blacks often looked to their masters to protect them against the depredations and viciousness of the poorer whites. We may therefore understand how, during race riots like that in Atlanta in 1906, blacks reportedly ran to whites—or at least to some whites—for protection.

The residency of the planters and their hegemony across the South gave American slavery its particular quality and especially set it off from Caribbean slavery. Between the Revolutionary War and the War for Southern Independence the treatment of slaves, defined as day-to-day conditions of life (housing, food, rigor of work routine, leisure time, incidence and character of corporal punishment) improved steadily and perceptibly. Although manumission was made increasingly difficult and escape from the system was sealed off, the harsh slave codes were steadily tempered by community sentiment and the interpretations of the state supreme courts. During the late antebellum period steady pressure built up to reform the slave codes in order to protect slave family life and to check glaring abuses of the slave's person. The purpose and effect of this amelioration in practice and at law was not to pave the way to freedom, but to consolidate the system from within and without. Like all liberal reformism it aimed to strengthen the social system.

For the planters these trends formed part of a developing world view within which paternalism became the specific manifestation of class consciousness. Paternalism did not mean kindness or generosity or love, although it embraced some of each; essentially it meant a special notion of duty and responsibility toward one's charges. Arbitrary power, harshness toward disobedience, even sadism, constituted its other side. For our immediate purposes, paternalism and the trend of treatment are especially noteworthy in confronting the slave with a world in which resistance could be quickly, severely and legitimately punished, whereas obedience placed him in a position to benefit from the favor of a master who more often than not had a genuine interest in his welfare. The picture of the docile and infantilized Sambo, drawn and analyzed so brilliantly by Stanley M. Elkins, is one-sided, but he is not far from the mark when he argues that the Southern regime greatly encouraged acceptance of and dependence upon despotic authority.[6] Elkins errs in thinking that the Sambo personality arose only in the United States, for it arose wherever slavery existed. He does not err in thinking that it was especially marked and extensive in the United States, where recourse to armed resistance was minimal and the tradition of paternalism took such firm root.

To say that slaves generally accommodated is not to say that they were so dehumanized as to be incapable of all forms of protest. Historians are quick to claim rebelliousness every time a slave broke a plow or stole a hog, but at least some room might be left for lack of initiative, thoughtlessness, stupidity and venality. Yet, we do know of enough instances of deliberate acts of day-to-day resistance to permit us to speak of a strong undercurrent of dissatisfaction and hostility, the manifestations of which require analysis.

One of the more prominent and irritating habits of recalcitrant slaves was stealing. Plundering the hog pen and the smokehouse was an especially happy pastime. Radical and liberal historians have taken particular delight in insisting that slaves might "steal" from each other but only "took" from their masters. After all, their labor being unpaid, they only took that which was rightfully theirs. I can understand this viewpoint from liberals because I can understand almost anything from liberals; I cannot understand it from Marxists. Since Marxists regard all surplus value as deriving from unpaid labor time, we ought, by the same logic, to be delighted every time a worker commits robbery at his plant. I do not wish to discuss the general problem of ethics in relation to class oppression, but I do insist that the encouragement given by the slave system to thefts had dangerous effects on the slaves themselves. The slaves understood the link between conventional morality and the civilized behavior of the whites; by rejecting that morality they registered a protest, but they simultaneously underscored their own isolation from that standard of civilization. Few masters got upset over slave thefts. They expected their slaves to steal, and by doing so, the slaves accepted their master's image of themselves.

Southern folklore abounds with charming stories of slaves outwitting masters by behaving like black versions of the Good Soldier Schweik. The trouble is that too often the masters enjoyed being outwitted in the same way that a tyrannical father sometimes enjoys being outwitted by a child. Every contortion necessary to the job implied inferiority. It proved the slave a clever fellow; it hardly proved him a man. It gained a few privileges or crumbs but undermined self-respect and confirmed the master's sense of superiority. The postslavery tradition of obsequiousness, indirection and the wearing of a mask before white men has played a similar role in the South ever since.

Arson and the mishandling of tools stand out as more positively rebellious acts. As expressions of frustration and resentment they are understandable, and might, in a general context of rebellion, have had considerable social value. As it was, they amounted to individual and essentially nihilistic thrashing about. With luck a few slaves might do enough damage to ruin a planter, in which case he would be forced to sell out and perhaps have to break up slave families and friendships. Advocates of the philosophy of "burn-baby-burn," whether on a Mississippi plantation in the 1850's or in a Northern ghetto in the 1960's, would do well to bear in mind that of necessity it is primarily the blacks who get burned. On occasion a slave took direct action against a particularly unpleasant master or overseer and killed him. For that manly act he would, if lucky, be hanged.

As we review these actions, which by no means exhaust the range, we find the formation of a tradition of recalcitrance but not revolution, action but not politics, dim awareness of oppression but not cumulative, ideological growth. Thus, whereas most slaves came out of slavery with a psychology of dependence conditioned by paternalism, the most active spirits came out having learned little more than that they could get away with individual acts of undirected, misdirected or naively directed violence. What was missing was that sense of group consciousness, collective responsibility and joint political effort which is the essence of a revolutionary tradition.

The formation of class leadership presents another side of this development. Legend has it that house slaves and drivers, by virtue of their special positions, arrayed themselves on the side of the master against the field hands, who as the most oppressed were of course the most revolutionary and pure. Examination of plantation documents casts grave doubts on this legend. Few plantations were big enough to carry a staff of servants large enough to constitute a separate caste. Even then the social life of the plantation proved too enticing for them to maintain total separation. With much of their everyday world conditioned by contacts with field slaves, they could ill-afford to be wholly on the side of the whites. The range of behavior was wide, but there were many instances of identification and sympathy.

The drivers, or slave foremen, present an even clearer case. These men often dominated the everyday life of the plantation. On the whole masters trusted them more than they trusted their white overseers; overseers came and went after a year or two, but drivers usually stayed on in positions of authority for many years. Masters relied on their drivers to tell them if an overseer was too lax or too harsh and if the hands respected him. Rarely did a planter take his overseer's word against that of a trusted driver. Some drivers undoubtedly were themselves severe taskmasters who lorded it over their fellow slaves, but drivers, too, had no social life apart from that of the slave quarters and had to live with the others. In general, they compromised as best they could between the master to whom they had pledged loyalty and to whom they were indebted for special favors, and the slaves who constituted their everyday fellows. Often the driver stood as a protector or interpreter between slave and master or overseer. Drivers and house slaves often, although certainly not always, comprised a leading stratum in the eyes of the blacks as well as in the eyes of the whites.

In the Caribbean these privileged slaves led revolts; in the United States they served as agents of accommodation. Toussaint L'Ouverture was only the most prominent of insurrectionary leaders who had been trained to leadership within the system. The problem in the United States was not that the system did not create such privileged strata, nor that these strata were more docile or less courageous than those in the Caribbean. The problem was that the total environment reduced the possibilities for successful insurrection virtually to zero, and therefore made accommodationists out of the most high-spirited slave leaders. When the mass exodus from the plantations took place during the War for Southern Independence, drivers and house slaves often led their people to the Union lines. Not docility but lack of a tradition of armed resistance conditioned their leadership.

Potential recruitment of insurrectionary leaders was hampered by many other circumstances, of which three are especially noteworthy. For reasons already indicated little anti-Christian religious sentiment could develop. Religion (Islam, voodoo, or Afro-Catholic syncretisms) proved to be an essential ingredient in slave cohesion and organized resistance throughout the hemisphere, but in the United States the enforced prevalence of Protestant Christianity played an opposite role. The second group of potential leaders recruited from all strata were those who had sufficient strength, daring and resourcefulness to flee. The runaways are black folk heroes, with good reason, but they also drained the best elements out of the slave class. In much of Brazil and the Caribbean runaways had nowhere to go except into the back country to form maroon colonies, the existence of which encouraged slave disorder and resistance. Finally, the free blacks and mulattoes in the United States had little opportunity for self-development and rarely could or would provide leadership to slaves. Elsewhere in the hemisphere, where whites were relatively few, these free blacks and mulattoes were needed to fill a wide variety of social and economic functions. Often they prospered as a middle class. In some cases, feelings of racial solidarity or, as in Haiti, the racist stupidity of the whites, led them into partial identification with the cause of black freedom. Thus, with the exception of a rare Nat Turner, black leadership fell to those whose position within the plantation itself encouraged accommodation and negated the possibilities of effective political organization.

The War for Southern Independence brought these tendencies to a head. The staggering truth is that not one full-scale revolt broke out during a war in which local white police power had been drastically reduced. In only a few isolated cases did slaves drive off their masters and divide the land among themselves. Many, perhaps most, struck for freedom by fleeing to Union lines at the first opportunity. The attitude of the slaves toward the federals varied, but the great majority welcomed them with an adulation, trust and dependence that suggests the full force of the old paternalism.[7] Many blacks, free and slaves, Northern and Southern, entered the Union Army, where despite humiliating discrimination they gave a creditable account of themselves in action.

For all that, the record of the slaves and ex-slaves during the war constituted a disaster. Having relied previously on the protection and guidance of their masters, they now threw themselves on the mercies of the Union Army. As might be expected, untold thousands died in and out of virtual concentration camps, countless women were raped by Union troops, black soldiers generally found themselves used as menials or cannon fodder. Many decent and selfless white and black abolitionists accompanied the Union Army South and earnestly worked to educate and organize the freedmen; they deserve all the praise and attention historians are now heaping on them. The fact remains that no black movement and only a weak black leadership emerged from the war.

As the war years passed into the period of Reconstruction, these patterns were reinforced. The blacks could and did fight for their rights, but rarely under their own leadership. When they offered armed resistance under competent leadership they did well enough, but mostly they relied on the leadership of white politicians, or on the protection of federal troops, or on the advice of their own inexperienced leaders who in turn relied on whites. As Vernon Lane Wharton has observed, "The lesson learned was that the Negroes, largely unarmed, economically dependent, and timid and unresourceful after generations of servitude, would offer no effective resistance to violence."[8] When Whitelaw Reid asked black school children what they would do if someone tried to reenslave them, most responded that the troops would not permit it. No wonder Northern public opinion asked contemptuously in 1875 why a black majority in Mississippi constantly had to call for outside help.

The blacks sealed their own fate by relying on the protection of others. The Republican Party, the Union Army and the Freedman's Bureau all took on the role of protectors, but, if anything, the new paternalism proved much more flimsy and more insincere than the old. The best illustration may be found in the history of the Republican-sponsored, largely black militias. Ex-slaves, urged on and even threatened by their women, who were generally more militant than the men, responded to the calls of Republican governors and filled the ranks of state militias, which were put to effective use in guaranteeing Republican electoral victories. In several instances, especially toward the end of Reconstruction, militia units opposed each other on behalf of rival Republican factions. In the most appalling of these instances, the so-called Brooks-Baxter War in Arkansas in 1874, the Republican machine so discredited itself that the Democrats soon rode back to power. As Otis A. Singletary has sardonically observed, "The Negroes had been called to arms to fight in behalf of two white claimants for the governorship, as a consequence of which the Negro was eliminated as a political factor in Arkansas." [9] In Mississippi the radical governor, Adelbert Ames, called the blacks to arms in 1875 to counter Democratic violence, and then lost his nerve and disarmed them in return for a worthless pledge from the opposition. Significantly the black politicians in his party almost unanimously opposed using the black troops in a showdown. The militia movement failed because it faced greater force, but no less because its leaders were never willing to see it steeled in battle, especially in defense of specifically black interests.

In other respects the Reconstruction experience followed parallel lines. In the famous Sea Island experiment the blacks placed their trust in white generals, some of whom meant well and tried hard but could not prevail in the face of Washington's duplicity. When the old plantation owners returned with federal support, the blacks protested but ultimately accepted defeat without recourse to arms. Here, as with the militias, the masses seem to have been well ahead of their leaders. Demands for resistance were heard, anti-white feeling was manifest and the desire for land grew apace, but the leadership proved timid or mortgaged, and action independent of whites was deemed impractical. Black Congressmen and state legislators rarely fought for basic black interests and even opposed disfranchisement of ex-Confederate whites. With no powerful separate organizations and paramilitary units, without experience in leading their masses, they temporized and collapsed. Their fault did not lie in having coalesced with Northern whites, but in having coalesced from a position of weakness, without independent demands, organization and force. The masses moved sharply to the left and expressed an intense desire for land, but the old pattern persisted; they could not cut loose from accommodating leaders and from dependence on the ultimate authority of the whites. They did not so much demand, much less fight for, land, as they hoped it would be given them as a Christmas present.

The black leaders saw the duplicity of their white Republican allies, but had nowhere to go. Most had been Northerners or privileged Southern mulattoes; their links with the masses had never been firm. When election time arrived they swallowed their doubts and frustrations and, with the best of intentions, lied to their people. Without adequate traditions and without confidence in their masses they made the best deals they could. This lying carried on an old habit. Every slave, at some time or other, would outwit the white folks by pretending to be stupid or docile; unfortunately too often he simultaneously outwitted himself. When carried into slave leadership, it was generally impossible to outwit the whites without also outwitting the blacks. During the war, for example, the respected black pastor of a Baptist Church in Virginia offered a prayer for the victory of Confederate arms. Subsequently he was berated by his deacons for betraying the cause of the slaves, but he pacified them by saying, "Don't worry children; the Lord knew what I was talking about." [10] Undoubtedly, the Lord did, but the good pastor apparently never wondered whether or not his flock did also.

Some of the Reconstruction leaders simply sold out. As a distinguished South Carolina planter noted, they promised their people land and mules at every election but delivered only offices and jobs for themselves and their friends. [11] (Any resemblance to the War on Poverty is not of my making.)

Slavery and its aftermath left the blacks in a state of acute economic and cultural backwardness, with weak family ties and the much-discussed matriarchal preponderance. They also left a tradition of accommodation to paternalistic authority on the one hand, and a tradition of nihilistic violence on the other. Not docility or infantilization, but innocence of organized effort and political consciousness plagued the black masses and kept plaguing them well into the twentieth century. As a direct result of these effects and of the virtually unchallenged hegemony of the slaveholders, the blacks had little opportunity to develop a sense of their own worth and had every opportunity to learn to despise themselves. The inability of the men during and after slavery to support their families adequately, and especially to protect their women from rape or abuse without forfeiting their own lives, has merely served as the logical end of an emasculating process.

The remarkable ascendancy of Booker T. Washington after the post-Reconstruction reaction must be understood against this background. We need especially to account for his enormous influence over the black nationalists who came after him. Washington tried to meet the legacy of slavery on its own terms. He knew that slavery had ill-prepared his people for political leadership; he therefore retreated from political demands. He knew that slavery had rendered manual labor degrading; he therefore preached the gospel of hard work. He knew that slavery had undermined the family and elementary moral standards; he therefore preached the whole gamut of middle-class virtues and manners. He knew his people had never stood on their own feet and faced the whites as equals; he therefore preached self-reliance and self-help. Unhappily, apart from other ideological sins, he saw no way to establish self-reliance and self-respect except under the financial and social hegemony of the white upper classes. Somehow he meant to destroy the effects of paternalism in the long run by strengthening paternalism in the short run. It would be easy to say that he failed because of this tactic, but there is no way to be sure that the tactic was wrong in principle. He failed for other reasons, one of which was his reliance on the paternalistic, conservative classes at a time when they were rapidly losing power in the South to racist agrarian demagogues.

Washington's rivals did not, in this respect, do much better. The leaders of the NAACP repeatedly returned to a fundamental reliance on white leadership and money. Even Du Bois, in his classic critique of Washington, argued:

> While it is a great truth to say that the Negro must strive and strive mightily to help himself, it is equally true that unless his striving be not simply seconded, but rather aroused and encouraged by the initiative of the richer and wiser environing group, he cannot hope for great success.[12]

The differences between these militants and Washington's conservatives concerned emphases, tactics and public stance much more than ideological fundamentals. The differences were important, but their modest extent was no less so. The juxtaposition of the two tendencies reveals how little could be done even by the most militant without white encouragement and support. The wonder is that black Americans survived the ghastly years between 1890 and 1920 at all. Survival —and more impressive, growing resistance to oppression—came at the price of continuing many phases of a paternalistic tradition that had already sapped the strength of the masses.

The conflict between Washington and Du Bois recalled many earlier battles between two tendencies that are still with us. The first has accepted segregation at least temporarily, has stressed the economic development of the black community and has advocated self-help. This tendency generally prevailed during periods of retrogression in race relations until the upsurge of nationalism in our own day.

Washington was its prophet; black nationalism has been its outcome. The second has demanded integration, has stressed political action and has demanded that whites recognize their primary responsibility. Frederick Douglass was its prophet; the civil rights movement has been its outcome. Yet, the lines have generally been blurred. Du Bois often sounded like a nationalist, and Washington probably would have thought Malcolm X a madman.[13] This blurring reflects the dilemma of the black community as a whole and of its bourgeoisie in particular: How do you integrate into a nation that does not want you? How do you separate from a nation that finds you too profitable to release?

To probe the relationship between this past and the recent upsurge of the black masses requires more speculation and tentative judgment than one would like, but they cannot be avoided. Let us, at the risk of being schematic and one-sided, select several features of the developments of the last few decades and especially of the recent crisis for such analysis. In doing so let us bear in mind that the majority of blacks today live outside the South; that they are primarily urban, not rural, in all parts of the country; that whole cities are on the way to becoming black enclaves; that the problem increasingly centers on the urban North and West.[14] Let us bear in mind also that the only large-scale, organized black mass movements until recently have been nationalist. Garvey commanded an organization of hundreds of thousands; the Muslims have tens of thousands and influence many more. No integrationist organization has ever acquired such numerical strength; none has ever struck such deep roots in the black ghettoes.

Garvey's movement emphasized blackness as a thing of beauty, and struggled to convince the black masses to repudiate white leadership and paternalism. The pompous titles, offices, uniforms and parades did and do evoke ridicule, but their importance lay, as Edmund David Cronon says, "in restoring the all but shattered Negro self-confidence." There was enormous ideological significance in Garvey's delightful description of a light-skinned mulatto opponent as "a white man passing for Negro." [15]

A decisive break with the white man's church, if not wholly with his religion, has formed a major part of black nationalist thinking. In view of the central role of anti-Christian ideology in the slave risings of Brazil and the Caribbean and the generally accommodationist character of American Christianity, this has been a rational response to a difficult problem. Garvey tried to organize his own African Orthodox Church. The Islamic tendency, including Elijah Muhammed's Nation of Islam, has followed the maxim of Noble Drew Ali's Moorish

Science Movement, "Before you can have a God, you must have a nationality." Garvey's Black Jesus and Muhammed's Allah have had many attributes of a tribal deity. Of special importance in Muhammed's teaching is his decidedly un-Islamic denial of an afterlife. In this way Black Muslim eschatology embodies a sharp reaction against accommodationist ideology. The tendency to turn away from the white man's religion has taken many forms, including conversion to Catholicism ostensibly because of its lack of a color line. In Catholic Brazil, on the other hand, an equivalent reason is given by blacks who embrace Protestantism.[16]

Black Protestants in the United States have largely attended self-segregated churches since Reconstruction. With the collapse of Reconstruction these churches, especially in the South, played an increasingly accommodationist role, but they also served as community centers, protective agencies, marriage counseling committees and leadership training schools. As objective conditions changed, so did many ministers, especially the younger ones. One of the great ironies of the current struggle for integration has been the leading role played by ministers whose training and following have been made possible by segregated organizations. The experience of the Protestant churches and their anti-Christian rivals brings us back to slavery's legacy of accommodationist but by no means necessarily treasonable leadership, of an absence of collective effort, of paternalistically-induced dependence and of emasculation. Theoretically, a militant mass leadership could have arisen from sources other than enforced segregation; historically there seems to have been no other way.[17]

The first difficulty with the integrationist movement arises not from its ultimate commitment, which may or may not be desirable, but from the determined opposition of the whites, whose hostility to close association with blacks recedes slowly if at all. Integration may only mean desegregation, and outstanding black intellectuals like Killens and Baldwin insist that that is all they want it to mean; it need not mean assimilation. In fact, however, the line is difficult to hold, and segregationists probably do not err in regarding one as the prelude to the other. In any case, de facto segregation in education and housing is growing worse, and many of the professed goals of the civil rights movement look further away than ever. Communities like Harlem face substantially the same social problems today as they did forty years ago.[18] I need not dwell on the worsening problem of black unemployment and its implications.

Even where progress, however defined, occurs, the frustration of the black masses deepens. The prosperity of recent decades has widened the gap between blacks and whites even of the same class. The rise of the African peoples has inspired blacks here but has also threatened to open a gap in political power and dignity between Africans and Afro-Americans.[19]

The resistance of whites and the inflexibility of the social system constitute only half the problem. A. James Gregor, in an article published in *Science & Society* in 1963, analyzes an impressive body of sociological and psychological literature to demonstrate that integration under the disorderly conditions of American capitalist life more often than not undermines the development and dignity of the participating blacks. He shows that the problems of the black masses, in contradistinction to those of the bourgeoisie, become intensified by an integration which, in the nature of things, must pass them by. As Gregor demonstrates, black nationalism has been the political reply of these masses and especially of the working class.[20] Similarly, in his honest and thoughtful book, *Crisis in Black and White*, Charles E. Silberman analyzes cases such as that in New Rochelle, in which poor black and rich children had the wonderful experience of integrating in school. Why should anyone be surprised that the experiment proved a catastrophe for the black children, who promptly lost whatever ambition they might have had.[21]

When liberals and academics speak of a "crisis of identity," they may sometimes merely wish to divert attention from the prior fact of oppression, but, by whatever name, that crisis exists. Slavery and its aftermath emasculated the black masses; they are today profoundly sick and shaking with convulsions. It does us no good to observe, with Kardiner and Ovesey, that a psychology of oppression can only disappear when the oppression has disappeared.[22] It does us no good to admit that the sickness of white racism is more dangerous than the sickness it has engendered. We face an aroused, militant black community that has no intention of waiting for others to heal themselves. Those who believe that emasculation is the figment of the liberal imagination ought to read the words of any militant leader from David Walker to W.E.B. Du Bois, from Frederick Douglass to Martin Luther King, from Robert F. Williams to Malcolm X. The cry has been to assert manhood and renounce servility. Every outstanding black intellectual today—Killens, Baldwin, Ellison—makes the point in one way or another. Let me quote only one, Ossie Davis on the death of Malcolm X:

> [Negroes knew] that Malcolm—whatever else he was or was not— *Malcolm was a man!*
> White folks do not need anybody to remind them that they are

men. We do! This was his one incontrovertible benefit to his people. Protocol and common sense require that Negroes stand back and let the white man speak up for us, defend us, and lead us from behind the scene in our fight. This is the essence of Negro politics. But Malcolm said to hell with that! Get up off your knees and fight your own battles. That's the way to win back your self-respect. That's the way to make the white man respect you. And if he won't let you live like a man, he certainly can't keep you from dying like one.[23]

Is it any wonder, then, that Dr. King could write, almost as a matter of course, that the blacks of Birmingham during the summer of 1963 shook off 300 years of psychological slavery and found out their own worth? [24] It is no less instructive that his aide, the Reverend Wyatt T. Walker, denounced as "hoodlums" and "winos" those who responded to the attempt on King's life by attacking the white racists. King himself put it bluntly when he pleaded that the black militant be allowed to march and sit-in, "If his repressed emotions do not come out in these nonviolent ways, they will come out in ominous expressions of violence." [25]

King and his followers apparently believe that concerted action for integration can cure the ills engendered by slavery and subsequent oppression and break down discrimination at the same time. In one sense they are right. Their greatest achievement has been to bring order and collective effort to a people who had learned little of the necessity for either. But King must deliver victory or face grave consequences. As we have seen, not all slaves and freedmen yielded meekly to the oppressor. Many fought, sometimes with great ferocity, but they generally fought by lashing out rather than by organized revolutionary effort. It would be the crowning irony if the civil rights movement has taught just enough of the lesson of collective effort to guarantee greater and more widespread nihilism in the wake of its inability to realize its program.

More and more young black radicals are currently poring over Frantz Fanon's psychopathic panegyric to violence. Fanon argues that violence frees the oppressor from his inferiority complex and restores his self-respect.[26] Perhaps, but it is also the worst way to do either. Black Americans, like colonials, have always resorted to violence without accomplishing those goals. A slave who killed his overseer did not establish his manhood thereby—any wild animal can kill—he merely denied his docility. Violence can serve Fanon's purpose only when it is collective and disciplined—that is, political—but then it is precisely the collective effort, not the violence, that does the healing.[27]

The legend of black docility threatens to betray those who perpetuate it. They are ill-prepared for the yielding of one side of the slave tradition—accommodation and servility—to the other side—antisocial and nihilistic action. The failure of integration and the lawlessness to which the blacks have for so long been subjected and subject combine to produce that result. James Baldwin and Malcolm X, especially in remarks on the prestige of the ghetto hustler, have each warned of this danger.[28] Bayard Rustin has made a similar point with gentle irony:

> From the point of view of motivation, some of the healthiest Negro youngsters I know are juvenile delinquents: vigorously pursuing the American Dream of material acquisition and status, yet finding the conventional means of attaining it blocked off, they do not yield to defeatism but resort to illegal (and sometimes ingenious) methods. They are not alien to American culture.[29]

Those historians who so uncritically admire the stealing of hogs and smashing of plows by slaves might consider its modern equivalent. In the words of Silberman:

> There are other means of protest, of course: misbehaving in school, or dropping out of school altogether; not showing up for work on time, or not showing up at all (and lying about the reason); breaking school windows or ripping telephone receivers out of outdoor phone booths; or the oldest form of protest of all, apathy—a flat refusal to cooperate with the oppressor or to accept his moral code.[30]

Black nationalism, in its various manifestations, constitutes a necessary response on the part of the black masses. The Muslims, for example, have understood the inner needs of the working-class blacks who have filled their ranks and have understood the futility—for these people at least—of integrationist hopes. Their insistence on the forcible assertion of a dignified, disciplined, collectively responsible black community represents a rational response to a harsh reality.[31] We need not dwell on what is unrealistic, romantic or even reactionary in the Nation of Islam or other nationalist groups; they are easy to see. Ralph Bunche, in his radical days, Gunnar Myrdal and many others have for years pointed out that the idea of a separate black economy is a will-o-the-wisp and that the idea of a separate territory is less than that. Yet I am not sure how to answer Marc Schleifer who in 1963 asked whether these goals were less realistic than those of equality under capitalism or a socialist revolution in the foreseeable future.[32] I am not sure, either, that Malcolm X, Harold W. Cruse and Stokely Carmichael have not been wiser than their Marxist critics in

demanding black ownership of everything in Harlem.[33] Such ownership will do little toward the creation of a black economy, but many
of its advocates are easily bright enough to know as much. The point
is that it may, as Malcolm X suggested, play a decisive role in the
establishment of community stability and self-respect.

The black struggle for equality in America has always had two
tendencies—integrationist and separatist—and it is likely to retain
both. Since a separate economy and national territory are not serious
possibilities, the struggle for economic integration will undoubtedly
be pressed forward. For this reason alone some degree of unity between the civil rights and nationalist tendencies may be expected.
The black bourgeoisie and its allied stratum of skilled and government
clerical workers will certainly continue its fight for integration, but
the interest of the black workers in this fight is, at bottom, even
greater. At the same time there will clearly be serious defeats, as well
as some victories, and the slogan "Freedom Now!" may soon turn to
ashes.

The cumulative problems of past and present nonetheless demand
urgent action. The assertion of black hegemony in specific cities and
districts—nationalism if you will—offers the only politically realistic
hope of transcending the slave heritage. First, it seems the only way
for black communities to police themselves, to curb antisocial elements and to enforce adequate health and housing standards, and
yet break with paternalism and instill pride and a sense of worth.
Second, it seems the best way to build a position of strength from
which to fight for a proper share of jobs and federal funds as a matter
of right, not privilege. Black nationalism may yet prove to be the only
force capable of restraining the impulse to violence, of disciplining
black rebelliousness and of absorbing the nihilistic tradition into a
socially constructive movement. If this seems like a conservative
rendering of an ostensibly revolutionary movement, I can only answer
that there are no ingredients for a successful, independent black revolution, and that black nationalism can ultimately go only a few steps
further to the left than the white masses. The rise of specifically black
cities, counties and districts with high quality black schools, well
paid teachers, as well as political leaders, churches and community
centers, could and should uproot the slave tradition once and for all,
could and should act as a powerful lever for structural reform of the
American economy and society.

I do not offer these remarks as a program for a black movement,
for the time is past when white men can offer programs to black
militants. They are, happily, no longer listening. But I do submit that

they are relevant to the formation of a program for ourselves—for the American left. If this analysis has merit, the demands of the black community will increasingly swing away from the traditional appeal to federal power and toward the assertion of local and regional autonomy. Even now Bayard Rustin and others warn that federal troops can only preserve the status quo. I should observe, further, that the appeals to Washington reflect the convergence of two powerful and debilitating traditions: slave-engendered paternalistic dependence and the growing state paternalism of white America. Let us admit that the naive fascination of leftists for centralized power has, since the 1930's, greatly strengthened this tendency. With such labels as "progressive" and even "socialist," corporate liberalism has been building what William Appleman Williams has aptly called a nonterroristic totalitarian society. Yet American socialism has never even posed a theoretical alternative. When Professor Williams called for a program of regional and local reassertion and opposition to centralization, he was dismissed by most radicals as a Utopian of doubtful mental competence. We may now rephrase his question: How do we propose to support an increasingly nationalistic black radicalism, with its demands for local hegemony, unless we have an ideology and program of opposition to the centralization of state power?

The possible courses for the black liberation movement include a total defeat in an orgy of violence (we ought to remember that there is nothing inevitable in its or our victory), a compromise with imperialism in return for some degree of local rule or the integration of its bourgeois strata, and the establishment of black power on the basis of a developing opposition to American capitalism. Since its future depends to a great extent on the progress of its integrationist struggle for a place in the economy, the black community must for a while remain well to the left of the current liberal consensus by its demands for public works and structural reform. But reform could occur under the auspices of an expansion rather than a contraction of state centralization, and the most militant of the black leaders may have to settle for jobs and local political control in return for allegiance to a consolidating national and international empire. The final result will be decided by the struggle within white America, with the blacks playing the role of an increasingly independent ally for one or another tendency. Notwithstanding some offensive and pretentious rhetoric, the advocates of black power have judged their position correctly. They are determined to win control of the ghettoes, and we would be foolish not to bet on them. The use to which they put that power, however, depends not on our good wishes or on their good intentions, but on what they are offered as a *quid pro quo*. For American socialism the black revolt opens an opportunity for relevance that has been missing for decades. What we do with that opportunity, as the leaders of SNCC have rather rudely reminded us, is our problem, not theirs.

NOTES

1 Aptheker, Herbert, *American Negro Slave Revolts* (New York, 1943, 1963).
2 Carneiro, Edison, *O Quilombo dos Palmares, 1630–1695* (Sao Paulo, 1947).
3 Cf., Abbé Ignace Etienne, "La Secte musulmane des Malès du Brésil et leur révolte en 1835," *Anthropos*, IV (1909), 99–105; 405–415.
4 Cf., esp. C. L. R. James, *The Black Jacobins: Toussaint L'Ouverture and the San Domingo Revolution* (2nd ed., rev.; New York, 1963), which deserves to rank as a classic of Marxian historiography but has been largely ignored, perhaps because of the author's Trotskyist politics.
5 For example, Palmares was established by Angolans. See "Carta do Governador Fernao de Souza Coutinho . . ." in Ernesto Ennes, *As Guerras nos Palmares* (Sao Paulo, 1938), pp. 133–138, Nina Rodrigues, *Os Africanos no Brasil* (3rd ed., Sao Paulo, 1945), Ch. III.
6 Elkins, Stanley M., *Slavery: A Problem in American Institutional and Intellectual Life* (Chicago, 1959), esp. Ch. III.
7 Wiley, Bell Irvin, *Southern Negroes, 1861–1865* (New Haven, 1965; first pub., 1938), esp. pp. 14–15.
8 Wharton, Vernon Lane, *The Negro in Mississippi, 1865–1900* (New York, 1965; first pub. 1947), p. 190.
9 Singletary, Otis A., *Negro Militia and Reconstruction* (Austin, 1952), p. 65.
10 Wiley, *Southern Negroes*, p. 107.
11 Manigault, Charles, "Souvenirs of Our Ancestors & of My Immediate Family," ca. 1873. Ms. in the Manigault Papers, University of North Carolina.
12 Du Bois, W. E. Burghardt, *The Soul of Black Folk* (New York, 1964; first pub. 1903), p. 53.
13 For the period 1890–1915 see August Meier's careful and illuminating *Negro Thought in America: Racial Ideologies in the Age of Booker T. Washington* (New York, 1964).
14 For a perceptive discussion of these trends see Charles E. Silberman, *Crisis in Black and White* (New York, 1964), esp. pp. 7, 29–31.
15 Cronon, Edmund David, *Black Moses: The Story of Marcus Garvey and the Universal Negro Improvement Association* (Madison, 1955, 1964), p. 174. It was never Garvey's intention to send all blacks back to Africa; he wanted a strong African nation to serve as a protector to blacks everywhere. See esp. the interview with Garvey in James Weinstein, ed., "Black Nationalism: The Early Debate," *Studies on the Left*, IV, no. 3 (1964), pp. 50–58.
        The idea of black nationality in America stretches back to the beginnings of the nineteenth century, if not earlier. See esp. Herbert Aptheker, "Consciousness of Negro Nationality to 1900," *Toward Negro Freedom* (New York, 1956), pp. 104–111; also, Benjamin Quarles, *The Negro in the Making of America* (New York, 1964), p. 157.
16 Bastide, Roger, and Fernandes, Florestan, *Brancos e negros em Sao Paulo* (2nd ed.; Sao Paulo, 1959), p. 254.

17 This recent experience, especially of SCLC, reveals the legacy of the past in other ways as well. Louis E. Lomax has criticized Dr. King for organizational laxness and has related the problems of the SCLC to the structure of the Baptist Church, "The Negro Baptist Church is a nonorganization. Not only is each congregation a sovereign body, dictated to by no one, but it would appear that the members who come together and form a Baptist Church are held together only by their mutual disdain for detailed organization and discipline." *The Negro Revolt* (New York, 1962), p. 86. As a result, according to Lomax, the SCLC is a loose, scattered organization that mobilizes itself only with great difficulty. Lomax makes good points but fails to note the extent to which this weakness flows from the entire history of black America and especially the black South. With justice, one could argue that the remarkable strength of SCLC in the face of this amorphousness is a singular tribute to Dr. King's political genius. He has mobilized masses who are ill-prepared for the kind of puritanical discipline preached by Elijah Muhammed.

18 Osofsky, Gilbert, *Harlem: The Making of a Ghetto* (New York, 1966), p. 179.

19 See the perceptive remarks on these two kinds of gaps in Oscar Handlin, *Fire-Bell in the Night: The Crisis in Civil Rights* (Boston, 1964), pp. 21–22, 53; C. Eric Lincoln, *The Black Muslims in America* (Boston, 1961), p. 45; and James Baldwin, *The Fire Next Time* (New York, 1964), pp. 105–106.

20 Gregor, A. James, "Black Nationalism: A Preliminary Analysis of Negro Radicalism," *Science & Society*, XXVII (Fall 1963), 415–432.

21 Silberman, *Crisis in Black and White*, p. 298. Even under more favorable conditions, as John Oliver Killens has noted, black children in the South often have a feeling of belonging that is undermined when they move north. *Black Man's Burden* (New York, 1965), pp. 84–85.

22 Kardiner, Abram, and Ovesey, Lionel, *The Mark of Oppression: Explorations in the Personality of the American Negro* (New York, 1951, 1962), p. 387.

23 Davis, Ossie, "On Malcolm X," in *The Autobiography of Malcolm X* (New York, 1965), p. 453.

24 King, Martin Luther, Jr., *Why We Can't Wait* (New York, 1964), p. 111.

25 Silberman, *Crisis in Black and White*, pp. 122, 199.

26 Fanon, Frantz, *The Wretched of the Earth* (New York, 1965). But see also two good critiques in *Studies on the Left*, VI, no. 3 (May–June, 1966): Samuel Rohdie, "Liberation and Violence in Algeria," pp. 83–89, and esp. A. Norman Klein, "On Revolutionary Violence," pp. 62–82.

27 The warning of so humane and sensitive a man as Killens on this matter is worth quoting: "The advocates of absolute non-violence have reckoned without the psychological needs of Black America. Let me state it plainly: There is in many Negroes a deep need to practice violence against their white tormentors." *Black Man's Burden*, p. 113. The Muslims understand this very well, as does Dr. King; they try to substitute internal discipline and collective effort for the violence itself.

28 Baldwin, *The Fire Next Time*, pp. 35–37; *The Autobiography of Malcolm X*, pp. 315–316.

29 Rustin, Bayard, "From Protest to Politics: The Future of the Civil Rights Movement," in F. L. Broderick and A. Meier, eds., *Negro Protest Thought in the Twentieth Century* (Indianapolis, 1965), p. 410.

30 Silberman, *Crisis in Black and White*, pp. 47–48.

31 The best study of the Muslims is E. U. Essien-Udom, *Black Nationalism: A Search for Identity in America* (New York, 1964). Elijah Muhammed has demonstrated remarkable awareness of the persistence of the slave tradition, even in its most elusive forms. His denunciation of black conspicuous consumption, for example, correctly views it as essentially a reflection of the mores of the slaveholders and counterposes to it standards that recall those of revolutionary petty-bourgeois puritanism.

32 Schleifer, Marc, "Socialism and the Negro Movement," *Monthly Review,* XV
   (Sept. 1963), pp. 225–228.
33 For a suggestive theoretical defense of such a demand see Harold W. Cruse,
   "Revolutionary Nationalism and the Afro-American," *Studies on the Left,* II,
   no. 3 (1962), 12–25; and his subsequent communication in III, no. 1 (1962),
   esp. p. 70. See also *The Autobiography of Malcolm X,* p. 318.

Whenever historians of the black experience discuss slave revolts and debate their significance, two uprisings are inevitably mentioned: Gabriel's Insurrection and Nat Turner's Revolt. Both of these are described in the pages to follow.

In an essay written especially for this volume, Gerald W. Mullin offers an impressive account and analysis of the well-planned "rebellion that did not happen" in Richmond, Virginia, in 1800. Piecing together the evidence, Mullin first tells the story of Gabriel's hopes and plans and ultimate failure. He then examines the social status of Gabriel's co-conspirators, the highly political character of their goals, and the nature of the world in which they lived and moved.

3

Gerald W. Mullin

GABRIEL'S INSURRECTION

In the summer of 1800 a group of slave artisans organized an attack on Richmond, the capital of Virginia.[1] Because the conspirators' plan was essentially an expression of their class and its understanding of the values and norms of the American Revolution, Gabriel's Rebellion was exceptionally political in character. It never took place; and the following interpretation is divided into a narrative conveying the conspiracy's meaning for its participants, and an explanation for its failure.[2] The evidence for this slave rebellion is remarkably ample.[3]

"A Society to Fight the White People for [Our] Freedom"

Friday noon, 12 September 1800. At the gallows in Richmond, Colonel John Mayo questioned slaves awaiting execution for their part in

Original for the volume. A version of this essay was read at the Wayne State University Convocation on "The Black Man in America, 350 Years: 1619–1969," Detroit, May 5–6, 1969.

53

Gabriel's Rebellion. Mayo asked about his runaway slave, "George," who was implicated in the conspiracy.[4] George, a waitingman, was a very special type of slave whose most distinguishing physical and psychological characteristics had been described in a newspaper advertisement:

One Hundred and Fifty Doll[ar]s

REWARD

For stopping the Villain!!!

RAN-AWAY on the 25th of July last from the subscriber, near this city

GEORGE

A likely stout made mulatto man, 24 or 25 years of age, five feet eight or nine inches high, with a conspicuous [sc]ar under his left jaw, occasioned b[y] a defective tooth, a large scar on the back of his right hand from the cut of a knife——and a small one inclining obliquely downwards, in the middle of his forehead, occasioned by some accident when a child—stutters a little when about to speak, a bushy head of hair,—legs rather small from the constant use of boots, and of sulky looks and temper, except when he chooses to force a deceitful smile———He has served an apprenticeship to the barber's trade,— knows a little of shoemaking, and is, when he pleases, a very complete domestic servant.

———As he has several times travelle[d] with me into the Northern states, it is possible he may obtain a forged certificate of freedom, and endeavor to go that way.[5]

As a fugitive and insurrectionist, Mayo's George typifies the men who led Gabriel's Rebellion—born in Virginia not Africa, highly assimilated, well-traveled, and versatile in a variety of skilled tasks.

Mayo also asked about his friend and neighbor, William Young, whose slaves instigated the rebellion. Although it was necessary for him to publicly defend himself in the Richmond newspaper, Young was merely negligent.[6] His actions were representative of the permissive, confused, and disordered state of slavery in the final years of the Colonial Order—so careless and permissive that such critical features of the slave code as the system of written passes for slaves who traveled and the supervision of gatherings of slaves were simply ignored. The state of slavery was confused and indecisive also because, in this period of revolutionary and religious idealism, the slaveowners expressed antislavery views in efforts to ameliorate the blacks' condition, by liberalizing manumission procedures,[7] restricting the slave trade, and discouraging the separate sales of slave children and their mothers.[8] But apparently the slaveowners' "humani-

tarianism" was to no avail; the most puzzling and ominous development in their society was the fact that the conspirators were the same
highly advantaged type of slaves who typically ran off to towns and
passed as free men for considerable periods of time, if indeed they
were ever recaptured. With this avenue of escape and freedom as
accessible as ever before, why, the whites asked themselves, did this
class of men turn, organize, and fight for their freedom in 1800. As
John May rode slowly back into Richmond, pondering this unprecedented reaction of a few very unusual slaves, we can imagine that he
was preoccupied with questions such as this.

Six miles south of the city, two months earlier, late evening 10
July, one of these slaves stands before a woodpile, axe in hand. He is
Ben Woolfolk, a shrewdly intelligent man, hired out to William
Young. George Smith, one of the conspiracy's most active recruiters,
steps from the scrubby pine woods and asks Woolfolk, "Would you
join a free Mason society?"

> All free Masons would go to hell.
> It [is] not a free mason society I have in mind [but] a society to
> fight the white people for [our] freedom.[9]

Woolfolk hedged, he would give "the idea" some thought; but Smith
persisted and invited him to a meeting at a neighboring plantation.

Within the next few weeks Woolfolk, who was to become the
state's principal witness, met several conspirators. One of these was
Jack Bowler, a proud and physically overpowering man, who ultimately placed the insurrection above his own ambitions. Bowler was
hired out to a widow who lived in Urbana, a small, decaying tobacco
port on the lower Rappahannock River. He was twenty-eight years of
age, six feet, five inches tall, scarred above one eye, and wore his
long hair in a queue and twisted at the sides. One white man described
him as "stra[i]ght made and perhaps as Strong a man as any in the
State." [10]

Bowler and Gabriel were rivals, and the nature of the recruitment
procedure intensified their contest for over-all command. Leadership
positions were presumably open to anyone, but only those who obtained men and arms came to be leaders and, for a while, no one was
really in charge. Gabriel, for example, once mentioned that he first
heard about the insurrection from Bowler; and one slave testified that
the latter "was determined to raise and Enlist Men and Contend for
Command with Gabriel." To this end, Bowler often visited the Prosser
blacksmith shop and "repeatedly" mentioned seven pounds of gun-
powder he had obtained and two Frenchmen, who were implicated
in a number of depositions as his contact. But because both he and

Gabriel were adept at converting slaves to soldiers, and at temporarily overcoming the enlistee's profound caution and conservatism, the issue of leadership was for a time unresolved.

"I Could Kill a White Man as Free as Eat"

The one-to-one contact between the leaders and their potential followers reveals the conspiracy's meaning for many slaves, while indicating how the first group lost the initiative to Gabriel and his brothers—Martin, a preacher; and Solomon, a blacksmith. Recruitment usually followed a pattern. The organizer contacted a man in a small group of slaves and in words like this asked, "was he willing to fight the white people for his freedom?" The enlistee often responded by declaring his hatred for whites and willingness to dispatch them without compassion, by sharing the recruiter's views of the insurrection's goals, and by requesting a command position. Sometimes the leader's questions were put in the context of the slave's manhood or toughness. "Charles," for example, asked Patrick "if he was a Man"; Woolfolk told Jacob that he "looked so poor and weakly that he could not kill a man." The response was perhaps predictable. Jacob struck back: "do not take me by my looks, I could kill a white man as free as eat." Following a Sunday barbecue, Gabriel revealed his plan to his brothers, who locked hands and exclaimed "here are our hands & hearts. We will Wade to our Knees in blood sooner than fail in the attempt." But the leaders were seldom so effusive, and some in the face of certain death were quietly eloquent: "my name is Solomon, and [I] am good, what is of me, for fighting." [11]

Challenges were often made before other men. One witness for the state said that when he recruited the defendant he asked if he was one of George Smith's men.

> He said yes, by God I am—He asked him if he thought he could kill White people stoutly; Yes says he by God I can; and I will fight for my freedom as long as I have breath, and that is as much as any man can do. [12]

The enlistee's little boy, standing nearby while the boy was "minding" one of their master's children, "gave" his father "offence," for which "he was whipt." When the master's son also cried, the black man turned and said "if you were big enough you would have my shirt off, but I hope you never will be big enough." [13]

Two members of the rank-and-file have left fuller accounts of their transformation from fugitives to insurrectionists.[14] Gilbert, a sensitive and intense man, held deep and positive feelings about his master. King, a valet, was a deeply embittered man, whose hatred for whites, unlike Gilbert's, was unadulterated.

King's life changed dramatically one July market day in Richmond. While lounging with a group of black men before Francis Vanne's Shop, Woolfolk mentioned that he was "encouraged" by King's "language and deportment." The slave replied, he "never intended, or suffered white people to have much their way with him," and the ritual proceeded in this manner:

> Are you a true man?
> Pris[one]r: I am a true hearted man.
> Witn[ess]: Can you keep a *proper,* or *important* secret?
> Pris[one]r: Yes
> Witn[ess]: The Negroes are about to rise and fight the White people for their freedom.[15]

"They ought to have taken the rebellion into consideration a long time ago," King said. Yes, he "was ready to join them at any moment," and he would "slay the white people like sheep."

After the conspiracy's discovery, King and another slave entered Mary Martin's Grog Shop "as the Guards were going out." "In a surly & abrupt style," he demanded a drink on credit. Mary refused, "I trust nobody." So King paid and turned to his friend, who was journeying to visit his wife, and said he wished he could do the same. Mary joined in; well, "why didn't he visit his wife?" "It was too far," King said, "and the white people ha[ve] turned so comical a man can't go out of his house now but he's taken up to be hanged." He then asked his companion to tell a mutual friend:

> We are all alive as yet, looking hard at the bacon, but can't get at it, "as we are doing what we can." "What we can't do with our Guns, we will do with our Bayonets." [16]

Placing his finger to his forehead, King concluded, "nobody knows what is here yet." Mary indulged the court further, "she had no bacon in her shop—nor had they any that she saw." Even though his master petitioned for a pardon, King was condemned and executed on October 3.

Few conspirators outside the small leadership clique were as active in promoting the rebellion as William Young's Gilbert.[17] But in his eagerness to get at whites, he encountered a number of petty, frustrating situations. At the Young's Spring meeting (see p. 59), he replied to Martin's vow to "turn out & fight with [his] stick," with, "he [Gilbert] was ready with his pistol, but it was in need of Repair." When approached by Gabriel and asked if he had a sword, Gilbert "replied that his Master had one hanging up in the house, which he would get and make himself a belt for it." He also depended on the use of his master's horse, but on the day before the rebellion, he expressed "regret . . . that their master was up the Country," he would "take the Bald." There were larger disappointments compounded by Gilbert's feelings about himself and his owner. During the conversation regarding the sword, he "asked to be made a Captain," but Gabriel refused, "saying he stuttered too much to give the word of Command." Later Gilbert also said that his "Master and Mistress should be put to death, but by the men under him (as he could not do it himself) because they raised him."

"The Main Spring and Chief Mover"

Gilbert first enlisted with George Smith, whose recruitment of men in itself indicated that his group was moving too slowly, indecisively, and ceremoniously. In fact, Smith seemed unable to distinguish between a plan and its execution. So Gilbert joined Gabriel because, as he later testified, he realized that Gabriel "would carry the business into execution." [18]

This explanation focuses sharply on the style of Gabriel's leadership. More than any other organizer he sensed the narcotic and self-justifying effects of revolutionary rhetoric and organization, while recognizing the critical necessity for careful planning. Because he was able to make decisions, delegate responsibilities, and pursue onerous tasks to their completion in order to avert the strong possibility of military disaster, the rebellion came to be his. And it bore his own quietly methodical, businesslike character. Gabriel cannot be characterized like Woolfolk and Bowler, because his most essential qualities remain hidden and unrecoverable in the manuscripts. Gabriel was a powerful force pushing the conspiracy toward fruition; a man imbued not so much with messianic fervor as a sense of what had to be done. The whites also recognized his unusual abilities; a county justice, using an especially appropriate mechanical metaphor, noted that Gabriel was "the Main Spring and Chief Mover." [19]

Thus the direction of the rebellion shifted to Prosser's blacksmith shop, where Gabriel and his brothers gave form and substance to the notion of revolution. During the early summer months the conspiracy matured under their direction.

THE YOUNG'S SPRING MEETING

In the second week of August, William Young left his plantation for a fortnight, and the insurrectionists returned there ostensibly to bury a Negro child. Saturday afternoon, August 10, the mourners drifted back from the black infant's grave.[20] Gabriel, who often used religious gatherings for his own political purposes, invited the slaves to drink grog with him on the banks of the spring. Understanding that he must build a following among the country people, secrecy was ignored. He asked those assembled who wished to join him to stand, and those who did not to sit. He and Bowler moved among the men, promoting the war and enlisting fighters. Unsatisfied with this cooperative arrangement, Bowler asked rhetorically what Gabriel would do for war material, and before Gabriel replied, he rushed on and asked that those "who have agreed to engage in the Insurrection to give him their Voice for General." "The Votes [were] taken," and "Gabriel [had] by far the greater number." Although he had miscalculated Gabriel's hold on the slaves, Bowler was made second in command, a "Captain of Lighthorse."

Following the election they debated the critical issue of when to attack. Although the vernacular was religious, the deliberations were practical and realistic. Some, including a few leaders, were apprehensive. While recruiting in the countryside, George Smith came to understand the "plantation negro's" dual nature: his bitter hatred for whites and his inability for one reason or another to do much about it. So Smith argued that they defer "the business some time longer." But Young's Gilbert said "the Summer was About over, & he wished them to enter upon the business before the winter got too cold." Following Gilbert's lead, Gabriel suggested that "the Subject should be refered" to his brother Martin, the preacher, who stepped forward and intoned: "there was this expression in the Bible that delays breed danger." But religion was not the binding for this rebellion and Martin was not a prophet. Turning from Scriptural sanction to more rational, secular considerations, he argued that the time for revolution was very near. The country was at peace, the soldiers were discharged, their arms "all put away," and "there were no patrols in the Country." He paused, then crossing what for many was an insurmountable barrier, he spoke from within. "I can no longer bear what [I have] borne." The proceedings were open and the silence was broken by "others who spoke to the company" and said that Woolfolk had "something to say." Woolfolk also used the Bible but to loosen the spectre of defeat. "He had heard in the days of old, when the

Israelites were in Servitude to King Pharaoh, they were taken from
him by the power of God—& were carried away by Moses. . . . But
I can see nothing of that kind in these days." Martin quickly replied
that "their cause was familiar to [the] Israelites;" but that he had
read in his Bible "where God Says, if we worship him, we should
have peace in all our land," and "five of you shall conquer an hundred
& a hundred a thousand of our enemies." At this point the preacher
held the floor and made the most important decision: "after this
they went into consultation upon the time they should execute the
plan. Martin spoke & appointed for them to meet in three weeks
which was to be a Saturday night [August 30]." With this achieved,
Bowler and Gabriel withdrew into "secret conversations," which were
"interrupted" by the "appearance" of Young's overseer. The conspirators dispersed after agreeing to meet in front of Moore's Schoolhouse the following Sunday (while their masters met within the
schoolhouse), "where a final Conclusion on the business would take
place."

The Conspiracy had peaked at the Young's Spring meeting. In
the few weeks before the attack a certain indefinable but no less real
revolutionary élan was dissipated—if sustained it might have carried
the rank-and-file from words to deeds. Portions of the meeting itself
were symptomatic of profound and potentially destructive divisions
among the slaves, such as Woolfolk's comment upon the unfulfilled
search for a Moses, George Smith's desire to postpone the rebellion,
and the recruiters' deceptive responses to questions concerning the
number they had actually enlisted.

The recruiters' reports reflected the character of the enlistment
process and the nature of the rank-and-file's commitment to the rebellion. When asked to produce their lists the organizers often
couched their responses in vague allusions to the "warehouse boys,"
the "boys across the river" or the "boys in town." Sam Byrd was asked
for his record at the Young's Spring meeting and he said, while he
did not have his list "about him" he "supposed he had about five
hundred, who were to be assembled by him and given up to Gabriel
on the Night [of] the Attack." Some sensed what was going on. Gilbert asked a Richmond free Negro, Matt Scott, who said he had a
hundred men, for his list. "Some other time," Scott answered, and
Gilbert testified that he "never did see the list." [21]

The recruiters' imprecise, dangerously misleading feedback was
further distorted by the leaders—but only on occasion; that is, when
they addressed groups of slaves in the countryside. In one instance,
Gabriel himself (while displaying two bullet moulds which he said
he had worn out producing several pecks of shot) proclaimed that

he "had nearly 10,000 men: 1000 in Richmond, about 600 in Caroline
County and nearly 500 at the Tuckahoe Coal Pits, "besides others at
different places." Significantly, estimates of the number prepared to
fight diminished as the point of departure approached. Gabriel's was
made three weeks before the attack while addressing the gathering at
Young's Spring. A week later, August 20, a slave asked Solomon how
many would follow them: the answer was 3000; and nine days later,
Gabriel's wife, Nanny, told a black man "that 1000 Men were to meet
her husband near Prosser's Tavern the ensuing Night." [22]

But Gabriel understood what was and was not happening with
regard to recruitment in the countryside. He only talked of 10,000
men before gatherings of slaves of all kinds; in the privacy of Prosser's blacksmith shop, he carefully assessed his limited resources and
planned accordingly. In its tactical dimensions his insurrection was a
coup; a small guerrilla force of about two hundred fifty men would
sweep down upon Richmond, thoroughly terrorize that city by burning its warehouse district, capturing stores of arms, initially killing
indiscriminately, and taking the Governor as a hostage. [23]

The Governor, James Monroe, also understood the real nature of
the rebellion. He referred to it as an "experiment," a "project," undertaken by "bold adventurers," who relied on a "successful . . . first
effort," rather than a "very extensive preconcerted combination." [24]
Against this strategic background the slaves' prolific discussions and
the recruitment procedure is more understandable. The organizers,
the "bold adventurers," sought to build a viable following among the
country people, who, they hoped, would follow up their first attack.
Thus Gabriel's strategy: he recognized that unless he struck suddenly
and sensationally—presenting the blacks as well as the whites with
a *fait accompli*—there would be no mass uprising. [25]

War material materialized no more readily than foot soldiers
(There is hard evidence of 500 bullets, 12 dozen swords, six "guns,"
several kegs of gun powder, and Jack Bowler's 50 spears.). Consequently, Gabriel was forced to arm on the night of the attack and
plans to this end involved meeting various janitors and caretakers at
taverns and public buildings and obtaining "keys" to arms rooms.

Tactics were also a source of weakness because they were need-
lessly complicated. Since the city was the key to their plan it is perhaps surprising that they chose to rendezvous six miles out in the
countryside. Once gathered the insurrectionists would enter Richmond in three wings (two would be unarmed) from the north and
the south. One group would fire the wooden buildings in Rocketts, the
warehouse district, in order to draw off the townsmen from the residential district. Gabriel's group would take the capital buildings, the

store of arms in the Penitentiary, and capture the Governor. When the whites returned from the fires, the insurgents would close with them.

Sound in strategy but bogged down by confusing tactics, imperiled by a lack of men, arms, and military leadership, the conspiracy moved into its final days. Noon, Saturday August 30, it began to rain. By midevening the thunderstorm had swelled streams and washed out roads and bridges; communication movements and morale—fragile at best—collapsed. The whites later repeatedly referred to the storm as "Providential." [26]

Although it is a moot point how many men would have met at Prosser's midnight August 30, no one rendezvoused on either Saturday or Sunday night when the attack was rescheduled.[27] And, in the meantime, security suddenly collapsed. For months hundreds of slaves, including women and children, maintained secrecy while listening to the discussions and pondering their places in the new scheme of things. By Saturday morning, however, at least three slaves had informed their masters about the attack. Monroe dispatched two cavalry troops, which swept back and forth through the area of the rendezvous. But this was unnecessary because the leaders postponed the attack; one man who came to the Prosser plantation that stormy Saturday night was told by Gabriel to return the next evening. But another slave informed (her report was that three or four hundred, "some from Town & some from the Country" would meet) and again the troop commanders' reports were negative. So Monroe noted: "I was on the point of concluding there was no foundation for the alarm." And even when he came to a partial understanding of what he was confronting, his deployment of men in the capital indicated the Governor's profound misgivings regarding the extent of the conspiracy's penetration among the plantation Negroes.[28]

In the aftermath the State proceeded cautiously and confidently while making arrests, using informers, and conducting the trials.[29] Within a few days of the storm, twenty slaves were captured in Henrico and Caroline Counties. Thereafter arrests proceeded more slowly. On September 15, Monroe wrote Jefferson that to date ten slaves had been executed and "at least" twenty would be condemned and "perhaps forty." [30] This last figure is probably close to the total number executed. The exact number of convictions is unknown, however, because the records of payments to their masters are incomplete. At least twelve slaves were acquitted, one of whom was Sam Byrd's father, who was accused of recruiting in Hanovertown. Another seven condemned slaves were pardoned.[31]

"The Business Only Required a Beginning"

For Gabriel the final scene comprised many of the elements which made slavery such a tragic and crazy reality. In his last moments of real freedom, he was aided by a white and betrayed by a black man.

Richardson Taylor, who tried to carry Gabriel to safety, was the master of the schooner, *Mary,* and an embodiment of the fiercely contradictory values of his postwar society.[32] Taylor was a family man, an exoverseer, a ship captain with a crew of slaves, and an antislavery Methodist. Although he later feigned innocence by virtue of his ignorance of the matter, Taylor knew about Gabriel. Before he weighed anchor in Richmond and dropped down the James for Norfolk, several insurrectionists were tried and executed. Late Saturday night, September 17, the *Mary* conveniently ran on to Ward's Reach, four miles below the capital. The following morning Gabriel ran from a patch of woods, crossed the sand bar, and after tossing his bayonet into the water, he was taken aboard. Taylor later claimed that he was "unwell" during this episode; when he awoke the ship was underway. Coming on deck he questioned his strange passenger, who said he was a free Negro, "Daniel," but unfortunately, he had left his manumission papers ashore. While Taylor let the matter drop, his slave crewmen, Isham and Billy, insisted that the man was Gabriel; and, "it was their opinion that he was the person [for whom] the reward was offer[e]d."

The *Mary* was eleven days in passage. Taylor overlooked numerous opportunities to put ashore and either inquire or dispose of his strange passenger. When he was finally boarded by an official in Norfolk, he said nothing about Gabriel. But Isham, who later testified that he was to be freed if he converted to Methodism, brought the officials back to the ship. They were amazed: "Capt. Taylor is an old inhabitant been an overseer & must have known that neither free blacks nor slaves could travel in this Country without papers." This time Gabriel left in chains; and, although he said he would talk only to Monroe, there is no evidence that he did so while he awaited execution.

In the grim days following the conspiracy's discovery, it became clearly evident that rebellion waited on Gabriel. In court the following testimony was typical: "all the negroes in Petersburg were to join him [Gabriel] after he had commenced the insurrection"; and, "as soon as the boys on this side made a brake the boys from Manchester would come over and join them." On the weekend following the storm, about one-hundred fifty slaves actually gathered at Whitlock's

Mill outside Norfolk. "They never left this neighborhood until the Tuesday after it was known that the Richmond plan had failed," reported one planter. When a number of "mulattoes, negroes, & some whites whose connections were with the negroes" were examined, they said that the Negroes at the mill were "to do what those of Richmond were about to do." [33] Nor did the slaves' expectations readily subside. Three months later one Benjamin DuVal wrote Monroe that he had overheard a "parcel" of Richmond Negroes talking about the "Norfolk Cowards." "Cowards & Liberty," were "Several times expressed conjoined with other words that I could not distinctly hear." And one Negro said "that there never was or would be a better time than the present" and observed "that the business only required a beginning." [34]

An old road runs out past the Gloucester County Court House to Ware's Neck. One hundred seventy years ago one of Gabriel's recruiters hurriedly shoved a note into the neck of a bottle which he dropped alongside that road. It concerned Jacob, a black man who carried refugees into the Southside after the conspiracy was uncovered.

> September 20: 1800
>
> dear frind
> Tel jacob at john Williams johny is taken up and wil be hanged i is a afraide-so all you in gloster much keep still yet-brother X will come and prech a sermon to you soon, and then you may no more about the bissiness. i must be killed if the white people catch me and carry me to richmon
>
> i am your tru frind
> A. W.[35]

In the bitter aftermath of the rebellion that did not happen, running away was once again the only alternative for slaves who refused to accept slavery. Even though insurrection was in the air, and "only required a beginning," the slaves "looked at the bacon" but "couldn't get at it."

A Society "Ill at Ease"

"It is always the individual that really thinks and acts and dreams and revolts," wrote Edward Sapir many years ago.[36] Although the meaning of Gabriel's Insurrection lies in its narration, in its tragic and personal dimension, a discussion of the most strategic preconditions for rebellion in 1800 completes our view of the revolutionary situation.[37]

There are essentially two ways of talking about the insurrection's setting, and about what accounted for its failure.[38] These categories are the nature of the conspirators' tasks and their understanding of the values of the American Revolution.

In slavery much of a man's life was expressed in his job; and the insurrectionists of 1800 were unified by a common work experience. But, even though the human meaning of their work set them apart from other slaves, it does not in itself explain—at least at the production level—the insurrectionists' experience of slavery. Depositions and lists supplied by informers offer a fairly complete picture of the conspirators' place and function in society. Many worked either in coal mines, iron foundries, and rope walks—industries whose growth in scale and number was accelerated by the Revolutionary War—or, in such "new" industries as the Public Canal Works at the falls of the James. Privileged domestics who have not fared too well in studies of American Negro slavery were as well represented as any other group: Robin and Charles, waiters at the Eagle Tavern and Priddy's Ordinary; janitors and custodians who worked in the Capitol buildings and the Penitentiary, as well as the valets and waitingmen, King and John Mayo's fugitive slave George. Blacksmiths from Goochland, Caroline, and Henrico counties, the only type of highly esteemed craftsmen represented, played crucial roles as recruiters. Several warehousemen also participated. Others were men whose tasks meant extensive travel; they included several boatmen (from the upper waters of the James between Powhatan and Buckingham counties) and a postman who rode a route between Richmond and Charlottesville. These men may have been more independent than all the others because they usually worked at their own pace and among their own people. The insurrectionists' work experiences cut across several categories, including semi-skilled and skilled, stationary and mobile, routine and artistic. But common denominators of their reality of slavery were, structurally, the location of their work—outside the field and usually beyond the confines of the staple-producing plantation; and functionally, their mobility—they were comparatively highly mobile men who moved through their slave society while working in a variety of roles and coping with different kinds of whites and blacks.[39]

The conspirators were probably freer, more autonomous, than any other type of slave. Because nearly half of them were hired out, they were at least a step or two away from their masters (several of whom were women, thus it is assumed their slaves came from estates). Allowing slaves to hire their own time (or simply hiring them out) was an illegal but highly popular and profitable practice in this period of economic readjustment and diversification. Some conspirators were so far removed from their owners that their provenance was difficult to determine. One confused official described William Young's Gilbert in the following manner: "at the time the Fire took place at Mr. Percells, he was then living with John Young in Caroline County." And Brutus, "Alias Julius," who belonged to William Anderson, was hired to a prominent Richmond physician and public servant, Dr. William Foushee, at which time Brutus ran off and joined the rebellion.

Slaves who often ran away, like John Mayo's George, men who possessed the requisite linguistic and occupational skills for passing as free men, are in fact a key to the relationship between the conspiracy's social and personal dimensions.[40] In writing in 1801 about fugitives and insurrectionists as a type of slave, St. George Tucker, aristocrat and lawyer, analyzed the conspiracy's preconditions. His letter to the state legislature discussed the artisans' exceptionally rapid material and spiritual development in the "few short years" following the Revolutionary War. He attributed the "striking" increase in the slaves' awareness to acceleration of the literacy rate, which was complemented by the growth of towns and trades. This educational process, pervasive among slaves in commercial areas, brought about a "prodigious change" in their outlook, which Tucker referred to as the "love of freedom," and that "evolving spirit we fear." And he demonstrated its effects by comparing the slaves' reaction to the Royal Governor's Emancipation Proclamation in 1775 and their support of Gabriel. Although only a few disorganized runaways, a "few solitary individuals," joined the British fight against Tidewater patriots, the insurrectionists of 1800 organized extensively in order to "assert their claims, while rest[ing] their safety on success alone." Consequently, the difference between the two rebellions, Tucker argued, was basically ideological: whereas in 1775 "they fought [for] freedom merely as a good; now they also claim it as a right." [41]

Thus in the closing years of the century, revolutionary conflict and ideology were resolved for most free men, but not black men, especially if they were artisans. Between 1775 and 1800 a type of slave who was literate, skilled, and at work in a commercial environment came to be sufficiently marginal to believe, really believe, that the values and "right[s]" of the Revolutionary Era were his. He also came to be sufficiently resourceful and gifted to do something about his situation with the aid of other men like him. Thus those slaves who usually resisted as fugitives came to see slavery as more than an individual matter. And to the extent that the artisans were motivated by ideas, their expanded revolutionary consciousness was also representative of their particular view of the system, for these ideas also established boundaries for revolutionary action.

The insurrectionists' goals were essentially political. While using the rhetoric of their generation to clearly distinguish between their oppressors and slavery's victims, white as well as black, they displayed a keen sense of their own time and place. One man testified that he wanted "to fight for his Country," and another said they were to "subdue the whole of the Country where Slavery was permitted but no further." "As far as I understand all the whites were to be massacred, except the Quakers, the Methodists & Frenchmen," Woolfolk testified, and "they were to be spared on account as they conceived of their being friendly to liberty." Prosser's Ben, an eighteen-year-old who worked beside Gabriel in the blacksmith shop, mentioned that "whites were to [be] murdered & killed indiscriminately excepting French Men none of whome were to be touched." And another said simply they "intended to spare all poor white women who had no slaves." Thus the cathartic, sometimes posturing demonstrations, and the continual discussions of who was to be spared or killed, that characterized recruitment, seldom impaired the participant's expression of his understanding of the leading principles of his day.

The organizers' discussions regarding Richmond are even more informative of both the origin and political character of their revolutionary style. These rational and calculating men were neither self-indulgent nor really self-destructive; for at times, it seemed, they wanted a political settlement, not a reformation. Gabriel once said that all townsmen excepting those who agreed to fight with them would be killed. His brother remarked in passing that they were to possess themselves of the whites' property; and George Smith asked that they preserve the brick storehouse in Rocketts "for their own use." Recall their strategy: the insurgents would fortify the city, take the Governor hostage and then—it is assumed—they would negotiate. At this point, Gabriel again sets the tone. When the capital was secured, "on the day it should be agreed to," he "would dine and drink with the merchants of the City." [42]

These progressive ideological and occupational values isolated the artisans of 1800; and cut them off from the new economic realities of the ante-bellum period as well as from their own people. There is in their conspiracy, then, a note of cultural despair. Since the South

was again moving away from manufactures and economic diversification, the occupational strata and milieu productive of this type of
slave was rapidly becoming anachronistic. Hence from this threat
to their way of life came this group's despair. Isaac declared that
"if the [insurrection] was not soon he would run off, as he was determined not to serve a white man [for] another year," and Martin
said "he could no longer bear what he had borne." To a third, the
transformation from a slave to a free man was simply expressed, "I
will kill or be killed." And, Solomon, one of the few mulattoes in the
conspiracy, joined and died even though he was to be legally free
at age 31.[43]

But where were the other slaves? The reality of slavery in postwar
Virginia was radically different for leaders and followers. An elite
initiated, planned, and dominated Gabriel's Rebellion. In the four
months before the insurrection they lived and were sustained by it;
they knew one another well. Living with death, they accepted it;
slowly and profoundly, freedom, revolution, and death came to be a
large part of their lives. Meanwhile, the rank-and-file simply raised
their hands at meetings; a few personalized their commitment by
volunteering for specific responsibilities and acquiring weapons. Enlisting in the most inauthentic manner, they did not share the leaders'
distinctive revolutionary awareness. Thus their commitment was
fragile at best, and in the end Gabriel and his men stood alone.

NOTES

1 By artisan I mean a type of slave who enjoyed considerable mobility within
   and without the plantation world, while employed in a variety of nonfield
   tasks. (See pp. 53–55, 67.)
2 The Evidence. The slaves were imprisoned separately; and, although about
   four of the accused were pardoned, only a small number were spared because they confessed. The following endorsements of depositions indicate the
   careful and critical handling of evidence by the officials concerned: "the
   Witness was at Mr. Young's on the night spoken of by Prosser's Ben (whose
   testimony is Confirmed by him in every Part)."—the trial of William Young's
   William; "He (William—the trial of William Young's Gilbert) confirms Ver-
   batem Prosser's Ben's Testimony"; and, when the clerks or justices consciously
   imposed themselves between what was said and what they heard, they usually
   made a note of it: "This statement is made with the aid of some notes, but
   principally from recollection; minute circumstance is detailed in it, they feel
   assured that no material circumstance is omitted."
3 Unless otherwise indicated the sources for this paper are the Executive Papers (September–December 1800) in the Virginia State Library (Richmond).
   These two boxes contain several 8 x 11 folders marked "Negro Insurrection
   1800," and their approximately 105 items include the following types of
   documents: letters chiefly from officials and ranking state politicians to

Governor James Monroe; "certificates from the Examining Magistrates (the Justices of Henrico and Caroline Counties)," who recorded the conspirators' depositions; resolutions concerning the conspiracy from the Richmond, Williamsburg, and Petersburg Common Halls; "Informations" taken from slave informers and transcribed by clerks of the court; court transcripts and depositions submitted as evidence, including the testimony of the most important slave informers, Paul Grayham's Ben Woolfolk, Thomas H. Prosser's Solomon, and Ben and William Young's Gilbert; and many bits and pieces of undated and unendorsed documents, including some very important lists of suspects used by officials while making arrests.

About two-thirds of this material is reprinted in Henry W. Flournoy, ed., *Calendar of Virginia State Papers and Other Manuscripts Preserved in the Capital at Richmond* (11 vols., Richmond, Va., 1875–1893), Vol. 9. Some depositions are also reprinted ("Documents respecting the Insurrection of the Slaves") in the *Richmond Recorder,* April 13, 1803, State Library microfilm.

4 *Virginia Argus,* October 3, 1800.

5 *Virginia Gazette and General Advertiser* (Richmond), February 7, 1800.

6 *Virginia Argus,* October 3, 1800.

7 William W. Hening, ed., *The Statutes at Large; Being a Collection of all the Laws of Virginia, From the first Session . . . in the Year 1619* (13 vols., Richmond, 1809–1823), Vol. 11, 24–25, 390–1340. See also Robert E. and B. Katherine Brown, *Virginia 1705–1786; Aristocracy or Democracy?* (East Lansing, Mich., Michigan State University Press, 1964), pp. 285ff; and Robert McColley, *Slavery and Jeffersonian Virginia* (Urbana, Ill.: University of Illinois Press, 1964), Vols. 7–8.

8 The following plantation records and newspaper advertisements offering slaves for sale indicate that Virginians in the last quarter of the century were reluctant to separate slave children from their mothers. *Virginia Herald and Fredericksburg Advertiser,* October 11, 1792 (subscriber, James Lewis); October 24, 1793 (John Minor, Jr.); July 25, 1793 (Burges Ball); November 14, 1793 (Charles Taylor), and October 30, 1794 (Robert Patton and John Mercer). See also Hawkes and McGehee Family Papers, Will of Young Short (September 4, 1795); Thomas Jefferson to T. M. Randolph, Sr., October 22, 1790, Edgehill-Randolph Papers, University of Virginia Archives.

9 Ben Woolfolk's testimony at the trial of Smith's George; of "Confessions of Ben Alias Ben Woolfolk Sept 17th 1800 Nos. 4." The latter is the most important document in the collection, and hereafter it will be cited as "Woolfolk's Confessions" (it is reprinted in Flournoy, ed., *Calendar,* pp. 150–152).

10 Bowler's description is taken from a small and battered slip of paper which reads: "Jack Bowler alias Jack Ditcher, the property Wm Bowlers wife [?] of Urrbina [Urbana] is a Black man [passages cited above are deleted] . . . he has a Scare over one of his Eyes But which I do not Recollect His hair Grows Wiry down his forehead He by trade a Ditcher Rick Bowler Septr 17. 1800."

11 "Evidence adduced against Solomon the property of Thomas Henry Prosser on his trial on the 11th September 1800;" and Prosser's Ben's testimony at Jack Bowler's trial.

12 Woolfolk at the trial of Jacob and Solomon.

13 "Woolfolk's Confession."

14 The pertinent material in the Executive Papers which deals with these two slaves is the following: for Gilbert see, "Information from Mr. Foster respecting the intended Insurrection 1800 September 23d" (on the document's cover), material within is endorsed, "The above information given by Gilbert 23d. Sepr. 1800 to Jno. Foster." See also (the trial of) "Sam Bird (Byrd), James & others no date. . . . Communications made by Gilbert." For King see: (Cover) "The Application, by Philip N. Nicholas, esqr. to the court of

Oyer & terminer, which tried & condemned a negroe man Slave named *King*.
. . ." See also the testimony of the following slaves and free men: Ben Woolfolk, Mrs. Mary Martin, "Colonel Goodall's Man"; Mr. (Philip N.) Nicholas,
and Larkin Stanard.

15 Woolfolk's and Mary Martin's testimony.

16 *Ibid.*

17 The testimony of William Young's Gilbert at the trial of William Galt's
    Armstead; for additional information on the French see Prosser's Ben at
    Gabriel's trial; Woolfolk's testimony also at Gabriel's trial; Woolfolk at Sam
    Byrd, Jr.'s trial; and "Woolfolk's Confessions."

    Because of the "cold war" with France and the candidacy of Thomas
    Jefferson for President of the United States, the slave society was remarkably
    involved with the French Revolution and the French in America in the late
    1790s. There were references to the French throughout the trials: since
    Frenchmen were "friendly to liberty" they would not be harmed; Frenchmen
    in Richmond were allegedly fanning the fires of revolution among the "town
    negroes"; two Frenchmen had actually agreed to fight with the slaves; and
    "they [the conspirators] understood that the French were at war with this
    Country—for the money which was due them & that an army was landed at
    South Key which they hoped would assist them."

18 Woolfolk at the trial of William Young's Gilbert; Prosser's Ben at Gabriel's
    trial. Only one slave demonstrated a strong attachment to Gabriel; John
    Williamson's Laddis told the gathering at Young's Spring that "he would
    join Gabriel & stand by him till the last."

19 "Certificate of the examining Magistrates respecting the intended insurrection
    . . . 8th Sept. 1800 To the Governor of Virginia at Richmond."

20 For the Young's Spring meeting see, "Woolfolk's Confessions," Prosser's Ben
    at Jack Bowler's trial; and a letter "from a gentleman in this city [Richmond],
    to his friend in New-York" (dated September 20, 1800) in *Virginia Argus,*
    October 14, 1800.

21 "Communications made by [William Young's] Gilbert" (no date); Woolfolk
    at the trial of Thomas Goode's Michael; Prosser's Ben at the trial of Mrs.
    Price's John; Woolfolk at Sam Byrd's trial; and Billey and Ben at the trial
    of Mr. Gregory's Martin.

22 Prosser's Ben at the trials of Gabriel, Solomon, Pharaoh, and John Holman's
    Doby; William Burton's Daniel at the trial of Mary Jones' John.

23 "Information" on Ned, the property of Judith Owen; see also the trial of
    Philip Sheppard's Pharaoh.

24 Monroe to the Speakers of the General Assembly, Richmond, December 5,
    1800 in Stanislaus M. Hamilton, ed., *The Writings of James Monroe* (7
    vols., New York; G. P. Putnam's Sons, 1898–1903), Vol. 3, pp. 239ff.

25 The testimony of Woolfolk and Prosser's Ben at Gabriel's trial.

26 The conspirators also made back-up plans. Recognizing that the whites were
    especially vulnerable in their towns, Gabriel said that if they "sustained any
    considerable loss" they "would bend their course" for one of two small towns,
    Hanvertown or Yorktown. But "they were not decided which [one]." At this
    point their plans trailed off into a vague notion of attempting to "form a
    junction" with some slaves who "they understood from Mr. Gregory's overseer
    were in rebellion in some quarter of the country."

    The question of who was to direct the military operations also seemed to
    portend disaster. Slaves knew little of arms and less of tactical leadership.
    When asked by his brother whether or not Bowler knew "anything about
    carrying on war," Gabriel replied negatively. Solomon then asked who would
    he "employ?" A Frenchman from Caroline County "who was at the Siege
    of Yorktown and was to meet him [Gabriel] at the Brook." He was to be
    "Commander & manager the first day, After exercising the Soldiers" fol-
    lowing the attack, "the command was to be resigned to Gabriel."

27 Herbert Aptheker states that 1000 slaves met Saturday night. See *American Negro Slave Revolts* (New York, International Publishers, 1943), pp. 221–222, 222n; see also John Killens, "The Confessions of Willie Styron," in John Henrik Clarke, *Ten Black Writers Respond* (Boston, Beacon Press, 1968), p. 39.

28 See Monroe to the General Assembly, December 5, 1800, *Writings of Monroe*, Vol. 3, pp. 235–236. "The close of the day [August 30] was marked by one of the most extraordinary falls of rain ever known in our country. . . . Nothing occured in the night, of the kind suspected." It is noteworthy, however, that the one movement of slaves in support of Gabriel came from the city, not the countryside. Monroe continued, "In the morning the officer commanding the Horse reported he had seen but one circumstance unusual in the neighbourhood, which was, that all the negroes he passed on the road, in the intervals of the storm, were going from town, whereas it was their custom to visit it every Saturday night. This circumstance was not otherwise important than as it was said the first rendezvous of the negroes was to be in the country." See also, William Mosby to Governor James Monroe, Henrico County, September (?), and November 10, 1800; Monroe to Colonel David Lambert, Richmond, September 2, 1800; Monroe to the Mayor of Richmond, December 27, 1800, *Writings of Monroe*, Vol. 3, pp. 203, 246–247.

29 *Virginia Argus*, October 14, 1800.
     A "gentleman" who witnessed the trials wrote to his "friend in New-York":

> The judges conduct themselves with a degree of humanity highly honorable. The least doubt, the smallest suspicion, or contradiction on the part of the witnesses (who are kept in separate apartments) will often acquit Negroes who are really criminal.

This is probably a fairly accurate picture. The court on at least one occasion silenced a slave informer who implicated some Petersburg black men who had not been formally charged. The slaves' legal counsel, James Rind, seems to have conducted himself in an unexceptional way; he and other officials secured a number of pardons.

30 Monroe to Jefferson, Richmond, September 15, 1800, *Writings of Monroe*, Vol. 3, p. 208.

31 Professor Aptheker has made a careful study of the appropriate vouchers and warrants dealing with the executions. See *American Negro Slave Revolts*, pp. 222–223, 223n. "Altogether merely in executed slaves the Gabriel plot cost the State of Virginia $14,242.31, plus one hundred pounds paid to a Mr. Michael Ocletree. Other expenses, as for slaves banished, rewards, costs of guards and militia, would bring the plot's expense to about $25,000 (Auditor's Papers, Box 187, Archives, Va. St. Lib.), no small item," he concludes, "when it is remembered that the total planned budget of the State for the fiscal year 1801–1802 was $377,703." On Sam Byrd Sr., a free black man, see Monroe to William Prentis, Richmond, October 11, 1800, *Writings of Monroe*, Vol. 3, p. 215.

32 Monroe to the President and Members of the Council of State, Richmond, September 27, 1800. For letters dealing with Captain Richardson Taylor and Gabriel see, Thomas Newton (Recorder for the City of Norfolk) to Monroe, Norfolk, September 24, 1800; John Moss to Monroe, September 28, 1800; Richard E. Lee to Monroe, September 28, 1800; Newton to Obadiah Gunn and Robert Wilson, Norfolk, September 23, 1800.
     Newton's letter to Monroe (September 24) reads in part: "I confess I think Mr. Taylor knew much better than he acted, what to do in such a case, having Long had the management of negroes. . . . His conduct appears extraordinary to me. . . . Taylor told the men that he had emancipated his negro Isham, but on (exa)mination Isham he told me that he had never given him any papers but promised him to do it, when he was a methodist, but as

he was now turn'd again he was afraid he should not be given his freedom—
both Billy & Isham say they saw the Negroes hung before they left Richmond. . . . Mr. Taylor must have known that circumstance & undoubtedly
have heard of Gabriels before he left. . . . I hope for the sake of his family,
he may be able to clear himself of the opinion entertained of him here.
Gabriels says he will give your Excy. a full information he will confess to
no one else. . . . Billey one of Taylors men has a wife at a Mr. Harris's on
Scockoe hill she may probably know whether Gabriel had concerted any
measure, to get on board this vessel with the hands. Gabriel will set off this
day under a guard, in a vessel . . . should your Excy think proper a guard
may be sent down the River & take him from Osborns by land but they will
proceed by water as fast as possible & I believe there will be no danger of
a rescue."
33 (Lexington) *Kentucky Gazette,* November 3, 1800.
34 Benjamin DuVal to Monroe, Richmond, December 26, 1800.
35 Jacob's letter was sent in a cover endorsed: "Thomas Booth to Captain Alex-
     ander McCrae Gloucester County, October 5, 1800."
36 Edward Sapir cited in Elman R. Service, *Primitive Social Organization* (New
     York: Random House, 1964), p. 10; Henry Adams, *The United States in
     1800* (Ithaca, N.Y.: Cornell University Press, 1961), p. 98, characterized
     Virginian society in 1800 as "ill at ease."
37 Two overviews of a period that needs reinterpretation are Winthrop D. Jor-
     dan, *White over Black* (Chapel Hill, N.C.: The University of North Carolina
     Press, 1968), Part IV; and Kenneth M. Bailor, "John Taylor of Caroline:
     Continuity, Change and Discontinuity in Virginia's Sentiments toward Slav-
     ery," *Virginia Magazine of History and Biography,* 75 (July 1967), 290–304.
        The discussion of economic and demographic changes in postwar Vir-
     ginia is based on Chapter 5 of my dissertation "Patterns of Slave Behavior in
     Eighteenth-century Virginia" (unpublished doctoral dissertation, University
     of California, Berkeley, 1968). There are surveys of social and economic de-
     velopments in late eighteenth-century Virginia in Louis Morton's excellent
     study *Robert Carter of Nomini Hall* (Charlottesville: University of Virginia,
     1941); Vols. 6–8; Louis G. Grey, *History of Agriculture in the Southern
     United States to 1860* (2 vols., Washington, D.C.: Carnegie Institute, 1933),
     Vol. 2, pp. 611ff; Charles R. Lingley, *The Transition in Virginia from Colony
     to Commonwealth* (New York: Columbia University Press, 1910), pp. 14ff.
38 The following general statements on "internal war" have been especially use-
     ful. Harry Eckstein, "On the Etiology of Internal War," *History and Theory,*
     4 (1965), 133–163, particularly, pp. 148–152 for a discussion of structural
     and behavioral hypotheses (action theory and the "orientation process");
     Chambers Johnson, *Revolutionary Change* (Boston: Little, Brown, 1966),
     Vol. 4, pp. 60ff; and James C. Davies, "Toward A Theory of Revolution,"
     American Sociological Review, 27 (1962), 5–19, especially pp. 17ff for his
     attempts to drive in harness the views of Marx and de Tocqueville on the
     antecedents of revolution.
39 "Patterns of Slave Behavior," II, "The African as a 'New Negro': Adjust-
     ment to Slavery on the Staple-producing Plantation," and "Slavery in Colo-
     nial Virginia: the African Background," paper read by Gerald W. Mullin
     at the AHA, Pacific Coast Branch, August 1968.
40 Descriptions of runaways in newspaper advertisements reflected the times.
     See *Virginia Gazette and General Advertiser* December 29 (?), 1790, Alex-
     ander Quarrier's Anthony who was "supposed to be on his way to Pennsyl-
     vania, where he has been informed, by those who now call themselves
     'Friends of Liberty,' he will find asylum." He "stammers when questioned
     closely," . . . is "a preacher . . . and while out before hired himself to a
     French gentleman."; March 11, 1795, M. Anderson; July 15, 1795, John
     Tyler; *Virginia Herald and Fredericksburg Advertiser,* September 29, 1795,

Peter Bower's Tom who "has worked some time with blacksmith, and professes to be a baptist."

41 (St. George Tucker) *Letter to a Member of the General Assembly of Virginia on the Subject of the Late Conspiracy of the Slaves, with a Proposal for their Colonization* (Richmond, 1801). State Library microfilm.

Imbued with the mood and themes of the Enlightenment and revolutionary idealism, Tucker's prescient analysis is worth citing at length, for it deals with nearly all of the major preconditions for insurrection.

There is a progress in human affairs which may indeed be retarded, but which nothing can arrest. . . . Of such sort is the advancement of knowledge among the negroes of this country. . . . Every year adds to the number of those who can read and write; and he who has made any proficiency in letters, becomes a little centre of instruction to others. This increase of knowledge is the principal agent in the spirit we have to fear. The love of freedom, sir, is an inborn sentiment . . . long may it be kept under by the arbitrary institutions of society, but, at the first favorable moment, it springs forth, and flourishes with a vigour that defies all check.

In our infant country, where population and wealth increase with unexampled rapidity. . . . The growth and multiplication of our towns tend a thousand ways to enlight and inform them. The very nature of our government, which leads us to recur perpetually to the discussion of natural rights, favors speculation and enquiry.

But many of those, who see and acknowledge this change in the temper and views of the Negroes, ascribe it principally to the mild treatment they have of late years experienced. . . .

We have hitherto placed much reliance on the difficulty of their acting in concert. Late experience has shewn us . . . they have maintained a correspondence, which, whether we consider its extent, or duration, is truly astonishing. . . . Fanaticism is spreading fast among the Negroes of this country, and may form in time the connecting link between the black religionists and the white. Do you not, already, sir, discover something like a sympathy between them? It certainly would not be a novelty, in the history of the world, if Religion were made to sanctify plots and conspiracies.

42 "Woolfolk's Confessions"; Prosser's Ben at Gabriel's trial; Solomon's "Communications" (September 13); "Information from Mr. Foster"; Woolfolk at Gabriel's trial.

43 Prosser's Ben at the trial of James Allen's Isaac; Ben at the trial of William Burton's Isaac; "Information" of William Young's Gilbert given to John Foster (September 23)

Unlike Gabriel's Rebellion, Nat Turner's Revolt was not well documented. Yet of the bits and pieces of information still extant, one is most remarkable: Nat's own confession. This is reprinted in its entirety, exactly as told to the lawyer Thomas Gray in 1831 while Nat awaited his execution in the jailhouse of Jerusalem in Southampton, Virginia.

The selection also includes the charge of the court and its sentence upon Nat, a list of victims, and the names of many of the slaves who participated in the revolt.

4

Nat Turner

THE CONFESSIONS OF NAT TURNER
AS TOLD TO THOMAS R. GRAY

District of Columbia, To Wit:

BE IT REMEMBERED, That on this tenth day of November, Anno Domini, eighteen hundred and thirty-one, Thomas R. Gray of the said District, deposited in this office the title of a book, which is in the words as following:

"The Confessions of Nat Turner, the leader of the late insurrection in Southampton, Virginia, as fully and voluntarily made to Thomas R. Gray, in the prison where he was confined, and acknowledged by him to be such when read before the Court of Southampton; with the certificate, under seal, of the Court convened at Jerusalem, November 5, 1831, for his trial. Also, an authentic account of the whole insurrection, with lists of the whites who were murdered, and of the negroes brought before the Court of Southampton, and there sentenced, &. the right whereof he claims as proprietor, in conformity with an Act of Congress, entitled "An act to amend the several acts respecting Copy Rights."

(Seal.)

EDMUND J. LEE, Clerk of the District.
In testimony that the above is a true
copy, from the record of the District
Court for the District of Columbia, I,
Edmund J. Lee, the Clerk thereof, have
hereunto set my hand and affixed the
seal of my office, this 10th day of November, 1831.

EDMUND J. LEE, C. D. C.

To the Public.

The late insurrection in Southampton has greatly excited the public
mind, and led to a thousand idle, exaggerated and mischievous reports. It is the first instance in our history of an open rebellion of the
slaves, and attended with such atrocious circumstances of cruelty and
destruction, as could not fail to leave a deep impression, not only
upon the minds of the community where this fearful tragedy was
wrought, but throughout every portion of our country, in which this
population is to be found. Public curiosity has been on the stretch
to understand the origin and progress of this dreadful conspiracy,
and the motives which influence its diabolical actors. The insurgent
slaves had all been destroyed, or apprehended, tried and executed
(with the exception of the leader), without revealing any thing at all
satisfactory, as to the motives which governed them, or the means by
which they expected to accomplish their object. Every thing connected with the sad affair was wrapt in mystery, until Nat Turner,
the leader of this ferocious band, whose name has resounded throughout our widely extended empire, was captured. This "great Bandit"
was taken by a single individual, in a cave near the residence of his
late owner, on Sunday, the thirtieth of October, without attempting
to make the slightest resistance, and on the following day safely
lodged in the jail of the County. His captor was Benjamin Phipps,
armed with a shot gun well charged. Nat's only weapon was a small
light sword which he immediately surrendered, and begged that his
life might be spared. Since his confinement, by permission of the
Jailor, I have had ready access to him, and finding that he was willing
to make a full and free confession of the origin, progress and con-
summation of the insurrectory movements of the slaves of which he
was the contriver and head; I determined for the gratification of
public curiosity to commit his statements to writing, and publish
them, with little or no variation, from his own words. That this is

a faithful record of his confessions, the annexed certificate of the County Court of Southampton, will attest. They certainly bear one stamp of truth and sincerity. He makes no attempt (as all the other insurgents who were examined did) to exculpate himself, but frankly acknowledges his full participation in all the guilt of the transaction. He was not only the contriver of the conspiracy, but gave the first blow towards its execution.

It will thus appear, that whilst every thing upon the surface of society wore a calm and peaceful aspect; whilst not one note of preparation was heard to warn the devoted inhabitants of woe and death, a gloomy fanatic was revolving in the recesses of his own dark, bewildered, and overwrought mind, schemes of indiscriminate massacre to the whites. Schemes too fearfully executed as far as his fiendish band proceeded in their desolating march. No cry for mercy penetrated their flinty bosoms. No acts of remembered kindness made the least impression upon these remorseless murderers. Men, women and children, from hoary age to helpless infancy were involved in the same cruel fate. Never did a band of savages do their work of death more unsparingly. Apprehension for their own personal safety seems to have been the only principle of restraint in the whole course of their bloody proceedings. And it is not the least remarkable feature in this horrid transaction, that a band actuated by such hellish purposes, should have resisted so feebly, when met by the whites in arms. Desperation alone, one would think, might have led to greater efforts. More than twenty of them attacked Dr. Blunt's house on Tuesday morning, a little before day-break, defended by two men and three boys. They fled precipitately at the first fire; and their future plans of mischief, were entirely disconcerted and broken up. Escaping thence, each individual sought his own safety either in concealment, or by returning home, with the hope that his participation might escape detection, and all were shot down in the course of a few days, or captured and brought to trial and punishment. Nat has survived all his followers, and the gallows will speedily close his career. His own account of the conspiracy is submitted to the public, without comment. It reads an awful, and it is hoped, a useful lesson, as to the operations of a mind like his, endeavoring to grapple with things beyond its reach. How it first became bewildered and confounded, and finally corrupted and led to the conception and perpetration of the most atrocious and heart-rending deeds. It is calculated also to demonstrate the policy of our laws in restraint of this class of our population, and to induce all those entrusted with their execution, as well as our citizens generally, to see that they are strictly and rigidly enforced. Each particular community should look to its own safety, whilst the general guardians of the laws, keep a watchful eye over all. It Nat's statements can be relied on, the insurrection in this county was entirely local, and his designs confided but to a few, and these in his immediate vicinity. It was not instigated by motives of revenge or sudden anger, but the result of long deliberation, and a settled purpose of mind. The offspring of gloomy fanaticism, acting upon materials but too well prepared for such impressions. It will be long remembered in the annals of our country, and many a mother as she presses her infant darling to her bosom, will shudder at the recollection of Nat Turner, and his band of ferocious miscreants.

Believing the following narrative, by removing doubts and conjectures from the public mind which otherwise must have remained, would give general satisfaction, it is respectfully submitted to the public by their ob't serv't,

T. R. GRAY.

Jerusalem, Southampton, Va. Nov. 5, 1831.

We the undersigned, members of the Court convened at Jerusalem, on Saturday, the 5th day of Nov. 1831, for the trial of Nat, *alias* Nat Turner, a negro slave, late the property of Putnam Moore, deceased, do hereby certify, that the confessions of Nat, to Thomas R. Gray, was read to him in our presence, and that Nat acknowledged the same to be full, free, and voluntary; and that furthermore, when called upon by the presiding Magistrate of the Court, to state if he had any thing to say, why sentence of death should not be passed upon him, replied he had nothing further than he had communicated to Mr. Gray. Given under our hands and seals at Jerusalem, this 5th day of November, 1831.

JEREMIAH COBB,	[Seal.]
THOMAS PRETLOW,	[Seal.]
JAMES W. PARKER,	[Seal.]
CARR BOWERS,	[Seal.]
SAMUEL B. HINES,	[Seal.]
ORRIS A. BROWNE,	[Seal.]

State of Virginia, Southampton County, to wit:

I, James Rochelle, Clerk of the County Court of Southampton in the State of Virginia, do hereby certify, that Jeremiah Cobb, Thomas Pretlow, James W. Parker, Carr Bowers, Samuel B. Hines, and Orris A. Browne, esqr's are acting Justices of the Peace, in and for the County aforesaid, and were members of the Court which convened at Jerusalem, on Saturday the 5th day of November, 1831, for the trial of Nat *alias* Nat Turner, a negro slave, late the property of Putnam Moore, deceased, who was tried and convicted, as an insurgent in the late insurrection in the county of Southampton aforesaid, and that full faith and credit are due, and ought to be given to their acts as Justices of the peace aforesaid.

[Seal.]

> In testimony whereof, I have hereunto set my hand and caused the seal of the court aforesaid, to be affixed this 5th day of November, 1831
> JAMES ROCHELLE, C. S. C. C.

Confession.

Agreeable to his own appointment, on the evening he was committed to prison, with permission of the jailer, I visited NAT on Tuesday the 1st November, when, without being questioned at all, he commenced his narrative in the following words:—

SIR—You have asked me to give a history of the motives which induced me to undertake the late insurrection, as you call it—To do so I must go back to the days of my infancy, and even before I was born. I was thirty-one years of age the 2nd of October last, and born the property of Benj. Turner, of this county. In my childhood a circumstance occurred which made an indelible impression on my mind, and laid the ground work of that enthusiasm, which has terminated so fatally to many, both white and black, and for which I am about to atone at the gallows. It is here necessary to relate this circumstance —trifling as it may seem, it was the commencement of that belief which has grown with time, and even now, sir, in this dungeon, helpless and forsaken as I am, I cannot divest myself of. Being at play with other children, when three or four years old, I was telling them something, which my mother overhearing, said it had happened before I was born—I stuck to my story, however, and related something which went, in her opinion, to confirm it—others being called on were greatly astonished, knowing that these things had happened, and caused them to say in my hearing, I surely would be a prophet, as the Lord had shewn me things that had happened before my birth. And my father and mother strengthened me in this my first impression, saying in my presence, I was intended for some great purpose, which they had always thought from certain marks on my head and breast—[a parcel of excrescences which I believe are not at all uncommon, particularly among negroes, as I have seen several with the same. In this case he has either cut them off or they have nearly disappeared]—My grandmother, who was very religious, and to whom I was much attached—my master, who belonged to the church,

and other religious persons who visited the house, and whom I often
saw at prayers, noticing the singularity of my manners, I suppose,
and my uncommon intelligence for a child, remarked I had too much
sense to be raised, and if I was, I would never be of any service to
any one as a slave—To a mind like mine, restless, inquisitive and
observant of every thing that was passing, it is easy to suppose that
religion was the subject to which it would be directed, and although
this subject principally occupied my thoughts—there was nothing
that I saw or heard of to which my attention was not directed—The
manner in which I learned to read and write, not only had great
influence on my own mind, as I acquired it with the most perfect
ease, so much so, that I have no recollection whatever of learning
the alphabet—but to the astonishment of the family, one day, when
a book was shewn to me to keep me from crying, I began spelling the
names of different objects—this was a source of wonder to all in the
neighborhood, particularly the blacks—and this learning was constantly improved at all opportunities—when I got large enough to
go to work, while employed, I was reflecting on many things that
would present themselves to my imagination, and whenever an opportunity occurred of looking at a book, when the school children
were getting their lessons, I would find many things that the fertility
of my own imagination had depicted to me before; all my time, not
devoted to my master's service, was spent either in prayer, or in
making experiments in casting different things in moulds made of
earth, in attempting to make paper, gun-powder, and many other
experiments, that although I could not perfect, yet convinced me
of its practicability if I had the means.* I was not addicted to stealing in my youth, nor have ever been—Yet such was the confidence
of the negroes in the neighborhood, even at this early period of my
life, in my superior judgment, that they would often carry me with
them when they were going on any roguery, to plan for them.
Growing up among them, with this confidence in my superior judgment, and when this, in their opinions, was perfected by Divine inspiration, from the circumstances already alluded to in my infancy,
and which belief was ever afterwards zealously inculcated by the
austerity of my life and manners, which became the subject of
remark by white and black.—Having soon discovered to be great,
I must appear so, and therefore studiously avoiding mixing in society,
and wrapped myself in mystery, devoting my time to fasting and
prayer—By this time, having arrived to man's estate, and hearing
the scriptures commented on at meetings, I was struck with that
particular passage which says: "Seek ye the kingdom of Heaven
and all things shall be added unto you." I reflected much on this

---

* When questioned as to the manner of manufacturing those different articles, he was found well informed on the subject.

passage, and prayed daily for light on this subject—As I was praying one day at my plough, the spirit spoke to me, saying "Seek ye
the kingdom of Heaven and all things shall be added unto you."
Question—what do you mean by the Spirit. *Ans.* The Spirit that
spoke to the prophets in former days—and I was greatly astonished,
and for two years prayed continually, whenever my duty would
permit—and then again I had the same revelation, which fully confirmed me in the impression that I was ordained for some great
purpose in the hands of the Almighty. Several years rolled round,
in which many events occurred to strengthen me in this my belief.
At this time I reverted in my mind to the remarks made of me in
my childhood, and the things that had been shewn me—and as it
had been said of me in my childhood by those by whom I had
been taught to pray, both white and black, and in whom I had the
greatest confidence, that I had too much sense to be raised, and
if I was, I would never be of any use to any one as a slave. Now
finding I had arrived to man's estate, and was a slave, and these
revelations being made known to me, I began to direct my attention to this great object, to fulfil the purpose for which, by this
time, I felt assured I was intended. Knowing the influence I had
obtained over the minds of my fellow servants (not by the means
of conjuring and such like tricks—for to them I always spoke of
such things with contempt) but by the communion of the Spirit
whose revelations I often communicated to them, and they believed
and said my wisdom came from God. I now began to prepare them
for my purpose, by telling them something was about to happen
that would terminate in fulfilling the great promise that had been
made to me—About this time I was placed under an overseer, from
whom I ranaway—and after remaining in the woods thirty days, I
returned, to the astonishment of the negroes on the plantation, who
thought I had made my escape to some other part of the country,
as my father had done before. But the reason of my return was,
that the Spirit appeared to me and said I had my wishes directed
to the things of this world, and not to the kingdom of Heaven, and
that I should return to the service of my earthly master—"For he
who knoweth his Master's will, and doeth it not, shall be beaten
with many stripes, and thus have I chastened you." And the negroes
found fault, and murmured against me, saying that if they had
my sense they would not serve any master in the world. And about
this time I had a vision—and I saw white spirits and black spirits
engaged in battle, and the sun was darkened—the thunder rolled
in the Heavens, and blood flowed in streams—and I heard a voice
saying, "Such is your luck, such you are called to see, and let it
come rough or smooth, you must surely bare it. I now withdrew
myself as much as my situation would permit, from the intercourse

of my fellow servants, for the avowed purpose of serving the Spirit
more fully—and it appeared to me, and reminded me of the things
it had already shown me, and that it would then reveal to me the
knowledge of the elements, the revolution of the planets, the operation of tides, and changes of the seasons. After this revelation in
the year of 1825, and the knowledge of the elements being made
known to me, I sought more than ever to obtain true holiness before the great day of judgment should appear, and then I began
to receive the true knowledge of faith. And from the first steps of
righteousness until the last, was I made perfect; and the Holy Ghost
was with me, and said, "Behold me as I stand in the Heavens"—
and I looked and saw the forms of men in different attitudes—and
there were lights in the sky to which the children of darkness gave
other names than what they really were—for they were the lights
of the Savior's hands, stretched forth from east to west, even as
they were extended on the cross on Calvary for the redemption of
sinners. And I wondered greatly at these miracles, and prayed to
be informed of a certainty of the meaning thereof—and shortly
afterwards, while laboring in the field, I discovered drops of blood
on the corn as though it were dew from heaven—and I communicated it to many, both white and black, in the neighborhood—
and I then found on the leaves in the woods hieroglyphic characters,
and numbers, with the forms of men in different attitudes, portrayed
in blood, and representing the figures I had seen before in the heavens. And now the Holy Ghost had revealed itself to me, and made
plain the miracles it had shown me—For as the blood of Christ
had been shed on this earth, and had ascended to heaven for the
salvation of sinners, and was now returning to earth again in the
form of dew—and as the leaves on the trees bore the impression
of the figures I had seen in the heavens, it was plain to me that
the Savior was about to lay down the yoke he had borne for the
sins of men, and the great day of judgment was at hand. About
this time I told these things to a white man (Etheldred T. Brantley)
on whom it had a wonderful effect—and he ceased from his wicked-
ness, and was attacked immediately with a cutaneous eruption, and
blood oozed from the pores of his skin, and after praying and fasting
nine days, he was healed, and the Spirit appeared to me again, and
said, as the Savior had been baptised so should we be also—and
when the white people would not let us be baptised by the church,
we went down into the water together, in the sight of many who
reviled us, and were baptised by the Spirit—After this I rejoiced
greatly, and gave thanks to God. And on the 12th of May, 1828, I
heard a loud noise in the heavens, and the Spirit instantly appeared
to me and said the Serpent was loosened, and Christ had laid down

the yoke he had borne for the sins of men, and that I should take it on and fight against the Serpent, for the time was fast approaching when the first should be last and the last should be first. *Ques.* Do you not find yourself mistaken now? *Ans.* Was not Christ crucified? And by signs in the heavens that it would make known to me when I should commence the great work—and until the first sign appeared, I should conceal it from the knowledge of men—And on the appearance of the sign (the eclipse of the sun last February) I should arise and prepare myself, and slay my enemies with their own weapons. And immediately on the sign appearing in the heavens, the seal was removed from my lips, and I communicated the great work laid out for me to do, to four in whom I had the greatest confidence (Henry, Hark, Nelson, and Sam)—It was intended by us to have begun the work of death on the 4th July last—Many were the plans formed and rejected by us, and it affected my mind to such a degree, that I fell sick, and the time passed without our coming to any determination how to commence—Still forming new schemes and rejecting them, when the sign appeared again, which determined me not to wait longer.

Since the commencement of 1830, I had been living with Mr. Joseph Travis, who was to me a kind master, and placed the greatest confidence in me; in fact, I had no cause to complain of his treatment to me. On Saturday evening, the 20th of August, it was agreed between Henry, Hark and myself, to prepare a dinner the next day for the men we expected, and then to concert a plan, as we had not yet determined on any. Hark, on the following morning, brought a pig, and Henry brandy, and being joined by Sam, Nelson, Will and Jack, they prepared in the woods a dinner, where, about three o'clock, I joined them.

Q. Why were you so backward in joining them.

A. The same reason that had caused me not to mix with them for years before.

I saluted them on coming up, and asked Will how came he there, he answered, his life was worth no more than others, and his liberty as dear to him. I asked him if he thought to obtain it? He said he would, or lose his life. This was enough to put him in full confidence. Jack, I knew, was only a tool in the hands of Hark, it was quickly agreed we should commence at home (Mr. J. Travis') on that night, and until we had armed and equipped ourselves, and gathered sufficient force, neither age nor sex was to be spared, (which was invariably adhered to). We remained at the feast, until about two hours in the night, when we went to the house and found Austin; they all went to the cider press and drank, except myself. On returning to the house, Hark went to the door with an axe, for the purpose of breaking it open, as we knew we were strong enough to murder the family, if they were awaked by the noise; but reflecting that it might create an alarm in the neighborhood, we determined to enter the house secretly, and murder them whilst sleeping. Hark got a ladder and set it against the chimney, on which I ascended, and hoisting a window, entered and came down stairs, unbarred the door, and removed the guns from their places. It was then observed that I must spill the first blood. On which, armed with a hatchet, and accompanied by Will, I entered my master's chamber, it being dark, I could not give a death blow, the hatchet glanced from his head, he sprang from the bed and called his wife, it was his last word, Will laid him dead, with a blow of his axe, and Mrs. Travis shared the same fate, as she lay in bed. The murder of this family, five in number, was the work of a moment, not one of them awoke; there was a little infant sleeping in a cradle, that was forgotten, until we had left the house and gone some distance, when Henry and Will returned and killed it; we got here, four guns that would shoot, and several old muskets, with a pound or two of powder. We remained some time at the barn, where we paraded; I formed them in a line as soldiers, and after carrying them through all the manoeuvres I was master of marched them off to Mr. Salathul Francis', about six hundred yards distant. Sam and Will went to the door and knocked. Mr. Francis asked who was there, Sam replied it was him, and he had a letter for him, on which he got up and came to the door; they immediately seized him, and dragging him out a little from the door, he was dispatched by repeated blows on the head; there was no other white person in the family. We started from there for Mrs. Reese's, maintaining the most perfect silence on our march, where finding the door unlocked, we entered, and murdered Mrs. Reese in her bed, while sleeping; her son awoke, but it was only to sleep the sleep of death, he had only time to say who is that, and he was no more. From Mrs. Reese's we went to Mrs. Turner's, a mile distant, which we reached about sunrise, on Monday morning. Henry, Austin, and Sam, went to the still, where, finding Mr. Peebles, Austin shot him, and the rest of us went to the house; as we approached, the family discovered us, and shut the door. Vain hope! Will, with one stroke of his axe, opened it, and we entered and found Mrs. Turner and Mrs. Newsome in the middle of a room, almost frightened to death. Will immediately killed Mrs. Turner, with one blow of his axe. I took Mrs. Newsome by the hand, and with the sword I had when I was apprehended, I struck her several blows over the head, but not being able to kill her, as the sword was dull. Will turning around and discovering it, despatched her also. A general destruction of property and search for money and ammunition, always succeeded the murders. By this time my company amounted to fifteen, and nine men mounted, who started for Mrs. Whitehead's (the other six were to go through a by way to Mr. Bryant's, and rejoin us at Mrs. Whitehead's), as we approached the house we discovered Mr. Richard Whitehead standing in the cotton patch, near the lane fence; we called him over into the lane, and Will, the executioner, was near at hand, with his fatal axe, to send him to an untimely grave. As we pushed on to the house, I discovered some one run round the garden, and thinking it was some of the white family, I pursued them, but finding it was a servant girl belonging to the house, I returned to commence the work of death, but they whom I left, had not been idle; all the family were already murdered, but Mrs. Whitehead and her daughter Margaret. As I came round to the door I saw Will pulling Mrs. Whitehead out of the house, and at the step he nearly severed her head from her body, with his broad axe. Miss Margaret, when I discovered her, had concealed herself in the corner, formed by the projection of cellar cap from the house; on my approach she fled, but was soon overtaken, and after repeated blows with a sword, I killed her by a blow on the head, with a fence rail. By this time, the six who had gone by Mr. Bryant's, rejoined us, and informed me they had done the work of death assigned them. We again divided, part going to Mr. Richard Porter's, and from thence to Nathaniel Francis', the others to Mr. Howell Harris', and Mr. T. Doyles. On my reaching Mr. Porter's, he had escaped with his family. I understood there, that the alarm had already spread, and I immediately returned to bring up those sent to Mr. Doyles, and Mr. Howell Harris'; the party I left going on to Mr. Francis', having told them I would join them in that neighborhood. I met these sent to Mr. Doyles' and Mr. Harris' returning, having met Mr. Doyle on the road and killed him; and learning from some who joined them, that Mr. Harris was from home, I immediately pursued the course taken by the party gone on before; but knowing they would complete the work of death and pillage, at Mr. Francis' before I could get there, I went to Mr. Peter Edwards', expecting to find them there, but they had been here also. I then went to Mr. John T. Barrow's, they had been here and murdered him. I pursued on their track to Capt. Newit Harris', where I found the greater part mounted, and ready to start; the men now amounting to about forty, shouted and hurraed as I rode up, some were in the yard, loading their guns, others drinking. They said Captain Harris and his family had escaped, the property in the house they destroyed, robbing him of money and other valuables. I ordered them to mount and march

instantly, this was about nine or ten o'clock, Monday morning. I
proceeded to Mr. Levi Waller's, two or three miles distant. I took
my station in the rear, and as it was my object to carry terror and
devastation wherever we went, I placed fifteen or twenty of the
best armed and most relied on, in front, who generally approached
the houses as fast as their horses could run; this was for two purposes, to prevent escape and strike terror to the inhabitants—on
this account I never got to the houses, after leaving Mrs. Whitehead's, until the murders were committed, except in one case. I
sometimes got in sight in time to see the work of death completed,
viewed the mangled bodies as they lay, in silent satisfaction, and
immediately started in quest of other victims—Having murdered
Mrs. Waller and ten children, we started for Mr. William Williams'
—having killed him and two little boys that were there; while engaged in this, Mrs. Williams fled and got some distance from the
house, but she was pursued, overtaken, and compelled to get up
behind one of the company, who brought her back, and after show-
ing her the mangled body of her lifeless husband, she was told to
get down and lay by his side, where she was shot dead. I then
started for Mr. Jacob Williams, where the family were murdered—
Here he found a young man named Drury, who had come on business with Mr. Williams—he was pursued, overtaken and shot. Mrs.
Vaughan was the next place we visited—and after murdering the
family here, I determined on starting for Jerusalem—Our number
amounted now to fifty or sixty, all mounted and armed with guns,
axes, swords and clubs—On reaching Mr. James W. Parker's gate,
immediately on the road leading to Jerusalem, and about three
miles distant, it was proposed to me to call there, but I objected,
as I knew he was gone to Jerusalem, and my object was to reach
there as soon as possible; but some of the men having relations at
Mr. Parker's it was agreed that they might call and get his people.
I remained at the gate on the road, with seven or eight; the others
going across the field to the house, about half a mile off. After
waiting some time for them, I became impatient, and started to
the house for them, and on our return we were met by a party of
white men, who had pursued our blood-stained track, and who
had fired on those at the gate, and dispersed them, which I knew
nothing of, not having been at that time rejoined by any of them—
Immediately on discovering the whites, I ordered my men to halt
and form, as they appeared to be alarmed—The white men, eighteen
in number, approached us in about one hundred yards, when one
of them fired (this was against the positive orders of Captain Alexander P. Peete, who commanded, and who had directed the men
to reserve their fire until within thirty paces)—And I discovered

about half of them retreating, I then ordered my men to fire and rush on them; the few remaining stood their ground until we approached within fifty yards, when they fired and retreated. We pursued and overtook some of them who we thought we left dead; (they were not killed) after pursuing them about two hundred yards, and rising a little hill, I discovered they were met by another party, and had halted, and were re-loading their guns (this was a small party from Jerusalem who knew the negroes were in the field, and had just tied their horses to await their return to the road, knowing that Mr. Parker and family were in Jerusalem, but knew nothing of the party that had gone in with Captain Peete; on hearing the firing they immediately rushed to the spot and arrived just in time to arrest the progress of these barbarous villians, and save the lives of their friends and fellow citizens). Thinking that those who retreated first, and the party who fired on us at fifty or sixty yards distant, had all fallen back to meet others with ammunition. As I saw them reloading their guns, and more coming up than I saw at first, and several of my bravest men being wounded, the others became panick struck and squandered over the field; the white men pursued and fired on us several times. Hark had his horse shot under him, and I caught another for him as it was running by me; five or six of my men were wounded, but none left on the field: finding myself defeated here I instantly determined to go through a private way, and cross the Nottoway river at the Cypress Bridge, three miles below Jerusalem, and attack that place in the rear, as I expected they would look for me on the other road, and I had a great desire to get there to procure arms and ammunition. After going a short distance in this private way, accompanied by about twenty men, I overtook two or three who told me the others were dispersed in every direction. After trying in vain to collect a sufficient force to proceed to Jerusalem, I determined to return, as I was sure they would make back to their old neighborhood, where they would rejoin me, make new recruits, and come down again. On my way back, I called at Mrs. Thomas's, Mrs. Spencer's, and several other places, the white families having fled, we found no more victims to gratify our thirst for blood, we stopped at Majr. Ridley's quarter for the night, and being joined by four of his men, with the recruits made since my defeat, we mustered now about forty strong. After placing out sentinels, I laid down to sleep, but was quickly roused by a great racket; starting up, I found some mounted, and others in great confusion; one of the sentinels having given the alarm that we were about to be attacked, I ordered some to ride round and reconnoitre, and on their return the others being more alarmed, not knowing who they were, fled in different ways, so that I was reduced to about twenty again; with this I determined to attempt to recruit, and proceed on to rally in the neighborhood, I had left. Dr. Blunt's was the nearest house, which we reached just before day; on riding up the yard, Hark fired a gun. We expected Dr. Blunt and his family were at Maj. Ridley's, as I knew there was a company of men there; the gun was fired to ascertain if any of the family were at home; we were immediately fired upon and retreated, leaving several of my men. I do not know what became of them, as I never saw them afterwards. Pursuing our course back and coming in sight of Captain Harris', where we had been the day before, we discovered a party of white men at the house, on which all deserted me but two (Jacob and Nat), we concealed ourselves in the woods until near night, when I sent them in search of Henry, Sam, Nelson, and Hark, and directed them to rally all they could, at the place we had had our dinner the Sunday before, where they would find me, and I accordingly returned there as soon as it was dark and remained until Wednesday evening, when discovering white men riding around the place as though they were looking for some one, and none of my men joining me, I concluded Jacob and Nat had been taken, and compelled to betray me. On this I gave up all hope for the present; and on Thursday night after having supplied myself with provisions from Mr. Travis's, I scratched a hole under a pile of fence rails in a field, where I concealed myself for six weeks, never leaving my hiding place but for a few minutes in the dead of night to get water which was very near; thinking by this time I could venture out, I began to go about in the night and eaves drop the houses in the neighborhood; pursuing this course for about a fortnight and gathering little or no intelligence, afraid of speaking to any human being, and returning every morning to my cave before the dawn of day. I know not how long I might have led this life, if accident had not betrayed me, a dog in the neighborhood passing by my hiding place one night while I was out, was attracted by some meat I had in my cave, and crawled in and stole it, and was coming out just as I returned. A few nights after, two negroes having started to go hunting with the same dog, and passed that way, the dog came again to the place, and having just gone out to walk about, discovered me and barked, on which thinking myself discovered, I spoke to them to beg concealment. On making myself known they fled from me. Knowing then they would betray me, I immediately left my hiding place, and was pursued almost incessantly until I was taken a fortnight afterwards by Mr. Benjamin Phipps, in a little hole I had dug out with my sword, for the purpose of concealment, under the top of a fallen tree. On

Mr. Phipps' discovering the place of my concealment, he cocked his gun and aimed at me. I requested him not to shoot and I would give up, upon which he demanded my sword. I delivered it to him, and he brought me to prison. During the time I was pursued, I had many hair breadth escapes, which your time will not permit you to relate. I am here loaded with chains, and willing to suffer the fate that awaits me.

I here proceeded to make some inquiries of him, after assuring him of the certain death that awaited him, and that concealment would only bring destruction on the innocent as well as guilty, of his own color, if he knew of any extensive or concerted plan. His answer was, I do not. When I questioned him as to the insurrection in North Carolina happening about the same time, he denied any knowledge of it; and when I looked him in the face as though I would search his inmost thoughts, he replied, "I see sir, you doubt my word; but can you not think the same ideas, and strange appearances about this time in the heaven's might prompt others, as well as myself, to this undertaking." I now had much conversation with and asked him many questions, having forborne to do so previously, except in the cases noted in parenthesis; but during his statement, I had, unnoticed by him, taken notes as to some particular circumstances, and having the advantage of his statement before me in writing, on the evening of the third day that I had been with him, I began a cross examination, and found his statement corroborated by every circumstance coming within my own knowledge or the confessions of others who had been either killed or executed, and whom he had not seen nor had any knowledge since 22d of August last, he expressed himself fully satisfied as to the impracticability of his attempt. It has been said he was ignorant and cowardly, and that his object was to murder and rob for the purpose of obtaining money to make his escape. It is notorious, that he was never known to have a dollar in his life; to swear an oath, or drink a drop of spirits. As to his ignorance, he certainly never had the advantages of education, but he can read and write, (it was taught him by his parents,) and for natural intelligence and quickness of apprehension, is surpassed by few men I have ever seen. As to his being a coward, his reason as given for not resisting Mr. Phipps, shews the decision of his character. When he saw Mr. Phipps present his gun, he said he knew it was impossible for him to escape as the woods were full of men; he therefore thought it was better to surrender, and trust to fortune for his escape. He is a complete fanatic, or plays his part most admirably. On other subjects he possesses an uncommon share of intelligence, with a mind capable of attaining any thing; but warped and perverted by the influence of early impressions. He is below the ordinary stature, though strong and active, having the true negro face, every feature of which is strongly marked. I shall not attempt to describe the effect of his narrative, as told and commented on by himself, in the condemned hole of the prison. The calm, deliberate composure with which he spoke of his late deeds and intentions, the expression of his fiend-like face when excited by enthusiasm, still bearing the stains of the blood of helpless innocence about him; clothed with rags and covered with chains; yet daring to raise his manacled hands to heaven, with a spirit soaring above the attributes of man; I looked on him and my blood curdled in my veins.

I will not shock the feelings of humanity, nor wound afresh the bosoms of the disconsolate sufferers in this unparalleled and inhuman massacre, by detailing the deeds of their fiend-like barbarity. There were two or three who were in the power of these wretches, had they known it, and who escaped in the most providential manner. There were two whom they thought they left dead on the field at Mr. Parker's, but who were only stunned by the blows of their guns, as they did not take time to re-load when they charged on them. The escape of a little girl who went to school at Mr. Waller's, and where the children were collecting for that purpose, excited general sympathy. As their teacher had not arrived, they were at play in the yard, and seeing the negroes approach, she ran up on a dirt chimney, (such as are common to log houses,) and remained there unnoticed during the massacre of the eleven that were killed at this place. She remained on her hiding place till just before the arrival of a party, who were in pursuit of the murderers, when she came down and fled to a swamp, where, a mere child as she was, with the horrors of the late scene before her, she lay concealed until the next day, when seeing a party go up to the house, she came up, and on being asked how she escaped, replied with the utmost simplicity, "The Lord helped her." She was taken up behind a gentleman of the party, and returned to the arms of her weeping mother. Miss Whitehead concealed herself between the bed and the mat that supported it, while they murdered her sister in the same room, without discovering her. She was afterwards carried off, and concealed for protection by a slave of the family, who gave evidence against several of them on their trial. Mrs. Nathaniel Francis, while concealed in a closet heard their blows, and the shrieks of the victims of these ruthless savages; they then entered the closet, where she was concealed, and went out without discovering her. While in this hiding place, she heard two of her women in a quarrel about the division of her clothes. Mr. John T. Baron, discovering them approaching his house, told his wife to make her escape, and scorning to fly, fell fighting on his own threshold. After firing his rifle, he discharged his gun at them, and then broke it over the villain who first approached him, but he was overpowered, and slain. His bravery, however, saved from the hands of these monsters, his lovely and amiable wife, who will long lament a husband so deserving of her love. As directed by him, she attempted to escape through the garden, when she was caught and held by one of her servant girls, but another coming to her rescue, she fled to the woods, and concealed herself. Few indeed, were those who escaped their work of death. But fortunate for society, the hand of retributive justice has overtaken them; and not one that was known to be concerned has escaped.

The Commonwealth,

vs.

Nat Turner

Charged with making insurrection, and plotting to take away the lives of divers free white persons,

&c. on the 22d of August, 1831.

The court composed of ——, having met for the trial of Nat Turner, the prisoner was brought in and arraigned, and upon his arraignment pleaded *Not guilty;* saying to his counsel, that he did not feel so.

On the part of the Commonwealth, Levi Waller was introduced, who being sworn, deposed as follows: (*agreeably to Nat's own Confession.*) Col. Trezvant * was then introduced, who being sworn, narrated Nat's Confession to him, as follows (*his Confession as given to Mr. Gray.*): The prisoner introduced no evidence, and the case was submitted without argument to the court, who having found him guilty, Jeremiah Cobb, Esq. Chairman, pronounced the sentence of the court, in the following words: Nat Turner! Stand up. Have you any thing to say why sentence of death should not be pronounced against you?

Ans. I have not. I have made a full confession to Mr. Gray, and I have nothing more to say.

Attend then to the sentence of the Court. You have been arraigned and tried before this court, and convicted of one of the highest crimes in our criminal code. You have been convicted of plotting in cold blood, the indiscriminate destruction of men, of helpless women, and of infant children. The evidence before us leaves not a shadow of doubt, but that your hands were often im-

* The committing Magistrate.

brued in the blood of the innocent; and your own confession tells us that they were stained with the blood of a master; in your own language, "too indulgent." Could I stop here, your crime would be sufficiently aggravated. But the original contriver of a plan, deep and deadly, one that never can be effected, you managed so far to put it into execution, as to deprive us of many of our most valuable citizens; and this was done when they were asleep, and defenseless; under circumstances shocking to humanity. And while upon this part of the subject, I cannot but call your attention to the poor misguided wretches who have gone before you. They are not few in number—they were your bosom associates; and the blood of all cries aloud, and calls upon you, as the author of their misfortune. Yes! You forced them unprepared, from Time to Eternity. Borne down by this load of guilt, your only justification is, that you were led away by fanaticism. If this be true, from my soul I pity you; and while you have my sympathies, I am, nevertheless called upon to pass the sentence of the court. The time between this and your execution, will necessarily be very short; and your only hope must be in another world. The judgment of the court is, that you be taken hence to the jail from whence you came, thence to the place of execution, and on Friday next, between the hours of 10 A.M. and 2 P.M. be hung by the neck until you are dead! dead! dead! and may the Lord have mercy upon your soul.

A LIST OF PERSONS MURDERED IN THE INSURRECTION, ON THE 21ST AND 22ND OF AUGUST, 1831.

Joseph Travers and wife and three children, Mrs. Elizabeth Turner, Hartwell Prebles, Sarah Newsome, Mrs. P. Reese and son William, Trajan Doyle, Henry Bryant and wife and child, and wife's mother, Mrs. Catharine Whitehead, son Richard and four daughters and grand-child, Salathiel Francis, Nathaniel Francis' overseer and two children, John T. Barrow, George Vaughan, Mrs. Levi Waller and ten children, William Williams, wife and two boys, Mrs. Caswell Worrell and child, Mrs. Rebecca Vaughan, Ann Eliza Vaughan, and son Arthur, Mrs. John K. Williams and child, Mrs. Jacob Williams and three children, and Edwin Drury—amounting to fifty-five.

A LIST OF NEGROES BROUGHT BEFORE THE COURT OF SOUTHAMPTON, WITH THEIR OWNERS' NAMES, AND SENTENCE.

| Daniel | Richard Porter | Convicted. |
| Moses | J. T. Barrow | d[itt]o. |

Tom	Caty Whitehead	Discharged.
Jack and Andrew	Caty Whitehead	Con. and transported.
Jacob	Geo. H. Charlton	Disch'd without trial.
Isaac	Ditto	Convi. and transported.
Jack	Everett Bryant	Discharged.
Nathan	Benj. Blunt's estate	Convicted.
Nathan, Tom, and	Nathaniel Francis	Convicted and transported.
Davy (boys)	Elizabeth Turner	Convicted.
Davy	Thomas Ridley	Do.
Curtis	Do.	Do.
Stephen	Benjamin Edwards	Convicted and transp'd.
Hardy and Isham	Nathaniel Francis	Convicted.
Sam	Joseph Travis' estate	Do.
Hark	Do.	Do. and transported.
Moses (a boy)	Levi Waller	Convicted.
Davy	Jacob Williams	Do.
Nelson	Edm'd Turner's estate	Do.
Nat	Wm. Reese's estate	Do.
Dred	Nathaniel Francis	Do.
Arnold, Artist (free)		Discharged.
Sam	J. W. Parker	Acquitted.
Ferry and Archer	J. W. Parker	Disch'd. without trial.
Jim	William Vaughan	Acquitted.
Bob	Temperance Parker	Do.
Davy	Joseph Parker	
Daniel	Solomon D. Parker	Disch'd without trial.
Thomas Haithcock (free)		Sent on for further trial.
Joe	John C. Turner	Convicted.
Lucy	John T. Barrow	Do.
Matt	Thomas Ridley	Acquitted.
Jim	Richard Porter	Do.
Exum Artes (free)		Sent on for further trial.
Joe	Richard P. Briggs	Disch'd without trial.
Bury Newsome (free)		Sent on for further trial.
Stephen	James Bell	Acquitted.
Jim and Isaac	Samuel Champion	Convicted and trans'd.
Preston	Hannah Williamson	Acquitted.
Frank	Solomon D. Parker	Convi'd and transp'd.
Jack and Shadrach	Nathaniel Simmons	Acquitted.
Nelson	Benj. Blunt's estate	Do.
Sam	Peter Edwards	Convicted.
Archer	Arthur G. Reese	Acquitted.
Isham Turner (free)		Sent on for further trial.
Nat Turner	Putnam Moore, dec'd.	Convicted.

Along with Stanley Elkins' Slavery *and* Daniel P. *Moynihan's report* The Negro Family, William Styron's *Confessions of Nat Turner* has *become the target of many black critics and the subject of heated debate among all who study the black experience.*

The previous selection tells Nat's story, but what of Styron's? How did he, a white southerner, come to attempt to probe the psyche of the slave in his "meditation on history"? Here, answering questions posed by George Plimpton, Styron explains what he was trying to do—and why.

5

George Plimpton

WILLIAM STYRON: A SHARED ORDEAL

[Mr. Styron] would you say something about the chronological history of the book?

I've had the idea of writing about Nat Turner ever since the late forties, when I read Nat's original "Confessions," a brief transcript taken down while he was awaiting trial, by a lawyer named Thomas Gray. It was the book I wanted to write when I started out writing —and yet something inside me was hesitant and reluctant. I think I realized that I had a tremendous theme—one that I simply wasn't able to cope with at the time. Furthermore, I was overly smitten by the violent aspects of the revolt, the bloodiness, the massacre itself, which appealed to me as a kind of melodrama. At one point, I remember describing it to Hiram Haydn, my editor then at Random House, with full bloodcurdling delight, and when I told him it was the next book I wanted to write (I had just finished "Lie Down in Darkness") he said to me, "I don't think you have a real understanding of the thing." He thought that the "gothic" part of

From *The New York Times Book Review,* October 8, 1967, pp. 2–3, 30, 32, 34. © 1967 by The New York Times Company. Reprinted by permission.

my nature was too predominant just then to allow me to write a good book about the revolt and its implications. He was right. I don't mean to say that he dictated the choice, but I sensed that he was right.

What finally jogged you into beginning?

The project stayed with me through all those years though I was unable to cope with the writing of it. I kept up with the subject, constantly reading books on slavery, simply because it fascinated me. Then along about 1962, a couple of years after "Set This House on Fire" was published, I was up on Martha's Vineyard and I had just read for the first time Camus' "The Stranger." It is a brilliant book, the best of Camus, and it impressed me enormously: there was something about the poignancy of the condemned man sitting in his jail cell on the day of his execution—the existential predicament of the man—that hit me. And so did the use of the first person, the book being told through the eye of the condemned. The effect of all this was so strong that I suddenly realized that my Nat Turner could be done the same way: that, like Camus, I would center the novel around a man facing his own death in a jail cell, which of course was true of Turner and how his life ended. And so there, suddenly provided, was the architecture of the book, its framework, along with the idea of telling the story in the first person.

Did it ever give you pause that by writing in the first person you would be telling the story as a Negro?

It was a challenge, of course, since I don't think anything of the sort has been done by a white American writer—to assume the *persona* of a Negro and make it convincing.

What made you feel that you could try what no one else had?

Rank intuition. I doubt that the feelings of the dispossessed, whatever their color, are all that different. If you can sympathize with the dispossessed, you can certainly take on the lineaments of the Negro. To assume that one can't would raise a most dangerous esthetic point, such as to deny Jimmy Baldwin's right to write from the point of view of white people, as he has done, or to suggest that the races are so far apart that even "Othello" cannot be considered valid art.

Did you make any concession in the style of the book to the times of Nat Turner?

The language of the book is in my own literary style, 20th-century *literary* style, which after all is not too different from 19th-century *literary* style. One can read Matthew Arnold and, to be sure, there's a difference, but it's not all that much. So when I set out to write the book, I didn't strive to write like a 19th-century preacher. I tried to write as spontaneously as I could in the form and language I would have written a contemporary novel, at every point, of course, trying to avoid obvious anachronisms like slang phrases and figures of speech which are peculiarly 20th-century. It was a risk, call it arrogance.

What about the accuracy of the 19th-century Negro dialects?

There's enough on record to show that Negroes in the early part of the 19th century spoke very much as rural Negroes in the South speak today. It is a distinct dialect and I believe that with some modifications it has remained frozen for several hundred years. Fanny Kemble, Frederick Law Olmstead and other chroniclers of the era set down Negro speech and it sounds very much like the rhythms of the speech I heard as a boy when I grew up in the Virginia Tidewater. It's with the urban class that the language evolves. As soon as you learn to spell and write, the language becomes educated American English, whatever one might call it, and the dialect disappears. I'm not speaking, of course, of the "hip" sub-language that rises in the city.

Can you say something about your research?

What there is to know about Nat Turner can be learned in a single day's reading. But there is a whole canon of slavery literature. It begins in this century with Ulrich B. Phillips, a Georgia-born historian who tends to sympathize with slavery, his position being that slavery was a relatively benign institution. He was not exactly an apologist, but then the plight of the historiography of slavery is that positions of polarity are always taken—Southern apologists who offer the captious argument that slavery, after all, was a great blessing compared to the lot of the working man in the stews of Leeds, Lancashire, Sheffield; and then you have the Northern neo-abolitionists who state that slavery was so abominably oppressive that nothing decent existed within the framework of the institution at all.

How would you state your own position?

One must assume that slavery was an abomination and a horror. But among other things, I simply wanted to tell in the book the truth about what it was to be a slave of a certain sort in the early years of the last century—to portray the horror but at the same time not to shirk what must have been after all the tolerable aspects of the situation.

In this slave society what personal characteristics enabled Nat Turner to conduct his revolt?

His impulses were, historically speaking, those of the traditional revolutionary—that is to say puritanical, repressive and sublimated. Such impulses seem an authentic part of the revolutionary drive: Luther, Castro, Danton, Mao—all of them are basically puritanical.

They are trying to find a release and they find it, partially, in revolt. I mean it's amazing that Martin Luther, for example, was an ascetic, a monk, and it wasn't until after his revolution that he got married suddenly and had a large family. It's not only involved in the impulse, but also in practicality. All revolutionary movements have a puritanical side; if you allow loose conduct to get the upper hand, you don't have much of a revolt. Castro, for instance, at least by report, headed a revolutionary movement that was obsessively puritanical: no fooling around in the camps up in those hills. Nat Turner was no exception. In the book he never has a sexual experience directly with a woman. He has an adolescent homosexual experience, quite innocent. Beyond that, Turner lived a sexual life of fantasy, fantasies of women, mainly white women, which in turn led to imagined revelations, and then finally to what Turner supposed were revelations from the Divine Spirit. Of course, I can't prove that this is Nat's psychological history, but I think something like it was part of his psychic makeup.

How much of a socio-political thinker was Nat Turner?

I'm sure Nat Turner was aware in a rudimentary way of the social horrors he was struggling against, but the wellsprings of his revolt were largely religious. His actual dream was two-pronged in a sense—one apocalyptic, that he was divinely ordained to destroy all the white people he could lay his hands on because they were evil; the other, the practical one, that he would capture the armory in the county seat, Jerusalem, and outfitted with weapons march the thirty miles or so to the Dismal Swamp, where he would set up an empire, an enclave, and live there out of sight of the detested white people.

Not unlike Elijah Muhammad's plan for a separate state for Negroes.

Except, of course, that Nat Turner and his crowd would have fled and lived as fugitives. Yet it was not all that unpractical a plan. Runaway slaves did live successfully in the swamps of the South. Nat Turner must have had a plan of refuge when he headed out on his revolt. It would have been quixotic of him if he hadn't *something* planned. He was not stupid, after all.

Is there any mention of his plan in the original "Confessions"?

Gray, the lawyer who took down the "Confessions," avoids asking him; or if he did, he never records it. I suspect Gray didn't want to have the outline of the plot generally known. It was one of those things which, if it got around and seeped down to other Negroes, might have caused them to try the same thing again.

The failure of Turner's revolt was due in large part to the lack of support from fellow Negroes, wasn't it? And indeed because many opposed him and fought against him?

It must have been the bitterest part of his ultimate feeling about what he had done, though it's nowhere mentioned in the actual confession. It's *hinted* at, and I think if you read between the lines you can feel that regret. It is historically true that while Nat had a number of very staunch and valiant cohorts, and a bunch of good killers, they did not comprise nearly the number he thought would join him.

What were the after-effects of Turner's rebellion?

For one thing, terrible reprisals: several hundred Negroes were killed by rampaging whites. Then, too, it seems unmistakable that the revolt caused the first actual laws to be passed in the Virginia Legislature prohibiting Negro education, assembly without white supervision, the establishment of patrols, and so forth—all comprising the so-called Black Laws. Before, it had been a passive consensus among white people that it wasn't a good idea to let Negroes learn to read and write; afterward, the restrictions and repressions became both legal and severe, not only in Virginia but throughout the South. Most ironic of all, of course, is the fact that Virginia had been edging toward emancipation, with fierce debates raging in the Legislature. It seems likely that Nat Turner's revolt closed down the issue of emancipation once and for all. Can you imagine the enormous effect on our history if Virginia—then one of the most prestigious of states—freed her slaves? It might have forestalled the Civil War.

Can you describe the process involved in turning characters mentioned in the original "Confessions" into the fictional characters of your book?

The description of the revolt adheres very closely to the original "Confessions" and also to the details outlined in William S. Drewry's book on the revolt, "The Southampton Insurrection," which came along 70 years later. Every character in the book has a prototype. For example, Gray, the lawyer who took down the "Confessions": I don't know if he was the way I described him. After all I had to create him out of whole cloth because there is no sense of his personality in either the "Confessions" or the trial records. So he is a product of my imagination. I remember specifically that when I started the book with Nat sitting in the cell on the day of his trial, suddenly Gray entered and I could see him: I envisioned him as a portly, very condescending Southern type of his time—that is to say, a racist, a man with an equal combination of meanness and vindictiveness, and yet I think he had human warmth, a kind of humanity.

What about Will, the killer? Were you thinking in any way of the contemporary militants?

Will is mentioned in the original "Confessions." He was the slave of a man named Nathaniel Francis. It turns out that three of Francis's slaves participated in the revolt, which would suggest that Francis was a pretty mean son of a bitch. If you had a thoroughly cruel master—and they did exist—it made you all the more liable to want to participate in the revolt, even to the extent of Will's madness. He just loved to swing that axe. He was very adept at decapitation and other niceties.

Why do you think that Nat, in antithesis to Will, had so much difficulty bringing himself to kill?

It's intriguing that Nat was only able to kill the one person he did—Margaret Whitehead. Throughout his original confession he states over and over that, for accidental reasons of one sort or another, he couldn't kill, Will had to do it. But it doesn't hold water that "the sword was dull," as he often says: I'm convinced that he was suddenly overtaken by his own humanity. It is partially why the revolt fails.

Why was it the one girl—Margaret Whitehead—who is indicated as not only having great admiration for Nat, but even a passion for him?

I was trying to suggest that—insofar as the phrase signifies anything—she was a white Southern liberal, meaning that she deeply sympathized with the plight of the Negro, which was not at all unusual for certain young ladies of the time, oddly enough. True, she might have had a buried passion for Nat because he was so much smarter than the white people she was associating with. Nat's feelings for her were just as I described them in the book: he was smitten by her, this paragon of the unobtainable, in some obscure and perilous way so that the killing of her was not only a matter of working out his frustration but possessing her soul and body as well.

What about the character Samuel Turner, Nat's first master, who, if unwittingly, started Nat on the route to the revolt? Who was his prototype?

Nothing is known about Nat's first real master; I had to invent his character. But the prototype of this person would be Gen. John Hartwell Cocke, a man I admire very much. He was a Virginia landowner and would have been a contemporary of Nat. Cocke was a man of magnificent bearing and decency who was tormented over slavery. He inherited over a hundred slaves which made him a large slaveowner in terms of his era. But he found it impossible to free them, because he didn't have the means to educate them, which was the moral requirement among decent white men as necessary to the process of freeing a slave. The only possible way was to educate him as Nat Turner's master did in my book, and try to send him to a place like Richmond in the employ of a liberal-minded person and let him work for several years as an apprentice to find his bearings in the town and then give him his emancipation. That was a common procedure. There were freedmen in the cities of the upper South who lived reasonably good lives. It was a terrible dilemma for people like Cocke—in a constant frenzy over slavery—to be faced with the self-righteous proclamations from New England referring to all Southerners as fiends and monsters.

Do you suppose such idealists as Cocke and Thomas Jefferson ever privately wondered if education would lead to such acts as Turner's rebellion?

I rather doubt it. However, in Turner's case, history went tragically awry because he was not given his freedom—at least that is my assumption. The two keys to Nat Turner and his revolt are that, first, education gave him a sense of his own worth as a human being—given it by a master who was truly solicitous of his welfare. Second, the promise of freedom which had been proffered, was suddenly snatched away from him. If there is a historical parallel to be made between Nat Turner and what is happening to Negroes *en masse* today it is surely that of the disparity between the promise and the fulfillment. Basic psychology dictates that when you are offered the sweetest of promises and you experience only total frustration of it, you're driven round the bend. America is, and always has been, a great tease.

In Turner's time, the two institutions which sold the Negro down the river were the legal system and the church. Either, or both, could have at one time exerted their influence for the better. But they didn't, and it was perhaps the cruelest sell-out of all time.

The church abandoned the Negro in the 19th century and took up Hugh Hefner in the 20th. Churchmen in America have always been followers instead of leaders.

The parallel between contemporary times and Turner's anguish is compelling. . . .

I began the book and was concerned with the subject back in the forties, long before the civil-rights struggle was truly joined. The central meaning of the book is not consciously contemporary, though I would be the first to admit that the parallels are unavoidable. If there is a focus to Nat Turner's vision, it is surely that of the Bible. One must remember that he is a religious fanatic. And the book, as you can tell is a sort of religious parable and a story of exculpation. The last words of the book are the last words of the Bible, the last words of the Book of Revelation. I mean without revelation the book doesn't make sense. It should be apparent that the book expresses the idea of Old Testament savagery and revenge redeemed by New Testament charity and brotherhood—affirmation. It's in there somewhere, *hoped* for, lurking in the terrible story.

William Styron once wrote that "one of the most egregious of southern myths—one in this case propagated solely by southerners—is that of the white southerner's boast that 'he knows the Negro.'" Mike Thelwell, a black critic, agrees and thinks that Stryon would have done well to have heeded his own admonitions.

To Thelwell (and to many other critics), in writing his novel Styron was unable to put himself into Nat's position. Thus he transformed him from what he really was into the white, southern author's conception of what he should have been. Thelwell sees the novel as "a symbol and an example of an entire process of definition and evaluation of black history, culture, and experience in terms created by and necessary to white people."

6

Mike Thelwell

THE WHITE NAT TURNER

Dr. Robert Coles' review of William Styron's *Confessions of Nat Turner* is an attempt to dismiss certain very real problems presented by this novel which is "less an historical novel . . . than a meditation on history." He considers irrelevant comments on the book's "psychological accuracy or historical inaccuracy" and does not believe that "it is the validity or historical accuracy that count all that much," yet goes on to predict that "the book will make history" and finds "it all valid." But Dr. Coles cannot have it both ways.

The contradictory nature and strangely defensive tone of the review seem to derive from Dr. Coles' determination to endorse the undertaking—and if not the accomplishment, then at least the attempt. While he appears to be aware, as earlier reviewers were not, of certain racial issues raised by the book, he never discusses them. As a psychologist who has worked with Southern Negroes

"Arguments: The Turner Thesis" appeared first in *Partisan Review*, 35:3 (Summer 1968).

(the anecdote about the Mississippi sharecropper which comprises the first third of the review establishes his credentials) and who presumably knows the "Negro mind," he simply pronounces the book "valid."

Indeed, Dr. Coles' basic argument, which appears to be that this book is to be seen simply as a "hauntingly luminous novel" rather than a social and cultural phenomenon with significant implications, is undercut by the fact that a journal in which distinguished critics are willing to write decided to consult someone outside the "profession" on this novel.

The novel is about an historical event and personality and is presented to us as a kind of historical "nonfiction" novel, which, according to its publishers, "reveals the agonizing essence of Negro slavery" and which in the words of the New York Times reviewer, "shows us our American past, our present, ourselves, in a dazzling shaft of light," and according to Dr. Coles, is "redemptive and will be read and cherished for generations." Clearly we are in the presence of an American "classic" in the making. It is in this sense, as a determinant of attitudes, that the book will "make history."

The question of historical accuracy cannot be dismissed, since in the terms the author sets up, which is the context in which the book has been praised, and one assumes (if criticism has any function) is being read, he burdens his novelist's sensibility with the historian's responsibility to "accuracy."

The changing of a few of the known facts of Turner's life is not itself the issue. What offends black critics of this novel is the entire process of selection and emphasis, and the coherent and cumulative pattern which emerges from the selective use of the materials surrounding Turner's life. We question not merely isolated incidents of omission or invention (was Turner married as is suggested by all available sources, for example) but the manner in which these distortions serve Mr. Styron's commitment to a view of black history which is seriously being questioned. The novel is a symbol and an example of an entire process of definition and evaluation of black history, culture, and experience in terms created by and necessary to white people. Black critics of the book, in objecting to the "symbolic" and psychological "truth" of the novel, are objecting not simply to answers presented, but to the questions asked (and unasked) and to the assumptions underlying those questions.

Nothing is clarified by saying, as a historian of slavery did recently by way of explaining black responses to the book, that "it does not meet the need of black militants to create a tradition of revolutionary forebears." Nor is it any more useful to dismiss the entire undertaking as another case of "white cultural terrorism" which "titillates white fantasies and reduces black reality to terms acceptable to whites." Even if both statements are partially true— and they are not at all incompatible—to accept them would be to assume an insurmountable division "white history vs. black history" which can hardly be the case. The nation may be two societies, as a presidential commission belatedly discovered recently—but they have a common history. The polarization which is becoming evident in the discussion of this novel can only be self-defeating.

Why is it that most black readers find the characterization of Nat Turner in the novel unacceptable, while most whites, to judge from the reviews, find him perfectly credible and perhaps even comforting? The answer to this question lies in the very real differences in attitude, world-view, and self-definition so glibly glossed over by the currently fashionable terms "black consciousness" and "white consciousness." Part of this response does have to do with what Christopher Lasch calls a search for "a usable past" on the part of blacks. But this does not entail creating one by subjecting American history to "the meatgrinder of black nationalist historical revision" with its implications of reckless invention and ideological rewriting. It is more a question of revising and expanding certain orthodox white assumptions, and contributing to the currently limited arsenal of terms, categories, and definitions through which white historians have structured black history. Black necessity has less to do with manufacturing a history, than with the excavation, articulation, and legitimization of what has been ignored or misunderstood in our history.

To the extent that this novel, and its reception in the black and white communities, provides an opportunity to bring some of these admittedly vague generalizations into sharp focus, it is useful.

Writers are at the mercy of their experience—actual or literary— and can rarely transcend the mythic and psychological framework that is the legacy of class and race, and through which their perceptions of the world are structured and evaluated. In electing to render this novel through the mind and voice of Nat Turner, Mr. Styron had almost inevitably to end up in the position of appearing to define black emotions, responses, and experience from white perspectives.

Assume that it is possible for a white southern writer to tune in on the thought pattern, beliefs, impulses, and world-view of a black slave in the 1830's. There are undoubtedly literary terms in which such a psychological and historical leap is possible. Mary Renault's recreation of ancient Greek culture (admittedly, in the

light of modern assumptions) in her novels on the Theseus legends
is such an instance. But for a white southerner writing about black
slaves such a leap necessitates his completely disengaging himself
from that pervasive body of mythology concerning black people,
slavery, and his ancestors, created and preserved by his class, and
from that vast tradition of literary cliché, racial stereotyping, and
the romantic and sentimental version of history that is the cultural
heritage of the literary southerner.

Having discarded large portions of this heritage, he must acquire
a sensitivity to a series of aspirations and sensibilities, to a black
cultural tradition which contradicts most of his class assumptions,
the existence of which the slaveholding south in particular and
whites in general seem at some pains to deny.

That Mr. Styron was not oblivious to these problems can be
seen from his brilliant and candid essay "This Quiet Dust" (*Harper's
Magazine*, April 1965). There is an interesting, but tangential, problem of literary form implicit in the way that Mr. Styron was able
in his essay to engage questions which he could not in the novel,
perhaps because that form is so much more intimate, less detached
and cerebral than the essay.

"My boyhood experience," he tells us in the essay, "was the
typically ambivalent one of most native southerners, for whom the
Negro is simultaneously taken for granted and the object of unending concern. . . . My feelings seem to have been confused and
blurred, tinged with sentimentality, colored by a great deal of folklore, and wobbling always between a patronizing affection . . . and
downright hostility. Most importantly my feelings were completely
uninformed by that intimate knowledge of black people which
most southerners claim as their special patent; indeed they were
based on almost total ignorance."

This knowledge, he writes, came from a distance, "as though I
had been watching actors in an all black puppet show." He concludes that "one of the most egregious of southern myths—one in
this case propagated solely by southerners—is that of the white
southerner's boast that 'he knows the Negro,' " is fanciful.

A major factor in this distance is the effect of "the sexual myth,"
which he says "needs to be re-examined." "Surely a certain amount
of sexual tension between the races continues to exist," he writes,
"and the southern white man's fear of sexual aggression on the part
of the Negro male is still too evident to be ignored. . . . While it
cannot be denied that slavery times produced a vast amount of
inter-breeding . . . it is impossible not to believe that theories involving a perpetual sexual 'tension' have been badly inflated."

Later in the essay when he discusses the insurrection, he finds
it interesting that "the Negroes did not resort to torture, nor were
they ever accused of rape. Nat's attitude toward sex was Christian
and highminded, and he had said: 'we will not do to their women
what they have done to ours.'"

His comments on the literary effect of this ignorance on the part
of whites is significant. "Most southern white people cannot know
or touch Negroes" a gulf reflected even in "the work of a writer
supremely knowledgeable about the south as William Faulkner, who
confessed a hesitancy about attempting to 'think Negro,' and whose
Negro characters, as marvellously portrayed as most of them are,
seem nevertheless to be meticulously *observed* rather than *lived*."
Faulkner, in retrospect, proves the wiser, as we shall see, and Styron
should have given a great deal more thought to the reasons behind
the canny Mississippian's "hesitance."

The comments about the historical Turner and the rebellion in
this essay seem much more plausible and objective than the account
found in the novel. Of Nat Turner: "His gifts for preaching, for
prophecy, and his own magnetism seem to have been so extraordinary that he grew into a rather celebrated figure among Negroes of
the County, his influence even extending to whites, one of whom—
a poor, half-cracked, but *respectable,* overseer named Brantley—he
converted to the faith and baptized in a mill pond."

Of the political nature of the insurrection: "That the insurrection
was not purely racial, but perhaps obscurely premarxist, may be
seen by the fact that a number of dwellings belonging to poor white
people were pointedly passed by."

These observations in the essay—on Turner's personal charisma
and influence, the absence of sexual incident, and the sympathy or
at least lack of resentment on the part of the slaves for poor whites—
are important departures from certain southern myths about slavery.
These beliefs were to the effect that the perennial desire of black
men for white women made it imperative that slaves be kept in
constant subjugation, that the real enemies and oppressors of slaves
were poor whites rather than the enlightened and benevolent aristocratic master class, for whom the blacks bore a dog-like affection
and fidelity.

One point needs to be made about white southerners' knowledge of blacks. In his essay, Mr. Styron assumes this ignorance to
be a recent phenomenon. But the evidence is that slave masters
and overseers had no more intimate an understanding of blacks
than their descendants do. As the first real leisure class produced
in this country, and under the clear pressure of their morally ambiv-

alent position the slaveholding south devoted much energy to ra-
tionalizing and justifying their situation. They created an elaborately
articulated regional mythology—an intelligence-perverting, guilt-
generated composite of biased and self-serving interpretations of
reality intended to prove black moral, mental, cultural, and genetic
inferiority while creating a pseudo-aristocratic tradition of white
cultural and moral superiority—which was enshrined into a way
of seeing, understanding, and structuring experience. Its basic terms
and assumptions—with a few concessions to changed social realities—still provides the intellectual substructure for white racism in
the national subconscious.

In its terms, slaveholders were much maligned, benevolent Christians whose concern for and services to their chattel far outweighed
the labor they extracted in return. The slaves were simple, childlike
subhuman types of limited intelligence and potential who were
basically happy and contented with their lot. But it is clear from
the most cursory look at plantation records, letters, and journals
kept by slave owners, that only the most obtuse of them ever really
believed this. What emerges from these documents was that the
more perceptive whites recognized that they were almost totally
ignorant of what really went on in the minds of their property.

Kenneth Stampp cites evidence of this in his book, *The Peculiar
Institution*. One Virginian observed that his slaves had "sharp faculties" and "extremely fine and acute perceptions." Another found
them "so deceitful" that he could never "decipher their character"
or "get at the truth." An overseer expressed the opinion that any
white man who trusted a Negro "was a damned fool." In public
documents intended for northern consumption adjectives to do with
simplicity, contentment, and fidelity occur with great frequency. But
we learn from private papers and reflections of "the cunning, shrewd-
ness, and reticence" of blacks and their "habitual distrust of the
white race," along with a high frequency of adjectives like "surly,
sullen, resentful, insolent, impudent" and "artful, secretive, and in-
scrutable."

That the slaves had a caste system independent of and coexistent
with the one imposed by the whites, in which house servants and
coachmen and drivers considered themselves a kind of aristocracy,
is clear, as is the fact that they had their own loyalties, values, social,
legal, and moral codes. In 1851 one slave master bemoaned the
"notorious fact that on every large plantation of Negroes, there is
one among them who holds a kind of magical sway over the minds
and opinions of the rest; to him they look as their oracle . . . The

influence of such a Negro, often a preacher, on a quarter, is incalculable."

These are considerations which are important to black people in search of their heritage. More important, they are essential to any understanding of what must *really* have taken place in Southhampton county in 1831.

How does what we know of the historical Nat Turner fit into this framework of a slave "culture" and society which was zealously protected from white scrutiny?

All available sources indicate that Turner's roots and support came from this kind of organization in the slave community. Turner's own brief confession recorded by a white lawyer in 1831 has hardly any mention of whites until the passages where the violence is described. The other source to which Mr. Styron appears to have resorted is *The Southhampton Insurrection* (1900) a book written by one William S. Drewry, an unabashed apologist for the "benign" institution. (He does not appear to have considered two earlier accounts, one in 1867 by William Wells Brown, a black historian, or that of Thomas Wentworth Higginson, a white abolitionist, whose account appeared in the *Atlantic Monthly* in 1869.)

However, despite Drewry's repeated conviction of the "faithful and affectionate" qualities of Virginia's slaves who were "the happiest laboring class in the world," he includes much information that contradicts his basic position. While he triumphantly cites cases of slaves hiding or protecting their masters, he is baffled by evidence that many slaves who did not participate apparently knew of the planned uprising yet failed to denounce it. While Turner was motivated by a "hideous fanaticism" and his followers "weak, misguided and ungrateful" he never denies the political basis of the rebellion, which he attributes to abolitionist agitation and the blacks' knowledge of the Haitian revolution, refugees from which were present in the county. Another factor, according to Drewry, was the presence of 1,745 free blacks in a county with a slave population of 7,756. These freemen were "prosperous, many owned land" and their presence "encouraged the slaves to the possibility of freedom."

Drewry notes that "news travelled among the slaves rapidly and mysteriously" as was reported among "natives of the Congo." He believes that the insurrection plot extended to neighboring counties and into North Carolina. (Turner's denial from his jail cell of any implication in the North Carolina plot must be weighed in the light of his circumstances.)

Drewry's comments on Turner's personal history are instructive. Turner's education he attributes to his master, "assisted by his parents who were intelligent Negroes." Nancy, Nat's mother, came "direct from Africa" and was "so wild" that she had to be tied to prevent her from murdering Nat at birth. (Infanticide by mothers who preferred to see their children dead rather than slaves seems to have been frequent.) His father was also "high-spirited" and ran away when Nat was a boy and was never recaptured.

Nat's role as youthful strategist and leader of stealing expeditions is mentioned. But Drewry attributes Nat's importance in the slave community to charlatanry, reporting that "he spat blood at will" having previously filled his mouth with dye, and reports that "he wrote hieroglyphics and prophecies on leaves of grass, which subsequently being found according to his prophecies, caused the slaves to believe him a miraculous being."

Higginson reports that as late as the 1860's, there were traditions among Virginia slaves of the "keen devices of Prophet Nat." "If he were caught with lime and lamp black conning over a half-finished county map on the barn door, he was always 'planning what to do if he were blind' or 'studying how to get to Mr. Francis' house.' "

Poor whites who came eavesdropping at his meetings immediately became the subject of discussion. "He incidentally mentioned that the Masters had been heard planning to drive them away; one slave had been ordered to shoot Mr. Jones' pigs, another to tear down Johnson's fences. Johnson and Jones ran home to see to their homesteads, and were better friends than ever to Prophet Nat."

Drewry's treatment of Turner's lieutenant proceeds with characteristic perverseness. To have followed so quixotic and fanatical a leader these men had to be the least intelligent, most suggestible, and superstitious of the slaves. Yet he can in the same breath describe the slave Hercules, who is prominent in the novel, as "a black Apollo" and the most intelligent and enthusiastic conspirator. Drewry says of this slave, "the name Hark was the more readily assumed because Hark Travis had heard of a famous Negro general named Hark who served under Saood (sic) the leader of the Wahabees, the reforming Mohammedans of Arabia, who about 1810 carried his arms across the Euphrates and threatened Damascus." During the insurrection Hark and the other leaders took the title General, and were referred to by that title by the slaves in the county afterwards.

In a similar vein William Wells Brown mentions a slave Will

who joins the rebellion as being "a lifelong rebel who scorned to take his master's name" and whose last words after committing great carnage with his axe were "bury my axe with me." "For he religiously believed," Brown explains, "that in the next world, the blacks would have a contest with the whites and he would need his axe." This is hardly a belief arising from the culture of the whites.

What is the point of all these comments? To those white historians who maintain that the slave population never developed any coherent, independent form of social organization or modes of collective response to their condition, but simply lapsed into a mindless infantile depression and spiritual inertia, such comments as these are probably ephemeral. But as evidence of a slave worldview and self-image this information is essential to a novelist intent upon presenting a figure like Nat Turner from the "interior." Further, taken together, these considerations present a real alternative to the accepted white assumptions about black responses to slavery on which Mr. Styron bases his recreation of this event.

The very survival of the slaves is the most persuasive rebuttal of the "passive-inertia-cultural-shock" theory since less resilient and adaptable races like the Arawak Indians of the West Indies succumbed entirely to slavery and are now extinct.

But, in any event, the search for a credible Nat Turner, and an objective reconstruction of his rebellion must certainly include the effects on his young mind of his "militant" family. What passed between the young Nat and his "wild and intelligent" African mother? What was the legacy of his "high-spirited" father who successfully escaped? Or did he have nothing to say to his son before leaving? To what extent was the slave "society" that Nat refers to sustained and structured by memories and legends of Africa? Is no glimmering of the slaves' understanding of their situation to be found in their quick acceptance and adaptation to their own needs of the Book of Exodus as both a metaphor of their condition and a promise of deliverance? By what devices did news circulate "rapidly and mysteriously" among the "surprisingly well-informed" but "passive and inert" Sambos? Was that haunting, dirge-like melody with its not quite "civilized" melodic patterns and antiphonal scheme the words to which were "Steal 'way, Steal 'way, Lord, ah ain't got long to stay heah," just more evidence of the darkies' simple faith?

We find no answers in Mr. Styron's meditations. Indeed, these questions which must surely have comprised a large part of the historical Turner's consciousness are not raised, and black people having lost the African heritage, are by the implications of this void in the novel, in danger of being deprived of the tragic, grim, yet infinitely moving and inspiring heritage created for us by those "many thousands gone" who found ways to endure and myths and concepts to comfort and sustain themselves.

What does it mean, for example, that the Nat Turner of the novel speaks in a highly literary, convoluted, latinate prose reminiscent of one of Charles Dickens' Victorian pedagogues? Mr. Styron has said that the language was in part determined by his desire "to make him every bit as intelligent as I possibly could." The implication is that this man, conceded even by his enemies to be supremely intelligent, had no language.

The language that Turner must have spoken, preached, exhorted, and plotted in still exists in the rural south. The true tenor of that language—apocalyptic, poetic, richly allusive, and moving—can be seen in the spirituals and bitter blues poetry, which is a familiar part of the national culture. It is a language coming out of suffering and oppression, a language of subterfuge, of sharp metaphor and parable, which implies a world-view. It is a functional, living language, rather than a formal literary one, depending on vivid similes, effective juxtaposition of images and contrasts rather than large vocabulary for its range and flexibility. It is capable of communicating incredibly subtle nuances of meaning through variation of rhythm, cadence, and intonation. A credible characterization of Nat Turner demands some literary approximation of this language for many reasons, beyond the objections of many black readers that there is an implicit insult in Mr. Styron's giving Turner an abstract "white" language to make him "intelligent."

In the act of giving Turner a white language his creator invests him with a white consciousness. He is removed from the slave cabins and installed in the great house from which he observes blacks from a distance "like actors in an all black puppet show." Constantly in the novel he is watching "lines of Negroes etched against the sky," or in coffles going south.

The most striking characteristic of this Nat Turner is that he accepts and operates within the context of white nineteenth-century assumptions about black people. The voice and consciousness which operates in this novel perceives and defines black existence in terms which black people *have never accepted about themselves*. His racism is no more virulent than that of one of Faulkner's white characters, but with those characters one recognizes that one is in the presence of a self-justifying class rhetoric quite unrelated to black consciousness.

But this black preacher, teacher and revolutionary sees his "black shit-eating people" as "flies," "God's mindless outcasts, lacking that will to destroy . . . their unending anguish." He describes field hands as "a disheveled ragged lot" whose voices "babble, with loutish nigger cheer" and fill him with "a loathing so intense it was akin to disgust and belly sickness." From his position in the great house, he regards "Negroes of the mill and field as creatures beneath contempt." He describes an old slave as being "simple headed and in a true state of nigger ignorance." He is revulsed again by a group in church who are "picking their noses, scratching, sweating and stinking to high heaven" with "faces popeyed with nigger credulity." Nowhere do his descriptions and reflections on his fellow slaves escape the exaggerated, parodic, pseudo-anthropological language of the slave-auction announcement. The only slave of any accomplishment, with any psychological integrity and purposefulness is a driver, which means that his sense of self-worth is a gift of the whites.

On the other hand, all of the inflated, self-congratulatory, sentimental white myths about their genteel and chivalric past are accepted by Nat, who views his master "in terms of such patriarchal and spiritual grandeur as glows out from Moses on the Mount." To him white ladies possess "the disembodied, transparent beauty of an imagined angel," and appear to float "in an immaculate effulgence of purity and perfection." His master's household (in which it is not clear that the historical Turner ever set foot) where the First Families of Virginia gather for formal balls and feasts, and where he is "pampered, fondled, nudged, pinched," and educated as the "black jewel" and "spoiled child" is presented to us through his eyes, as a virtual temple to the "lost" elegance and gentility of the golden age of southern chivalry, a world peopled by Patriarchs, demigods, and angels. That southerners wish to think that their slaves viewed their masters in these terms is clear, but that the slaves in fact did is highly questionable. The real Nat Turner was not too awed by his master's patriarchal grandeur to organize raiding forays against his property.

This point of departure and the mythic version of southern history on which it is based forms the ideological skeleton of the novel, and all incidents and detail flow logically from it. Turner is isolated from Blacks, and influenced and motivated by "white" considerations. This denies the tradition of independent black leadership typified by Turner, since in the novel his authority is based on his master's favor and preference, and those attributes coming from his exposure to white influences. Turner hates and despises his blackness and aspires to the culture and enlightenment of his masters. His rebellion is a consequence of the inevitable frustration of these aspirations.

The sexual myth, which Mr. Styron would have re-examined in 1965, becomes a dominant theme. Turner is an onanistic, repressed neurotic who scorns women of his own race and is plagued with a fierce and obsessive lust for white women that drives him to rebel. In this case it is not white "blood" that generated his militance as was the accepted explanation of past generations of southern writers, but his exposure to white "culture," and his repressed sexuality.

General Hark, the "black apollo" and "the most enthusiastic and intelligent conspirator" who Drewry believed to have taken the name of an African warrior, becomes a dumb, shuffling darkie who is reduced to quivering paralysis in the presence of whites and is terrorized in a humiliating manner by a white woman and a boy.

Brantley, the "respectable" overseer converted by Turner, becomes a retarded, child-molesting pederast, which apparently is the price he pays for abandoning his class position and the protocol which decrees that normal whites do not relate to blacks in terms of genuine respect and equality.

The slave Will who "scorned to take his master's name" and who is reported by Turner to have joined the insurrection because "his life was worth no more than others and his liberty as dear" and who was "resolved to obtain it (liberty) or lose his life" becomes another figure out of the pages of plantation melodrama. He is a ravening, demented, hate-maddened monster who "sidles" unto the scene stinking, licking his fangs, and motivated by blood lust and a desire to rape white women. In this case, the bestiality of the figure is attributed to the abuses of a cruel master rather than natural depravity, but the figure is a familiar one from a certain school of southern writing.

The rebellion is defeated by the actions of loyal slaves, "owned by the gentry" who armed by their masters attack the insurrectionists with, in Turner's words, "as much passion and fury and *even* skill" as their white masters. When three black coachmen maul the rebel Hark with "exuberance and glee," it is another indication of the benignity of the enlightened aristocratic Virginia gentleman, whose slaves were contented, loyal, and believed themselves superior to "field niggers." Not only did no such confrontation take place, but all the evidence suggests that the majority of slaves placed more importance on their standing in the slave community, with its rules and values, than on the goodwill of their masters. Quite apart from this, this emphasis on the slaves' worshipful affection for "the quality" is at odds with the "obscurely pre-marxist" element Mr. Styron mentioned in his essay.

There are other examples of the influence of the myth on Mr. Styron's recreation of the situation. (Nat's doubting of his ability to cope with the freedom, promised by his master who is presented, with no discernible irony, as being inhibited from freeing all his slaves only by his fears for their survival in that unaccustomed condition, is inexplicable in light of what Drewry reports about the free black population of the county.)

The presence and dominance in the novel of these reductive and mythical views of black reality is in itself distressing. But the literary implication of this book and its reception is more far-reaching.

In the fictional Turner's white consciousness is the implicit statement that blacks have synthesized no independent attitudes toward this society and their involvement in it. This novel represents an invasion, and appropriation of areas of black heritage into which it imposes white definitions.

It would be unwarranted optimism for blacks to expect the white literary and scholarly establishment to abandon the comfortable myths, habits, and traditions of many lifetimes to undertake the reassessment of black historical and cultural contributions to the nation. But we must insist—a burden no other minority appears to have—on our prerogative to define and present this heritage in *terms* of our own choice. This is necessary not only to black needs of the moment, but to fill a vacuum in the total history, consciousness, and sensibility of the nation. By glossing that vacuum over, and denying by implication the existence of these terms, this novel reinforces the foolish and dangerous notion that the black community participates emotionally in the myths of their oppressors and shares the same perceptions of historical experience. It is in this sense that the novel is "reactionary."

SUGGESTED READINGS

Aptheker, Herbert. *American Negro Slave Revolts.* New York: Columbia University Press, 1943.
A history of slave unrest.

Aptheker, Herbert. *Nat Turner's Slave Rebellion.* New York: Humanities Press, 1966.
An assessment of Turner's rebellion originally written in 1935. The book also contains the "Confessions" as told to Thomas Gray and its appendices.

Clarke, John Henrik. *William Styron's Nat Turner: Ten Black Writers Respond.* Boston: Beacon Press, 1968.
A series of essays critical of Styron's treatment of the Nat Turner Rebellion.

Halacz, Nicholas. *The Rattling Chains.* New York: McKay, 1966.
A recent study of slave uprisings in the antebellum South.

Litwack, Leon. *North of Slavery, The Negro in the Free States, 1790–1860.* Chicago: University of Chicago Press, 1961.
One of the few studies of free Negroes in the days of Southern slavery. Of special interest here is the section on "The Black Abolitionists."

Styron, William. *The Confessions of Nat Turner.* New York: Random House, 1967.
The controversial novel based on the original "Confession" (which appears herein).

Freedom Now!

What happens to a dream deferred?
Does it dry up
like a raisin in the sun?
Or fester like a sore—
And then run?
Does it stink like rotten meat?
Or crust and sugar over—
like a syrupy sweet?

Maybe it just sags
like a heavy load.

Or does it explode?

LANGSTON HUGHES

The following section moves the reader from the debates about slave resistance in the ante-bellum South to more contemporary matters. In a series of essays the efficacy of various strategies that have been (and are being) used to overcome institutionalized segregation is discussed. In the first, written especially for this volume, August Meier and Elliott Rudwick trace the history of the civil rights movement.

Here the authors explore the plans and problems of such disparate figures as Booker T. Washington, W. E. B. DuBois, Marcus Garvey, Bayard Rustin, Stokely Carmichael, and many others. And here too they point out how frequently yesterday's heroes became anathema to each new generation (and/or each new leader) seeking solutions to the same old issue.

7

August Meier
Elliott Rudwick

RADICALS AND CONSERVATIVES: BLACK PROTEST IN TWENTIETH-CENTURY AMERICA

Black protest in the United States extends back to the slave revolts and the activities of the Free People of Color in the generations before the Civil War. But the dramatic developments of the 1960's stem from the work of the organizations that arose in opposition to the ideology of accommodation which was in the ascendancy among Negroes at the beginning of the twentieth century. The purpose of this essay is to describe the principal trends in twentieth-century Negro protest down to the emergence of the black power movement in 1966.

I

The course of Negro protest in the twentieth century is naturally a unique social phenomenon. Yet in many respects it can be regarded

Original for this volume.

119

as representative of the black man's attempts to improve his lot throughout his history in America.

The racial ideologies of American Negroes can be analyzed from various points of view. One can examine how Negroes have adapted to their needs various elements in American social thought, such as belief in political democracy, advocacy of thrift and industry, and faith in the efficacy of education. One can describe how in some situations and in certain periods Negroes have protested against their status, in some instances even advocating—and in the slave revolts attempting—violent rebellion; while in others they felt compelled to accommodate to their subordinate position. Finally, one can describe Negro social thought as ranging along a continuum of ideologies from assimilation to nationalism.

At one end of this continuum have been the advocates of complete biological amalgamation and cultural assimilation with members of the dominant society, and the complete disappearance of Negroes as a racial group. At the other end have been those who urged complete withdrawal from American society and the creation of independent Negro states. Between these two extremes have been a great variety of ideologies recognizing Negroes as American citizens, yet emphasizing their distinctiveness as an ethnic group. These intermediate categories have included the advocacy of attaining constitutional rights through self-help and racial solidarity, an insistence upon racial equality combined with preference for separate clubs and churches, and the espousal of all-Negro communities within the United States. This ethnic dualism, this ambivalence, which has been produced by the contradiction between the values of American democracy and the facts of race discrimination, was best articulated by W. E. B. Du Bois. In an essay written early in this century, he said, "One ever feels his two-ness, — an American, a Negro; two souls, two thoughts, two unreconciled strivings; two warring ideals in one dark body, whose dogged strength alone keeps it from being torn asunder. . . . He simply wishes to make it possible for a man to be both a Negro and an American, without being cursed and spit upon by his fellows, without having the door of opportunity closed roughly in his face."

In no case have Negroes, even those completely favoring integration and assimilation, been able to forget their connection with an oppressed group. From this very alienation came the thrust for separate institutions operated without white interference, such as the church and the mutual benefit society, calls for race pride and a cultural pluralism, and, most recently, the demands of the black power advocates. The gap between ideal and practice in American society has meant that Negroes not only wanted to be a part of that society, but that they also found it desirable to develop their own group life within it.

It should be emphasized that the whole subject of the Negro's response to discrimination and his search for freedom and human dignity is a highly complex one. For one thing, the diverse ideologies have been combined in a bewildering variety of ways. Both protest and accommodating leaders have advocated thrift, industry, and economic accumulation. Usually these values have been associated with the idea of Negroes securing equality in the United States by assimilating American middle-class ways. These economic ideas have also been combined with the advocacy of race pride and race solidarity to stimulate Negro support of Negro business, and by thus achieving material success, to gain acceptance in American society. Finally, certain highly nationalist movements, like the Black Muslims, have combined the Puritan ethic with complete rejection of American white society.

Negro thinking has varied under the impact of changing conditions. Gunnar Myrdal described the situation perceptively. Noting that to a large degree Negroes are "denied identification with the nation," he observed:

> to them social speculation, therefore, moves in a sphere of unreality and futility. Instead of organized popular theories or ideas, the observer finds in the Negro world, for the most part, only a *fluid and amorphous mass of all sorts of embryos of thoughts. Negroes seem to be held in a state of eternal preparedness for a great number of contradictory opinions*—ready to accept one type or another depending on how they are driven by pressures or where they see an opportunity. Under such circumstances, the masses of American Negroes might, for example, rally around a violently anti-American, anti-Western, anti-white, black chauvinism of the Garvey type, centered around the idea of Africa as the mother country. But they might just as likely, if only a slight change of stimulus is provided, join in an all-out effort to fight for their native country . . . for the Western Civilization to which they belong, and for the tenets of democracy in the entire world. . . . Or they might develop a passive cynicism toward it all.*

In surveying the development of Negro protest ideologies in the twentieth century, certain major themes stand out. Externally there has been an impressive shift in white public opinion. Internally, what was once a liberal white and Negro upper-class movement, has become a completely Negro-led and largely working-class movement. There has been a shift in strategy from agitation, legislation, and court litigation aimed at securing the colored man's constitutional

---

* Gunnar Myrdal, *An American Dilemma.* New York: Harper & Row, 1944, Vol. II, p. 782.

rights, to emphasis on direct-action techniques and finally, to mobilizing the potential power of the masses in the ghettos along political
and economic lines. When, in the 1960's, the nation moved closer
toward protecting the rights guaranteed by the Constitution, goals
were redefined, and the Negro protest organizations went beyond
constitutional rights to demand special efforts to overcome the poverty
of the black masses. Interwoven in complex patterns with these trends
were two other themes that periodically waxed and waned as conditions—and Negro perception of conditions—changed: various
schools of economic interpretation and Marxist thinking, on the one
hand, and elements of nationalist ideology on the other.

It is also noteworthy that the twentieth-century protest movement
has been preeminently urban. At the opening of the century Negroes
were 75 percent rural, and nine-tenths of them lived in the South.
Nevertheless until mid-century the base of Negro protest lay principally in Northern cities where Negroes enjoyed greater freedom of
action. Beginning with World War I Negroes have moved in growing
numbers to the North, and to the cities of both regions, so that today
three-quarters of them are urban, and about half live outside the old
slave states. One concomitant of the migration has been the mounting strength of the black vote in the Northern cities. This has served
as a vital element in drawing the federal government into defense of
civil rights and making it more responsive to the needs of the black
masses. Today rural Negroes in the South still suffer from enormous
disabilities because of their race, but the major unsolved problems
now facing Negroes stem from discrimination embedded in urban
patterns of housing, employment, and education. And the urban
ghetto, rather than the rural black belt of Alabama or Mississippi
is the base upon which the advocates of black power must work if
their goals are to have any possibility of fulfillment.

Finally, a salient characteristic of twentieth-century Negro protest
has been an extraordinary amount of controversy within the black
community over the tactics and strategies to follow—a nearly constant
warring between "radicals" and "conservatives." Over the years, as
conditions changed, definitions of these two terms and the contents
of the argument have naturally shifted. At the beginning of the century "radical" black militants who helped to found the NAACP
denounced the accommodator, Booker T. Washington, for his "conservatism." Later the NAACP in turn found itself denounced as
"conservative," gradualist, even in effect accommodating, by a suc-
cession of groups who regarded themselves as the genuine militants—
from the radical Socialists led by A. Philip Randolph and the militant
nationalists led by Marcus Garvey in the early 1920's, to the direct-
action organizations and the black power advocates of the 1960's.

This counterpoint of "radical" and "conservative" has been so pervasive in the dialogue over Negro strategies and tactics in the course of the past two generations, that the dynamic course of the twentieth-century protest can be understood only in terms of it.

II

As the nineteenth century drew to a close, the Negro's position in American society was declining steadily. Disfranchisement, lynchings, Jim Crow laws, and farm tenancy were the Negroes' lot in the South. Throughout the country labor unions excluded them from the skilled trades. After 1900 race riots became commonplace in both North and South, with the Negroes being victims in what were essentially pogrom-like mob attacks upon the black minority. Under these conditions protest and agitation waned, and a philosophy of accommodation gained the upper hand. The most prominent representative of this trend was Booker T. Washington, principal of the Tuskegee Institute in Alabama. Between his famous Atlanta Exposition Address in 1895 and his death in 1915 Washington was the most prominent Negro in America. Though he covertly spent thousands of dollars fighting disfranchisement and segregation laws, he publicly advocated a policy of conciliation and gradualism. Largely blaming Negroes themselves for their condition, and describing the Southern white man as the Negro's "best friend," he minimized the extent of racial prejudice and discrimination, accepted segregation and the separate-but-equal doctrine, deprecated political activity, favored vocational training and working with the hands at the expense of higher education and the professions, and recommended economic accumulation and the cultivation of Christian character as the best methods for advancing the status of Negroes in America. By helping themselves, by proving their usefulness to society through the acquisition of wealth and morality, Negroes, he believed, would earn the respect of the white man and thus eventually gain recognition of their constitutional rights. Washington's ultimate aims were stated so vaguely and ambiguously that Southern whites mistook his means for his ends. But his Negro supporters understood that through tact and indirection he hoped to secure the goodwill of white men and the ultimate recognition of the Negro's citizenship rights.

There was another side to Washington's emphasis upon Negroes helping themselves. He advocated racial unity—or racial solidarity as it was called at the time—especially in economic matters. He maintained that it was essential for Negroes to support Negro business in order to advance the race to the point where it would be respected

by whites. While holding Negroes themselves largely responsible for
their lowly status, he possessed a deep racial pride and a profound
belief that Negroes could shape their own destiny in America. By
helping themselves, and organizing to help each other, they would
advance the race and achieve equality in American society. Thus
Washington's separatist ideology functioned both as a mechanism of
accommodation to American racism and as a device for overcoming
it.

Despite Washington's prominence, Negro protest, though temporarily muted, did not completely disappear. The media of mass
communication, and the public at large, both black and white, regarded the Montgomery, Alabama, bus boycott of 1955–1956 as a
radical innovation. But at the opening of the century Negroes conducted boycotts of trolley-car segregation in more than twenty-five
Southern cities, in protest against Jim Crow arrangements then being
introduced in state after state throughout the South. Curiously, these
boycotts were ordinarily led by some of the most conservative members of the Negro community—businessmen and clerics who were
often close friends of the accommodator Booker T. Washington.
Trolley-car boycotts were a "conservative" protest movement. They
were conservative in the generic sense that they attempted to preserve the status quo against a radical change pushed by lower-class
whites. They were also conservative as a form of protest because they
constituted a withdrawal, avoiding rather than precipitating a confrontation with the racist whites. It is undoubtedly for these reasons
that this widespread protest movement, unsuccessful though it was,
occurred at all in a period of severe racial oppression in the South
and concomitant Negro accommodation.

After the turn of the century accommodation and separatism were
also challenged by a small band of militant black intellectuals. Led
by the noted scholar and professor at Atlanta University, W. E. B.
Du Bois, they formed in 1905 the all-Negro Niagara Movement to
oppose Washington's program, which they denounced as a failure.
On nearly every issue they stood in direct contrast to Washington. In
sharp language, the Niagara group placed full responsibility for the
race problem squarely on the whites. They denounced the iniquities
of segregation, the separate-but-equal doctrine, and the disfranchisement laws. They maintained that economic progress was not possible
in a democratic society without the protection afforded by the ballot,
and insisted above all that Negroes could gain their rights only by
agitation and complaint. Partly because of Washington's vigorous
opposition, his critics in the Niagara Movement accomplished little.
But these militant black integrationists were significant because they
spoke out against accommodation and Negro separatism at a time

when nearly all influential whites and the most powerful among the Negro leaders endorsed these ideas as the appropriate solution for the race problem in America.

Ardent integrationists though they were, it should be noted that some of the Negro "radicals," as they were called in contrast to the "conservative" followers of Booker T. Washington, were themselves advocates of self-help and racial solidarity. This was particularly true of Du Bois. As early as the 1890's he had advocated "Pan-Negroism"— that sense of identity with Africa and black men everywhere which is today called "Pan-Africanism," and he was a prominent leader in the first Pan-African Conference held in 1900, and in the five later Pan-African Congresses held between 1919 and 1945. Moreover, like Washington he advocated black economic nationalism, or what he called the creation of a "group economy." Where Washington, however, spoke of developing "captains of industry," Du Bois' vision shifted from capitalism to the advocacy of a socialistic system of producers and consumers' cooperatives. In fact, Du Bois and several of the other radicals were strongly influenced by Socialist doctrines.

Despite all of Washington's efforts to crush them, these Negro radicals carried the message of protest and the demand for integration to prominent white Progressives and Socialists. Together, in 1909–1910, they formed the National Association for the Advancement of Colored People, with the announced goal of fighting for the black man's constitutional rights and the undeclared aim of curbing Booker T. Washington's power. Given the context of the times, it was the wealth, prominence, and influence of this small band of concerned whites that made it possible for the radical Negroes to push their program with some degree of effectiveness. From the start the NAACP branches were typically Negro both in members and leaders; but at the national headquarters Du Bois, as editor of *The Crisis* and director of research, was the only Negro executive until James Weldon Johnson became the Association's Secretary in 1921. The legal work was handled mainly by volunteer white attorneys until 1935 when Charles Houston became chief counsel. Today, all the national staff but two are Negroes, as is the overwhelming majority of the National Board of Directors.

It is very difficult today, with the NAACP under attack as gradualist and conservative, to understand that in 1910 contemporaries regarded its position on the race question as exceedingly radical. Through propaganda and publicity, through litigation in the courts and lobbying in the legislatures, the NAACP hoped to topple the edifice of discrimination. Almost at the outset of its career, the NAACP convinced the Supreme Court to declare unconstitutional two discriminatory statutes. In 1915, the Court overruled the "grandfather clause," a provision in several Southern state constitutions that, in effect, excluded from the vote those whose ancestors were ineligible to cast ballots in 1860. In 1917, the Supreme Court outlawed municipal residential segregation ordinances. Thus were taken the first legal steps in the lengthy struggle against disfranchisement and segregation.

Negroes moved slowly toward the radical camp. Despite much uncertainty and vacillation, the radicals steadily gained influence. In 1916, the year after Washington's death, the NAACP appointed as its national organizer, the author James Weldon Johnson, among the most brilliant men in Booker T. Washington's camp.

III

Between the two World Wars, the NAACP program was in the ascendancy. The Association gained strength from the large numbers of Southern Negroes who had migrated to Northern cities; from a small but growing black bourgeoisie of professionals and businessmen who served them; from an upsurge of confidence among the "New Negro," race-proud and self-reliant, believing in racial cooperation and self-help and determined to fight for his constitutional rights; from writers and artists of the "Harlem Renaissance" who used their own cultural tradition and experiences as materials for their works. W. E. B. Du Bois, as *Crisis* editor, symbolized the new mood and exerted great influence.

The NAACP did extraordinary service, giving legal defense to victims of race riots and unjust judicial proceedings. It obtained the release of the soldiers who had received life sentences on charges of rioting against intolerable conditions at Houston in 1917. It successfully defended Negro sharecroppers in Elaine, Arkansas, who in 1919 had banded together to gain fairer treatment, had become the objects of a massive armed hunt by whites to put them "in their place," and were charged with insurrection when they resisted. It secured the acquittal, with the help of Clarence Darrow, of Dr. Ossian Sweet and his family who had moved into a white neighborhood in Detroit, shot at a mob attacking their home, killed a man, and were eventually judged to have committed the act in self-defense. A major effort of the NAACP during the 1920's was to secure passage of an anti-lynching bill. Though the law was not enacted, the NAACP rallied a great deal of public support, and the number of lynchings gradually declined in the nation.

In the long run the most important of the NAACP's activities was the litigation designed to secure the enforcement of the Fourteenth and Fifteenth amendments. It continued the battle against disfran-

chisement and residential segregation. With the outlawing of municipal residential segregation ordinances in 1917, white property-owners
and realtors retreated behind other subterfuges, particularly restrictive covenants, under which homeowners' associations excluded Negroes through agreements among themselves. The decade of the
1920's saw the beginning of the lengthy legal battle against this form
of Jim Crow. At the same time the NAACP embarked upon the almost
endless fight against the white primaries. The Association, despite its
immediatist philosophy, was compelled to use an essentially gradualist approach, attacking one small aspect of discrimination at a time,
hacking away piece by piece at the structure of discrimination.
Though recognition of the Negroes' constitutional rights was still a
long way off, the NAACP could at least point to a corpus of definite
accomplishment. Less successful, however, were the attempts to prevent the development of school segregation in Northern cities. Gerry-
manders of school boundaries and other devices initiated by boards of
education were fought with written petitions, verbal protests to school
officials, legal suits, and in several cities school boycotts, but in the
end all proved to be of no avail.

The Association, considering itself heir to the abolitionist tradition,
and regarded as radical during the ascendancy of Booker T. Washington, after World War I found itself in the curious position of being
classed as a conservative organization by militant Marxists and nationalists on the left. In the Socialist *Messenger* magazine, editor A.
Philip Randolph even roasted and satirized Du Bois as a political
opportunist and a "handkerchief head . . . hat-in-hand" Negro. The
Messenger condemned the NAACP as basically a middle-class organization oblivious to pressing economic problems. Taking a Marxist
position on the causes of prejudice and discrimination, Randolph
called for a new and radical Negro unafraid to demand his rights as
a member of the working class. He advocated physical resistance to
white mobs, and believed that only united action of black and white
workers against capitalists would achieve social justice.

Although Randolph addressed himself to the urban masses, few of
them knew or understood the intellectual theories of the *Messenger,*
which circulated chiefly among elite Negroes. The one man who really
reached the frustrated and disillusioned residents in the Northern
ghettos was a Jamaican citizen, Marcus Garvey. Garvey, founder in
1914 of the Universal Negro Improvement Association, aimed to liberate both Africans and American Negroes from their oppressors. His
utopian means of accomplishing both goals was the wholesale migration of American Negroes to Africa. He contended that whites would
always be racist and insisted that the Negro must develop "a distinct
racial type of civilization of his own and . . . work out his salvation

in his motherland. . . ." On a more practical level he urged Negroes to support Negro businesses, and the UNIA itself organized a chain of groceries, restaurants, laundries, a hotel, and a printing plant. Thousands bought stock in the UNIA's Black Star Steamship Line, which proposed to establish a commercial link between the United States, the West Indies, and Africa. Garvey's followers proudly waved the Association's flag (black for Negro skin, green for Negro hopes, and red for Negro blood), and sang the UNIA anthem, "Ethiopia, Thou Land of Our Fathers." Stressing race pride, Garvey gloried in the African past and taught that God and Christ were black.

Garvey condemned the light-skinned, integrationist, upper-class Negroes active in the NAACP for being ashamed of their black ancestry and desiring to amalgamate with the white race. He insisted that the UNIA was the only agency able to protect the darker-skinned Negro masses against the Du Bois-led "caste aristocracy" of college graduates. Thus while *The Messenger* denounced Du Bois as a cowardly renegade Socialist, Garvey charged him with preferring white men to black. In turn both *The Messenger* and *The Crisis* joined in denouncing Garvey. The established Negro leaders resented and feared the "provisional President of the African Republic" and several of them called the attention of the United States government to irregularities in the management of the Black Star Line. Once Garvey had been jailed and then deported on charges of using the mails to defraud, the movement collapsed. But Garvey dramatized as never before the bitterness and alienation of the Negro slum dwellers who, having come North to seek the Promised Land, found only overcrowded and deteriorated housing, mass unemployment, and race riots.

Regardless of Randolph's and Garvey's castigation of the NAACP, the true conservatives in the era between the two World Wars counseled gradualism and tactful moral suasion as the most expedient way to attain racial justice. This approach was best represented by the National Urban League, founded about the same time as the NAACP by whites and Negroes, sympathetic toward Booker T. Washington. The League attained most success during the prosperous 1920's, seeking jobs for Negro migrants to the cities and using arguments that appealed to the white businessman's sense of economic self-interest as well as to his conscience.

IV

Despite the contribution of the NAACP and the interest of philanthropic whites in the Urban League and Harlem Renaissance during the 1920's, it was only during the 1930's that a clear-cut reversal in the attitudes of white Americans started to become evident. The New Deal marked a turning point in American race relations, although its programs were not free of discrimination. Federal housing expanded urban ghettos; the Agricultural Adjustment Administration subsidized white landowners, while crop restrictions forced many Negro share-croppers off the land. Nevertheless, Negroes shared in relief, jobs, and public housing, and Negro leaders, who felt the open sympathy of many highly-placed New Dealers, held more prominent political positions than at any time since President Taft's administration. The concern of people like Eleanor Roosevelt and Secretary of Interior Harold Ickes was part of the larger humanitarian interest in the wel-fare of the underprivileged in American society. At the same time, the Negro vote had reached sizeable proportions in many Northern cities, creating an additional motivation for the attention to Negro welfare among New Deal politicians. By 1936, Negroes had deserted their traditional allegiance to the Republican party. Finally, the emer-gence of the Congress of Industrial Organizations, which attempted to erase racial discrimination, gave some substance to the dream of an alliance of black and white workers for the first time since the decline of the Knights of Labor nearly a half century earlier.

The Depression, the New Deal, and the CIO together produced in the Negro protest movement a greater concern with economic problems. For example, Negroes staged "Don't Buy Where You Can't Work" campaigns in a number of cities, boycotting and picketing commercial establishments owned by whites that depended on the Negro market.

Massive unemployment and the general radicalization of Ameri-can thinking during the 1930's led to bitter attacks on the NAACP's program. Du Bois resigned as editor of *The Crisis* in 1934 largely because he became convinced that the NAACP was so identified with the black bourgeoisie that it would continue protesting disfranchise-ment and segregation without pursuing basic economic goals. Du Bois, furthermore, had never given up completely his belief in the value of collective racial economic endeavor. His ardent advocacy of a separate Negro cooperative economy as a solution to the problems posed by the Depression led to a clash with those who backed the NAACP's traditional position of opposing any form of segregation, and resulted not only in his withdrawal from his position with the NAACP, but also, as a consequence, in his withdrawal from a position of effective leadership. Younger critics of the NAACP like Ralph Bunche, who was then a professor at Howard University, also assailed the Association for its gradualism, and its blindness to the problems of the masses. Under these pressures, the organization not only spent

much effort attacking discrimination in New Deal agencies, but by
the end of the decade came out in full support of the new interracial
industrial unions.

The organization also expanded its legal program, fought a vigorous though unsuccessful campaign to abolish the poll tax, and finally
won its attack on the white primaries in a Supreme Court decision of
1944. But the heart of its litigation was a long-range campaign against
school segregation. It adopted the tactic of focusing on the most obvious inequities in the Southern school systems: the lack of professional and graduate schools and the low salaries received by black
teachers. Not until about 1950 would the NAACP make a direct assault against school segregation on the legal ground that separate
facilities were inherently unequal.

V

The changes in white attitudes that began with the New Deal accelerated during and after World War II. Thoughtful whites had been
painfully aware of the contradiction in opposing Nazi racial philosophy while doing nothing about racism at home. The revolution against
Western imperialism in Asia and Africa brought new respect for the
nonwhite people of the world. American racial attitudes liberalized
in large part because new nonwhite nations emerged and took increasing responsibilities in international councils. Moreover, Negroes
benefited from the Cold War, since the Russians raised the issue of
American racism to embarrass the United States in the eyes of the
world.

The early part of World War II witnessed two new movements
that anticipated later developments: the March on Washington Movement and the Congress of Racial Equality. In 1941 A. Philip
Randolph, president of the Brotherhood of Sleeping Car Porters,
threatened a mass march on Washington unless President Roosevelt
secured employment for Negroes in the discriminatory defense industries. The President's Executive Order 8802 establishing a federal
Fair Employment Practices Commission forestalled the demonstration. Even without enforcement powers, the FEPC set a precedent
for treating fair employment practice as a civil right. The short-lived
March on Washington Movement prefigured future trends in three
ways: (1) it was an explicitly all-black organization; (2) it based
its strategy on mass action by the urban slum dwellers; (3) it concentrated on economic problems.

Randolph's March on Washington Movement was greatly influenced by the tactics of Gandhi's movement of nonviolent resistance in India, but it was the Congress of Racial Equality that was chiefly responsible for projecting the use of nonviolent direct action as a civil rights strategy. CORE's origins lie in the activities of the Fellowship of Reconciliation, a Christian pacifist organization founded during the First World War. Certain leaders of the FOR, interested in the use of nonviolent direct action to fight racial discrimination, founded CORE in 1942 with the hope of enlisting persons whose major concern was in race relations instead of pacifism. CORE combined Gandhi's techniques with the sit-in, derived from the sit-down strikes of the 1930's. Until about 1959, CORE's main activity was attacking discrimination in places of public accommodation in the cities of the Northern and Border states. A cornerstone of its philosophy was that American racism could be destroyed only through an interracial movement. It was thoroughly interracial—even "color-blind" in its internal operations; as late as 1961, two-thirds of its membership and the majority of its national officers were white.

In the post-World War II period, the campaign for Negro rights gained new strength. The Truman administration in some ways opened a new era in the history of American race relations. The political impact of the heavy Negro migration to Northern and Western cities now became evident. The presidential election of 1948, which Truman won by a narrow majority, but with the overwhelming support of Negroes, showed that the black vote had become a balance of power in national, as well as many state and local elections. This was the first election since Reconstruction in which the Negro's status was a major issue. Though the Democratic Congress failed to enact a civil rights law, the Truman administration took some significant forward actions, most notably the desegregation of the armed forces. The report, *To Secure These Rights,* issued by a presidential commission, called for the full integration of Negroes in all aspects of American society. The principle value of this document, largely symbolic and educational, was its help in paving the way for new norms in American race relations.

Thus at mid-century, the accelerating migration to the industrial centers was about to usher in the most momentous changes in Negro-white relationships since the Civil War. The context and texture of Negro life had changed, and the process of future racial adjustment was to take place in a chiefly urban environment. The urban ghetto was at one and the same time the force which constricted Negro life and aspirations and yet formed the base for Negro political power and the activities of the civil rights organizations. Because the Negro vote was often closely tied to Democratic city machines, it was not as effective a voice of protest as some believe it could have been. Nevertheless, without the urban base the Negro protest movement would have remained small, and without the political leverage the urban masses provided, it would have remained impotent. Though no one realized it at the time, and though other factors were also essential in bringing about the events that were to follow, by mid-century the vote of the black ghetto in the North had reached the proportions that made possible the civil rights revolution.

VI

In the context of changing international trends and shifting American opinion the campaign for Negro rights broadened. The growing size of the Northern Negro vote not only made civil rights a major issue in national elections but ultimately, in 1957, led to the federal Civil Rights Commission, which had the power to investigate discriminatory conditions throughout the country and to recommend corrective measures to the President. Under pressure from the NAACP and other organizations, both black and white, more and more Northern and Western states outlawed discrimination in employment, housing, and public accommodations. The NAACP, in successive court victories, secured decisions against racially restrictive covenants in housing, segregation in interstate transportation, and discrimination in publicly owned recreational facilities. Finally, the Supreme Court ruling of 1954 became the triumphant climax to the NAACP's campaign against educational segregation in the South. The NAACP continued to conduct voter-registration drives and established housing and labor departments to improve its program in these two areas. Thus in the 1950's the NAACP was strengthening its traditional legal and legislative activities. Meanwhile, during and after the Second World War, the backbone of its expanding membership came to rest among the working-class urban Negroes.

CORE, by mid-century, was embarking upon demonstrations in the Border states. And as early as 1947, CORE, in cooperation with the Fellowship of Reconciliation, had conducted a "Journey of Reconciliation"—or what would later be called a "Freedom Ride"—in the states of the Upper South. Its purpose was to test compliance with the *Morgan* v. *Virginia* decision of the preceding year, in which the Supreme Court had outlawed segregation on interstate buses. The riders met resistance in some areas, and the pacifist Bayard Rustin, who was to become a prominent civil rights leader of the 1960's, was one of those sentenced to a thirty-day term on a North Carolina road gang.

But what captured the imagination of the nation and of the Negro community in particular, and what was chiefly responsible for the growing use of direct-action techniques, was the Montgomery, Alabama, bus boycott of 1955–1956, which catapulted into national prominence the Reverend Martin Luther King, Jr. Like the founders of CORE (but unlike most civil rights demonstrators), King held to a Gandhian belief in the principles of pacifism. In King's view, white oppressors who beat and jailed civil rights activists were transformed by seeing the unmerited suffering of their victims.

Even before a court decision obtained by NAACP attorneys in November, 1956, desegregated the Montgomery buses, a similar movement had started in Tallahassee, Florida. Afterward, another one developed in Birmingham, Alabama. In 1957, Tuskegee Negroes boycotted local merchants for three years after the Alabama legislature gerrymandered nearly all the Negro voters outside the town's boundaries. In response to a lawsuit filed by the NAACP, the Supreme Court outlawed the Tuskegee gerrymander. Today Negroes hold public office in the community where Booker T. Washington used to preach that Negroes had erred by starting in politics instead of at the plow.

These events were widely heralded. A "New Negro" had emerged in the South—militant, no longer fearful of white hoodlums or mobs, and ready to unite with other Negroes to achieve racial justice. Capitalizing upon this mood, King established the Southern Christian Leadership Conference to coordinate direct action activities in Southern cities. Negro protest had now moved in a vigorous fashion into the South; like the Northern protest activities, it was concentrated in the urban ghettoes.

Nonviolent direct action attained popularity not only because of the effectiveness of King's leadership but because the older techniques of legal and legislative action had had limited success. Impressive as the advances in the fifteen years after World War II were, in spite of state laws and Supreme Court decisions, something was still clearly wrong. Negroes were still disfranchised in much of the South, though in the twelve years following the outlawing of the white primary in 1944, the NAACP and other groups had raised the total number of Negroes registered in Southern states from about 250,000 to nearly a million and a quarter. Supreme Court decisions desegregating transportation facilities were still being largely ignored in the South. Discrimination in employment and housing continued not only in the South but also in Northern states boasting of civil rights laws. The Negro unemployment rate moved steadily upward after 1954. The South reacted to the Supreme Court's decision on school desegregation by outlawing the NAACP, intimidating civil rights leaders, bringing "massive resistance" to the Court's decision, curtailing Negro voter registration, and forming White Citizens' Councils.

At the very time that legalism was proving to be of limited usefulness, other events were bringing about a change in Negro attitudes: Negroes were gaining a new sense of self-respect and a new self-image as a result of the rise of the new African nations; King and others were demonstrating that nonviolent direct action could succeed in the South; new laws and court decisions and increasing support of white public opinion gave American Negroes a new confidence in the future. There occurred what has been described as a "revolution in expectations." Negroes no longer felt that they had to accept the humiliations of second-class citizenship, and consequently these humiliations—somewhat fewer though they now were—appeared to be more intolerable than ever. Ironically, it was the NAACP's very successes in the legislatures and the courts that more than any other single factor led to this revolution in expectations and the resultant dissatisfaction with the limitations of the NAACP's program. This increasing impatience accounted for the rising tempo of nonviolent direct action in the late 1950's, culminating in the student sit-ins of 1960 and the inauguration of what is popularly known as the "Civil Rights Revolution" or the "Negro Revolt."

The Negro protest movement would never be the same again. The Southern college student sit-ins set in motion waves of events that shook the power structure of the Negro community, made direct action temporarily pre-eminent as a civil rights technique, ended NAACP hegemony in the civil rights movement, speeded up incalculably the whole process of social change in race relations, largely destroyed the barriers standing against the recognition of the Negro's constitutional rights, and ultimately turned the Negro protest organizations toward a deep concern with the economic and social problems of the masses. Involved was a steady radicalization of tactics and goals: from legalism to direct action and ultimately to Black Power, from participation by the middle and upper classes to mass action by all classes, from guaranteeing the protection of the Negro's constitutional rights to securing economic policies that would insure the welfare of the culturally deprived in a technologically changing society, from appeal to the white Americans' sense of fair play to demands based upon the power in the black ghetto.

VII

The successes of the student movement in desegregating lunch counters in scores of communities in the Upper South, the Atlantic Coastal states, and Texas, brought a decisive break with the pre-eminence of legalistic techniques and threatened the existing leadership arrangements in the black community. There ensued a spirited rivalry among all civil rights organizations. Both the NAACP and SCLC attempted to identify themselves with the student movement. The organizing meeting of the Student Nonviolent Coordinating Committee held at Raleigh, North Carolina, in April, 1960, was called by Martin Luther King. The SNCC platform expressed the same ideas of religious pacifism as did King himself. But within a year the youth had come to consider King as too cautious, and not dedicated enough to the cause, and had broken with him and SCLC. The NAACP, which had previously engaged in demonstrations only in a peripheral way, now decided to make direct action a major part of its strategy. In many cases eager youths pushed reluctant adults into backing direct action. The young demonstrators, especially in the NAACP branches, depended heavily on the legal and financial aid which adult citizens supplied. CORE, which was still unknown to the general public, installed James Farmer as national director in January, 1961, and moved to the front rank of civil rights organizations with the famous Freedom Ride to Alabama and Mississippi that spring. Designed to dramatize the lack of transportation desegregation in those states, the Freedom Ride eventuated in a bus burning in Alabama, hundreds spending a month or more in Mississippi prisons, and partial compliance with a new order from the Interstate Commerce Commission desegregating all facilities used in interstate transportation.

Disagreements over strategy and tactics inevitably became intertwined with rivalries between personalities and organizations. The clashes between individuals and organizations, both nationally and locally, were often very severe, and the lack of unity was often deplored. Actually, down to about 1964, the overall effect of the competition was to stimulate more and more activity as organizations attempted to outdo each other in city after city. On the other hand, even among the strictly direct-action organizations, there developed differences in style. SCLC appeared to be the most cautious and to engage chiefly in a few major projects. From the beginning SNCC staff workers lived on subsistence allowances and appeared to conceive of going to jail as a way of life. More than any of the other groups, SNCC workers were "True Believers."

Direct actionists often criticized the NAACP for being dominated by a conservative Black Bourgeoisie wedded to a program of legal action and gradualism. Actually in the 1960's, the NAACP's program became the most highly varied of all the protest organizations. It retained a strong emphasis on court litigation. Acting in part through the Civil Rights Leadership Conference, consisting of many Negro and interracial organizations interested in promoting civil rights legislation, it maintained an extraordinarily effective lobby in the nation's capital. It also engaged in many direct-action campaigns. Some branches disdained direct action, but others enthusiastically adopted the tactic.

In the absence of carefully collected empirical data, it is impossible to speak with precision about the sources of membership in either the NAACP or the other groups. Individuals of middle-class and upper-class background or attainments have predominated in the leadership of all the national organizations, for they alone are likely to possess the necessary skills of administration and communication. This is true today, although SNCC and CORE have consciously worked to create indigenous grass-roots leadership, and many purely local groups formed since 1965 have also developed leaders from among the poor themselves. The college students who founded SNCC and formed the backbone of the demonstrations in 1960–1961 tended to be mainly from an upward-mobile, lower-class background, or what they themselves often described as "striving lower class." By 1962, however, SNCC had ceased to be a coordinator of college groups but had become a staff of activists whose field-workers stimulated direct action in Southern communities. Both SNCC community projects and SCLS affiliates have appealed mostly to working-class people rather than to the bourgeoisie. The NAACP since the 1940's has also drawn most of its members from the working-class, although certain branches with a mass membership base, like those in Newark and Chicago, have been closely allied with the urban political machines, which have used the organization to siphon off protest rather than to articulate it. CORE, by 1962 and 1963, when it was turning its attention to employment problems in the Northern cities, attracted a number of blue-collar workers and even people from the chronically unemployed lower class, and during 1963–1965 its Southern staff created and closely cooperated with working-class community organizations. But frequently CORE chapters, which were principally in the North and West, continued to have leaders and members alike who were mainly middle-class. In fact, in many localities the range of members and leaders in the NAACP, in CORE, and in the SCLC affiliates was such that one found it hard to distinguish among them on the basis of social class, though the activist groups drew almost entirely from younger people in their twenties and thirties. Rather, the NAACP and the more activist organizations often seemed to attract different personality types from roughly the same social backgrounds.

VIII

Meanwhile, the role of whites in the movement was changing. Instead of occupying positions of leadership, they found themselves relegated to the role of foot soldiers and followers. Negroes in the movement had come to feel less dependent on whites, and more confident of their own power, and demanded that their leaders be black. The NAACP had acquired Negro leadership some years before; and both SCLC and SNCC were from the start Negro-led and Negro-dominated. CORE, having acquired a new image in 1961 after the Freedom Ride, became predominantly Negro as it expanded in 1962 and 1963. Today all its national officers are Negro, and its 1965 convention adopted a constitutional amendment that officially limited white leadership in the chapters.

White liberals, socialists, and pacifists found themselves increasingly under suspicion in the activist organizations, especially if they did not endorse the most militant steps. Many of them must have felt rather like the Girondists did when overtaken by the Jacobins. In the labor movement, black workers grew restive over the failure of even the most liberal unions to place Negroes on their international boards or to eliminate discrimination in Southern locals. Consequently, the Negro-labor alliance forged during the 1930's disintegrated. "Farewell to Liberals," as an article in *The Nation* by an NAACP vice-president was called, expressed the idea well enough.

Thus by 1962 "white liberal" had joined "Black Bourgeoisie" as an epithet of opprobrium in the vocabulary of the civil rights militants. The phrase "white liberal" was also employed in a pejorative sense by white revolutionary Marxists who had jumped on the direct-action bandwagon. But beginning about 1963 they too found themselves in the ranks of those being "race-baited" by their Negro colleagues in the Movement.

Nevertheless, whites continued to play an essential supporting role. Involved were many individuals, hitherto not sensitive to the civil rights issue, whom we can call the "white moderates." Such whites, most notably leaders of the three major religious faiths, were of critical importance in the coalition of forces that was represented in the March on Washington in 1963, and it was this coalition that made possible the Civil Rights Acts of 1964 and 1965. More recently, in the wake of the annual wave of summer rioting and the emergence of the black power movement, white businessmen have been playing an increasingly important supportive role, most notably through the Urban Coalition.

IX

The white radicals had been attracted to the activist cause because they regarded it as the key to a socialized America. Yet the precise role of the white—and Negro—revolutionary leftists is difficult to ascertain. Actually, purely as a result of its own dynamics the Negro protest movement of the 1960's has undergone a continuous radicalization in tactics and ideology. As already noted, it was disappointment with the results of the NAACP's legal-legislative strategy that led to the triumph of direct action as a technique. Then, as lunch counters were desegregated, sit-ins and boycotts were used to attack exclusion from other places of public accommodation in the South, racist housing developments in the North and, most important of all, discrimination in employment. Large sections of the NAACP enthusiastically embraced direct action. The National Urban League, under the leadership of Whitney M. Young, Jr., executive director since 1961, became outspoken and militant in dealings with businessmen whom it had previously treated with the utmost tact and caution. It was principally the new climate provided by the activists that made this change in Urban League strategy possible. As businessmen came to fear demonstrations at their doorsteps or factory gates, they listened more carefully to requests and suggestions from the Urban League.

Meanwhile, as the excitement created by the earlier demonstrations dissipated, and as it became evident that many places of public accommodation remained firmly segregated, more dramatic forms of direct action became essential. To desegregate the more intransigent Southern communities, it was necessary to persuade dozens and even hundreds of people to go to jail and stay there. It became quite obvious that the unmerited suffering of the direct actionists did not bring a change in the hearts of the oppressors. Rather it was the economic pinch created by sit-ins and boycotts, the publicity obtained through mass arrests, and the national and international pressure generated by the violence of white hoodlums and police which forced social change. At the same time there occurred a secularization of those Southern Negro activists who remained in the movement for any length of time. Few of them had ever been pacifists in the first place; yet an important reason for the initial attraction of nonviolent direct action had been its consonance with their Christian faith. But by 1963, instead of speaking of love and Christianity, activists were coming to talk in terms of power. They thought less of convincing the white man of the moral righteousness of their aspirations and more of forcing him to change his policies through the power of black bodies to create social dislocation.

A major factor leading to the radicalization of the civil rights movement was unemployment and poverty—and an important force awakening the protest organizations to this problem was the meteoric rise of the Black Muslims to national prominence. Paradoxically, this nationalist sect, established around 1930, reached the peak of its influence when more progress toward equal rights was being made than ever before in American history. But this was also a time of deteriorating economic opportunity for the lower classes in the urban ghettos. Due to automation and other forms of technological change, Negro unemployment rose steadily. By 1962 it was two and a half times that for whites, and in some industrial cities the differential was even greater.

More than anything else this growing problem of employment, combined with the rapidly escalating expectations of the masses, produced an environment in which the Black Muslims flourished. To those willing to submit to its rigid discipline, the Black Muslims organization gave a sense of purpose and destiny. Its program offered them four things: an explanation of their plight (white devils); a sense of pride and self-esteem (black superiority); a vision of a glorious future (black ascendancy); and a practical program of uplift (working hard, saving money, and uniting to create Negro enterprise and prosperity). With this Puritan ethic the Muslims appealed to an upward-mobile group of the lower social class of Negroes. In the same way that the Garvey Movement was a lower-class counterpart of the New Negro of the 1920's, so the Black Muslims were a counterpart of the new "New Negro" of the early 1960's. Ironically, until split by internal dissension, the Black Muslims were of distinct assistance to the civil rights organizations, for their talk of violence and their hatred of blue-eyed devils frightened white people into becoming more amenable to the demands of the integrationists. As happened in the case of the black power movement later, to many whites the Black Muslims sounded so extreme that integration seemed to be a conservative program.

Paradoxically, the trials and successes of the integrationist protest movement after 1960, by producing heightened self-esteem among black men, encouraged other nationalist tendencies. For one thing as Negroes grew in racial pride, they displayed a sharply rising interest in Negro history. Another nationalistic manifestation was the call for black leadership within the civil rights movement, based upon the growing belief that Negroes could, through their own power, bring about drastic changes in American society. As early as 1963 there were proposals for the formation of an all-black political party. At the same time there were other proposals along the lines of self-help and racial cooperation in order to attack the economic needs of the rural and urban poor. Finally, a group of writers expressed their alienation by questioning the values of middle-class white America and militantly calling for preservation of the unique aspects of the Negro subculture. Subsequently, after 1965, this cultural pluralism was to become a widely held ideology, described by the phrase "black consciousness."

As the direct-action tactics took more dramatic form, as the civil rights groups began to articulate the needs of the masses and draw some of them to their demonstrations, the protest movement in 1963 assumed a new note of urgency and immediatism, a demand for complete "Freedom Now!" Moreover direct action returned to the Northern cities, taking the form of massive protests against economic, housing, and educational inequities. The new mood of militance suffused the events of 1963: from the fresh wave of demonstrations that swept the South to the fruitless Northern street demonstrations against the discriminatory building trade unions, and, the following winter, the equally fruitless school boycotts against *de facto* segregation. The frustration of the expectations of 1963 largely accounted for the further radicalization and increasing nationalism of the most militant activists that was to begin in 1964.

X

At first the new militance of the early 1960's tended to propel the more "conservative" Negro community leaders, whether prominent in the NAACP or not, into a more radical tactical position. It was notable that in crisis situations engendered by mass arrests, especially if these were accompanied by blatant police brutality, temporary unity was achieved between organizations and classes— generally on the militants' terms. For example, before the Birmingham demonstration conducted by SCLC in early 1963, the wealthy Negro citizens there had opposed King's decision to use that citadel of segregation as the site of a direct-action campaign. But after hundreds of children had gone to jail, after the police had used firehoses and dogs, even the opponents of direct action rushed to SCLC's support.

Though a superb example of how to run a direct-action demonstration, the Birmingham project resulted in a compromise that

brought the city's Negroes not "Freedom Now" but token concessions that later were not carried out. Nevertheless the demonstration was enormously important because it compelled the United
States to face the problem of Southern discrimination in a way it
had never done before. It forced President Kennedy to ask Congress
for major civil rights legislation. The Civil Rights Act of 1964, in
contrast to the token civil rights laws of 1957 and 1960, outlawed
discrimination in places of public accommodation, instituted a modest program for protecting the Southern Negroes' right to vote,
created a federal fair employment practices agency with mild enforcement powers, and—potentially most significant of all—gave the
national Executive the power to withdraw federal funds from state
and local agencies that discriminated against Negroes.

The Civil Rights law of 1964 settled the public accommodations
issue in the South's principal cities. Its voting section, however,
promised more than it accomplished. Again Martin Luther King
and SCLC dramatized the issue, this time at Selma, Alabama, in
early 1965. Yet, as President Johnson pointed out in his address to
Congress and the nation urging passage of the voting rights law
of 1965, beyond the protection of constitutional rights lay the as
yet unsolved problems of the poor.

XI

Where Birmingham had made direct action respectable, the Selma
demonstration, drawing thousands of white moderates from the
North, made direct action fashionable. Nevertheless, as early as 1964
it was becoming evident that like "legalism," direct action was but
a limited instrument. This was the result of two converging developments.

One of these was the failure of the sit-ins of 1960–1961 to desegregate public accommodations in Deep South states like Mississippi and Alabama, and the realization, first grasped by Robert
Moses of SNCC, that without the leverage of the vote, demonstrations there would be failures. Beginning in 1961 Moses, with the
cooperation of CORE and the state NAACP as well as SNCC, established voter registration projects in the cities and county seats of
Mississippi. He succeeded in registering only a handful, but by
1964 had generated enough support throughout the country to enable the Mississippi Freedom Democratic Party, which he had
created, to challenge dramatically the seating of the official white
delegates from the state at the Democratic National Convention.

Direct action also failed when applied to the difficult economic and social problems facing the Negroes in the black ghettos of the North. Inferior schools, rat-infested slum housing, and police brutality did not prove vulnerable to an attack of this kind. Street demonstrations did compel employers, ranging from banks to supermarkets, to add many Negroes to their work force. But technological innovation was leading to a steady decline in the number of unskilled jobs available, and the masses of Negroes, half of whom had not gone beyond the eighth grade, were unable to qualify for positions requiring higher skill and education. As a result, while the Negro "job-mix" changed because of the new hiring policies on the part of business, the basic pattern of mass unemployment remained.

Faced with the intransigence of the Deep South and with the inadequacy of direct action to solve the problems of the slums, the programs of the civil rights organizations diverged. The tendency toward a unity of strategy, if not between personalities, that was emerging during 1963 was being dissipated by the middle of 1964. At the very time that white support for the movement was actually rising, its most militant members felt increasingly isolated from the American scene. People in this radical left-wing of the movement were growing disdainful of American society and the middle-class way of life, cynical about liberals and the leaders of organized labor. Any compromise, even if a temporary tactical device, had become anathema to them. They talked more and more of the necessity for "revolutionary" changes in the social structure, even of violence. They became increasingly skeptical of the value of white participation in the movement, racially chauvinistic in their insistence that black power alone could compel concessions from the "power structure" of capitalists, politicians, and bureaucratic labor leaders. The black nationalist, Malcolm X, after his assassination in 1965, became the symbolic hero for the militants. At the extreme left wing of the movement Marxism and nationalism coalesced into a truly revolutionary ideology. In contrast, the conservative wing, impressed by changes in public attitudes, came to view its role as exercising influence within established institutions rather than fighting them from the outside. Between the two poles of thought there existed a group who recognized the new willingness of the nation's decision-makers to move toward greater racial justice, but perceived also that powerful pressure would be needed to push them in that direction. While it would be a gross oversimplification to pigeon-hole Negro protest leaders and organizations, broadly speaking it can be said that the militant left-wing was composed of SNCC and many individuals in CORE; that the conservative right-wing consisted of Urban League officials and a substantial group in the

NAACP; and that varieties of the centrist position, while found among many CORE and NAACP people, were best articulated by Bayard Rustin, A. Philip Randolph, and Martin Luther King.

Although by the middle of 1965 all segments of the movement were agreed that future protest activity would focus on the problems of the urban ghettos, and that rather than direct action the major weapon would be the political potential of the black masses, programatically there were wide differences. The most radical advocated "independent" politics, and the creation of Negro political organizations like the Black Panther Party of Lowndes County, Alabama. It was evident, however, that the future of this tactic would necessarily lie with the urban ghettos; there the main emphasis was on organizing the masses to challenge the Democratic machines from within the party, and elect officials who really represented the interests of the poor. The right wing, impressed by the legislation of 1964 and 1965, and the selection of prominent protest leaders for high public office, viewed the Democratic party establishment and city machines not as enemies but as allies. The centrist group, on the basis of experience with the civil rights laws of 1964 and 1965 developed a theory of "coalition politics." Under no illusions about alliances with the Democratic party leadership, they based their strategy on a coalition of Negroes with white liberals, white clergy, and organized labor.

The success of the coalition strategy from 1963–1965 had been due in no small part to the role of Martin Luther King. He served as an extraordinary symbol to blacks and whites alike. On the one hand, he was the most effective interpreter of Negro aspirations to white America in the country's history. On the other hand, during the early 1960's he occupied a position of strategic importance as a "vital center" within the Negro protest movement. Identified as militant and activist, his SCLC nevertheless was the most deliberate of the direct-action groups. This not only gave King respectability in the eyes of white moderates, but also enabled him to act as a bridge between the radical and conservative wings of the movement. For example, it is unlikely that the Urban League and the NAACP would have joined the 1963 March on Washington if King had not done so.

Yet between 1964 and 1966 the Negro protest movement became increasingly fragmented and ineffective. King found it more difficult, and finally impossible, to continue his unifying role. Fundamentally the growing disunity in the protest movement was rooted in the frustration of radically heightened expectations, and in the extraordinary problems involved in achieving genuine equality for the black poor. In the face of these circumstances, the various segments of the movement became increasingly divided on how to tackle the situation.

The 1964 Democratic Party Convention foreshadowed this trend. Events there, in the eyes of the militants, thoroughly discredited both the Democratic Party Establishment and the white liberal elements in the interracial coalition backing the national civil rights legislative program. The black militants believed that the Party's compromise offer of two delegates-at-large for the Mississippi Freedom Democratic Party, was mere tokenism, proving the insincerity of the Johnson administration. Moreover their growing distrust of the white liberals became complete when many of the latter, having originally supported the challenge, in the end advocated accepting the compromise. Finally, the Negroes themselves were deeply divided, with SNCC and CORE refusing to approve the compromise, while NAACP elements in the Freedom Democratic Party and men like King argued for its acceptance.

The war in Vietnam exacerbated the growing cleavages. Some believed that the war diverted attention and funds away from solving the country's leading domestic problem. Others went further, and regarded the war as cut of the same cloth as domestic racism, charging that both involved the attempt of the American "white power structure" to keep a colored race in a colonial status. A number of people, heretofore devoting their full energies to fighting racial discrimination, were diverted to working against the war in Vietnam. At the opposite pole were those who held that the Vietnam issue was irrelevant as far as the Negro protest was concerned, and that to mix the two issues was tactically dangerous, since it would lose some support for the Negroes' cause. The Urban League and the NAACP refused to identify themselves with the Vietnam issue. King, previously a key figure in the coalition strategy, openly attacked United States policy in Vietnam, as did SNCC and CORE. The white supporters of the coalition were similarly split, with organized labor particularly endorsing the war program.

Meanwhile, by 1965, white funding of the direct-action organizations was drying up. All along, the NAACP had been financed primarily by Negroes, and the Urban League continued to receive money from white businessmen. Various factors accounted for the financial problems of CORE, SLCL, and SNCC—the riots of 1964 and 1965, annoyance with the refusal of SNCC and CORE to accept the compromise offered at the 1964 Democratic Convention, and the position of all three organizations on the Vietnam War. Even King, who had urged the MFDP to accept the compromise at the 1964 Democratic Convention, found that his opposition to the war produced a sharp drop in SCLC's income. The financial situation exacerbated the distrust for the white liberals and accelerated the decline in the activities of CORE and SNCC. Not only did many individuals in these organizations turn to peace activities, but others, including many among the most effective local leaders, were siphoned off into well-paying administrative positions in the War on Poverty.

The antipoverty act, passed in 1964, had several effects on the protest movement. It accelerated the shift, already evident, from an emphasis on a national legislative program to local community action led by grass-roots people from among the poor themselves. The struggle within the black community over who would administer the community action programs exacerbated the polarization between the more moderate middle-class leaders, often identified with the NAACP and Urban League, and the more radical types. Finally, the antipoverty program unintentionally served to increase the frustration and discontent among the black poor by further escalating their expectations, but failing to deliver anything substantial. Yet one legacy of the War on Poverty was the feeling that the government should allocate resources to the ghetto, to be spent for programs initiated and administered by the ghetto-dwellers themselves. Thus, paradoxically, the OEO projects, while not solving the problems of the poor, led to a heightened militance among them.

The disillusionment with the national administration and the white liberals, the fragmentation of the Negro protest movement, the enormous difficulties that stood in the way of overcoming the problems of the black masses, and the riots that erupted spontaneously in 1964 and 1965 as a consequence of the anger and frustration of the urban slum dwellers, all set the stage for the dramatic appearance of the black power slogan in the summer of 1966.

XII

Black power first articulated a mood rather than a program—disillusionment and alienation from white America, race pride, and self-respect, or "black consciousness." The precipitating occasion was the Meredith March from Memphis to Jackson in the early summer of 1966, but the slogan expressed tendencies that had been present for a long time and had been gaining strength in the Negro community. Having become a household phrase, the term generated intense discussion of its real meaning, and a broad spectrum of ideologies and programatic proposals emerged.

In politics, black power meant independent action—Negro control of the political power of the black ghettos and its conscious use to better the slum dwellers' conditions. It could take the form of organizing a black political party or controlling the political machinery within the ghetto without the guidance or support of white politicians. Where predominantly Negro areas lacked Negroes in elective office, whether in the rural Black Belt of the South or in the urban centers, black power advocates sought the election of Negroes by voter registration campaigns, and by working for redrawing electoral districts. The basic belief was that only a well-organized and cohesive bloc of Negro voters could provide for the needs of the black masses. Even some Negro politicians allied to the major political parties adopted the term "black power" to describe their interest in the Negro vote. In economic terms, black power meant creating independent, self-sufficient Negro business enterprise, not only by encouraging Negro entrepreneurs but also by forming Negro cooperatives in the ghettos and in the predominantly black rural counties of the South. In the area of education, black power called for local community control of the public schools in the black ghettos. Throughout, the emphasis was on self-help, racial unity, and, among the most militant, retaliatory violence, the latter ranging from the legal right of self-defense to attempts to justify looting and arson in ghetto riots, guerrilla warfare and armed rebellion.

Phrases like "black power," "black consciousness," and "black is beautiful" enjoyed an extensive currency in the Negro community, even within the NAACP and among relatively conservative politicians. Expressed in its most extreme form by small, often local, fringe groups, among the national organizations the black power ideology was most closely associated with SNCC and CORE.

Generally regarded as the most militant among the leading Negro protest organizations, CORE and SNCC have had different interpretations of the black power doctrine. Though neither group is monolithic in its viewpoint, broadly speaking it can be said that SNCC called for totally independent political action outside the established political parties, as with the Black Panther Party in Lowndes County, Alabama; questioned the value of political alliance with other groups until Negroes themselves built a substantial base of independent political power; applauded the idea of guerrilla warfare; and regarded riots as rebellions. CORE, while not disapproving of the SNCC strategy, advocated working within the Democratic Party and forming alliances with other groups. It sought to justify riots as the natural explosion of an oppressed people against intolerable conditions, but it urged violence only in self-defense. While favorable toward cooperatives, it was more inclined toward job-training programs and developing a Negro entrepreneurial class, based upon the market within the black ghetto.

Paradoxically, the popularity of the term represented both a sense of power produced by the earlier successes of the movement, and an escape into the rhetoric of power caused by the powerlessness to achieve continued rapid progress toward full equality. The slogan emerged when the Negro protest movement was slowing down, when it was finding increased resistance to its changing goals, when it discovered that nonviolent direct action was no more a panacea than legal action, when CORE and SNCC were declining in terms of activity, membership, and financial support. Impotent to make any fundamental changes in the life of the masses, the advocates of black power substituted a separatist program for the platform of integration. Ironically, this occurred at the very time that Negroes were closer to the goal of integration than ever before. Where sixty years earlier the themes of racial unity and separatism had functioned primarily as part of an ideology of accommodation, while the black radicals demanded integration, now, among the latest generation of black radicals, it was fashionable to decry integration as a white man's strategy of tokenism aimed at holding Negroes in a subordinate position. Racial separatism had become part of a platform of radicalism and militance, while the erstwhile radical program of integration was now denounced as conservative, and sometimes as downright racist.

XIII

Yet it should be remembered that traditionally and today the central thrust of Negro protest has always struck at discrimination and segregation (the radicals of today distinguishing between voluntary separatism and enforced segregation); the central demand has always been for equal treatment with other citizens. The nationalist emphasis in militant Negro thought today is the latest expression of the ethnic ambivalence of American Negroes that is rooted in the contradictions in American society. Behind the revolutionary phrases of the black power militants is a profound desire for an equal share and an equal status in American society. "Radical" is, of course, a relative term; and indeed the central thrust of Negro protest, aiming at the inclusion of black men in America on a basis of full equality is not truly radical at all. For Negro protest has always been firmly embedded in the basic values of American society. It aims not at their destruction but at their fulfillment.

In the early 1960s the Anti-Defamation League commissioned a series of studies on prejudice and discrimination in America. One of these focused on a survey of attitudes of black Americans toward their situation and concerning their struggle.

Here Gary T. Marx reports on and interprets his findings about "The Social Context of Militancy." His analysis offers some generalizations about who feels what, where. The emphasis is on how a militant orientation develops rather than on modes of action. Three clusters of variables are correlated with militancy: the nature of an individual's value system, the extent of "social privilege," and the degree of "social involvement."

8

Gary T. Marx

THE SOCIAL CONTEXT OF MILITANCY

Beat and cuff your slave, keep him hungry and spiritless, and he will follow the chain of his master like a dog; but feed and clothe him well, work him moderately, surround him with physical comfort, and dreams of freedom intrude.

—*Frederick Douglass*

Many [slave owners] agreed that bondsmen should not visit neighboring estates. . . . By keeping them at home "they do not know what is going on beyond the limits of the plantation, and feel satisfied. . . ."

—*Kenneth Stampp*

. . . While militancy is undoubtedly influenced by both social and psychological factors, we do not mean to treat these as entirely separate classes of variables. Clearly, much that is treated as a psychological characteristic of persons is in turn greatly shaped by social circumstances. Thus, while both kinds of factors are investi-

From "The Social Context of Militancy," *Protest and Prejudice* by Gary T. Marx, New York: Harper & Row, 1967, pp. 49–79. Copyright © 1967 by Anti-Defamation League of B'nai B'rith. Reprinted by permission of Harper & Row, Publishers.

gated separately, ultimately their joint influence upon militancy will be examined. In this way it will be possible to assess the extent to which certain psychological factors seem to be the mechanisms by which social circumstances produce militancy. For example, I shall try to show that high social status produces militancy to the extent that status produces hope which in turn makes militancy seem realistic. But this anticipates what is to come. First we must see the extent to which social factors have consequences for Negro militancy.

For the sake of understanding, it is necessary to violate the seamless web of life and make analytic distinctions. Some of these are hierarchical or vertical distinctions; others are nonhierarchical or horizontal. Education, income, and occupational prestige serve to differentiate persons vertically. Other variables, such as region or sex, may be thought of as horizontal categories. In addition we distinguish between *attributes* of persons, such as their age, sex, or education, and their *behavior*, for example, participation in voluntary organizations or reading newspapers. In searching for the social determinates of militancy, we examine horizontal distinctions first, then the hierarchical, and finally various aspects of behavior bearing on social involvement and participation.

To avoid errors in interpretation, it should be clearly noted that our concern is with understanding the social and psychological factors that affect attitudes toward the civil rights struggle rather than the factors that affect actual participation in the civil rights movement. However, there is a strong relation between participation, as measured by membership in a civil rights organization, and attitudes toward civil rights, as measured by the Index of Conventional Militancy. Those classified as militant on the index were much more likely to report membership in a civil rights organization and to indicate willingness to take part in a civil rights demonstration than were those who were scored as conservative or moderate. If the definition of participation is broadened to include financial and other contributions, boycotting of products and stores, keeping children out of schools on protest days, and voting for more outspoken pro-civil rights candidates, then no doubt almost all of those termed militant have at one time or another been mobilized to some degree of participation.

However, our interest is not simply in civil rights activism, but rather in how a militant orientation develops and where it is located in the social structure. What we have done is characterize three main styles of response to the civil rights struggle among members of a "mass." "Mass" refers to a number of separate individuals each responding independently to the same stimulus (here the civil rights struggle). It implies a common focus of attention, but it is less than a collectivity since it lacks interaction tying the group together, as would be found among members of a civil rights group.[1] Thus, what we are exploring are the moods of the Negro community, not its modes of organization. However, when activism is analyzed the results are the same. In addition, as with any social movement, the civil rights struggle does not exist in isolation. In a society such as the United States which, ideally at least, permits groups to openly pursue their goals, civil rights leaders direct much attention toward mobilizing mass opinion in the black community. It is from this community that activists are recruited and that various forms of support so crucial for success in a direct action movement are obtained. Thus there is important reason for analyzing the response of the Negro community as a whole to the civil rights struggle.

Exposure to Race Relations Values of the Traditional South

The desire for radical social change and the belief that things are not as they should be requires an informing vision or perspective. In the case of race relations, such a vision must compete with contradictory perspectives on the proper place of the Negro. The extent to which modern American Negroes hold a perspective legitimating a struggle for equality ought to be partly contingent upon their exposure to and acceptance of the opposing value system of the traditional South.

Until very recently, the normative system governing race relations in the South was massive, and covered the most minute details of daily life down to segregated pet cemeteries, telephone party lines, blood plasma, and courtroom Bibles. In South Carolina, Negroes and whites were forbidden to look out of the same windows. This system was buttressed by a large set of formal laws, informal mores, and (white) economic, police, and juridical power. There is an ongoing debate among scholars about the role of coercion versus voluntary compliance in maintaining the patterns of Southern race relations both during and after slavery. Until recently the cheerful-compliance side has no doubt been overemphasized. However, the fact remains that the system rested (and rests) on something more than the police power of the white community.

This something is, of course, acquiescence in (to a greater or lesser degree) the system on the part of many oppressed by it. In the absence of sustained contact with an alternative pattern of race relations, or a different normative system, acceptance of the dominant pattern is easily understood. However, as the Negro's life circumstances operate to reduce his exposure to the Southern value system (and conversely, as exposure to the equalitarian value system of the rest of the country increases), individuals should increasingly question the legitimacy of the Southern "way of life" and militancy should increase.

We do not have a direct measure of the extent to which an individual has been exposed to the race relations values of the traditional South. However, certain indirect measures are available. The least ambiguous is whether a person was raised in the South or not.

Region and Type of Community

It is not surprising that among those raised in the deep South (but not necessarily still living there) only 19 per cent scored as militant (Table 1). This proportion increases steadily for those born in the border states and outside the South, up to 40 per cent for those raised outside the United States.

TABLE 1   *Militancy by Region Where Most of Childhood Was Spent*

	DEEP SOUTH	BORDER STATES	NON-SOUTH	OUTSIDE OF U.S.
Militant	19%	31%	35%	40%
Number	(523)	(260)	(293)	(20)

Africans and West Indians in the United States have occasionally been critical of what they regard as the docility of American Negroes. Marcus Garvey and Denmark Vesey, two prominent protest leaders of the past, were both born outside the United States, as were Stokely Carmichael and a number of other contemporary civil rights leaders. However, while those raised outside the United States had the highest percentage militant, they were only slightly higher than those raised in the North.

TABLE 2   *Militancy by Type of Community Raised in*

	FARM	SMALL AND MEDIUM CITIES	BIG CITY
Militant	15%	28%	37%
Number	(321)	(483)	(287)

Being raised in a rural rather than in an urban area would also seem to be a good indicator of the value system to which an individual has been exposed. Rural areas, in the South and elsewhere, have traditionally been bastions of cultural conservatism, in addition to being a source of occasional populist reform. Today it is in the cities of the South that the traditional social structure is crumbling most rapidly. The anonymity of the city, its greater heterogeneity and mobility, its more cosmopolitan and sophisticated atmosphere, and its greater integration into the national life all militate against traditional Southern patterns. The data show that militancy increases from 15 per cent among those raised on farms to 37 per cent for those raised in big cities (Table 2). This finding holds independent of region.

Age and Sex

The color line in America, despite periods of regression, has slowly been shifting since the turn of the century, and each successive generation is born into a social milieu where less and less consensus exists over the traditional inferior position of Negroes in American life. The shifts in the color line have been particularly pronounced since the beginning of World War II and have gained increasing momentum in recent years. In view of this changing climate of opinion, it can be inferred that most of the old were raised to accept segregation and to limit their aspirations.

TABLE 3 *Militancy by Age*

	18–29	30–44	45–59	60–75	75+
Militant	31%	34%	23%	16%	9%
Number	(243)	(368)	(271)	(179)	(32)

The old should therefore be less likely to be militant than the young, and Table 3 shows that this is so. About one out of three under 44 scored as militant; this figure decreases to about one in ten for those 75 and over. The greater militancy of the young is also indicated by their visible prominence in picket lines, sit-ins, and voter registration drives. The Congress of Racial Equality estimates that as of early 1961 more than 95 per cent of demonstrators who had been arrested were in their early twenties or late teens.[2]

Sex differences are also relevant. Men, being generally less insulated from society than women, are less traditional. This is true even in the Negro community, which in some respects, and partly for economic reasons, tends to be matriarchal. Men are more likely to be involved in the secular world and hence more likely to be exposed in a sustained way to values which would lead to rejection of the *status quo*. Negro males have traditionally been treated worse than females. It can be seen that about one in three of the men in the sample were militant while only about one in five of the women were (Table 4).

TABLE 4   *Militancy by Sex*

	MEN	WOMEN
Militant	32%	22%
Number	(495)	(600)

It has been observed that region, size of the community that one was raised in, age, and sex are each related to militancy, confirming the expectation that those most likely to be exposed to the values of the traditional South are the least likely to be militant. The effect of any one of these factors is independent of the effect of the others and, indeed, is independent of additional factors yet to be discussed.

A stronger measure of exposure to Southern values may be obtained by combining the four variables into a single Index of Exposure to Values Legitimizing Protest. This index shows that among those whose life circumstances combine to insure maximum exposure to the race relations values of the traditional South, only 11 per cent scored as militant while, at the other end of the index, among those least exposed to Southern values, 44 per cent were militants.

Thus, older Southern women reared in insulated rural areas are the least militant,[3] and younger Northern men reared in big cities are the most militant. When scores on the index are collapsed into categories of low (0, 1, 2), medium (3, 4), and high (5, 6, 7), the percentages militant are 12, 26, and 40, respectively (Table 5).

Heretofore it has been argued that exposure to values legitimating protest (or conversely lack of exposure to values precluding protest) seems to be required if militancy is to develop.[4] Being removed from the influence of the normative system of the traditional South seems to make it possible to adopt a new value system from which an individual can question the existing system. However, much more than this is involved in the development of militancy. An additional factor which ought to influence militancy is a certain amount of social privilege and the things associated with it.

Social Privilege

Militancy has already been located along some horizontal dimensions of social organization. Consideration will now be given to the vertical

TABLE 5   *Militancy by Index of Exposure to Values Legitimizing Protest*

SCORE ON INDEX [a]

High on Presumed Exposure to Values of Traditional South				High on Presumed Exposure to Equalitarian Values			
0	1	2	3	4	5	6	7

	0	1	2	3	4	5	6	7
Militant	11%	12%	13%	24%	29%	38%	40%	44%
Number	(44)	(111)	(151)	(234)	(212)	(141)	(129)	(66)

COLLAPSED SCORES

	(0, 1, 2)	(3, 4)	(5, 6, 7)
Militant	12%	26%	40%
Number	(306)	(446)	(336)

[a] Includes age, sex, region, and type of community raised in. No point was given for each of the following: being over 60, a woman, brought up on a farm, and in the deep South. One point was given for being 45 to 59, a man, brought up in a small town, and raised in the upper South. Two points were given for being under 45, raised in a big city, and outside the South.

or hierarchical dimensions implied in social privilege. The effects of education, occupation, and income are investigated separately and then combined into a measure of social privilege.

Social groups differ markedly in the relative amounts of scarce social rewards distributed among their members. In some societies the gap between the privileged and less privileged is very pronounced while in others differences are small. But regardless of how great the relative gap between the "haves" and the "have nots," in all societies individuals differ in their share of social rewards. Laymen, and not only sociologists, categorize individuals by social class according to the relative amounts of social status, skill, and economic and political power they possess.

EDUCATION

James Vardaman, a Negro-baiting politician of another era, in commenting on Northern aid to Negro education stated, "What the North is sending South is not money but dynamite: this education is ruining our Negroes. They're demanding equality." [5] As a humanitarian Vardaman may leave something to be desired, but as a social analyst he was perceptive. As Table 6 indicates, education is strongly related to militancy. Among those with a grammar school education or less, only 15 per cent scored as militant, compared with 31 per cent of those who had attended high school and 42 per cent of those

TABLE 6   *Militancy by Education*

	GRAMMAR SCHOOL	AT LEAST SOME HIGH SCHOOL	AT LEAST SOME COLLEGE
Militant	15%	31%	42%
Number	(404)	(545)	(146)

with a partial or complete college education. This relation holds in both the South and the North.

OCCUPATION

Strongly associated with but still independent of education is the individual's occupation. In Tables 7–10 several measures of occupation are related to militancy.

In considering employment, among those currently employed, 32 per cent scored as militant while for the unemployed and housewives this figure drops to 22 per cent and to 14 per cent for the retired (Table 7).

TABLE 7   *Militancy by Employment Status*

	EMPLOYED	UNEMPLOYED OR LAID OFF	HOUSEWIFE	RETIRED
Militant	32%	22%	22%	14%
Number	(589)	(119)	(265)	(111)

These findings are consistent with figures noted earlier, where women and the aged were lower in militancy. The unemployed are somewhat lower in militancy than are the employed despite their greater actual deprivation.

Among those currently employed it can be seen that, in general, as the status of a given occupation increases, so does militancy. In the category of service occupations only 24 per cent were scored as militant, and this figure increases consistently to 48 per cent among professionals (Table 8).

When occupations are grouped by prestige (here considering those currently employed and the "usual occupation" of the unemployed and retired), militancy increases from 22 per cent among those in lower-status occupations to 47 per cent among those in higher-status jobs. When housewives are included and assigned the occupation of the head of the household, a similar pattern is found: The higher the status of the occupation, the higher the percentage militant.

TABLE 8 *Militancy by Occupation*

RESPONDENT'S OCCUPATION [a]

	Prof.	Semi-prof.	Man-agers	Cleri-cal	Sales	Crafts	Opera-tives	Labor	Service
Militant	48%	41%	54%	42%	42%	35%	27%	27%	24%
Number	(23)	(17)	(26)	(60)	(12)	(71)	(138)	(41)	(198)

PRESTIGE OF RESPONDENT'S OCCUPATION [b]

	High	Medium	Low
Militant	47%	36%	22%
Number	(77)	(189)	(549)

PRESTIGE OF OCCUPATION OF HOUSEHOLD HEAD [c]

	High	Medium	Low
Militant	45%	31%	22%
Number	(78)	(283)	(694)

[a] Among employed only.
[b] Professionals, semiprofessionals, managers, and proprietors were classified as high in occupational prestige; clerical, sales, and craftsmen as medium; and laborers, operatives, and service workers as low. Table includes the usual occupation of the unemployed and retired.
[c] Includes all respondents.

Since education is strongly related to both militancy and occupation, it is possible that those in higher-status occupations are more militant simply because they are more educated. However, Table 9 offers evidence that, even with education held constant, the higher the occupational position the higher the percentage militant. Similarly, the employed remain more militant than the unemployed even when education is controlled for. Among those in lower-status occupations, the employed are still higher in militancy than the unemployed (Table 10).

TABLE 9 *Militancy by Education and Occupation*

(PER CENT MILITANT)

PRESTIGE OF OCCUPATION	GRAMMAR SCHOOL	AT LEAST SOME HIGH SCHOOL	AT LEAST SOME COLLEGE
High	[a]	38%	57%
Number		(16)	(51)
Medium	27%	37%	44%
Number	(44)	(106)	(39)
Low	12%	32%	26%
Number	(250)	(272)	(27)

[a] Too few cases to compute percentages.

One of the reasons students are more active in the civil rights struggle is their relatively greater freedom, including freedom from the economic reprisals that may restrain employed people. Likewise, it has been theorized that one element in the civil rights activism of some Negro ministers is their independence of white employers. Although the present study did not inquire as to the race of the individual's employer, it did ask whether respondents were self-employed or employed by someone else. If one assumes that the self-employed are apt to be less subject to economic reprisal than those responsible to an employer, one might be led to predict greater militancy on their part. However, this is not the case. On the contrary, militancy is somewhat less pronounced among the self-employed than among those employed by others (Table 10).

TABLE 10   *Militancy by Prestige of Occupation and Employment Status*

EMPLOYMENT STATUS	PRESTIGE OF OCCUPATION (PER CENT MILITANT)		
	High	*Medium*	*Low*
Employed	55%	41%	26%
Number	(45)	(133)	(366)
Self-Employed	33%	0%	14%
Number	(21)	(10)	(15)
Unemployed or Laid Off	a	37%	18%
Number		(24)	(87)
Retired	a	19%	11%
Number		(21)	(81)
Housewife b	44%	21%	20%
Number	(9)	(58)	(178)

a Too few cases to compute percentages.
b For housewives, the prestige of husband's occupation is used.

This finding certainly does not invalidate the hypothesis that those subject to strong economic reprisals are apt to be less militant than those not, particularly in concrete situations where action is called for.[6] However, it does suggest that, by itself the threat of economic reprisal need not hinder the development of a militant orientation just as freedom from economic reprisal may fail to encourage it.

STATUS DISCREPANCY AND SOCIAL MOBILITY

It has sometimes been suggested that discrepancies among the various dimensions of social status—for example, being highly educated but in a low-prestige occupation, or being high on both of these

yet belonging to a lowly esteemed racial or ethnic group—may lead
to the development of radicalism.[7] It is argued that individuals in a
position of status discrepancy are subject to pressures by the social
order not experienced to the same extent by individuals with congruent statuses. This has often been thought to predispose them for
radical political movements. The eighteenth century revolutionary
zeal of the French bourgeoisie, denied recognition by the old aristocracy, and the support given in the fifties to Senator Joseph McCarthy
by some recently arrived and upwardly mobile ethnic groups are
often cited as examples.

How does militancy appear among those who manifest a pattern
of status discrepancy, such as having considerable education, but
being in a working-class occupation? It would seem that feelings of
resentment against the social order would be particularly pronounced
among this group whose education qualifies them for higher-status
occupations, yet who are presumably denied such occupations and
rewards simply because of society's arbitrary racial arrangement.
One of our educated militant respondents in describing his occupation of garbage collector said that it was "subhuman beast-of-burden
type work even though I was a student." Comments such as this
would lead to the expectation that status discrepancy of this type
would be an important factor in the development of militancy. However, in Table 9 it can be seen that this is not the case. Those with
this type of objective status discrepancy (high education–low occupation) do not show a greater predisposition for militancy. In fact,
among those whose consistent status stems from having a college education and being in a high-status occupation, 57 per cent were scored
as militant while among the status-discrepant group, this figure was
only 26 per cent.[8] Among American Negroes, apparently, rather than
marked status discrepancies leading to radicalism they seem more
likely to lead to resignation and a low morale. The joint effect of
education and occupation on militancy is additive—the greater one's
social status the greater one's militancy.

The notion of status discrepancy is closely related to the question
of social mobility and its effect on attitudes. It is possible to view
those who have been socially mobile as being status discrepants in the
sense that their past status is inconsistent with their current status
(independent of whether they have moved up or down in status).

The problem of intergenerational social mobility, or change in
social position relative to one's parents, is an important factor in social
behavior. It is becoming particularly relevant in the case of Negroes
as the opportunity structure becomes more open.

Past research on social mobility in the United States has generally revealed a tendency for those who move up in the social structure to become more conservative in their political orientations than both the group they enter and the group they left. In the same way, those who are moving downward are more likely to hold on to the conservative outlook of the class they left so that downward mobility, too, is associated with conservatism.[9]

However, in the case of the Negro American and civil rights militancy, one would not necessarily expect to find this pattern. Instead, it might be thought that rather than becoming more conservative the downwardly mobile Negro would become more radical since, to a much greater extent than the downwardly mobile white, he has a built-in explanation (whether right or wrong) for his failure, his skin color.

Similarly, those who move up out of the ghetto world, instead of becoming satisfied and less militant, may merely have had their appetites whetted. More to the point, perhaps, is that recently arrived Negroes rarely have the large stake in the economic system which Frazier and others have suggested makes some members of the Negro elite almost as resistant to positive racial change as the white elite. Thus it may be hypothesized that those who have been socially mobile, regardless of the direction of their mobility, should be both more militant than the class from whence they came or the class into which they have moved.

These conjectures receive support in Table 11. Here we see that mobility is indeed related to militancy. Among the three groups who have been downwardly mobile (those of high-status parents who moved either into medium- or lower-status occupations and those of medium-status parents who moved into lower-status occupations), in every case the percentage scoring as militant is higher than among those in the status position moved out of or the new one moved into. Among those who moved down from a high-status background to medium-status occupations, 56 per cent were militant, while among those who remained in medium-status positions this figure is only 30 per cent, and for those who remained in high-status positions it is 37 per cent. The pattern is the same for each of the three upwardly mobile groups. Among those who moved from lower-status and medium-status into relatively high-status positions, 48 and 76 per cent, respectively, are militant, while for those who remained in high-status positions only 37 per cent are militant. This finding is of particular interest because it suggests that although militancy is strongly related to social privilege, among those high in social privilege the *arrivistes* are more militant than others.[10] The higher-prestige, older, more-established Negro families may indeed have a vested interest

TABLE 11   *Militancy by Social Mobility*

PRESTIGE OF
RESPONDENT'S
OCCUPATION   PRESTIGE OF FATHER'S OCCUPATION ª (PER CENT MILITANT)

	High	Medium	Low
High	37%	76%	48%
Number	(19)	(17)	(27)
	(stationary)	(upwardly mobile)	(upwardly mobile)
Medium	56%	30%	41%
Number	(16)	(44)	(64)
	(downwardly mobile)	(stationary)	(upwardly mobile)
Low	39%	36%	20%
Number	(31)	(56)	(188)
	(downwardly mobile)	(downwardly mobile)	(stationary)

ª Because of difficulty of classification, farm proprietors are excluded, as are the approximately 10 per cent of the sample who did not know their father's occupation.

in the *status quo* and thus be less militant than those newly arrived to their positions of prestige. However, among persons who have not been mobile, the higher the prestige, the greater the militancy. Both higher prestige and mobility produce militancy.

INCOME

Due to discrimination, education and occupation are less closely related to income among Negroes than among whites. Nevertheless, the three are related. Table 12 shows the relation between income and militancy. The pattern is similar to that observed for the two other

TABLE 12   *Militancy by Income*

	LESS THAN $2,000	$2,000– $3,999	$4,000– $5,999	$6,000 AND OVER
Militant	13%	19%	38%	35%
Number	(205)	(258)	(268)	(298)

status variables: The more privileged are much more likely to be militant than are the less privileged. Thus, among those earning less than $2,000 a year, only 13 per cent are militant; this proportion increases to 38 per cent among those with incomes of $4,000 to $6,000. Beyond $4,000 there are no meaningful differences. A ceiling effect seems to obtain: Beyond a certain point increased income does not influence militancy. That the relation between income and militancy is independent of education can be seen in Table 13. Status discrep-

TABLE 13   *Militancy by Income and Education*

(PER CENT MILITANT)

EDUCATION	LESS THAN $2,000	$2,000–$3,999	$4,000–$5,999	$6,000 AND OVER
Grammar school	10%	13%	27%	20%
Number	(126)	(105)	(73)	(67)
At least some high school	15%	22%	43%	35%
Number	(68)	(135)	(157)	(153)
At least some college	36%	33%	40%	47%
Number	(11)	(18)	(37)	(79)

ancy, in this case between high education and low income, again fails to influence militancy.

A Combined Measure of Social Privilege

Since all three separate measures of social privilege are positively and indepedently related to militancy, it is proper to combine them into an over-all Index of Social Class. As is clear in Table 14, the joint effect of these three variables on militancy is very great. Among those lowest on the Social Class Index only 8 per cent scored as militant. This figure increases to 31 per cent for those in the middle of the

TABLE 14   *Militancy by Social Class*

INDEX OF SOCIAL CLASS [a]

	Lower Social Class				*Upper Social Class*		
	0	1	2	3	4	5	6
Militant	8%	19%	31%	31%	39%	49%	55%
Number	(182)	(252)	(269)	(210)	(105)	(47)	(32)

COLLAPSED SCORES

	(0, 1)	(2, 3)	(4, 5, 6)
Militant	14%	31%	45%
Number	(434)	(479)	(184)

[a] No point was given for a grammar school education or less; at least some high school and at least some college were given one and two points, respectively. Occupation was also scored 0, 1, or 2, according to low, medium, or high status. No point was given for incomes under $2,000; incomes from $2,000 to $3,999 were given one point; all higher incomes, two points.

class hierarchy and to 55 per cent for those with the highest social positions. When this measure is combined into categories of lower class, middle class, and upper class,[11] the percentage militant is 14 per cent, 31 per cent, and 45 per cent, respectively.

These data do not mean that there are not many lower-class people concerned with and involved in the struggle for equal rights or that those who are involved may not often be more militant than the involved of higher status. The data merely suggest that a militant orientation (as defined in terms of this index) increases as social position does. According to a number of observers, one of the distinguishing characteristics of the civil rights struggle is the fact that it draws support from all segments of the Negro community. For example, Rustin has stated that "Birmingham remains the unmatched symbol of grass-roots protest involving all strata of the black community."[12] However this is not to say that the civil rights struggle draws its support in equal proportions from the various class groups.

On the basis of knowing that an individual is very low in social position, it is possible to predict that he will not be militant and be correct nine times out of ten. With each increase in social class there is a concomitant increase in the percentage militant. However, for those in the highest social positions predictions of militancy would be wrong slightly more often than they would be right. There are factors associated with being more privileged that lead to greater likelihood of militancy. But the fact that slightly less than half of the most privileged group scored as militant shows that there are still other factors which determine militancy in this class (some of which may not affect those low in status).

One factor which may reduce militancy among the high-status group is the conservatism often associated with higher-status positions. As Frazier has noted, the existence of a segregated Negro community, which is an exploitable economic unit, results in some Negroes, as well as whites, having a vested interest in the continuance of segregation. Higher-status Negroes often have a captive market within the ghetto.[13]

Although our study does not have any direct measure of the kind of vested interest just mentioned, certain inferences can be made as to who among the more privileged are most apt to have a vested interest in the *status quo*.

While we have observed that in general militancy increases with social privilege, we also noted variations in militancy among the privileged with respect to occupation and social mobility. Among higher-status individuals those who have been socially privileged for a longer time are lower in militancy than those who have arrived at their positions more recently. Furthermore, those earning over $6,000 a year were slightly less likely to be militant than those earning $4,000 to $6,000. This suggests that those who have been upper status for a longer period of time are more likely to have developed a vested interest in the system than those who have recently arrived, and the former are therefore less militant. Furthermore, among those who are already privileged, the more wealthy and generally better off might be expected to profit more from the system and hence be more conservative than the relatively well off, but less wealthy, people.

TABLE 15   *Militancy by Home Ownership* [a]

	OWN HOME	RENT
Militant	35%	54%
Number	(93)	(87)

[a] Among those classified as upper social class only.

An additional indication of economic well-being is the ownership of a home. In Table 15 home ownership is related to militancy for those of higher social status. Here it can be seen that the relation between privilege and militancy noted for the rest of the sample is reversed. Among those who are already relatively well off, the less privileged rather than the more privileged are the most militant. *Over half of the nonhome owners are militant, while only about one-third of those who own their homes were scored as militant.*

This question of a vested interest in the *status quo* among some of those in the highest social positions certainly does not entirely explain why many members of the group are not militant. However, by inferring its effect an important qualification must be made to the generalization that militancy increases with social privilege. We have perhaps isolated one of the factors that keep militancy from reaching higher proportions within this group.[14]

However, rather than being concerned with what prevents some of those high in social privilege from also being high in militancy, let us address ourselves to the more important question posed by the over-all relation between privilege and militancy. Social privilege is strongly related to militancy. The more education an individual has, the higher the prestige of his occupation, and the greater his income, the more likely he is to be militant (even when the effect of education on each of these other variables is controlled). This fact is even more evident when these items are combined into a measure of social class.

Why should social privilege relate to militancy the way it does? One might imagine the more privileged to be more satisfied—since the system has treated them relatively well—and hence less likely to be militant. However, social theorists have questioned the seemingly obvious idea that concern for social change is likely to be greatest among those most disinherited, and social science research has tended to support their claims.

The relation of deprivation to social upheaval has long been of interest to scholars. One of the most perceptive statements made about this subject was offered by the French political scientist Alexis de Tocqueville, well over 100 years ago:

> So it would appear that the French found their condition the more unsupportable in proportion to its improvement. . . . Revolutions are not always brought about by a gradual decline from bad to worse. Nations that have endured patiently and almost unconsciously the most overwhelming oppression often burst into rebellion against the yoke the moment it begins to grow lighter. . . . Evils which are patiently endured when they seem inevitable become intolerable when once the idea of escape from them is suggested.[15]

Although Tocqueville was talking about revolutionary rather than reform movements, his statement has much relevance for understanding the increased tempo of the civil rights struggle within the United States in recent years. Protest has grown as the standard of living has risen (not fallen) and as the legal basis of segregation has been undermined (not strengthened). Tocqueville's analysis, which has led to theories of the revolution of rising expectations, is congruent with the regional differences we have observed. There is more militancy in the North, where living standards are higher and social justice more in evidence, than in the South, where objectively things are much worse. Thus, among Negro Americans, those who have experienced the most improvement and are least subject to objective deprivation are much more likely to be militant than those worse off.

Tocqueville suggested that the taste of better things serves, not to quell dissatisfaction, but to create and increase it. The many reforms and unprecedented prosperity of France just prior to the French Revolution, and the abolition of most of the remnants of serfdom prior to the Russian Revolution, are good examples of this. The situation seems similar for the pattern of militancy we have observed in this chapter. The more privileged recognize that change is possible and want more. The most deprived Negroes tend not to have a basis in experience for what "more" means.

Karl Marx, somewhat later than Tocqueville, stressed a different factor in his interpretation of why discontent is not necessarily related to the severity of objective conditions. He wrote in the *Communist Manifesto:*

Thus, although the enjoyments of the workers have risen, the social satisfaction that they [increased wages] give has fallen in comparison with the increased enjoyments of the capitalist. . . . Our desires and pleasures spring from society; we measure them, therefore, by society and not by the objects which serve for their satisfaction. Because they are of a social nature, they are of a relative nature.

Following through on the implications of Marx's idea, the authors of *The American Soldier*, a classic of survey research, develop the notion of relative deprivation to help understand why discontent among servicemen was not necessarily related to objective conditions of deprivation. The fact that soldiers in units with high rates of promotion were more critical of their chances of promotion than were soldiers in units where the chances for promotion "were about the worst in any branch of the army" is explained as follows: "such opinions represent a relationship between their expectations and their achievements relative to others in the same boat with them." [16]

In understanding discontent, what counts is not so much the individual's objective situation as that of the "others" with whom he compares himself. The group with whom the individual compares himself is called by sociologists his "reference group." If a person's reference group is as deprived as he is, the individual is apt to be content with his lot. If, however, a person's reference group is more successful than he is, the individual may have a sense of deprivation no matter how objectively well off he is.

The notion of relative deprivation and the related concept of reference group [17] have relevance for understanding the pattern of militancy observed in this chapter. The fact that militancy is more pronounced among the privileged than among the unprivileged suggests that the privileged have a broader perspective, derived from their greater education and social participation. With this perspective, an individual can evaluate his own and his group's position in relation to the more privileged segments of white society rather than the limited framework of the depressed ghetto world.[18] This shift in perspective comes from the ability of the more privileged to look horizontally at whites in similar positions and from their greater knowledge about how these whites live and are treated.[19] In addition to employing white society as the frame of reference, this perspective is likely to include greater intellectual sophistication, more substantive knowledge about the world, and an image of man more conducive to militancy.

The more privileged may be much more conscious of lack of acceptance due to race because they come so close to being accepted in every other way. They have reaped many of the fruits of middle-class existence and their image of themselves is likely to be severely contradicted when they find themselves assigned to an inferior racial status. The more deprived individual in the ghetto—uneducated, unskilled, underpaid or unemployed—may be less aware of the racial aspect of his low status because he is so consistently submerged. Thus, a subtle kind of status discrepancy may be an important impetus to militancy for the relatively privileged Negro.

There are far more concrete reasons, however, why militancy should vary directly with social privilege. These involve the energy, resources, morale, and self-confidence needed to challenge an oppressive and powerful system. The mental and physical energy of severely deprived people is occupied in simply staying alive. A concern with somewhat abstract principles of racial justice is a luxury of the more privileged, who need not worry where their next meal is coming from. They are freer in both a mental and a physical sense to challenge the *status quo*. In addition, their relatively well-to-do financial situation and the possession of occupational skills make them less vulnerable to economic reprisals for civil rights activities. Further, they are more likely to have the intellectual and organizational skills and the *savoir faire* that activism requires. Because they are less awed and overwhelmed by the power of society's institutions, and freer from concern for economic survival, they can more easily question and act.[20]

Those in very deprived positions may be less apt to feel the sense of solidarity needed for organized political challenge. A study of the effect of unemployment on "revolutionary attitudes" reports that experiences of unemployment "do not lead by themselves to a readiness for mass action. . . . They can easily lead to outbreaks of distress in the form of single acts, but they leave the mass inert, since they lead to ever-increasing mutual estrangement, isolation, dispersion, destruction of solidarity, even to hostility among the laborers. . . ."[21] Literary depictions of the junglelike character of life in the urban ghetto with its "war of all against all" seem further to support such claims.

Furthermore, militancy requires at least some degree of hope, a belief in the possibility of beautiful tomorrows. Morale is needed which, although linked with dissatisfaction, is the opposite of despair. One can be "down," but he must not believe that he is "out." A sense of futility would seem to work against the development of the morale and hope required for a militant vision. One of the reasons that militancy is more pronounced among those in higher social positions may be that this group is more likely to have the high morale needed to sustain it. No matter how dissatisfied and distraught an individual may be over his personal and group situation, unless his discontent is found together with a positive morale, it is likely to lead not to militancy but to apathy, despair, and estrangement.

This does not mean that the underprivileged are filled with love or respect for the system that oppresses them. But they are likely to lack the energy, incentive, and will to challenge it in the disciplined way of civil rights organizations. If their concern does lead to attack, it is more likely to take the form of violent outbursts such as those of Richard Wright's protagonist, Bigger Thomas.[22] An Oakland, California, CORE spokesman described the absence of organized civil rights protest among impoverished young males in the ghetto by remarking, "If you want to go blow up something or fight, they'll do it, but they're not interested in carrying picket signs."

Closely related to morale is the question of self-image. One of the frequent consequences of lower social status is an unfavorable self-image, or at least a disparaging image of one's group. In the case of protest among Negroes, the question of self-image or group disparagement may be an extremely important factor. To believe that most Negroes are lazy, if not inherently inferior to whites, or that they are loud, dirty, and prone to violence often leads whites to fight to preserve segregation. Among Negroes, the acceptance of such beliefs probably leads to resignation. An unstated assumption made by militants is that Negroes are every bit as capable as whites, if not superior, and that they have the same vices and virtues as their pale counterparts. To believe otherwise would seem to justify differential treatment of Negroes and to shift the blame away from changing the social structure to changing the behavior of individuals. More privileged Negroes are probably better able to resist derogatory stereotypes of the Negro, as are more privileged whites, and this, too, may be a factor in the greater militancy of those in higher social positions.

In this section it has been suggested that important factors in the positive impact of social class on militancy are the greater intellectual sophistication, the higher morale and expectations, and the more positive self-image of those in more privileged social positions. In the next chapter these hypotheses are tested empirically.

Social Participation: Actual and Symbolic

A great deal of social participation takes in interpersonal settings in which there is face-to-face contact and communication occurs by word of mouth. But social participation also occurs when the individual reads newspapers, magazines, or books, watches television, or goes to a movie. For want of better terms, we call the first "actual" social participation, the second "symbolic" participation. Both, however, are forms of communication, and both are the opposite of social isolation and estrangement. The spread of militancy in the Negro community presupposes lines of communication which bring the message of protest and its legitimating values. By the same token, it also presupposes social participation on the part of its members, whether actual or symbolic. In this section both modes of social participation are examined to see the extent to which they are related to militancy. We consider actual participation first and then symbolic participation.

We have already learned that one aspect of social participation, employment, is positively related to militancy. Work is a major means by which persons participate in the larger society, gain a sense of responsibility for it, and acquire an interest in public affairs. The fact that men and employed women are more informed on news events than are housewives is well-known. The finding that employed Negroes are more militant than the unemployed (among both men and women) can be partly understood as a result of this process.

A similar pattern appears in Table 16 where three measures of social participation are examined. Membership in voluntary organizations [23] is positively related to militancy. Of those who belong to no voluntary organization 23 per cent are militant compared with 30 and 38 per cent of those who belong to one or more than one such organization.

Furthermore, the more frequently an individual visits with friends, the more likely he is to be militant. Militancy ranges from 19 per cent among those who "almost never" visit to 34 per cent among those who do so every day.

An additional measure of social participation is voting. Those who failed to vote in 1960 were less likely to be militant (17 per cent) than were those who voted (31 per cent).

When these three aspects of social participation are combined into a single Index of Actual Participation, they show a powerful joint effect on militancy. Only 11 per cent of those scored zero on the index were militant as compared with 43 per cent of those high on the index (Table 16).

SYMBOLIC PARTICIPATION

Since the Civil War, Negro newspapers and magazines have been organs of racial protest (in spite of their advertisements for "straighteners" and "lighteners," which discredit black appearance). In fact, the existence of the Negro press can be traced to the desire to protest

TABLE 16   *Militancy by Index of Actual Social Participation*

NUMBER OF ORGANIZATIONAL MEMBERSHIPS [a]

	0	1	2+
Militant	23%	30%	38%
Number	(677)	(298)	(118)

SOCIALIZE WITH FRIENDS

	Almost Never	Often	Every Day
Militant	19%	23%	34%
Number	(216)	(737)	(134)

VOTED IN 1960

	No	Yes
Militant	17%	31%
Number	(346)	(625)

INDEX OF ACTUAL SOCIAL PARTICIPATION [b]

	Low				High
	0	1	2	3	4, 5
Militant	11%	18%	27%	33%	43%
Number	(76)	(273)	(397)	(238)	(112)

[a] Excludes church groups and civil rights organizations.
[b] Composed of number of organizations belonged to, frequency of visits with friends, and voting in 1960.

the treatment generally accorded Negroes by white newspapers. One observer has suggested that their singular dedication to the cause of Negroes "has been the prime reason for the effective organization of the Negro protest." [24] It is to be expected that those exposed to such publications should be more militant. Table 17 shows this to be the case. Of those who read no Negro newspapers, 19 per cent scored as militant, whereas this figure increases to 34 per cent for those who read two or more. Among those who read no Negro magazines only 13 per cent were militant, while among those reading two or more magazines this figure increases to 36 per cent. This phenomenon is not entirely due to the unique protest nature of the Negro media, since those who read general circulation newspapers or magazines are also more likely to be militant. Among those reading more than two general circulation magazines, 35 per cent were militant; among those who did not read such magazines this figure drops to 17 per cent. The questionnaire did not inquire how many general newspapers a respondent read, but it did ask how frequently he read a newspaper. It can be seen that the proportion of militants increases from 15 per cent among those who read newspapers less than once a week to 30 per cent for those reading a general newspaper every day. Thus, regardless of the medium, being plugged into channels of communication is associated with increased militancy. When these measures are combined into an Index of Symbolic Participation, the percentage militant increases from only 5 per cent among those who read no periodicals to 38 per cent for those who read a great many (Table 17).

TABLE 17   *Militancy by Index of Symbolic Social Participation*

NUMBER OF NEGRO NEWSPAPERS READ

	0	1	2+
Militant	19%	26%	34%
Number	(245)	(521)	(329)

NUMBER OF NEGRO MAGAZINES READ

	0	1	2+
Militant	13%	32%	36%
Number	(403)	(317)	(375)

NUMBER OF GENERAL MAGAZINES READ

	0	1	2+
Militant	17%	32%	35%
Number	(472)	(189)	(433)

READ OTHER NEWSPAPERS

	Less Than Once a Week	*Once a Week to Several Times a Week*	*Every Day*
Militant	15%	24%	30%
Number	(165)	(283)	(708)

SCORE ON INDEX OF SYMBOLIC SOCIAL PARTICIPATION [a]

	0	1	2	3	4
Militant	5%	14%	20%	30%	38%
Number	(62)	(158)	(225)	(252)	(382)

[a] The total number of magazines was combined, and those reading no magazines were scored 0; those reading one or two, 1; and those reading three or more, 2. A combined measure of newspaper reading was then built up. Reading no Negro newspapers was scored 0; one, 1; and two or more, 2. Reading a general newspaper less than once a week was scored 0; several times a week, 1; and every day, 2. This measure was then trichotomized (scores of 0, 1–2, 3–4) and combined with the score on the measure of number of magazines read.

The measures of actual participation and symbolic participation are strongly related to each other and for purposes of later analysis have been combined into an Index of Social Participation. On this combined index, the proportion militant increases from zero among those lowest on the index to 46 per cent among those scoring in the highest categories. Among collapsed categories of low, medium, and high, the proportions militant are 12, 25, and 39, respectively (Table 18). The advantage of combining these two measures is not that the percentage militant markedly increases at the extremes, but rather that cases become more evenly distributed over the index and subsequent analysis is facilitated.

TABLE 18   *Militancy by Index of Social Participation*

SCORE ON INDEX OF SOCIAL PARTICIPATION [a]

	Low								*High*
	0	1	2	3	4	5	6	7	8,9
Militant	0%	5%	17%	12%	20%	28%	36%	41%	46%
Number	(14)	(43)	(96)	(143)	(176)	(205)	(210)	(130)	(72)

COLLAPSED SCORES

	(0–3)	(4, 5)	(6+)
Militant	12%	25%	39%
Number	(296)	(381)	(412)

[a] Composed of indexes of Actual and of Symbolic Social Participation.

The social participation-militancy pattern just considered is similar to that which historians have noted in analyzing Negro protest during slavery. Elkins has pointed to differences in the social participation of slaves in the United States, as compared with that in Brazil, to help account for the wider scope and greater success of the Brazilian protest against slavery. In Brazil the slave was more involved in society and had greater opportunity to play a number of roles beyond that of mere slave. The Brazilian slave could be a father and husband (while the American slave often could not), a communicant in the church, and a member of a religious fraternity. The law guaranteed him the time to engage in activities such as being an artisan, peddler, and petty merchant, and even a share of the profits. Elkins notes that such roles were all legitimized and protected outside the plantation and offered a diversity of channels for the development of personality. He adds:

> Not only did the individual have multiple roles open to him as a slave, but the very nature of these roles made possible a certain range of

aspirations should he someday become free. He could have a fantasy-life not limited to catfish and watermelons; it was within his conception to become a priest, an independent farmer, a successful merchant, a military officer. The slave could actually—to an extent quite unthinkable in the United States—conceive of himself *as a rebel*.[25]

It is of more than passing interest that the three most noteworthy slave revolts in the United States were led by individuals with social involvements and perspectives that extended beyond the institution that bound them. Thus Gabriel Prosser, Denmark Vesey, and Nat Turner all had the chance to play a variety of social roles denied to the average slave of the time, and are presumed to have been literate.[26] The majority of plots for slave revolts which have been recorded developed in urban areas.

While present conditions are fundamentally different from those under slavery, the effect of social involvement seems to be the same. Broader perspective extending beyond the insulated ghetto world seems especially relevant.

Those higher in participation live in a less constricted social environment and have mentally escaped the ghetto without necessarily leaving it physically. They also stand a greater chance of coming into sustained contact with others who have similar problems. Through their greater involvement, both actual and symbolic, distant civil rights activities become meaningful. Lack of involvement, on the other hand, isolates the individual from channels of communication which might transmit protest values and a more extensive view of the world. Living in the narrow, fairly homogeneous ghetto environment, often untouched even by newspapers or magazines, belonging to no formal organizations, and interacting only occasionally with friends are likely to lead to resignation or despair, a narrow and immediate view of the world, and a concern largely with the problems of daily existence. With restricted spheres of experience, the morale of such persons may be lower and their mental imagery less apt to encompass the larger community and the vision of broad social change necessary to militancy.

The Combined Effect

We have found militancy to be related to three clusters of variables. The first has to do with the nature of the value system an individual is presumed to have been exposed to, the second with social privilege, and the third with social involvement. What effect can be achieved by taking these variables together?

It is well known that older people, those raised in the South, and people from rural areas have less education and lower incomes than younger people, those raised in the North, and people from urban areas. Therefore, it is possible that the pattern of the Value Exposure Index (which combines age, region, sex, and community size) is due to the fact that those low on this index are also low in social position. However, the impact of the Value Exposure Index remains strong when social class is controlled (Table 19). Among

TABLE 19 *Militancy by Social Class and Exposure to Values Legitimizing Protest*

VALUE EXPOSURE	SOCIAL CLASS (PER CENT MILITANT)		
	Lower	Middle	Upper
Low	9%	18%	20%
Number	(203)	(88)	(15)
Medium	14%	30%	41%
Number	(155)	(212)	(79)
High	30%	39%	52%
Number	(73)	(174)	(89)

those lowest on social class 9 per cent of those low on the Exposure Index are militant, while 30 per cent of those high on the index are militant. The effect of exposure remains strong within each class group. Reading across the table, the effect of social class also remains strong within all degrees of value exposure. Thus each has an independent effect on militancy. Together they strongly predict militancy, from 9 per cent militant among those low on both class and exposure to 52 per cent among those high on both.

A similar independence and joint effect can be seen when social participation and value exposure are simultaneously related to militancy (Table 20). Within categories of social participation, the greater the value exposure the greater the proportion militant.

TABLE 20 *Militancy by Social Participation and Exposure to Values Legitimizing Protest*

VALUE EXPOSURE	SOCIAL PARTICIPATION (PER CENT MILITANT)		
	Lower	Medium	High
Low	6%	13%	24%
Number	(142)	(98)	(64)
Medium	18%	23%	39%
Number	(107)	(166)	(161)
High	18%	36%	49%
Number	(46)	(114)	(175)

Within categories of value exposure, the greater the extent of social participation the greater the likelihood of militancy.

Nor is the effect of social participation merely a function of uncontrolled social class differences. Looking at Table 21, we see that

TABLE 21   *Militancy by Social Class and Social Participation*

SOCIAL PARTICIPATION	SOCIAL CLASS (PER CENT MILITANT)		
	Lower	*Middle*	*Upper*
Low	9%	17%	19%
Number	(190)	(92)	(16)
Medium	16%	28%	37%
Number	(151)	(184)	(46)
High	24%	40%	50%
Number	(90)	(202)	(120)

both indexes have an independent effect upon militancy. Among all social classes, militancy increases with social participation, while in all categories of social participation, militancy increases with social class.

Militancy is not an idiosyncratic state of mind. Rather it most often occurs among persons whose location in society is conducive to developing aspirations for a better life. Thus, lack of exposure to Southern values (or, conversely, exposure to non-Southern values), social privilege, and access to the message of protest through actual and symbolic social participation all independently and powerfully affect militancy.

We have seen that a sizable percentage of the black community consistently holds militant attitudes and have examined some correlates of these attitudes. However, only a very small minority of these people become deeply involved as activists. For militant attitudes to lead to consistent action in an organization such as CORE an individual must first be "available" and in a position to undertake the often considerable risks involved. It would seem that the young, those with few if any familial responsibilities, and those not in occupations subject to the punitive control of whites would be most likely to be involved in direct action. A study of CORE reveals that activists do disproportionately possess these characteristics.[27] Furthermore, in the South, individuals who hold militant attitudes and are "available" for direct action are more likely to actually engage in protest activity when they are in communities with certain characteristics. For example, other factors being equal, protest seems more likely in relatively urbanized communities, those with a higher socioeconomic level, those where organizations such as the NAACP were viable before the beginning of the current struggle and where a Negro college is located, and those where Negroes are a relatively smaller percentage of the population.

Before turning from social to psychological factors, we shall examine the extent to which the findings in this chapter are consistent with empirical findings from other studies.

Numerous studies have found that lower-status people and those socially isolated are more likely to be apathetic about issues of public policy. However, in times of crisis it is precisely these alienated and isolated individuals who are most likely to be attracted to movements that seek change outside the framework of traditional values.[28] In a later chapter it will be observed that although a very large majority of all Negroes reject the Muslim variety of black nationalism, lower-status, isolated people were relatively more receptive to it than were those higher in social position and participation.

When such people do express opinions, they are likely to be conservative on noneconomic issues. Past research has shown that those lower in social position and involvement are least supportive of the civil liberties of dissenters and the civil rights of minorities.[29] If the Militancy Index is viewed as a measure of noneconomic liberalism,[30] the pattern that has emerged is clearly to be anticipated.

Past research dealing with Negro militancy is generally consistent with the results reported here. Studies of the two most militant civil rights organizations, CORE and SNCC, indicate that in spite of their antibourgeoisie emphasis, members are disproportionately middle class and younger.[31] One study of Negro college students found expressions of militancy to be greatest among those of higher-status backgrounds and those who participate more fully in extracurricular activities.[32] Another study of students found civil rights activism to be greater among relatively more privileged students from the better Negro colleges, and among those raised in urban areas and those best informed and most in touch with the mass media.[33] Other researchers have found that, in one community, enrollment of children in the first integrated school was positively related to higher social status and an urban background.[34] A study done on use of the open occupancy law in New York City found most complainants to be middle class.[35] Another found that in one small New York State community the least militant tended to be older, less educated, Southern-born, lower in participation, and female.[36] Studying this community, and two others, still another found that "militant group pride" existed significantly more often among upper-status individuals.[37] Brink and Harris report that, of non-Southern middle- and upper-income Negroes, 44 per cent reported marching in a demonstration and 63 per cent reported boycotting various stores, while for those with low incomes these figures drop to only 13 and 6 per cent.[38] Over twenty years ago, research on the American soldier, referred to earlier, discovered that opposition to segregated army PX's was greatest among the more educated and the Northern-born Negroes.[39]

NOTES

1 The term "mass" is a familiar one in sociological literature; for example, Ralph Turner and Lewis Killian, *Collective Behavior,* Englewood Cliffs, N.J., Prentice-Hall, 1957, p. 167. Members of this "mass" are responding to what Blumer and Smelser have called "general social movements" as opposed to the specific "norm-oriented movements." (See Herbert Blumer, "Collective Behavior," in A. M. Lee, ed., *New Outline of the Principles of Sociology,* New York, Barnes & Noble, 1951, pp. 199–201, and N. Smelser, *Theory of Collective Behavior,* New York, Free Press, 1963, p. 273.)

2 As referred to in Jacob R. Fishman and Fredric Solomon, "Youth and Social Action: Perspectives on the Student Sit-In-Movement" in Bernard E. Segal, ed., *Racial and Ethnic Relations,* New York, Thomas Y. Crowell, 1966, p. 433.

In discussing age differentials among activists, Cothran notes that "a major source of conflict centers around adult conservatism and youthful aggressiveness" (Tilman C. Cothran, "The Negro Protest Against Segregation in the South," *Annals of the American Academy of Political and Social Science,* January 1965, p. 71). However, in considering the Negro community at large among those under 44, the percentage militant seems about the same, although it does drop down considerably as age increases beyond 44. This distinction roughly corresponds to those who reached maturity before and during or after World War II.

3 These older Southern women now live in urban areas and are probably more militant in their attitudes than those still living in rural areas.

4 The fact that one in ten of those who appear to be least exposed to equalitarian values were still scored as militant does not necessarily weaken this assertion. The index only imperfectly measures such exposure. No doubt some older women brought up on farms in the South have obtained a relatively good education and are high in social participation (all of the respondents live in cities where contact with ideas legitimizing protest is more likely) and hence may have overcome the effect of these other background variables.

5 Lerone Bennet, *Confrontation: Black and White,* Chicago, Johnson Publishing Company, 1965, p. 108.

6 The report of SNCC field workers with respect to difficulties in obtaining cooperation among some rural Negroes obviously supports such a hypothesis, as does the 1966 electoral loss of the Lowndes County Freedom Organization. See also *Voting in Mississippi,* Report of the United States Commission on Civil Rights, Government Printing Office, Washington, D.C., May 1965.

7 For example, G. Lenski, "Status Crystalization: A Non-Vertical Dimension of Social Status," *American Sociological Review,* 1954, pp. 405–413.

8 This measure suffers from the weakness of being an objective measure. As one school of sociology is continually reminding us, objective measures of social structure affect behavior most clearly when they lead to certain mental images

and self-indications. If we had inquired as to whether people were actively aware of this objective discrepancy and then contrasted percentage militant among the group who were aware of and bothered by their discrepancy with those not in discrepant status positions, the pattern might have been very different.

When the status discrepants are compared with another group of status consistents, those with only a grammar school education in workingclass occupations, the former appear as somewhat higher in militancy. However, this is no doubt due to their greater education rather than to tension in their status positions.

A recent study of status consistency and political attitudes similarly notes that social class is a much better predictor of attitudes than discrepancies in status (K. Dennis Kelly and William J. Chambliss, "Status Consistency and Political Attitudes," *American Sociological Review*, June 1966).

9 These studies are summarized in S. M. Lipset and R. Bendix, *Social Mobility in Industrial Society*, Berkeley, University of California Press, 1960, pp. 64–71.

10 A discussion of the background of SNCC workers (most of whom are young students) suggests that they are generally upwardly mobile. Zinn states: "These young people are not middle class reformers who became somehow concerned about others. . . . For the most part their fathers are janitors and laborers, their mothers maids and factory workers" (H. Zinn, *SNCC: The New Abolitionists*, Boston, Beacon Press, 1964, p. 9.

Similar findings are reported in a study of members of CORE (Ingeborg B. Powell, "Ideology and Strategy of Direct Action: A Study of the Congress of Racial Equality," Ph.D. dissertation, University of California in Berkeley, 1965, p. 191).

This pattern of upward mobility noted for both SNCC and CORE members suggests that exclusion from the entrenched Negro middle class is a factor encouraging militancy just as exclusion by the dominant white society encourages it.

11 It should be emphasized that these categories are relative. Negroes labeled upper class in this study would be mostly middle and lower middle class in the broader American class structure. Frazier notes: "If members of the Negro upper class were integrated into American society, their occupations and incomes would place them in the middle class." (E. Franklin Frazier, *The Negro in the United States*, New York, Macmillan, 1949, p. 291. A full discussion of Negro class structure in Chicago may be found in St. Clair Drake and Horace R. Cayton, *Black Metropolis*, New York, Harper Torchbook, 1962, pp. 521–715.) An important gap exists in knowledge about Negro class structure.

12 Bayard Rustin, "From Protest to Politics: The Future of the Civil Rights Movement," *Commentary*, February 1965. Meier notes that a recent development "has been the involvement of lower-lower class people, many of whom are unemployed or chronically so," and that "a large part of the increasing militancy of middle and upper class Negroes is derived from the new militancy of the involved lower class" (August Meier, "Negro Protest Movements and Organizations," *Journal of Negro Education*, Summer 1963, pp. 445 and 446).

It might be argued that lower-class Negroes are not concerned with integration per se, but rather with jobs and housing. However, the measure of militancy seems broad enough to cover these aspects as well, since it included questions about "equal rights," discrimination in employment, and civil rights demonstrations. In addition, the term integration has a symbolic meaning and refers to much more than simply equal treatment in expensive restaurants and residential areas. These items measuring militancy are all related to each other, and knowing how a person responded to any one of them helps predict his response to the remaining items. Most important, when the items are observed separately in relation to social class (even the items which did not mention integration, or discrimination in restaurants, or the sale of property), those lowest in social position were in every case the least militant.

Still the middle-class tone of the movement up until 1966 may help explain the lack of involvement of some working class Negroes. Much more as a result of a shared heritage and structural position in American society than of a common African past, a distinctive Negro working class culture does to some extent exist (for example, in language, food and music preferences, and perhaps in attitudes toward work and women). The fact that the civil rights movement has generally not worked within the framework of this subculture is no doubt relevant for the lack of involvement of some workingclass Negroes. The black power movement is trying to address itself to this lack.

13 E. Franklin Frazier discusses the conservatism of this group in "The Negro Middle Class and Desegregation," *Social Problems*, April 1957, pp. 291–301, and in *Black Bourgeoisie*, New York, Free Press, 1957. In addition, some higher-status individuals may enhance their own self-image by depreciating their own group and in no way identifying with the Negro masses.

14 It should be noted that even when this additional differentiation is made, even for those owning their own homes with their "relatively lessened" degree of militancy, militancy is still higher than among those in any of the less privileged groups. It is also interesting to note that the question of home ownership has slight effect on militancy among those lower in social status.

15 As quoted in J. Davies, "Toward a Theory of Revolution," *American Sociological Review*, February 1962, p. 5.

16 S. Stouffer *et al.*, *The American Soldier: Adjustment During Army Life*, Princeton, N. J., Princeton University Press, 1949, Vol. 1, p. 251.

17 Robert Merton, *Social Theory and Social Structure*, New York, Free Press, 1962, p. 237.

18 Studies of social mobility indicate that only as people rise in the class structure do they realize how far down they previously were.

19 From the mass media and employment by higher-status whites, lower-status people also come into contact with "white" values. However, such contact and whatever hope it may engender is, as Clark has indicated, more likely to involve "a pseudohope unaccompanied by an actual struggle to win better jobs, to get their children into college, to buy homes. Real hope is based on expectations of success; theirs seems rather a forlorn dream" (Kenneth Clark, *Dark Ghetto*, New York, Harper & Row, 1965, p. 32).

20 Hoffer notes: "Those who are awed by their surroundings do not think of change, no matter how miserable their condition" and ". . . The poor on the borderline of starvation live purposeful lives. . . . The goals are concrete and immediate. Every meal is a fulfillment" (Eric Hoffer, *The True Believer*, New York, New American Library, 1964, pp. 17 and 32).

21 B. Zawadski and P. F. Lazarsfeld, "The Psychological Consequences of Unemployment," *Journal of Social Psychology*, May 1935, p. 249. In summarizing the results of a number of studies dealing with deprivation and political attitudes Davies indicates: "Far from making people into revolutionaries, enduring poverty makes for concern with one's solitary self or solitary family at best and resignation or mute despair at worst" (*op. cit.*, p. 7).

22 In *Native Son*, New York, New American Library, 1961.

23 Civil rights and church organizations are excluded here. The literature has suggested that membership in voluntary organizations offers Negroes an opportunity for participation and recognition denied them in the general society. Some investigators have found Negroes to be higher in membership in such organizations than whites (Gunnar Myrdal *et al.*, *An American Dilemma*, New York, Harper and Row, 1944, p. 952, and more recently, N. Babchuk and R. Thompson, "Voluntary Associations Among Negroes," *Amer-*

ican Sociological Review, October 1962). However, when the data presented here are contrasted with data on whites obtained from the nation-wide study of anti-Semitism, differences in organizational membership by race are slight when social position is controlled for. A similar lack of difference in another nationwide sample is reported in C. Wright and H. Hyman, "Voluntary Association Memberships of American Adults: Evidence from National Sample Surveys," *American Sociological Review,* June 1958.

24 D. Thompson, "The Rise of Negro Protest," *Annals of the American Academy of Political and Social Science,* January 1965, p. 27.

25 Stanley M. Elkins, *Slavery,* New York, Grosset and Dunlap, 1963, p. 136.

26 H. Aptheker, *American Negro Slave Revolts,* New York, Columbia University Press, 1943, pp. 220, 268–269, 295–296.

27 Powell, *op. cit.,* pp. 215–216. Limitations of time and the importance of documenting the social and psychological factors associated with Negro response to the civil rights struggle have resulted in most of the analysis being directed toward factors which can be easily measured in an interview situation. A full understanding requires consideration of historical factors and variables related to the structure of a given community. Just because in most communities militants will share youth and higher social position or be alike in having a positive self-image and a high morale, this should not cause us to overlook the implications of variation in community structure for expressions of militancy. Nor should it be assumed that people with these common characteristics do not exhibit a wide variety of motives in becoming actively involved.

In contrasting regions, Breed explains the greater resistance of the Deep South to desegregation in terms of its being the least pluralistic area of the country. The one party system, the relative absence of labor unions, ethnic and religious homogeneity, and fewer associations all make it more difficult for competing definitions of the situation to emerge. Traditional elites committed to segregation have greater power and a monopoly on propaganda. (Warren Breed, "Group Structure and Resistance to Desegregation in the Deep South," *Social Problems,* Summer, 1962.) A consideration of these community structure variables also helps explain the greater ease with which protest has occurred in the North, the greater militancy of Negroes there, and the greater sympathy for the movement on the part of Northern whites.

28 Lipset notes: "In 'normal' periods, apathy is most frequent among such individuals (those in lower-status positions and isolated) but they can be activated by a crisis . . ." (S. M. Lipset, *Political Man,* New York, Doubleday, 1963, p. 116). Kornhauser states: "a greater proportion of people with few proximate concerns as compared to people with many such attachments, tend to be apathetic and uninformed on public matters; but . . . in times of crisis a greater proportion of people with few proximate concerns discard apathy and engage in mass movements outside of and against the institutional order." (W. Kornhauser, *The Politics of Mass Society,* New York, Free Press, 1961, p. 64.)

29 S. Stouffer, *Communism, Conformity, and Civil Liberties,* New York, Doubleday, 1955; Lipset, *op. cit.,* pp. 87–126. P. Sheatsley reports recent data on the attitudes of whites toward Negro rights ("White Attitudes Toward the Negro," *Daedalus,* Winter 1966, p. 229).

30 The index is certainly a measure of liberalism on civil rights issues, asking as it did about discrimination and demonstrations. Furthermore, it was strongly related to a measure of tolerance for religious dissent. Almost half of those scored as militant said "yes" to the following question: "Suppose a man admitted in public that he did not believe in God. Do you think he should be allowed to teach in a public high school?" Among those scored as conservative on the Militancy Index less than one in five said "yes."

31 On SNCC, see Zinn, *op. cit.;* on CORE, see Powell, *op. cit.,* p. 21. About

CORE, Powell states: ". . . the outstanding characteristic of the activists is their exceptionally high occupational and educational status." However, she adds that Negro activists are not "typical" of the entrenched and solidly established Negro middle class. Rather they are either recently upward mobile or have passed out of the established middle class ". . . into the same narrow layer of intellectual, left wing culture from which most [activist] whites are recruited" (pp. 21 and 22).

In addition, within CORE, those in the North, those brought up in larger urban areas, and those with more education have the most militant attitudes (*ibid.*, pp. 271–272).

32 R. Searles and J. A. Williams, Jr., "Negro College Students' Participation in Sit-ins," *Social Forces*, 1962, pp. 215–220.

33 D. Matthews and J. Prothro, *Negroes and the New Southern Politics*, New York, Harcourt, Brace & World, 1966, pp. 418, 423, 427. This study also notes that activism was most pronounced in private colleges and in communities where Negroes made up less than 20 per cent of the population. Also on the importance of urbanization and the percentage of Negroes in a county see Martin Oppenheimer, "Institutions of Higher Learning and the 1960 Sit-Ins: Some Clues for Social Action," *Journal of Negro Education*, Summer 1963.

34 E. A. Weinstein and P. N. Geisel, "Family Decision Making Over Desegregation," *Sociometry*, 1961, pp. 21–29.

35 H. Goldblatt and Florence Cromien, "The Effective Reach of the Fair Housing Law of the City of New York," *Social Problems*, Spring 1962.

36 Robert B. Johnson, "Negro Reaction to Minority Group Status," in M. Barron, ed., *American Minorities*, New York, Alfred Knopf, 1957, p. 204.

37 Donald Noel, Correlates of Anti-White Prejudice: Attitudes of Negroes in Four American Cities, Ph.D. dissertation, Cornell University, 1960, p. 225.

38 William Brink and Louis Harris, *The Negro Revolution in America*, New York, Simon and Schuster, 1964, p. 203.

39 Stouffer *et al., op. cit.*, pp. 568–580.

This essay offers another, and rather different, view of the social context of militancy. Nathan Wright's emphasis is on the differences between the traditional struggle for civil rights and the new impetus for black power.

According to Wright, the new movement speaks for a new day of candor and integrity. "Integration," he writes, "as we have sought to work it out over the past decade and more, has clearly failed. There can be no meaningful integration between unequals."

9

Nathan Wright, Jr.

THE CRISIS WHICH BRED
BLACK POWER

The current focus on Black Power may be seen as a logical result
of a crisis which had been developing for more than a decade in
the black communities across America.

The So-Called Decade of Progress

There have been at least several interrelated developments which
brought about our current crisis.

For one thing, there had been—since the early 1950's—a growing official commitment throughout the nation to what was defined
as civil rights. The historic Supreme Court school desegregation decision in 1954 was seen as symbolic of the new official attitude of
America in the area of civil rights. Indeed, so jubilant and optimistic were many black Americans concerning the import of the
1954 school desegregation ruling that some national civil rights

From *The Black Power Revolt*, Floyd Barbour, ed., Boston: Porter Sargent,
1968, pp. 103–118.

organizations at the time contemplated their own imminent extinction. In the mid 1950's a great debate took place in black and white academic circles as to the new role of the now seemingly anachronistic Negro colleges.

With the delayed (and presently questionable) implementation of the 1954 school desegregation ruling, it soon became clear that the battles of black America had not yet quite been won. By the late 1950's it was seen that there was at least some distance more to go.

Because of the intransigent attitude to school desegregation in the South, the focus of the civil rights forces turned southward. This fortunately threatened little the life patterns of northern whites, and so in the name of democracy and fair play in the Southland, eager and dedicated white northern ambassadors for southern freedom were enlisted. Then began a period of dramatic awakening and witness. It was staged in the late 1950's and early 1960's in such a magnificent and compelling manner that the very grandeur of the action seemed at least an appropriate substitute for a critical appraisal of the current goals.

Throughout the 1955–1965 "decade of progress" the dollar income gap between black and white Americans moved steadily toward a perilous proportion, relief roles mounted, northern school and residential segregation increased, and the economic control by black people of their local environments continued to decrease. Meanwhile the civil rights movement hailed a human rights revolution as black and white people fought and won fresh skirmishes over front seats on the buses and won the right to eat hamburgers at the corner coffee shop.

That black Americans were entitled to the enjoyment of full desegregation should have been clear to all. This, of course, gave the unquestionable stamp of validity for the increased pace of and massive involvement by white and black Americans in the sit-ins, the rallies and the marches which became the popular pattern in civil rights in the decade prior to 1965. Gains needed to be made in civil rights areas, as these were seen both by the leaders and by the masses. The national response to the program of the movement was evidenced in the glorious finale of the events leading up to and culminating in the great Civil Rights Act of 1964.

From the Montgomery Bus Boycott Movement started by Mrs. Rosa Parks in 1957, through the college student sit-ins in the early 1960's, the Birmingham demonstrations and the unforgettable "Letter from a Birmingham Jail" by Dr. Martin Luther King, and on to the moments of the monumental March on Washington, the civil rights movement had captured the hearts and the imagination of the land.

Yet assuredly all was not well in the now seen to be critical area of civil rights. In the late 1950's and early 1960's Malcolm X, militant young former prisoner and self-taught leader of the Muslims, grew in stature from an apparently minor menace to something of an enigmatic black hero. He haunted the nation's mind and dampened the gala mood of the marches and demonstrations as he posed an increasing challenge to the seeming certainty of the nation's perceived path of racial progress.

Malcolm X died early in 1965. He was cut down as his star took on an acknowledged brilliance and suddenly began to soar to national and international heights. His message contradicted the integrationist spirit and the mood of "making progress" on the part of the leaders for civil rights. Civil rights leaders, on the one hand, called upon the nation to be colorblind. Malcolm X spoke, on the other hand, of the need for racial self-awareness and for increased pride in blackness. The leaders of the civil rights movement called for increased help from white people. Malcolm X spoke contrarily of the need for at least a sense of sufficiency and self-respect. White people had come to lead, as well as control, much of the movement for civil rights. Malcolm X, against this state of affairs, demanded that organizations for black men's improvement—like those of the Jews by Jews and Irish by Irish—be black supported and black led. Civil rights leaders courted the friendship of white people. Malcolm X was unequivocal in his perception of each and every white man as being, whether consciously or unconsciously, by historical and cultural circumstance none other than the oppressor of black people.

With the demise of Malcolm X, other voices rose to echo repeatedly his crisp refrains. They were the voices of outraged black parents in the inner city and semi-suburban areas of New York, Boston, Washington, Chicago, Oakland, and in almost any other major American city which one might name. Black young people were not learning to read. Job opportunities were lost; college entrance was often barred to the children of chagrined black professional parents; and the mounting drop-out rate by black teenagers posed itself as a mushroom cloud to threaten the peace of our northern cities.

By the many signs the helping hand had not performed its ostensibly intended work. So beneath the surface of seeming success in the area of civil rights the ripples of restless uncertainty began to mount towards the proportions of a tidal wave.

To the voices of frustrated black parents, there were added other echoes of the late Malcolm X. They were heard in such cries as "Negro Removal," "War on the Poor," "Operation False-start," and the expressed alarm at what was seen to be the "Widening Gap" between black and white Americans in the economic sphere. Summer riots in the black urban ghettos in the early and mid 1960's seemed to be becoming a way of life. As the Anti-Poverty Program increased in its endeavors, relief rolls throughout the black sectors of the nation continued to mount.

By 1966, the gala festivities of the rallies, the marches, and the sit-ins were over. The Civil Rights Act of 1964 had effectively opened eating, sleeping, and recreational places to black Americans. Some relatively small and well publicized handfuls of black men had been elevated to new positions of higher visibility than ever before. Yet upon calm assessment the predicament of the overwhelming numbers of the black masses was one of growing economic attrition and a mounting inability to control or have investment in the local environment of their communities.

Despair and growing desperation were the unveiled products of ten years of deepening commitment to programs in civil rights which were largely uncritically assessed as to their priorities for the good of black people and the nation as a whole.

The 1967 Report of the United States Commission on Civil Rights, entitled *Racial Isolation in the Public Schools* tells in sober language the ever saddening story:

"The persistence of disparities in educational attainment has been accompanied by continuing and even widening social and economic disparities between Negro and white Americans.

True, there has been improvement in absolute terms in the position of Negroes. Levels of income are substantially higher now than before. More Negroes are attending college and entering professions; more skilled jobs are being filled by Negroes than ever before.

Despite this improvement, however, when the social and economic gains of Negroes are measured against the gains of white Americans, the gap is as wide as ever. The income of Negroes has risen over the years, but their situation relative to white Americans has worsened. In the 15-year period between 1949 and 1964, the median annual income for nonwhite families increased from $1,650 to $3,800. Median annual income for white families rose during the same period from $3,200 to more than $6,800. The disparity between white and nonwhite annual income in 1949 had been less than $1,600. By 1964, the gap was more than $3,000.

The distribution of occupations for Negroes and whites reveals much the same situation. The proportion of the total Negro labor force in white-collar occupations increased by one-third—to 11 percent—between 1950 and 1960. For whites, however, 33 percent were in white-collar jobs in 1950, three times the percentage attained by Negroes 10 years later.

Within the Negro population, there also is a growing gap separating the poor from the relatively affluent. For a comparatively small percentage of the urban Negro population, the decade of the 1950's brought real economic progress and even relative affluence. For the great majority of Negro Americans, however, there was little economic change in relation either to whites or to more affluent Negroes.

The great majority of Negroes still are "have-not" Americans. Small advances in their overall economic and social position have not altered significantly their situation relative to whites. The closer the promise of equality seems to come, the further it slips away. In every American city today, most Negroes inhabit a world largely isolated from the affluence and mobility of "mainstream America."

Signs of Crisis

There were no clearer concrete signs of a state of crisis for those in the black ghettos and for the nation as a whole than in the forecast revealed in the statistics of the 1965 report of the President's Commission on Technology, Automation, and Economic Progress.

The Commission's report depicts what is no less than a charted pathway toward peril, if the nation continues in the decade between 1965–1975 in the so-called pattern of progress adopted for the previous decade.

The report states in part:

> If nonwhites continue to hold the same proportion of jobs in each occupation as in 1964, the non-white unemployment rate in 1975 will be more than five times that for the labor force as a whole. In 1964, the unemployment rate for nonwhites was 9.8 percent, about twice that for whites. *If trends in upgrading the jobs of nonwhites continue at the same rate as in recent years,* the non-white unemployment rate in 1975 would still be about 2½ times that for the labor force as a whole. Thus nonwhites must gain access to the rapidly growing higher skilled and white-collar occupations at a faster rate than in the past 8 years if the unemployment rate is to be brought down to the common level.
>
> (*Technology and the American Economy,* page 31)

One may ask: can the nation as a whole, or its black community, hold still for such a situation as this to come to pass? It is clearly unthinkable that black people would *not* come to wholesale riot and revolution long before such a state of affairs would be realized.

According to trends even then apparent, some government economists predicted in the late 1950's that come 1972–73, this nation would experience the greatest racial conflagration this hemisphere has ever known. If the ominous facts in the report of the President's Commission on Technology, Automation, and Economic

Progress do not confirm this foreboding thesis, then the supposition cannot stand.

The use of the term "progress" as we have used it over the past decade may be an exercise in illusion. *Jobs for Negroes,* a special report from *Business Week,* dated June 12, 1965 cites the following measures of progress in defense jobs and in general business. Tables 1 and 2 respectively below.

TABLE 1   *Progress in Defense Jobs*

	1962	1964	% Increase
All employees			
Total	2,049,064	2,111,864	3.1%
White-collar	775,033	832,774	7.5%
Blue-collar	1,274,031	1,279,090	0.4%
Negro employees			
Total	136,613	146,880	7.5%
White-collar	12,079	15,782	30.7%
Blue-collar	124,534	131,098	5.3%

The interpretation for Table 1 is as follows:

Only a few of the statistical pictures of the progress of Negroes toward new and better jobs are reliable. The President's Committee on Equal Employment Opportunity is a prime source. It gets reports from prime contractors and first-level subcontractors who hold

TABLE 2   *Progress in General Business*

	1963	1964	% Increase
All employees			
Total	3,969,748	4,090,361	3.0%
White-collar	1,887,437	1,905,144	0.9%
Blue-collar	2,082,311	2,185,217	4.9%
Nonwhite employees			
Total	232,692	266,317	14.5%
White-collar	40,553	47,134	16.2%
Blue-collar	192,139	219,183	14.1%

government contracts for $50,000 or more and employ 50 or more workers. Reports from 3,471 plants show [the above] progress from 1962 to 1964.

The interpretation for Table 2 is as follows:

Plans for Progress is another program run by the same committee. It's a voluntary program in which 308 companies with 8.6 million employees have promised to go beyond legal requirements in giving employment opportunities to non-whites. [The above] is the picture of progress from 1963 to 1964 shown in reports from 100 of these companies with about 4 million employees.

The Report of the President's Commission on Technology, Automation, and Economic Progress details the "Employment by Major

Occupation Groups, 1964, and Projected Requirements, 1975" in Table 3 following:

TABLE 3 *

Major occupation group	Number (in millions)	Percent	Number (in millions)	Percent	Percent change 1964–75
Total employment	70.4	100.0	88.7	100.0	26
White-collar workers	31.1	44.2	42.8	48.3	38
Professional, technical, & kindred workers	8.6	12.2	13.2	14.9	54
Managers, officials, and proprietors, except farm	7.5	10.6	9.2	10.4	23
Clerical and kindred workers	10.7	15.2	14.6	16.5	37
Sales workers	4.5	6.3	5.8	6.5	30
Blue-collar workers	25.5	36.3	29.9	33.7	17
Craftsmen, foremen, and kindred workers	9.0	12.8	11.4	12.8	27
Operatives & kindred workers	12.9	18.4	14.8	16.7	15
Laborers, except farm & mine	3.6	5.2	3.7	4.2	**
Service Workers	9.3	13.2	12.5	14.1	35
Farmers, farm managers, laborers, and foremen	4.4	6.3	3.5	3.9	–21

* Projections assume a national unemployment rate of 3 percent in 1975. The choice of 3 percent unemployment as a basis for these projections does not indicate an endorsement or even a willingness to accept that level of unemployment.

** Less than 3 percent.

Note: Because of rounding, sums of individual items may not equal totals.

SOURCE: U.S. Department of Labor, Bureau of Labor Statistics, America's Industrial and Occupational Manpower Requirements, 1964–75.

From the foregoing charts it seems clear that major efforts of an unprecedented nature must be made in the future, if black Americans are to be dealt into the economic life of the nation in such a manner as to preserve or extend the nation's peaceable and ordered life. "Equal" opportunity will not suffice to make "progress" as black Americans start from a position of gross disadvantage.

Further, the nation's social and economic well-being call for the black American's being dealt into the nation's economic life with immediate equity *at all levels and according to existing potentialities.* This means, in effect, that no reasonable "progress" may be made in the employment patterns for black Americans unless some form of restitution or preferential device is employed to create a condition of equity. The staggering crippling effects of past and present discrimination must be overcome.

Far too often in the past have unrealistic pictures of Negro economic progress been painted. The painting of such pictures and the gross and repeated misuse of the term "progress" undoubtedly have played a major role in creating our present crisis in civil rights. To be helpfully realistic all "progress" must be defined in relation to at least two considerations. Progress must be gauged in part to economic trends and in part to the social needs of the nation as a whole. In regard to the painting of pictures in the light of economic trends, Table 4 is informative. Its heading is "Labor

TABLE 4   *Labor Force: Percentage Distribution over Broad Occupation Categories, 1900–1959*

Category	1900	1910	1920	1930	1940	1950	1959
White-collar	17.6	21.3	24.9	29.4	31.1	36.6	42.1
Manual and service	44.9	47.7	48.1	49.4	51.5	51.6	48.0
Farm	37.5	30.9	27.0	21.2	17.4	11.8	9.9
TOTAL	100.0	99.9	100.0	100.0	100.0	100.0	100.0

Note: Figures do not always add up to total because of rounding. The 1959 data contain almost 4 million unemployed not distributed among occupation groups. In order to make the series comparable, these unemployed are here distributed among the three categories in the proportion in which the figures for "economically active" for 1950 exceeded those for "employed" in 1950, according to the Current Population Report, Series P-60, No. 9 (April 1951), p. 36.

SOURCE: Fritz Machlup, The Production and Distribution of Knowledge in the United States (Princeton, N.J.: Princeton University Press, 1962), p. 381. Reprinted by permission of Princeton University Press. Copyright 1962, Princeton University Press; all rights reserved. Data for 1900 to 1950: US Bureau of the Census, Working Paper No. 5, "Occupational Trends in the United States, 1900–1950"; for 1959: Current Population Reports, Series P-60, No. 33, pp. 40–41.

Force: Percentage Distribution over Broad Occupation Categories, 1900–1959." It shows the percentage change by ten-year periods in the labor force of three categories of workers. These are white-collar workers, manual and service workers, and farm workers.

The percentage of workers in the manual and service category remained relatively constant over a sixty-year period. The approximately sixty-year percentage change was only 3.1, from 44.9 percent in 1900 to 48.0 percent in 1959. Meanwhile the percentage of farm workers moved downward from 37.5 in 1900 to 9.9 in 1959. This represented a drop within the total labor force of 25.6 percent. To turn the statistics around, there were approximately 4 times as many workers on the farms in 1900 as there were in 1959. The overwhelming majority of all Negroes lived on the farm in 1900. By 1959 the vast preponderance of farm jobs occupied in 1900 simply did not exist. Negroes moved to the city during this sixty-year period. (See

Table 5.) Farm workers have lower visible income than do non-farm workers. The shift by Negroes to the city would suggest an apparent economic upgrading for Negroes. In fact the seemingly higher echelon and higher income jobs which Negroes came to occupy in the cities had now become by a simple change in economic patterns the lower echelon jobs of 1959.

TABLE 5 *Percentage of Negro and White Population Living in Urban Areas, by Region, Conterminous United States, 1910–1960*

YEAR	UNITED STATES		SOUTH		NORTH & WEST	
	Negro	White	Negro	White	Negro	White
1910	27.4	48.7	21.2	23.2	77.5	57.3
1920	35.4	53.3	27.0	28.5	84.3	61.6
1930	43.7	57.6	31.7	35.0	88.1	65.5
1940	48.6	59.0	36.5	36.8	89.1	67.4
1950	62.4	64.3	47.7	48.9	93.5	70.1
1960	73.2	69.6	58.4	58.6	95.3	73.7

SOURCES:
1920–40: Sixteenth Census of the United States: 1940 Population, Vol. II, Characteristics of the Population, Pts. 1–7, tables 4, 5, for each State (US Bureau of the Census).
1950: Census of Population, 1950, Vol. II, Characteristics of the Population, Pt. 1, United States Summary, table 145 (US Bureau of the Census).
1960: Census of Population, Detailed Characteristics, United States Summary, Final Report PC(1) 1D, tables 158, 233; 1910: Abstract of the Thirteenth Census (1910), table 28, p. 103 (US Bureau of the Census).

The most visible sign of apparent economic success on the part of black Americans has been the entry of this group into the ranks of white-collar workers. This category of workers represented 17.6 percent of all workers in 1900. By 1959 this category had more than doubled to 42.1 percent. This represented an inroad of 24.4 percent into the total employment force of the nation. Here again, with automation and technology, nearly half of the employment force came to be represented in the white-collar category. The movement of the black American into this category by itself may not represent, as often we have been led to believe, upgrading for black workers, so much as it may reflect a relative downgrading or extension of white-collar category jobs.

The fact that we are in our imminently dire predicament today in spite of a pattern of seeming progress should be fair warning to us not to make uncritical assessments of apparent progress in the future. Progress must be made in relation to circumstances which bear clear comparison. If the overall economic picture has changed, simple percentages of Negro changes do not necessarily tell a tale of progress.

Again, the social needs of the nation as a whole must be a major factor in any assessment of employment progress by black Americans. Because black people have been isolated economically for so long a period in the nation's life, a black economic problem has become a social problem of major proportions for the nation as a whole. An entire ethnic group is perilously isolated in an arbitrary way from the economic and social mainstream of American life. Progress in the future must be gauged in substantial measure by the demands of the nation's internal peace and order. Social controls are always operative in ordering every aspect of the nation's life. The increasingly crucial concern for the future must be that social controls be exercised with the wisest possible judgment in the clear light of critically assessed priorities. That such judgments had not been made in the decade from 1965–1975 has played perhaps the most significant part in precipitating both the present crisis in civil rights and the perilously darker days which appear to lie ahead.

The Question of Power

The present crossroads or crisis in civil rights—and its possible resolution—must be associated with the issue of power.

The call on the part of black people for Black Power represents an unmistakable turnabout in both mood and direction in the area once appropriately described as civil rights.

There are certain clear differences between the civil rights movement and the impetus towards Black Power. The civil rights movement has asked for what was due to the Negro. The thrust toward Black Power does not ask what the black American is due. It seeks inherently to add the power, the latent and preciously needed potential, of black people for the enrichment of the life of the nation as a whole.

Black Power is not a negative concept. It is a positive, creative concept, seeking to bring a wanted maturity to our too long adolescent nation's life. To produce growth and a wholesome sense of maturity there must be equitable relationships of power. The gross imbalance between the power of black and white Americans has effectively subverted our democratic goals, blurred the nation's vision of the pathway towards the great destiny of which it dreams, and perverted its moral sense as an apparently all-powerful white America has confronted its seemingly powerless major ethnic minority.

Black Power seeks to bring to the nation's life the saving necessity of equitable and growth-producing power tension and extension.

Vice President Hubert Humphrey recently remarked that in spite of apparent disagreements concerning Black Power among some civil rights leaders, it should be clear to all familiar with American history that Black Power is within the basic American traditions. Black Americans, he asserted, need Black Power to achieve political, civic, and economic goals even as other ethnic groups have used the weight of their ethnic numbers to achieve their goals. In this way America has come thus far towards its own self-realization and fulfillment.

Black Power reflects the failure of the civil rights movement in at least several significant respects.

Above all else, black Americans have needed the power which comes from pride in one's own accomplishments. Black people have throughout this nation's history been *dependent* on other people. At first, this was due to necessity. Later it was due to long-standing cultural conditioning.

In the civil rights movement to a not inconsiderable degree the slave mentality of looking to others for direction and support is seen to have been kept in force. Black people manifestly must have the sense of pride and self-respect which can only come through the tradition of self-directed efforts at self-sufficiency. Black organizations and efforts for black self-improvement—as with Jewish organizations led by Jews and Italian organizations, by Italians—must be black led.

Black leadership must be able leadership. But the substitute of white competence for blackness in leadership cannot be said to have a clear advantage. White technical competence in educational matters, for example, may take Negroes much further down the road than black incompetence. But it will have—as the evidence in our inner cities plainly attests—a well-nigh impossible task in taking our youngsters over the bridge at the river or bringing them across the finish line. The ideal that is needed is the kind of black competence which affords pride and holds onto hope in uniquely saving ways. For these precious qualities there can be no effective substitute. We cannot and must not, as black men or white, settle for less, if we are to have the latent potential of our hopeless and increasingly desperate black masses come to its best flower.

Black Power does not negate the value of friendship and co-operation on the part of others. It speaks basically to the role of leadership. The basic American tradition is for each rising ethnic group to devise and execute its own plan for economic, political, and civic freedom and development. So it must be with the black people of our land. They have been the most assisted and the most greatly benighted. The civil rights movement focused upon cooperation and, in a way foreign to the American tradition and to all rising ethnic groups, accepted direction and leadership from outside its ranks. However wise it may be, no outside leadership has that crucially significant ingredient of that inner drive and urgency to be free which can come only from one who is a part of the oppressed.

The proof of the civil rights movement pudding has been in its eating. It has been tested severely especially in the decade ending in 1965; and the clear record of its sad legacy after a gloriously executed decade of battle tells its own sad story. We have seen that the black people of America are—as a whole—more benighted than ever in relation to the nation as a whole, and a white America faces a black future in which its rehabilitative and policing costs will stagger our minds and threaten the security of our institutions and our way of life.

Black Power speaks for a new day of candor and integrity. Integration, as we have sought to work it out over the past decade and more, has clearly failed. There can be no meaningful integration between unequals. Thus as black men have turned toward an illusive integrationist goal, with white men holding the reins of power, black men have lost both their identity and their self-respect.

No black man needs the presence of a white man to have a sense of worth. Increasingly black men are saying today that if they never saw white men in their lives, their being would not be diminished one bit. Nor is it necessary, as our government statistics seem daily to insist, for black children to have the presence of white children in order to learn as they should.

Where white children are present there is a pervasive sense that one has a future, that one might share in the shaping of the conditions of one's life. Black children, through the impetus toward Black Power, may have by themselves those same horizons. No one seeing life as one dark vast cavern of uncertainty would or could be moved or impelled to learn. But give a child hope, and his life may suddenly come to flower.

The integrationist mood of the civil rights movement has led to what some see as a dead-end street. White people in America overwhelmingly are not quite yet ready for open and honest friendship and brotherhood with black Americans. The integrationist mood of the civil rights movement asked black Americans to play a game of brotherhood where, almost universally, white men have welshed on the rules. If men and women will not be open and honest and fair and free when their children are of the age of courtship and marriage, how can they ask others to make full and free countercommitments? In all fairness, black Americans cannot be asked to make emotional commitments to white friendships into which white people have historically built a guarantee of soon or late frustration.

No rising ethnic group in this nation has, on its own, asked for integration. All have asked simply for desegregation. Desegregation involves some integration as a means to an end but not as an end in itself. Desegregation involves the clearing of the decks of all barriers to free choice relationships which do not interfere with the rights of others. It is permissive of growth and is not negative in its implications.

Black men, at this hour in our nation's life, need solidarity. They need pride in what they are. This means pride in blackness. They need the power implicit in their rising from their sitters and their standing on their feet. Black men want desperately to do just this. They want to pull themselves up by their own bootstraps, but where even bootstraps are so often lacking, some substitute must be supplied.

Because the black American's moving into self-sufficiency and pride and self-realization are the only means by which the mounting desperation of black people may be averted, Black Power is in the clear self-interest of all white Americans.

White Americans can and must facilitate Black Power by converting their neighbors and by encouraging in many creative ways the solidarity and self-respect which black Americans so sorely need. They can help also in the removal of many specific devices which debilitate black people. Black people are effectively barred from access not only to loans for large business properties, but also to many home ownership loans. Banks are threatened almost daily if they lend to Negroes in a way that breaks the unspoken racist code. Negroes are barred from consideration for many higher echelon civil or public service jobs vital to the well-being of the black and white community by screening committees with prevailing cultural perceptions and by non-objective oral examinations. White people concerned with the development of Black Power may help to insure that competent black men direct the human resources administrations of our states and shape the Model Cities plans at the local level. What most often appears to be black apathy is in substantial measure a black time-ingrained cynicism at the systematic way in which cards are stacked against black people.

Black Power, actively developed, and espoused and facilitated by all, may thus break through the present crisis and inaugurate a new day of hope. Peril may be averted when the powerless command a sense of power to find some semblance of fulfillment.

The current crisis in civil rights came about through an honorable, but faulty intent. Black Power now seeks a better way. It should be our purpose—for the sake of all who comprise and will come to comprise America—to encourage power for growth and for fulfillment on the part of all.

"Fanon . . . you'd better get this book. Every brother on the roof-tops can quote Fanon."

Although, as Aristide and Vera Zolberg point out, it is doubtful that every brother can quote Fanon, he has become one of the most important demigods of the black protest movement. His essay "On Violence" has become a paradigm to explain the oppression of all who live in a colonial situation and a blueprint for action to gain both physical and psychological freedom.

The Zolbergs assert that there are many problems in Americanizing Fanon, not least the fact that whatever else the United States may be, it is not the French Antilles, Algeria, Indochina, or Angola. They do not deny that the black American is seeking to solve his identity crisis (a quest indicated by many writers, including Fanon), but question whether the way to find it is through violent guerilla warfare.

10

Aristide Zolberg
Vera Zolberg

THE AMERICANIZATION OF
FRANTZ FANON

They moved in a tight-knit order, carrying sticks and clubs, shotguns and rifles, led by Ras the Exhorter become Ras the Destroyer upon a great black horse. A new Ras of a haughty, vulgar dignity, dressed in the costume of an Abyssinian Chieftain; a fur cap upon his head, his arm bearing a shield, a cape made of the skin of some wild animal around his shoulders. A figure more out of a dream than out of Harlem, than out of even this Harlem night, yet real, alive, alarming.

"Come away from that stupid looting," he called to a group before a store. "Come jine with us to burst in the armory and get guns and ammunition!"

The awesome presence Ralph Ellison conjured up twenty years ago is in our midst. But the Destroyer has moved with the times. In the Harlem of the twenties and thirties, he was an Ethiopian prince; in the Chicago South Side of the fifties, he was Jomo Freedom Kenyatta; today he still sometimes wears an animal skin, but more often a sweatshirt printed with the new symbols of a militant Third World. Now he is the warrior of Islam launching a new Jihad; he

From *The Public Interest*, 9 (Fall 1967), 49–63. © 1967 by National Affairs, Inc.

is the Black Panther; he is Simba, the Congolese lion, marching on
Stanleyville. His weapons have been modernized too: no more sticks,
clubs, and shotguns, but a precision rifle with telescope sight and a
Molotov cocktail. Like a good Fidelista or Maoist, he completes his
panoply with a book. Or at least some who dream of leading the
Black Guard have this vision. "You're going along thinking all the
brothers in these riots are old winos," Dan Watts, the editor of
Liberator magazine told Jimmy Breslin of the Chicago *Sun-Times*
after Newark and Detroit. "Nothing could be further from the truth.
These cats are ready to die for something. And they know why. They
all read. Read a lot. Not one of them hasn't read the Bible." "The
Bible?" "Fanon. . . . You'd better get this book. Every brother on a
rooftop can quote Fanon."

Well, perhaps not every brother on a rooftop, but at least every
brother who sits in an editor's chair or who travels on the lecture
circuit; every New Left intellectual, black or white; and especially
every war correspondent or strategy analyst. In *The New York Times*,
Paul Hoffman reported in May, 1967, that in New York, Chicago, and
Berkeley, Trotsky and Camus had given way to Che Guevara and
Fanon. In June, Gene Roberts reported from Atlanta that Fanon was
on SNCC's Revised New Syllabus; in July, Fanon made the *Times'*
editorial page in William V. Shannon's "Negro Violence vs. The
American Dream"; and in August, Gene Roberts explained that
SNCC's new pro-Arab stance was in keeping with Fanon's support
of the Algerian rebels against France. *The Wretched of the Earth*
has become *The Prince* of our age, its author a latter-day Old Nick.

The Transfiguration of a Man

Fanon himself came to America only as a dying man in 1961; he
died here of leukemia a month after *Les Damnés de la Terre* was
published in Paris. The book became available in English in 1964
and was published in the United States by Grove Press in 1965, a
few months before the Watts riots. Its most striking idea, that the
salvation of the colonial world lies in cataclysmic violence, was immediately broadcast in reviews which were granted prime space in
publications ranging from *Time* and *Newsweek* to *Commentary* and
The New York Review of Books. Many commentators saw it as an
allegory of our own situation. Fanon's 1959 work, *L'An V de la
Révolution Algérienne*, was brought out by the Monthly Review
Press as *Studies in a Dying Colonialism* the same year. His first book,
originally published in 1952, appeared in 1967 as *Black Skins, White
Masks*. Only *Pour la Révolution Africaine*, Fanon's political essays
and editorials for *El Moujahid*, written between 1952 and 1961 and

published posthumously in Paris in 1964, is now lacking to make the American corpus complete.

The appeal of Fanon's books stems not solely, and perhaps not even primarily, from their content but from their form and from their author's personality. In fact, his readers know but little about his life; but as with Patrice Lumumba, James Dean, Malcolm X, or Richard Fariña, early death contributed to the transfiguration of a man into a myth which infuses his ghost with fascinating powers. In Fanon's case, there are additional irresistible features. As he himself put it, "I attempt when I write . . . to touch my reader affectively, that is to say irrationally, almost sensually." His apocalyptic style gives new life to well-known sociopsychological hypotheses and ideological doctrines hitherto available only in dry scientific papers or turgid Germanic compendia. His visceral poetry transforms brilliant insights and trite half-truths into equally profound mysteries. His work embodies all the appropriate ingredients for selling an exotic product on the American market: it is made in France and contains sex, violence, psychoanalysis, Marxism, and it has been certified as an explosive intellectual contribution by Jean-Paul Sartre. But its contents too are timely. In an era of apparently inextricable American involvement in the sequels of European colonialism, in an epoch of growing incomprehension in the face of internal crisis, at a time when traditional religion is rejected even by theologians, in an age of rebellion against the tenets of time-worn liberal and radical ideologies, Fanon appears to provide a map which can guide the faltering steps of militant intellectuals in danger of being overtaken by events. But a cool look at the map reveals that its paths may take them in unexpected directions.

The French Colonial Experience

The specter who now haunts America is the Fanon of the first chapter of *The Wretched of the Earth*. But as one rereads his surrealistic essay, "On Violence," even in the light of burning American cities, it does not stand up as an allegory of our situation. In the face of imminent death, Fanon's single-minded passion was with birth, the birth of a new world in the colonies of Europe. His blunt assertion that "decolonization is always a violent phenomenon" is not a hyperbolic statement for someone who had gravitated in the French orbit since the end of World War II. It is merely an assertion of historic fact. By the time Fanon wrote, there had been an unbroken record of French warfare against its colonial possessions since 1947. It began with the little known, but extremely bloody, repression of an uprising in Madagascar, continued through seven years of war in

Indochina, and culminated in seven years of war in Algeria. Meanwhile, there were protracted conflicts in Morocco, Tunisia, the Ivory Coast, and Cameroun, and a nasty confrontation between de Gaulle and Sékou Touré in Guinea in 1958, following which the French discovered that the rest of their tropical African territories could be more easily manipulated as legally sovereign client-states. It was hardly an exaggeration to suggest that there appeared to be no choice available to those colonized by France except to rise against her or to accept her hegemony on her own terms. Nowhere was this more obvious than in Fanon's own West Indies, which to this day are governed according to a one-way-only theory of assimilation, recurrently reinforced by coercive measures against political dissenters.

Fanon's entire life was dominated by this unbearable fact which forced him—an "acculturated" West Indian psychiatrist—into permanent exile. In *The Wretched of the Earth,* he was angrily denouncing the false consciousness of his fellow-islanders; he was warning his Algerian friends who had undertaken negotiations with France not to jeopardize the revolutionary transformation of Algerian society (which he had forcefully described in *Studies in a Dying Colonialism*) by seeking a compromise peace; he was warning the Congolese leaders not to put their trust in the United Nations; he was pointing out to the Angolans the dangers of turning to international organizations for redress against the horrors of Portuguese domination. Most of all, he was providing the younger intellectuals of the new African states with the critical apparatus needed to evaluate the one-party states founded by the first generation of nationalists. He foresaw accurately that authoritarianism was a mere façade which hid an absence of authority and that, in the absence of political integration, these new regimes would remain at the mercy of any blow inflicted by an indigenous military group or by an external power.

A Murderous Encounter

The simple paradigm of "On Violence" is by now well known. The confrontation between colonizers and colonized is not based on their relationship to the means of production, but on the forcible establishment of hegemony by one society over another. While this has happened before in history, the special situation of the contemporary world stems from the fact that the conquerors and the conquered belonged to different races, or at least that they came to be defined in this manner. Through a fundamentally violent act, the world was torn asunder. Everything derives from this event. Fanon argues that the colonial world is not like the world of capitalist countries—

it does not constitute a single society but two, which are hierarchically related. Paralleling Rolf Dahrendorf's critique of Marx, he argues that political relationships are fundamental; in the colonial situation, even the economic infrastructure is a mere superstructure: "Cause is consequence. A man is rich because he is white, a man is white because he is rich."

History, then, proceeds dialectically. Colonialism is the rape of a society and the subsequent establishment of a totalitarian system—totalitarian in the sense that a completely new set of values is imposed, within which the situation of the colonized is fundamentally redefined. Through this cultural redefinition, initially enforced by a powerful coercive apparatus, the colonized becomes to the civilized colonizer as anti-matter is to matter. Some turn inward, becoming raging Calibans; others become "good natives," like Ariel, and are given a pittance in exchange for loss of freedom. There is therefore no solution except a self-assertion of the colonized which is as fundamental, as total, as violent, as the original act which brought colonialism into being. Nationalist agitation is but the first necessary phase in the process of emancipation. What is required is not merely the achievement of formal sovereignty but the full reintegration of each member of each colonized society into a new nation. This is to be achieved through mass participation in the process of decolonization, followed by equally intense participation in the struggle against underdevelopment. Intellectuals must lead, but they cannot trust themselves or be trusted by others, since they are most vulnerable to the temptations proffered by the colonizer. They can succeed in achieving their historic task only if they derive a new innocence from intimate contact with those least affected by colonialism, the peasants.

"If the last are to become the first, this can occur only as the result of a decisive and murderous encounter between the two protagonists." Was this dying man inciting the world to murder? As Sorel and others who before him viewed violence as a source of salvation, Fanon remains ambiguous on the subject. The need for violence in the struggle for national liberation, he argues, is a function of the size of resident white minorities and of its use by the colonial power to maintain hegemony. There is no doubt that he fully endorsed armed insurrection in the cases of Algeria and of Angola, and that he deplored the unwillingness of the leaders of the new African states around 1960 to support direct assaults against southern African bastions. But he also argued that, in other situations, political struggle would suffice, that violence may be symbolic only or channeled into other forms of pressure. Speaking of violence in the international context, for example, he merely advocates the use of boycotts as a major weapon to obtain from the developed countries aid which would be viewed as reparations for past exploitation. Although he rejected "non-violence" as a mere bargaining counter and reflecting a willingness to compromise, he wrote approvingly of the American freedom riders. Throughout, he refers to the political *or* armed phase of the struggle for national liberation without distinguishing qualitatively between them. What matters, then, is the determination to struggle, not violence *per se*.

Anyone attempting to adapt Fanon's scenario for the American stage must reflect on his critique of the intellectuals of the new states who, he believed, were too easily satisfied with mere ideological borrowing. He urged them to abandon European models, be they bourgeois or Marxist, and to draw their own maps. How is this to be done? Fanon offers no guidance except through his own analytic method. The fundamental key to an understanding of his method is the importance he attributes to the situational context. Even as an ideologue, Fanon remains the clinician who bases his diagnosis on *this* patient's case, on *this* patient's history, constitution, and environment, not merely on an understanding of systems in general. He repeatedly asserts that the colonial patient is unique, that even Marxist doctrine is inadequate in approaching his bedside. But if that is the case, then it follows that the physician's prescription for treatment cannot be unthinkingly administered to others.

On Negro Identity

Both *The Wretched of the Earth* and *Studies in a Dying Colonialism* are applied studies in revolutionary strategy appropriate to particular situations. They are linked not only by Fanon's Algerian experience but by an underlying theory of man in relation to society which he had developed in his first book, *Black Skins, White Masks*. Paradoxically, it is this book, his last to appear in America, which is potentially most relevant to the American situation, because it is concerned with the identity crisis of the Negro in a white world rather than with the special situation of colonialism.

Written while Fanon was a medical student, it reflects his clinical experiences, beginning with the belated discovery of his own alienation, reinforced by his observations concerning other Negroes from the Antilles and from Africa in a society which maintained that, unlike Anglo-Saxons on both sides of the Atlantic, it was not racist. He discovered in the course of his studies that Freud and Jung were culture-bound. Observing the interactions between North African proletarian patients and French middle-class doctors in a French hospital situation, he learned, as American medical students are only now beginning to be taught, that even somatic medicine is not independent of its sociocultural context. The book was conceived in the intellectual and political atmosphere of post-war France which included: the beginnings of the period of colonial warfare already mentioned; the repression of the more militant political movements in West Africa; and the apogee of the intellectual community of French intellectuals of African descent in diaspora on the basis of the concept of *négritude*—a concept developed since the late 1920's by two poet-politicians, Fanon's countryman Aimé Césaire and Léopold Sedar Senghor of Senegal. It was a time, also, when French intellectuals began to move beyond *Uncle Tom's Cabin* and were becoming somewhat more familiar with contemporary analyses of American race relations. The philosophic bastion erected by Bergson and Alain had already been rocked by the belatedly discovered batteries of Marxism and was crumbling under the onslaught of Merleau-Ponty's and Sartre's attacks.

Out of these ingredients Fanon fashioned a theory strikingly similar in many respects to the nascent paradigm of American sociology of race relations, which had already been fertilized by its encounter with psychoanalysis. Beginning with early socialization and finding many clues in language, he discovered that the black man living in a white world necessarily assumes an identity which is not congruent with his true being: he puts on a white mask. The consequences are obvious at another stage of human development: examining sexual relationships between adults of different races, he concludes that love is not possible because such relationships always involve the intrusion of another relationship which manifests itself through an inferiority complex or through its negation in the exaltation of domination. In passing, he criticizes the thesis then recently argued by Mannoni, in *La Psychologie de la colonisation* (in its English version: *Prospero and Caliban*) concerning the innate need for dependence in primitive societies, as demonstrated by ancestor-worship in Madagascar. This dependence, Fanon argues, is merely the result of the depersonalization which stems from a forcible imposition of European supremacy over traditional cultures. However, he expands Mannoni's notion that the European in a colonial situation suffers from a "Prospero complex" to encompass Western industrial society in general.

Like the Freud of *Civilization and Its Discontents*, or more recently Norman Brown, Fanon does not hesitate to psychoanalyze history. Racism, he argues, is a fundamental component of Western society, founded on the sexual repression Europeans underwent in the process of striving for high achievement, and embedded in the authoritarian family structure of European society as well as the socialization it entails. Not only the European in the colonies, but *all* men of European culture seek to overcome their own inferiority complex by dominating others. The mechanism always involves the projection of inner fears upon the Other: fear of Jewish brains, fear of Negro sexual power. The latter, for Fanon, is more ravaging than the former, because it concerns a more basic drive, anchored into European cultural archetypes. When the Black internalizes this European collective unconscious through contact with white society, he then becomes a victim, enslaved to the archetype. Unable to deal with this cultural neurosis on an individual level, forcibly prevented from seeking drastic solutions, Negroes resolve it in their dreams: they become white or disappear.

The Negro is less than a man, he is a Black; but the European is also less than a man, he is a White. Since the source of the neurosis stems from the creation of a manichean world in which race is a fundamental category of differentiation comparable to class, the neurosis cannot be extirpated through individual psychotherapy of Blacks or Whites. The task of the healer is not merely to analyze the psychodynamics of the situation, but to provide a collective solution.

Anti-négritude

Most of the book is devoted to a critique of the solution devised by Franco-African intellectuals, *négritude*. Fanon retraces his own discovery of pride in being black, based on the African past, but also relates how this solution became inadequate after Sartre praised its architects but condemned their work as mere "antiracist racism," a fleeting antithesis, which must in turn destroy itself and move on to a universal level through Marxism. Sartre was wrong to condemn it, Fanon argues, because it is a *necessary* stage; ultimately, however, he agrees with his master that the solution is not to oppose black narcissism to white narcissism, but to surmount both by changing the world. The self of the Black can become that of a man only through confrontation with others: citing Hegel, he concludes that the universality of the self must be recognized by others in order to acquire true existence. This recognition cannot merely be granted; it must be acquired through one's own efforts, in struggle.

Much of what Fanon had to say was profoundly original in the French world of 1952. The more lasting value of *Black Skins, White Masks*, however, lies in the consummate ability of its author to merge the role of the analyst and of the man of action by creating a myth without which, following Sorel, he believed no struggle could be successful. At the beginning there was a state of psychic peace. But this was violated by the Europeans, themselves the victims of their own history, who created a manichean world. By committing himself

to a human destiny, not to a black past or to a white present, not by
exploiting white guilt or by avenging black suffering, the Black will
become a Man and force the White to become a man as well:

> There is no Negro mission, there is no white burden. . . . No, I do
> not have the right to be a Negro. I do not have the duty to be this
> or that. . . . I find myself suddenly in the world and I recognize
> that I have one right alone: That of demanding human behavior from
> the other. One duty alone: That of not renouncing my freedom
> through my choices. I have no wish to be the victim of the *Fraud* of a
> black world. . . . There is no white world, there is no white ethic,
> any more than there is a white intelligence. There are in every part of
> the world men who search. I am not a prisoner of history. I should
> not seek there for the meaning of my destiny. I should constantly re-
> mind myself that the real *leap* consists in introducing invention into
> existence.

A Vision of Regeneration

Fanon rejected hatred and blackness for its own sake in favor of a
fierce humanism. Much as does Baldwin, he imposes upon the Negro
the immense burden of saving himself by saving a decaying world.
But he was an incorrigible optimist. Beyond violence, in *The
Wretched of the Earth* he foresaw the regeneration of the entire
world through the self-assertion of Third World nations and their
full integration into a world community from which the Manichean
heresy would have been expunged. His vision of America's fate was
more ambiguous. In his last book, America appears as a second Europe, more monstrous than the first. But in 1952 he had conjured up
for America a vision which paralleled, on the *national* level, his vision
of a regenerated world:

> The twelve million black voices howled against the curtain of the sky.
> Torn from end to end, marked with the gashes of teeth biting into the
> belly of interdiction, the curtain fell like a burst balloon. On the field
> of battle, its four corners marked by the scores of Negroes hanged by
> their testicles, a monument is slowly being built that promises to be
> majestic. And at the top of this monument, I can already see a white
> man and a black man *hand in hand*.

He appears to have believed, like many American liberals of the
pre-Little Rock period, that America had moved from lynchings to
mere discrimination, and that this in turn was now being overcome
as the result of the efforts of both Negroes and Whites. The mood of
the now distant era when the yearly affirmation of new legal rights
constituted tangible steps forward, and when the change of consti-

tutional doctrine concerning segregation was imminent, makes the
apotheosis appear less utopian than when we come upon it in the
year *Black Skins, White Masks* was published in the United States.
Yet, Fanon's vision was not merely the result of his ignorance of the
depths of the American racial problem. It was founded on a notion,
not well articulated but nevertheless present throughout his work,
that the special relationship which bound Blacks and Whites in
America constituted a source of national regeneration which was not
present in the nations of Europe. The problems of American society
were greater, but its ultimate potential was greater as well. He believed that America could bring about within itself the fundamental
transformation which elsewhere would necessitate action on an international scale.

The Anguish of Liberty

It is difficult to ascertain how well he knew the then already large
literature on race in America. Nowhere does he refer to the pre-
World War II works of Bogardus and Park, of Davis and Dollard;
to the great breakthrough of Myrdal; to the early post-war works
of Clark, of Cayton and Drake, of Allport, of Bettelheim and Jano-
witz. His references are to films such as *Home of the Brave* and *Lost
Boundaries*, to Richard Wright's *Native Son* and works by Chester
Himes, as well as to occasional articles in *Les Temps Modernes* such
as a piece analyzing the Uncle Remus stories. From these he derived
the conviction that the situation of the Negro in the United States
differed significantly from that of his counterpart in the French world,
the Negro of the West Indies.

While both are descendants of slaves, in the French world emancipation came as a paternalistic *fiat* from afar, followed by total
indifference, leaving the ex-slave with the frustration of having no
perception of strong feelings toward him. Hence, he has nothing to
fight against. "The former slave, who can find in his memory no trace
of the struggle for liberty or of that anguish of liberty of which
Kierkegaard speaks, sits unmoved before the young white man singing and dancing on the tightrope of existence." Doomed to be unchallenged, the French Negro turns his anger upon himself. "I say
'the French Negro,' for the American Negro is cast in a different
play. . . ." There is no question of indifference there, because unlike
Frenchmen who simply ignore the Blacks, white Americans are constantly confronted with the presence of Negroes—directly in the
South and, Fanon believed, vicariously through literary works in
the North. The White is inextricably involved with the Black. To the

White American the Negro represents freedom, gregariousness, passivity, contentment, exuberance; he is an unfrustrated animal. The White, constrained by his own civilization, envies this freedom. Fanon analyzed the White's response much as Conrad did: fearing the Negro as a potential rapist and aggressor, he tries to frustrate and constrain him to make him more like himself; but at the same time the Negro is his "secret sharer" who represents all that the white man would like to be. Wish fulfillment often takes the form of artistic fantasy: it is no accident, according to Fanon, that novels and films in which whites learn that they are Negroes, in which Negroes make love to white women or kill whites, become box-office successes and best-sellers; that whites become jazz musicians and that they put on blackface.

In America, whites oppress Negroes, but some necessarily participate in their struggle. Like Camus's *Stranger*, Fanon demanded that the Negro, as a man, be greeted with shouts of hatred. He believed that hatred and active oppression were a form of recognition and that, because these conditions determined his existence, the American Negro was less depersonalized than the Negro West Indian. The American slave, who was liberated in battle, has always fought discrimination and has always been fought against. But his existence has never been denied. "There is war, there are defeats, truces, victories."

Immersed in the Algerian situation to the end of his life, Fanon never wrote extensively about the changing American world. In *The Wretched of the Earth*, he alludes briefly to rumors of preparations for armed insurrection by Negroes in America. But his comments are cryptic: he cites these rumors, together with the efforts of counter-insurgency troops in Algeria and other incidents as evidence for the proposition that the two blocs may find it convenient to end violence on the international scene, while fostering it within each other's camp. Did he believe, anticipating some Americans, that racial conflict in the United States was the result of Communist efforts? Of greater interest are his remarks in a chapter "On National Culture," devoted to a demonstration of the dead-end to which *négritude* leads if it is pursued as an objective in itself. He traces the evolution of American Negroes in contact with African intellectuals from 1956 to 1959: initially, the Americans obtained from the apostles of *négritude* a reasonable birth certificate; but they soon realized that their problems were fundamentally different. All Negroes are confronted with a white world, but: "The principles and objectives of the freedom rides in which Black and White Americans attempt to roll back racial discrimination are but tenuously related to the heroic struggle of the Angolan people against the odious colonialism of Portugal."

This is as it must be, Fanon concludes, because "any culture is first of all national."

One Nation or Two?

Fanon remains silent on what concerns us most: Is the American situation analogous to the extreme colonial situation of *The Wretched of the Earth?* Is America one nation with an oppressed minority of Americans, or is it two nations? That is the debate which is now raging among the worshipers of Saint Fanon. Some, like LeRoi Jones, derive from him arguments on behalf of the impossibility of integration and for the assertion of the solidarity of the Negro nation, captive in America, with the Third World. But Daniel Watts castigates LeRoi Jones and others for their utopianism. He too invokes Fanon, but he argues that the struggle is meaningless unless it is organized around systematic demands for "a realistic piece of the action" in America.

In the spirit of Fanon's existential dialectic, the answer cannot be preordained but can only stem from choices made by both sides. If readers of Fanon, be they angry Negroes or frightened whites, neglect his own warnings and impose the scheme he extrapolated from Algeria on our own situation, then it is possible that the nation will be irremediably torn asunder. But if they do justice to Fanon by using his works as critically as he used those of other thinkers, from Marx and Engels to Jung and Sartre, then they may recognize as Fanon himself appears to have done, that the only path to salvation for both Negroes and whites in America lies in their determination to forge a common fate.

Fanon believed that self-emancipation requires participation in a struggle to bring about cultural and structural change, and that all means were useful to this end, "including, of course, violence." From his particular vantage point, he viewed passive acceptance of the dehumanization of the self by the colonized much as others have viewed the apparent acquiescence of Jews to their own slaughter in World War II. There is no dignity in permitting oneself to be brutalized and murdered. Defensive organizations of Negroes in Deep South counties, where justice is never done through legal channels and where more or less organized brutality by whites against a hitherto submissive Negro majority prevails, are in keeping with his call for the creation of a new man, one who says No to oppression and is willing to die for his dignity. But what of the urban areas, where—in Fanon's own view—the forces of oppression are not so palpable? There is no band of night-riders; oppression involves a complex of socio-economic factors in which no particular agent can be singled out as more responsible than others. Will the looting of a

shop transform the economic system? Will setting fire to the ghetto
purify America? Or are these acts, notwithstanding the temporary
elation they produce among the participants and spectators, to be
taken, as Fanon might have done, as evidence of the inability of the
damned to surmount the inhumanity that has been imposed on them?
The main consequence of uncontrolled fury may well be to bring
about, in America, an attitude similar to that of the *Cartieristes*, the
right-wing anticolonialists of France, who shrugged, "Let them be
independent and be damned." Then, black sovereignty would be
established over dead American cities. Lest we forget, Fanon never
excluded means *other* than violence and passionately rejected the
notion that regeneration would be brought about by a wonder-
working conflagration alone. Self-assertion in urban situations will
be infinitely more meaningful and effective if it takes the form of
political and economic pressure, of community organization, and
other strategies which alone can bring about structural change.

The Right to Be Violent

Ultimately, a consideration of the functions of violence in the emancipation of the Negro American cannot be divorced from its functions
in American society as a whole. If what is at stake is the resolution
of the identity crisis of Negroes, and particularly of young adult
males, through manipulation of the external world, then it is important
to recognize the constraints imposed by existing cultural patterns
upon the range of available means. Evidence of manhood can take
many forms, but a crisis can transform selected role-models into especially timely stimuli. This appears to be the case at present with
the oldest of all American heroes, the Minuteman. Lone and defiant,
judge and jury, he has reappeared throughout our history in his many
avatars as the vigilante, the cowboy, the gangster; he has been glorified in military doctrine and in the mass media; he is protected by
the Constitution in his right to bear arms and organized to defend
his rights in Congressional lobbies. The Molotov cocktail is but a
McLuhanish extension of his self through a new medium, gasoline.
The adoption of this role-model by the Negro is the greatest proof yet
that the Negro is an American.

That this choice should be made, literally on the rooftops or in
the streets, and more often vicariously as by carrying Fanon's Little
Black Book, is not surprising since the Negro male has been denied
the right to this role throughout most of our history. Negro men, as
analysts from Davis and Dollard on to Moynihan and Fanon himself
have pointed out, have been forced to suppress aggressive impulses
in the face of oppression in order to survive, with corresponding

damage to their psychic structures and a turning inward of violence upon themselves. While many outlets for male violence have been available to whites, either in fact or in approved fantasy, the Negro male until recently could be openly violent only when contained in the cage of the boxing ring; from Reconstruction to World War II, with some exceptions, even combatant roles in the Armed Forces were usually closed to him. Given the importance of violence in defining the role of the American male, the relative deprivation which has ensued for the Negro has been much greater than Fanon imagined.

Unfortunately, the Negro's assertion of his right to be a violent American comes at a time when traditional American views of violence are themselves being altered, especially among those who hitherto have been most sympathetic to Negro emancipation. While sex is being demystified through scientific objectivity, violence—at least in middle-class urban society—has taken over as the great source of anxiety. The same mothers who protest that science kits for children are defective because sex organs are omitted also protest against the diversity and quantity of war toys on the market; masturbation and "playing doctor" are approved as normal educational experiences, but children are told, "Don't get into a fight"; liberal PTA's insist that sexual education be included in the curriculum, but listen attentively for rumors of corporal punishment by teachers. This Victorianism-turned-on-its-head seems to be involving us in a process which parallels the earlier one stemming from the repression of sex. As violence is being extirpated from our institutional life, it begins to lurk around every corner as a mysterious force. The new novel and the new drama, the new art and the new cinema, drown us in a massive outpouring of gratuitous violence, literal or symbolic, which evokes the delights of pornotopia. Benefiting from the general liberalization of censorship, however, bloodshed can be displayed with impunity in spite of occasional mutterings by incipient liberal Watch and Ward societies.

This transformation seems to be expressed in white views of Negroes as well. The Negro remains the Other, but elementary knowledge generally available makes it difficult to believe the Negro male capable of prodigious sexual prowess. The abandonment of old beliefs is reflected in the disappearance of laws concerning miscegenation and in the appearance of interracial love scenes on the screen. Instead, there is a growing belief that the Negro male is in close touch with the source of the new mystery, violence, and that his potency in this respect is infinite. Faced with the moral duty to accept integration while mistrusting Negroes, Americans projected their fears onto other objects: from 1960 on, for example, the Congo, an-

other old cultural theme, became available in daily headlines re-
counting atrocities; events in other African countries, selectively
reported and selectively perceived, contributed to the process. It was
possible to believe that *our* Negroes were civilized and hence entitled to human rights, while conveniently holding the view that
elsewhere Blacks are still savages. But Negroes in America have been
exposed to the same information about Africa as whites, and their
perceptions are often similar. Of all the cultural materials Africa
makes available to those in search of *négritude,* it is noteworthy that
symbols connected with violence are so often selected. White fears
are confirmed: the savages are now in our midst.

In the atmosphere of panic which has been created, there is a
tremendous market for pseudo-scientific writing concerning violence,
the equivalent of early anthropology, which was often a mere veneer
for racialism, and of early sexology, which was often barely distin-
guishable from pornography. At a time when the prestige of science
in relation to social engineering is extremely high, pseudo-science is
extremely dangerous. Ardrey's theatrical theory, which extrapolates
from animal behavior a fundamental human drive—backed by violence—for territoriality, naturally acquires prestige in a society in
which areal segregation is a dominant feature; such a theory can
easily provide the underpinnings for one more instant ideology. But
the possibility of the existence of an aggressive drive in humans is
not to be taken as evidence that we are at its mercy, any more than
the recognition of our sex drive transformed us into erotomanes.
Fanon's interpretation of the role of violence in history is in the
same twilight zone between science and nonsense.

In the process of making himself, man has repressed, ritualized,
or replaced violence as a means of obtaining food, mates, or territory.
His recurrent lapses do not invalidate the efficiency of the substitute
means he has invented to achieve these ends. Similarly, violence has
often appeared in constituted society when new goals of political
and economic justice were set. It is not so long ago that culturally
homogeneous England could be viewed as two nations. As the history of the labor movement shows, however, it is possible to transform
riots into strikes, and to further institutionalize strikes as collective
bargaining sessions, while preserving the benefits which both sides
derive from membership in a common economic system and without
jeopardizing the dignity of the participants. Love is not enough for
the transformation to occur. What is required is a determination that
the society will not fall apart, a realistic appraisal of the costs of
different strategies, and the assumption that violence is not a cosmic
force, to be worshiped or exercised, but merely another complex facet
of the human phenomenon.

Lewis Killian is pessimistic about the future of race relations in the United States. Part of his pessimism lies in what he sees as a growing backlash among whites in response to the new militancy of blacks. Rejecting the traditional techniques of nonviolence and negotiation, an increasing number of young militants have set out to create in America "a new world in which racism will have been destroyed not by love but by fear of the power of colored revolutionaries."

Killian feels that, while successful in heightening tensions and sharpening lines, the black revolutionaries may be unable to realize their dream and may, instead, be hoist by their own petard.

11

Lewis M. Killian

THE REVOLUTIONARY MYTH

At its beginning in May, 1954, there was no place in the Negro Revolution for dissidents who would deny the professed values of the American democratic system. The NAACP had created a base of power to effect changes in the practices of society. It had done so, however, through skillful use of the white man's law. All that was asked was to make the application of the traditional values of the American system color-blind, not to change these values. The Communist party was caught flat-footed by the success of the NAACP in the school desegregation cases. It was still telling Negro Americans that there was no hope for them in a capitalist society in which they were an exploited nation. Black nationalism of the Muslim variety was an anachronistic hangover from the days of Marcus Garvey. To suspect that the Negro protest movement sought anything other than what white people wanted was the mark of the paranoid segregation-

From *The Impossible Revolution? Black Power and the American Dream*, by Lewis M. Killian, New York: Random House, 1968, pp. 125–146. © Copyright 1968 by Random House, Inc. Reprinted by permission.

ist. The Negro simply wanted to enter the mainstream of American life.

The Changing Values of the Revolution

During the years since the beginning of the revolution, the crystal clarity of the values has given way to confusion. How confused and diverse the values had become by 1966 is revealed by a letter from a Negro leader in Los Angeles. James H. Hargett spoke to the people of the city through a letter to the Los Angeles *Times*.[1] The letter read as follows:

> The indictments of Negro Leadership on the part of John McCone made it absolutely essential that I address myself to his seeming obsession on the question of Negro leadership.
>
> There is one thing the Negro community shares with almost every other ethnic group in its efforts to solve its problems and give direction to the basic aspirations of its people. They are three dominant ideas.
>
> The first idea is one of complete separation. This simply means the conviction that the Negro community would be better off if its white exploiters would leave or be driven out to permit self determination to express itself economically, socially, educationally, and religiously.
>
> The second idea is one of complete integration. This idea is best described in the speech of Dr. Martin Luther King at the famous March on Washington, which is best known by his words "I had a dream." In this dream Dr. King spoke of little black boys and little white boys, little black girls and little white girls, and all the rest of America living harmoniously in a totally integrated society.
>
> The third idea is the affirmation of America being a pluralistic society and an acceptance of the fact that the Negro American, like the Jew, will never be fully accepted into the mainstream of American society. Therefore, the drive should be towards instilling pride in Negro equality, developing the highest possible education and skills, broadening and deepening cultural appreciations and artistic endeavors all in the interest of strengthening the group but never pursuing the evasive dream of unconditional integration.
>
> Each one of these ideas has an articulate leader or leaders in the Negro community with a significant following. So far, these three ideas have experienced a kind of peaceful coexistence with the ever present possibility that one of the three might make a power grab and thus initiate the "fratricidal phase" of the Negro Revolution.
>
> I suspect that the traditional leadership image of the Negro whose primary value to the white community was his ability to keep down trouble that in any form or fashion inconvenienced the white community, no longer exists.

The real issue before us is which of the three expressed ideological points of view will emerge with the predominant power. With the other possibility being of the continuation of all three with almost equal power which will force them to peacefully co-exist. Such an outcome will complicate things for the white power structure for it will have to relate to all three of them in the search for consensus on certain policies, practices, political leadership and many other concerns.

The contrast between the complicated situation portrayed by Hargett and the clarity of goals of the early days of the movement is sharpened by the observation of Pat Watters, a member of the staff of the Southern Regional Council. Watters said of the early days, "It used to be so wonderfully simple, here were these Negroes and they were right. There were those segregated lunch counters. In an age of ambivalence, of moral ambiguity, the Negro movement gave us, at last, a choice, as clear cut as a sit-in, between good and evil." [2]

For the values of a social movement to change is not unusual. No matter how clear the vision of the holy grail is at the inception of the movement, the storm clouds of internal controversy and external opposition distort this vision as the movement progresses through its career. Characteristically there is a broadening and an elaboration of the values to include a larger number of specific goals and demands. Movements start with very limited and specific goals, but frequently end with almost global programs that demand a total reform of the society. During this process, vagueness and inconsistency in the specific goals may develop so that the total program becomes very diffuse and often contains contradictory propositions. It is this sort of process that Harold Isaacs has described when he says of the Negro movement, "The goal of integration, like freedom for the anti-colonialists stands like a great shining blur down at the far end of the struggle road, drawing and inspiring all who fight for it, but becoming not clearer, but blurrier, the closer one gets to it." [3]

Power as a Goal

As blurry as the goals may be, the longer the struggle to achieve them continues the greater and greater is the preoccupation with the over-riding goal of victory. Victory comes to mean achieving a position of power that will enable the members of the movement to work out their own destiny. The original goals become ultimate and, therefore, remote objectives. Consideration of the practical details and how they are to be implemented is deferred, supposedly until after the victory. The immediate objective becomes achieving sufficient power to permit the proponents of the ultimate objectives to work out their program without interference by the opponents of the movement. It is a commonplace of history that very often when revolutions do succeed in gaining power, the values with which they started get lost. In this manner the most idealistic value-oriented movement can become power-oriented. The power orientations of the Negro movement have been steadily increasing, as has been pointed out. Hence, the Black Power advocates represent the vanguard of the movement, not merely the lunatic fringe, as they are so often portrayed.

Why Black Power?

It is not difficult to envisage the reasons for the rise of the vision symbolized by the slogan "Black Power." Samual Dubois Cook suggests two reasons:

> First there is the experience of bitter disappointment, disgust, and despair over the pace, scope and quality of social change. . . . A second source of the myth of Black Power was the prolonged and direct encounter of certain civil rights workers—especially those connected with SNCC and CORE—with the grim and aching realities, the dark and brute actions and deceptions of certain sections of the Deep South.[4]

Ironically, the bitter disappointment of which Cook speaks arose not just from the adamancy of the resistance, but also from the experiences of Negroes in working with white allies. This helps to explain why the power the movement seeks came to be labeled Black Power. Even in the inner circles of SNCC and CORE the harsh reality that America is a white man's society intruded. Thus in the words of a young, white civil rights worker, Bruce Detwiler, there arose "a time to be black." Detwiler wrote, "Since the organizer's purpose is not to lead, but to get the people to lead themselves, being white is an insurmountable handicap. After a while organizers often wonder if they are not unwittingly developing a new breed of Uncle Tom, to put it harshly—a Tom who will do and think whatever the white civil rights worker wants him to."[5]

This is not to say that the new radicals have won control of the movement. There is no large, clearly defined following to whom Stokely Carmichael or his successor H. Rap Brown can appeal. SNCC is the smallest and most loosely structured of the major protest organizations. Floyd McKissick of CORE echoes Carmichael's theme, but how many of CORE's members subscribe to the philosophy of Black Power is undetermined. Certainly, the leaders of the larger organizations, the NAACP, SCLC, and the National Urban League, as well as the patriarch of the movement, A. Philip Randolph, have renounced the slogan in vigorous terms. Yet as Cook says of the slogan, "It makes crowds roar, conversations sparkle, and the television cameras click. It wins headlines. After all it made Stokely Carmichael a national figure over night." [6] [The volatility of the situation is clearly illustrated in the fact that Carmichael, Brown, and McKissick had already been replaced by others by the time Killian's book went to press in 1968.—P.I.R.]

The White Reaction

Even more important is the reaction of white Americans to the strident voices of the Black Power advocates. The bitter division within the Negro protest movement that was revealed by the confrontation between Stokely Carmichael and Martin Luther King during the Meredith march was conveniently overlooked or forgotten by many white Americans, particularly those opposed to any further extension of Negro rights. Particularly when set against the background of riots in Los Angeles and other cities, Carmichael's inflammatory words were perceived as ample evidence that civil rights demonstrations were getting completely out of hand. That King was still pleading desperately for adherence to nonviolent tactics; that far more violence had been initiated by white counter-demonstrators than by Negro demonstrators; that of thirty-four people killed in the Watts riots, thirty-one were Negro (and in Detroit, thirty-four of forty-two were Negro); were all conveniently overlooked. The Harris polls conducted in the fall of 1966 showed a dramatic rise in the percentage of white respondents who felt that Negroes were trying to go too fast in their demands for change and in the proportion who disapproved of the methods used by civil rights advocates. The public definition of the Negro protest movement as revolutionary was becoming even stronger.

The White Backlash: So-called or Real?

This public definition reflects the white backlash. Yet many liberal observers speak of the "so-called" white backlash, implicitly denying the reality of this much-discussed phenomenon. The reasons for this reluctance to accept the reality of a significant growth in white resistance to the Negro Revolution may be easily identified.

Opponents of the revolution are eager to point to the backlash as conclusive evidence that the movement has become self-defeating. They no longer need to seek moral justification for their opposition to militant tactics and the goals toward which these tactics are directed. With a great pretense of objectivity, and even a sympathy for the Negro, they can simply say, "Let's look at the facts." The liberal does not want to accept the fact of the white backlash because he does not want to fall into the trap thus set by the resistance.

In addition, to face squarely the reality and significance of both Black Power and the white backlash would be to accept the fact of the polarization of race relations and the applicability of a conflict model for interpreting them. This does great violence to liberal optimism that assumes that "the integrative effects of consensus about the American Creed as well as the cohesive qualities of the American social system will limit the destructiveness of the explosion triggered by the collision of white and Negro interest." [7]

An example of this kind of reluctance to accept the white backlash as a reality is found in an analysis of the victories of Mrs. Louise Day Hicks, chairman of the Boston School Committee, by J. Michael Ross, Thomas Crawford, and Thomas Pettigrew.[8] They attempted to answer the question, "Is there a 'white backlash'?" by analysis of attitudinal data collected in Boston, as well as the results of surveys by the National Opinion Research Center. They concluded: "The much touted 'white backlash,' the white counterattack to Negro civil rights activities, though much prophesied during the George Wallace and Barry Goldwater ascendancies, never materialized for Goldwater and has never been confirmed by social science research." [9]

They find evidence for this conclusion in the fact of steadily increasing white support for the *goals* of the civil rights movement. But they go on to say, "As in our Boston data, there were negative sentiments expressed about the *means* of achieving racial change, but this was nothing new. Such sentiments are expressed by many white Americans each time a new protest technique—sit-ins, freedom rides, street demonstrations—is introduced." [10]

But there *is* the reality of the white backlash. It is the newest version of the American dilemma. There has come to exist a new and popular acceptance of equality of opportunity for qualified Negroes. This is the modern, more enlightened application of the general valuations of the American creed to include the Negro literally as a member of the class of "all men" who, according to the Declaration of Independence, were created "equal." The white backlash consists of a reluctance to accept those *intermediate* steps that are necessary to make equality a reality for the many Negroes who are in no way prepared to live according to white middle-class standards. Desegregation has become respectable, or at least has been accepted as inevitable, in all parts of the land except the most recalcitrant sections of the Deep South. But the desegregation that has become respectable is token. It will continue to be so because of the sophistication of white people as to means of evading total integration, as well as the economic and educational incapacity of most Negroes to overcome the formally color-blind barriers to upward mobility. Certainly no later than a few days after the Los Angeles riot, it became inescapably clear that gradual and token integration was no longer acceptable to the Negro masses, nor to any but the most conservative Negroes.

David Danzig has described this shift from the civil rights movement to the Negro Revolution in these words:

> What we have here, in effect, is a radical departure from the traditional conception of civil rights as the rights of individuals. This departure lies at the heart of the "Negro Revolution" and may, indeed, almost be said to be that revolution. . . . What is now perceived as the revolt of the Negro amounts to this; the solitary Negro seeking admission into the white world through unusual achievement has been replaced by the organized Negro insisting upon a legitimate share for his group of the goods of American Society. The white liberal, in turn, who—whether or not he has been fully conscious of it—has generally conceived of progress in race relations as the one-by-one assimilation of deserving Negroes into the larger society, finds himself confused and threatened by suddenly having to come to terms with an aggressive Negro community that wishes to enter it *en masse*.[11]

The Real Backlash

It is the immediate steps necessary to make possible this entrance of the Negro community into society *en masse* that an increasing number of white people show themselves reluctant to accept. It is preferential treatment of Negroes in hiring practices in order to counterbalance the effect of years of discrimination. It is radical revision of patterns of school attendance to overcome the built-in tokenism maintained by the cherished neighborhood school and the homogeneous neighborhood. And the research of Ross, Crawford, and Pettigrew itself indicates strongly that "behind the resistance to school desegregation lies the greater fear of neighborhood desegregation; and even beyond that fear that the good old ways of life will change as Negroes move in."[12]

But the white people who are now resisting the movement are not the ancient foe, the southern whites. They are Jews, traditional liberal friends of Negroes, now defending their middle-class suburban neighborhoods and their neighborhood schools.[13] They are Americans of Irish, Italian, or Polish descent defending their labor unions, their neighborhood schools, and the imagined integrity of their neighborhoods. A labor leader said of these people, "a lot of blue-collar workers are first and second generation in this country and to them those nasty brick bungalows are almost holy." [14] And there are, finally, the old American Protestants as well.

As Danzig has pointed out, this does not mean that white people outside the South are becoming racist in the old tradition of southern white supremacy. As he says:

> Often they are merely a more coherent and readily identifiable segment of the working and middle-class urban population which may embrace integration as a plank in the democratic platform, but which is becoming militantly separatist at the local level where it lives under the heavy pressure of an expanding Negro population. The attempt of Negroes to penetrate adjacent white minority group neighborhoods not only arouses personal prejudice and individual defensiveness; it also arouses the fear that the cherished neighborhood culture will be destroyed.[15]

To put it very simply, an increasing number of white Americans will assent to the proposition that Negroes should share more fully, even equally, in the good things of American life. At the same time an increasing number are demonstrating that they are unwilling to give up any part of their share of these good things in order to provide equality for the Negro. On the local level these good things are schools that have not reached the tipping point; union locals toward which the members have a proprietary attitude; and neighborhoods that it is hoped will remain stable rather than undergoing transition and inundation by Negroes. On the national level, the matter is almost as simple as the tax dollar versus the welfare dollar. As the Viet Nam conflict drags on, it is also becoming an issue of guns versus butter. The "haves" of an affluent society are willing for the "have-nots" to gain only so long as it is not at their expense. These "haves" are not simply so many discrete, unrelated individuals, however. In the words of Nathan Glazer:

> The white community into which the Negro now demands full entrance is not actually a single community—it is a series of communities. And all of them feel threatened by the implications of the new Negro demand for full equality. . . . The Negro now demands entry into a world, a society that does not exist except in ideology. In that world

there is only one American community, and in that world, heritage, ethnicity, religion, race are only incidental and accidental personal characteristics.[16]

Black Pluralism

After a long and partially successful battle against the monolith of southern white resistance, the Negro has encountered a new, multifaceted resistance outside the South, arising partly out of the pluralism of white America. To this resistance one wing of the Negro movement has responded with a pluralism of its own. Even while the NAACP, at first, and CORE and SCLC, later, were giving the Negro protest movement an exclusively assimilationist theme, there was a glacial sort of pluralism among the Negro masses. While they applauded the prophets of integration from afar and sometimes followed them into the streets, thousands of Negroes continued to support the segregated institutions of the enduring Negro community. One of the major points of controversy in many local communities, between the liberals of the black bourgeoisie and the seemingly conservative poor Negroes, has been whether new but segregated institutions should be built, however great the need. Even after the militance of the Watts riot, a controversy raged between Negroes in the city of Los Angeles over the plea of some Watts residents for the construction of a junior college in the ghetto.

As disillusionment with the results of ten years of militant assimilationism set in, voices appeared in the Negro community advocating pluralism as a goal to be sought, not an unfortunate condition to be accepted only so long as necessary. New forms of black nationalism not burdened by the exotic religious ideology and the separatism of the Black Muslims began to appear. The open expression of hostility to Whitey by Negroes became commonplace. Supplementing the new black nationalism was what might be called colored anticolonialism, which linked the new radicals of the Negro Revolution with the new anarchists of the student movement. Both reflected the theme that white society and, specifically, an American society that was prosecuting the war against colored men in Viet Nam, were sick and defunct. A corollary of this theme was the denial that there was any hope of aid from the Establishment. To the new radicals of the Negro Revolution the Establishment was now a white liberal Establishment. The President of the United States himself became the foremost symbol of the moral bankruptcy of white liberalism. The values cherished by middle-class whites, including liberals, also lost their luster. Rather than wanting to enter the mainstream of American society, the new radicals called for a drastic diversion of that mainstream.

A New Variety of Pluralism

The pluralism of Negro Americans should not be confused with the historic pluralism of other American ethnic groups. It is a pluralism formed of frustration and disillusionment, not of hope and a long-established sense of peoplehood. Negroes do not have the pride in an ancient religion and the loyalty to a people who have suffered for this religion for centuries that the Jews possess. They do not have the identification with a nationality that has struggled for years or even centuries to achieve nationhood that gave the Italians, the Poles, and the Irish a ready-made identity and a fierce pride even as they sought political freedom and economic opportunity in a tolerant America. They do not even have the pride in *la raza y la gente* that has enabled Mexican-Americans to hold their heads high in the face of prejudice and discrimination. Removed by thousands of miles and three centuries from a homeland that they long since ceased to claim, Negro Americans lack even the sense of identity that characterizes the "Island centered community" of Puerto Ricans in New York.[17] Their religion tells them to worship a white God. Their cultural history stretches back only to the degradation of slavery, not to the glories of ancient African empires. In the struggle of the new nonwhite nations to achieve nationhood, Negro Americans see a corollary to their own colonial plight, not a black counterpart of *eretz Israel*. The successes of the new nations of Africa are as much a source of shame as of pride to Negro Americans because of their own failure to achieve freedom now. To put it bluntly, Negro Americans find little in their history as a people of which to be proud; pride must be in the future. As has been so often observed in recent years, Negro Americans are searching for an identity. L. Singer has observed that Negroes are just in the process of becoming an ethnic group after a long period of being a collection of unrelated individuals "without the community of tradition, sentiment and so forth that has marked other populations and given rise to ethnic groups such as the Italian Immigrants."[18] Singer observes further:

> As the Negroes become more an ethnic group—more focused and organized—it may be expected that rather than reacting to the actions of white [sic], they will increasingly act along paths of action chosen to achieve their goal of full, individual participation in the larger so-

ciety. It can be added that any successes can be expected to pave the way for increased activity. It may be further hypothesized that as the barriers to full participation yield and slowly crumble, frustration and impatience over the differences between actuality and aspirations may prompt segments of the Negro group to manifest radical and separatist (anti-white) sentiments such as the "black Muslim movement." It is doubtful that any of these organizations will be large. Size, however, should not be confused with importance. By defining one end of the spectrum of Negro responses, such groups will affect the thinking of all Negroes. Further, because of the impact upon the whites, they may contribute to the general struggle for Negro aspirations despite their separatist orientations.[19]

Black Power as Myth

Singer's words, written in 1962, were indeed prophetic. "Black Power" has arisen as a slogan that symbolizes the emerging pluralism and ethnicity of Negro Americans. It suggests a way in which pride, not to be found in the past, may be created in the future. Furthermore, Black Power has become the myth of the Negro Revolution, replacing the earlier myth, freedom now. It is the kind of myth of which the French syndicalist, Georges Sorel spoke when he wrote:

> Experience shows that the *framing of the future, in some indeterminate time,* may, when it is done in a certain way, be very effective, and have very few inconveniences; this happens when the anticipations of the future take the form of those myths, which enclose with them, all the strongest inclinations of the people, of a party or of a class, inclinations which recur to the mind with the insistence of instincts in all the circumstances of life; and which give an aspect of complete reality to the hopes of immediate action by which, more easily than by any other method, men can reform their desires, passions, and mental activity. . . . The myth must be judged as a means of acting on the present; any attempt to discuss how far it can be taken literally as future history is devoid of sense.[20]

Those rational, eminently practical observers who, with such confidence, denounce Black Power as the tragic fantasy of the lunatic fringe would do well to remember Browning's words, "If a man's reach does not exceed his grasp, then what's a heaven for?" Ironically, the Black Power proponents call for Negroes to do many of the same things that white people have criticized them for not doing. Thus Stokely Carmichael says, "If we are to proceed toward true liberation, we must cut ourselves off from white people. We must form our own institutions, credit unions, co-ops, political parties, write our own histories. . . . The charge may be made that we are 'racists,' but whites who are sensitive to our problems will realize that we must determine our own destiny." [21]

There is no objective or logical evidence that Negroes can create a viable parallel economy within the economic framework of the United States. Nor is it likely that they can create a black government even in the minority of counties in which Negroes are potentially the majority of the electorate. At the same time, any significant gain in Negro economic and political power will enhance the bargaining position of the Negro community.

This is not to imply, however, that Black Power is simply a vision of cultural pluralism. Nor is it to suggest that Stokely Carmichael regards it as a myth, as a vision that is not literally attainable. Carmichael points to another aspect of the issue when he says:

> The need for psychological equality is the reason why SNCC today believes that blacks must organize in the black community. Only black people can convey the revolutionary idea that black people are able to do things themselves. Only they can help create in the community an aroused and continuing black consciousness that will provide the basis for political strength.[22]

It is the demand for psychological equality and political power that frightens so many white people, and which causes Black Power to be equated with black violence and even black supremacy. Here the confusion in the goals of the Negro Revolution generates a confused and frightened white reaction. While Stokely Carmichael declaims of Black Power, Martin Luther King, Jr., leads marches demanding that white neighborhoods be opened for Negro occupancy. While the new radicals of the Negro movement talk about getting the white colonial occupation forces out of the Negro community, the earlier generation of Negro leaders still talks about getting Negroes into white neighborhoods, white schools, and white factories. While King talks about the power of nonviolent confrontation, Carmichael says, "As for initiating the use of violence, we hope that such programs as ours will make that unnecessary; but it is not for us to tell black communities whether they can or cannot use any particular form of action to resolve their problems." [23] H. Rap Brown cries, "If America don't come around, we're going to burn America down." Many white people respond to these confused signals by envisioning a society consisting not of proud, self-sufficient Negroes living in their own ethnic enclaves, but of thousands of dirty, lawless, uneducated, vice-ridden Negroes swarming out of the ghettoes into white neighborhoods. As Carmichael puts it, "To most whites, Black Power seems to mean that the Mau Mau are coming to the suburbs at night." [24] Those Negro leaders who try to drown the theme of Black Power by shouting over and over, "Freedom Now" and "Nonviolence" are not only fighting a losing battle, they are also contributing to the growth of white fears and the backlash which will make the appeal of Black Power even greater to Negroes.

Whatever nightmare visions of black supremacy they may have conjured up, the Black Power advocates, with their indubitably socialist orientation, have done what the previous generation of militant Negro leadership seemed incapable of doing. They have given their wholehearted support to the needs of the hard core of unassimilable Negroes without a backward glance at what this may do to the aspirations of the black bourgeoisie. The history of the tactics of love show clearly that while these tactics produce temporary feelings of pride and the illusion of victory, they also produce a hangover of frustration at the tokenism and broken agreements that have so often followed. David Danzig says of the Negro movement and Black Power:

> Though one cannot speak of the Negro movement as though it were monolithic and had clearly defined priorities and goals, one might describe its broad aspirations as directed toward "the good life." . . . But if the Negro movement can be said to be centered on material welfare it has a redemptive side as well; it seeks a rediscovery of pride and confidence and it couples communal self-assertion with individual self respect.[25]

Black Power, the first slogan to emphasize this idea of communal self-assertion, originally shocked white ears in the South. Yet it is essentially a northern product, having as it does a particularly profound meaning on the home ground of the liberal coalitions, in the cities where Negro expectations have escalated. In the ghettoes, the welfare goal has much higher salience in comparison to the status goal of integration than it does in the traditionally segregated South.

The emphasis of the new radicals of SNCC has not been limited to welfare goals, of course, nor has SNCC been the only organization emphasizing these goals. At the other end of the spectrum of militancy stands the National Urban League. For years it has endured the taunts of other organizations for emphasizing welfare and Negro self-improvement rather than integration. Whitney Young's Domestic Marshall Plan spells out the details of a radical revision of the economic structure. But SNCC is not the Urban League in dirty dungarees. Whitney Young has been an unofficial advisor to presidents; Stokely Carmichael calls the President of the United States a warmonger. The Urban League gains white support by warning that the "fire next time" will come if its program is not implemented. SNCC leaves the impression that it is ready to light the fire.

The Road to Black Power

Hence, the totality of the myth of Black Power must be considered, not just the economic, political, and social pluralism that it implies. First of all, the theme of Black Power as elaborated by its prophet Stokely Carmichael calls for a socialist America. Hear Carmichael's words:

> In Lowndes County 86 white families owned 90 percent of the land. What are black people in that county going to do for jobs; where are they going to get money? There must be reallocation of land, of money. Ultimately the economic foundations of this country must be shaken if black people are to control their lives.
>
> For racism to die a totally different America must be born. . . . The society we seek to build among black people, then, is not a capitalist one. It is a society in which the spirit of community and humanistic love prevail.[26]

When the new radicals speak, as they rarely do, of coalitions with white people, they do not have in mind coalitions with white liberals who wish to redeem the white man's society by making a place in it for the well-scrubbed, well-educated, "qualified" Negro. While Carmichael tells white civil rights workers that they are not wanted in SNCC, he does not mean that there is no place for them in the Negro Revolution. He makes their place quite explicit when he says, "It is purely academic today to talk about bringing poor blacks and whites together, but the job of creating a poor white power block must be attempted. The main responsibility for it falls upon whites." [27]

But the new radicals go farther than the Urban League or any other of the relatively moderate protest groups in rejecting the American system as it is. Not only do they reject the economic system, the existing political alignments, and the bourgeois values of America; they also reject the nationalism of late twentieth century America. The alliance of the radical wing of the Negro protest movement with the anti-Viet Nam war movement reflects the intrusion of the Third World theme into the ideology of the Negro Revolution. The Third World encompasses those peoples who are distinguished from the major powers not by their allegiance to capitalism or communism, but by being the victims of colonialism. In addressing themselves to poor Negroes and castigating the black bourgeoisie, the new radicals implicitly align the Negro movement with this Third World. In summarizing the areas of agreement between the various elements of the new radicalism, Howard Elinson observes:

> First, all share the view that American society is basically unsatisfactory and in need of changes too extreme to be brought about by gradual reforms. Second, they view the mainstream groups—King's SCLC, NAACP, liberal Democrats, etc.—as part of the Establishment or tools of the Establishment, who while pretending to work for change, are really helping to preserve the status quo. Finally, they agree that changes in the underdeveloped world are of great relevance to the American Negro. They believe that the struggle of the American Negro is not an isolated movement in American history, but, rather, is part of the broader worldwide struggle of the oppressed or nonwhite or colonial peoples.[28]

When Floyd McKissick denounces American participation in Viet Nam, and Stokely Carmichael labels Negro soldiers fighting there "mercenaries," they are reflecting more than a personal pacifism or a disloyalty born of despair. They are, instead, reflecting an inchoate faith in a new wave of the future. Despite the apparently overwhelming forces arrayed against the Impossible Revolution domestically, the hope remains that allies can be found abroad as the emerging nations of Africa and Asia and the revolutionary parties of Latin America grow stronger. The apparent inability of American military might to crush the Viet Cong and their Hanoi supporters lends credence to this hope. For the United States to leave the field to the nonwhite guerrillas would make the domestic Impossible Revolution appear a little more plausible. Carmichael reveals his faith in the Third World when he says:

> The colonies of the United States—and this includes the black ghetto within its borders, North and South—must be liberated. For a century this nation has been like an octopus of exploitation, its tentacles stretching from Mississippi and Harlem to South America, the Middle East, Southern Africa, and Viet Nam. The form of exploitation varies from area to area but the essential result has been the same—a powerful few has been maintained and enriched at the expense of the poor and voiceless colored masses. This pattern must be broken. As its grip loosens here and there around the world, the hopes of Black Americans become more realistic. For racism to die a totally different America must be born.[29]

Finally, arousing the greatest fear and righteous indignation among white Americans are the overtones of violence that distinguish the theme of the new radicals from the message of their militant rivals, such as SCLC. At one end of the spectrum is the justification

for retaliatory violence manifest in the existence of the Deacons for
Defense and Justice and sanctioned by the traditionally nonviolent
CORE under the new leadership of Floyd McKissick. At the other
end is the expatriate Robert F. Williams advocating a strategy of
guerrilla warfare and sabotage in the major metropolitan centers
where Negroes are concentrated. Every time a Negro throws a Molotov cocktail in a Negro ghetto, every time the National Guard must
be called in to put down a riot, the credibility of Williams' appeal
increases. During the summer of 1967, Stokely Carmichael moved to
a position identical to that of Williams. Both he and his successor,
H. Rap Brown, conjure up the vision of a Williams-style insurrection
if Black Power is pushed to its ultimate form. Carmichael rejects
exclusive reliance on tactics of nonviolence when he says, "Wherever
the honkies got injustice, we're going to tear their cities apart." [30]

The Choice for Negro Americans

Thus there has developed in the Negro protest movement a factional
division, and the course of the movement hangs in the balance. On
the one hand, there is the strategy of nonviolence, of negotiation, of
practical attempts to create coalitions with white Americans deemed
not beyond redemption, but capable of being brought to recognize
the true meaning of traditional American values. On the other hand,
there is the go-for-broke strategy that rests on the faith that there
will be a new America in a new world in which racism will have been
destroyed not by love but by fear of the power of colored revolutionaries. It is between these strategies that Negro Americans will choose
in the years ahead.

To argue to the new revolutionaries that their dream is an impossible one is as fruitless as it would have been to urge George
Washington to give up the struggle during the dark days at Valley
Forge. Revolutionaries have never been "summer soldiers"; it is faith,
not assurance of victory, that sustains them. Moreover, the new radicals can look to more recent examples to sustain their belief that not
even the power of modern centralized governments makes the revolution of the seemingly powerless irrelevant in today's world. They can
and do point to the victory of Castro and to the long and yet incon-
clusive struggle of the Viet Cong. They can even point to the failure
or inability of the federal government to repress white violence in the
South.

That the new radicals can find ample evidence to sustain their
belief that the Impossible Revolution can rebuild America in the

image they desire does not mean that their faith is justified. Whether they will gain enough support among Negro Americans to make the effort depends in part upon the reactions of white society to the latest phase of the crisis in race relations. It will depend also on events abroad and their repercussions on the home front. Finally there remains the ominous question, "Will the brave dreams of the revolutionaries end in a nightmare of violent repression in a new, fascist America that neither black radicals nor white liberals desire or even envision?"

NOTES

1 James H. Hargett, "Negroes and Leadership," Los Angeles *Times*, March 26, 1966, Part III, p. 4. Quoted by permission of the publishers.
2 Pat Watters, *Encounter With the Future* (Atlanta: Southern Regional Council, 1965), p. 1.
3 Harold Isaacs, "Integration and the Negro Mood," *Commentary* (December 1962), p. 494.
4 Samuel Dubois Cook, "The Tragic Myth of Black Power," *New South*, 21 (Summer 1966), p. 59.
5 Bruce Detwiler, "A Time to be Black," *New Republic* (September 17, 1966), p. 19.
6 Cook, *op. cit.*, p. 60.
7 Lewis M. Killian and Charles Grigg, *Racial Crisis in America* (Englewood Cliffs, N. J.: Prentice-Hall, 1964), p. 106.
8 J. Michael Ross, Thomas Crawford, and Thomas Pettigrew, "Negro Neighbors —Banned in Boston," *Trans-Action*, Vol. III (September–October, 1966), pp. 13–18.
9 *Ibid.*, p. 15.
10 *Ibid.*
11 David Danzig, "The Meaning of Negro Strategy," *Commentary* (February 1964), pp. 42–43.
12 Ross *et al.*, *op. cit.*, p. 16.
13 See Milton Himmelfarb, "Negroes, Jews, and Muzhiks," *Commentary* (October 1966), pp. 83–86.
14 "White Backlash Worrying Labor," Tampa *Tribune*, October 26, 1966, p. 6A.
15 David Danzig, "Rightists, Racists, and Separatists: A White Bloc in the Making?," *Commentary* (August 1964), p. 30.
16 Nathan Glazer, "Negroes and Jews: The New Challenge to Pluralism," *Commentary* (December 1964), pp. 33–34.
17 Nathan Glazer and Daniel Moynihan, *Beyond the Melting Pot* (Cambridge: The M.I.T. Press, 1963), pp. 99–110.
18 L. Singer, "Ethnogenesis and Negro-Americans Today," *Social Research*, Vol. 29 (Winter 1962), p. 429.
19 *Ibid.*, pp. 430–31.
20 Georges Sorel, *Reflections on Violence*, trans. T. E. Hulme and J. Roth (Glencoe, Ill.: The Free Press, 1950), pp. 124–26.
21 *The New York Times*, August 5, 1966, p. 1.
22 "What We Want," *The New York Review of Books*, September 22, 1966, p. 5.

23 *Ibid.*
24 *Ibid.*, p. 6.
25 David Danzig, "In Defense of Black Power," *Commentary* (September 1966), pp. 44–45.
26 "What We Want," *op. cit.*, pp. 6–7.
27 *Ibid.*, p. 6.
28 Howard Elinson, "Radicalism and the Negro Movement," in Raymond J. Murphy and Howard Elinson, eds., *Problems and Prospects of the Negro Movement* (Belmont, Calif.: Wadsworth, 1966), p. 370.
29 "What We Want," *op. cit.*, p. 6.
30 Quoted in St. Petersburg *Times,* April 19, 1967, p. 3.

SUGGESTED READINGS

Baldwin, James. *The Fire Next Time*. New York: Dial, 1963.
A prophetic essay in which the famous novelist predicted what was to become a frightening reality.

Bell, Inge Powell. *CORE and the Strategy of Non-violence*. New York: Random House, 1968.
A study of the Congress of Racial Equality, with particular focus on the "middle period," 1961–1963.

Brotz, Howard, editor. *Negro Social and Political Thought, 1850–1928*. New York: Basic Books, 1966.
Representative texts by black spokesmen.

Farmer, James. *Freedom, When?* New York: Random House, 1965.
The author's own story of CORE and his experience in the civil rights movement before the shift to Black Nationalism.

Handlin, Oscar. *Fire-Bell in the Night*. Boston: Atlantic-Little, Brown, 1964.
A social historian sounds a warning in this study of race relations at mid-century.

Lomax, Louis E. *The Negro Revolt*. New York: Harper & Row, 1962.
A history and commentary on the civil rights movement by a man who first called it "the Negro revolt."

Marx, Gary T. *Protest and Prejudice*. New York: Harper & Row, 1967.
The attitudes of black people toward their lot and their society are presented in this report of an extensive survey conducted in the mid-1960's.

Proudfoot, Merrill. *Diary of a Sit-in*. Chapel Hill: University of North Carolina Press, 1962.
A firsthand account of a sit-in in Knoxville, Tennessee.

Record, C. Wilson. *Race and Radicalism*. Ithaca: Cornell University Press, 1964.
An investigation of conflict between the aims and policies of the NAACP and the Communist Party in the United States.

Sugarman, Tracy. *Stranger at the Gates: A Summer in Mississippi*. New York: Hill & Wang, 1966.

An artist's commentary and sketches of the "Mississippi Summer" of 1964.

Warren, Robert Penn. *Who Speaks for the Negro?* New York: Random House, 1965.
Interviews with a variety of Negro leaders conducted and commented upon by the novelist.

IN QUEST OF COMMUNITY

Whither Black Power?

If ever the free institutions of America are destroyed,
that event may be attributed to the unlimited authority
of the majority, which may at some future time urge the
minorities to desperation, and oblige them to have recourse to physical force. Anarchy will then be the result,
but it will have been brought about by despotism.

ALEXIS DE TOCQUEVILLE

"We cannot be expected any longer to march and have our heads broken in order to say to whites: come on, you're nice guys. For you are not nice guys. We have found you out."

With words like these Stokely Carmichael offered an alternative to the traditional goal of integration and the techniques of nonviolent protest. "Black Power" would be the battle cry and black communalism the modus vivendi. He spelled out his new program in a SNCC position paper published in The New York Review of Books in September of 1966.

Carmichael has left SNCC, and the organization is quite different today than it was when he wrote the following essay. Yet, the paper remains one of the most important "period pieces" of the recent past.

12

Stokely Carmichael

WHAT WE WANT

One of the tragedies of the struggle against racism is that up to now there has been no national organization which could speak to the growing militancy of young black people in the urban ghetto. There has been only a civil rights movement, whose tone of voice was adapted to an audience of liberal whites. It served as a sort of buffer zone between them and angry young blacks. None of its so-called leaders could go into a rioting community and be listened to. In a sense, I blame ourselves—together with the mass media—for what has happened in Watts, Harlem, Chicago, Cleveland, Omaha. Each time the people in those cities saw Martin Luther King get slapped, they became angry; when they saw four little black girls bombed to death, they were angrier; and when nothing happened, they were steaming. We had nothing to offer that they could see, except to go out and be beaten again. We helped to build their frustration.

For too many years, black Americans marched and had their heads

From *The New York Review of Books* (September 22, 1966), pp. 5–8. Reprinted by permission of the Student Nonviolent Coordinating Committee.

broken and got shot. They were saying to the country, "Look, you guys are supposed to be nice guys and we are only going to do what we are supposed to do—why do you beat us up, why don't you give us what we ask, why don't you straighten yourselves out?" After years of this, we are at almost the same point—because we demonstrated from a position of weakness. We cannot be expected any longer to march and have our heads broken in order to say to whites: come on, you're nice guys. For you are not nice guys. We have found you out.

An organization which claims to speak for the needs of a community—as does the Student Nonviolent Coordinating Committee—must speak in the tone of that community, not as somebody else's buffer zone. This is the significance of black power as a slogan. For once, black people are going to use the words they want to use—not just the words whites want to hear. And they will do this no matter how often the press tries to stop the use of the slogan by equating it with racism or separatism.

An organization which claims to be working for the needs of a community—as SNCC does—must work to provide that community with a position of strength from which to make its voice heard. This is the significance of black power beyond the slogan.

Black power can be clearly defined for those who do not attach the fears of white America to their questions about it. We should begin with the basic fact that black Americans have two problems: they are poor and they are black. All other problems arise from this two-sided reality: lack of education, the so-called apathy of black men. Any program to end racism must address itself to that double reality.

Almost from its beginning, SNCC sought to address itself to both conditions with a program aimed at winning political power for impoverished Southern blacks. We had to begin with politics because black Americans are a propertyless people in a country where property is valued above all. We had to work for power, because this country does not function by morality, love, and nonviolence, but by power. Thus we determined to win political power, with the idea of moving on from there into activity that would have economic effects. With power, the masses could *make or participate in making* the decisions which govern their destinies, and thus create basic change in their day-to-day lives.

But if political power seemed to be the key to self-determination, it was also obvious that the key had been thrown down a deep well many years earlier. Disenfranchisement, maintained by racist terror, makes it impossible to talk about organizing for political power in

1960. The right to vote had to be won, and SNCC workers devoted their energies to this from 1961 to 1965. They set up voter registration drives in the Deep South. They created pressure for the vote by holding mock elections in Mississippi in 1963 and by helping to establish the Mississippi Freedom Democratic Party (MFDP) in 1964. That struggle was eased, though not won, with the passage of the 1965 Voting Rights Act. SNCC workers could then address themselves to the question: "Who can we vote for, to have our needs met—how do we make our vote meaningful?"

SNCC had already gone to Atlantic City for recognition of the Mississippi Freedom Democratic Party by the Democratic convention and been rejected; it had gone with the MFDP to Washington for recognition by Congress and been rejected. In Arkansas, SNCC helped thirty Negroes to run for School Board elections; all but one were defeated, and there was evidence of fraud and intimidation sufficient to cause their defeat. In Atlanta, Julian Bond ran for the state legislature and was elected—twice—and unseated—twice. In several states, black farmers ran in elections for agricultural committees which make crucial decisions concerning land use, loans, etc. Although they won places on a number of committees, they never gained the majorities needed to control them.

All of the efforts were attempts to win black power. Then, in Alabama, the opportunity came to see how blacks could be organized on an independent party basis. An unusual Alabama law provides that any group of citizens can nominate candidates for county office and, if they win 20 per cent of the vote, may be recognized as a county political party. The same then applies on a state level. SNCC went to organize in several counties such as Lowndes, where black people—who form 80 per cent of the population and have an average annual income of $943—felt they could accomplish nothing within the framework of the Alabama Democratic Party because of its racism and because the qualifying fee for this year's elections was raised from $50 to $500 in order to prevent most Negroes from becoming candidates. On May 3, five new county "freedom organizations" convened and nominated candidates for the offices of sheriff, tax assessor, members of the school boards. These men and women are up for election in November—if they live until then. Their ballot symbol is the black panther: a bold, beautiful animal, representing the strength and dignity of black demands today. A man needs a black panther on his side when he and his family must endure—as hundreds of Alabamians have endured—loss of job, eviction, starvation, and sometimes death, for political activity. He may also need a gun and SNCC reaffirms the right of black men everywhere to defend themselves when threatened or attacked. As for initiating the use of violence, we hope that such programs as ours will make that unnecessary; but it is not for us to tell black communities whether they can or cannot use any particular form of action to resolve their problems. Responsibility for the use of violence by black men, whether in self defense or initiated by them, lies with the white community.

This is the specific historical experience from which SNCC's call for "black power" emerged on the Mississippi march last July. But the concept of "black power" is not a recent or isolated phenomenon: It has grown out of the ferment of agitation and activity by different people and organizations in many black communities over the years. Our last year of work in Alabama added a new concrete possibility. In Lowndes County, for example, black power will mean that if a Negro is elected sheriff, he can end police brutality. If a black man is elected tax assessor, he can collect and channel funds for the building of better roads and schools serving black people—thus advancing the move from political power into the economic arena. In such areas as Lowndes, where black men have a majority, they will attempt to use it to exercise control. This is what they seek: control. Where Negroes lack a majority, black power means proper representation and sharing of control. It means the creation of power bases from which black people can work to change statewide or nationwide patterns of oppression through pressure from strength —instead of weakness. Politically, black power means what it has always meant to SNCC: the coming-together of black people to elect representatives and *to force those representatives to speak to their needs.* It does not mean merely putting black faces into office. A man or woman who is black and from the slums cannot be automatically expected to speak to the needs of black people. Most of the black politicians we see around the country today are not what SNCC means by black power. The power must be that of a community, and emanate from there.

SNCC today is working in both North and South on programs of voter registration and independent political organizing. In some places, such as Alabama, Los Angeles, New York, Philadelphia, and New Jersey, independent organizing under the black panther symbol is in progress. The creation of a national "black panther party" must come about; it will take time to build, and it is much too early to predict its success. We have no infallible master plan and we make no claim to exclusive knowledge of how to end racism; different groups will work in their own different ways. SNCC cannot spell out the full logistics of self-determination but it can address itself to the problem by helping black communities define their needs, realize their strength, and go into action along a variety of lines which they must choose for themselves. Without knowing all the answers, it can address itself to the basic problem of poverty: to the fact that in Lowndes County, 86 white families own 90 per cent of the land. What are black people in that county going to do for jobs, where are they going to get money? There must be reallocation of land, of money.

Ultimately, the economic foundations of this country must be shaken if black people are to control their lives. The colonies of the United States—and this includes the black ghettoes within its borders, north and south—must be liberated. For a century, this nation has been like an octopus of exploitation, its tentacles stretching from Mississippi and Harlem to South America, the Middle East, southern Africa, and Vietnam; the form of exploitation varies from area to area but the essential result has been the same—a powerful few have been maintained and enriched at the expense of the poor and voiceless colored masses. This pattern must be broken. As its grip loosens here and there around the world, the hopes of black Americans become more realistic. For racism to die, a totally different America must be born.

This is what the white society does not wish to face; this is why that society prefers to talk about integration. But integration speaks not at all to the problem of poverty, only to the problem of blackness. Integration today means the man who "makes it," leaving his black brothers behind in the ghetto as fast as his new sports car will take him. It has no relevance to the Harlem wino or to the cottonpicker making three dollars a day. As a lady I know in Alabama once said, "the food that Ralph Bunche eats doesn't fill my stomach."

Integration, moreover, speaks to the problem of blackness in a despicable way. As a goal, it has been based on complete acceptance of the fact that *in order to have* a decent house or education, blacks must move into a white neighborhood or send their children to a white school. This reinforces, among both black and white, the idea that "white" is automatically better and "black" is by definition inferior. This is why integration is a subterfuge for the maintenance of white supremacy. It allows the nation to focus on a handful of Southern children who get into white schools, at great price, and to ignore the 94 per cent who are left behind in unimproved all-black schools. Such situations will not change until black people have power—to control their own school boards, in this case. Then Negroes become equal in a way that means something, and integration ceases to be a one-way street. Then integration doesn't mean draining skills and energies from the ghetto into white neighborhoods; then it can mean white people moving from Beverly Hills into Watts, white people joining the Lowndes County Freedom Organization. Then integration becomes relevant.

Last April, before the furor over black power, Christopher Jencks wrote in a *New Republic* article on white Mississippi's manipulation of the anti-poverty program:

> The war on poverty has been predicated on the notion that there is such a thing as *a community* which can be defined geographically and mobilized for a collective effort to help the poor. This theory has no relationship to reality in the Deep South. In every Mississippi county there are *two* communities. Despite all the pious platitudes of the moderates on both sides, these two communities habitually see their interests in terms of conflict rather than cooperation. Only when the Negro community can muster enough political, economic and professional strength to compete on somewhat equal terms, will Negroes believe in the possibility of true cooperation and whites accept its necessity. En route to integration, the Negro community needs to develop greater independence—a chance to run its own affairs and not cave in whenever "the man" barks . . . Or so it seems to me, and to most of the knowledgeable people with whom I talked in Mississippi. To OEO, this judgment may sound like black nationalism. . . .

Mr. Jencks, a white reporter, perceived the reason why America's anti-poverty program has been a sick farce in both North and South. In the South, it is clearly racism which prevents the poor from running their own programs; in the North, it more often seems to be politicking and bureaucracy. But the results are not so different: In the North, non-whites make up 42 per cent of all families in metropolitan "poverty areas" and only 6 per cent of families in areas classified as not poor. SNCC has been working with local residents in Arkansas, Alabama, and Mississippi to achieve control by the poor of the program and its funds; it has also been working with groups in the North, and the struggle is no less difficult. Behind it all is a federal government which cares far more about winning the war on the Vietnamese than the war on poverty; which has put the poverty program in the hands of self-serving politicians and bureaucrats rather than the poor themselves; which is unwilling to curb the misuse of white power but quick to condemn black power.

To most whites, black power seems to mean that the Mau Mau are coming to the suburbs at night. The Mau Mau are coming, and whites must stop them. Articles appear about plots to "get Whitey," creating an atmosphere in which "law and order must be maintained." Once again, responsibility is shifted from the oppressor to the oppressed. Other whites chide, "Don't forget—you're only 10 per cent of the population; if you get too smart, we'll wipe you out." If they are liberals, they complain, "what about me?—don't you want my help any more?" These are people supposedly concerned about black Americans, but today they think first of themselves, of their feelings of rejection. Or they admonish, "you can't get anywhere without coalitions," when there is in fact no group at present with whom to form a coalition in which blacks will not be absorbed and betrayed. Or they accuse us of "polarizing the races" by our calls for black unity, when the true responsibility for polarization lies with whites who will not accept their responsibility as the majority power for making the democratic process work.

White America will not face the problem of color, the reality of it. The well-intended say: "We're all human, everybody is really decent, we must forget color." But color cannot be "forgotten" until its weight is recognized and dealt with. White America will not acknowledge that the ways in which this country sees itself are contradicted by being black—and always have been. Whereas most of the people who settled this country came here for freedom or for economic opportunity, blacks were brought here to be slaves. When the Lowndes County Freedom Organization chose the black panther as its symbol, it was christened by the press "the Black Panther Party"—but the Alabama Democratic Party, whose symbol is a rooster, has never been called the White Cock Party. No one ever talked about "white power" because power in this country *is* white. All this adds up to more than merely identifying a group phenomenon by some catchy name or adjective. The furor over that black panther reveals the problems that white America has with color and sex; the furor over "black power" reveals how deep racism runs and the great fear which is attached to it.

Whites will not see that I, for example, as a person oppressed because of my blackness, have common cause with other blacks who are oppressed because of blackness. This is not to say that there are no white people who see things as I do, but that it is black people I must speak to first. It must be the oppressed to whom SNCC addresses itself primarily, not to friends from the oppressing group.

From birth, black people are told a set of lies about themselves. We are told that we are lazy—yet I drive through the Delta area of Mississippi and watch black people picking cotton in the hot sun for fourteen hours. We are told, "If you work hard, you'll succeed"— but if that were true, black people would own this country. We are oppressed because we are black—not because we are ignorant, not because we are lazy, not because we're stupid (and got good rhythm), but because we're black.

I remember that when I was a boy, I used to go to see Tarzan movies on Saturday. White Tarzan used to beat up the black natives. I would sit there yelling, "Kill the beasts, kill the savages, kill 'em!" I was saying: Kill *me*. It was as if a Jewish boy watched Nazis taking Jews off to concentration camps and cheered them on. Today, I want the chief to beat hell out of Tarzan and send him back to Europe. But it takes time to become free of the lies and their shaming effect on black minds. It takes time to reject the most important lie: that black people inherently can't do the same things white people can do, unless white people help them.

The need for psychological equality is the reason why SNCC today believes that blacks must organize in the black community. Only black people can convey the revolutionary idea that black people are able to do things themselves. Only they can help create in the community an aroused and continuing black consciousness that will provide the basis for political strength. In the past, white allies have furthered white supremacy without the whites involved realizing it—or wanting it, I think. Black people must do things for themselves; they must get poverty money they will control and spend themselves, they must conduct tutorial programs themselves so that black children can identify with black people. This is one reason Africa has such importance: The reality of black men ruling their own natives gives blacks elsewhere a sense of possibility, of power, which they do not now have.

This does not mean we don't welcome help, or friends. But we want the right to decide whether anyone is, in fact, our friend. In the past, black Americans have been almost the only people whom everybody and his momma could jump up and call their friends. We have been tokens, symbols, objects—as I was in high school to many young whites, who liked having "a Negro friend." We want to decide who is our friend, and we will not accept someone who comes to us and says: "If you do X, Y, and Z, then I'll help you." We will not be told whom we should choose as allies. We will not be isolated from any group or nation except by our own choice. We cannot have the oppressors telling the oppressed how to rid themselves of the oppressor.

I have said that most liberal whites react to "black power" with the question, What about me?, rather than saying: Tell me what you want me to do and I'll see if I can do it. There are answers to the right question. One of the most disturbing things about almost all white supporters of the movement has been that they are afraid to go into their own communities—which is where the racism exists—and work to get rid of it. They want to run from Berkeley to tell us what to do in Mississippi; let them look instead at Berke-

ley. They admonish blacks to be nonviolent; let them preach non-
violence in the white community. They come to teach me Negro
history; let them go to the suburbs and open up freedom schools
for whites. Let them work to stop America's racist foreign policy;
let them press this government to cease supporting the economy of
South Africa.

There is a vital job to be done among poor whites. We hope to
see, eventually, a coalition between poor blacks and poor whites.
That is the only coalition which seems acceptable to us, and we see
such a coalition as the major internal instrument of change in
American society. SNCC has tried several times to organize poor
whites; we are trying again now, with an initial training program
in Tennessee. It is purely academic today to talk about bringing
poor blacks and whites together, but the job of creating a poor-
white power bloc must be attempted. The main responsibility for it
falls upon whites. Black and white can work together in the white
community where possible; it is not possible, however, to go into
a poor Southern town and talk about integration. Poor whites everywhere are becoming more hostile—not less—partly because they
see the nation's attention focussed on black poverty and nobody
coming to them. Too many young middle-class Americans, like some
sort of Pepsi generation, have wanted to come alive through the
black community; they've wanted to be where the action is—and
the action has been in the black community.

Black people do not want to "take over" this country. They don't
want to "get Whitey"; they just want to get him off their backs, as
the saying goes. It was for example the exploitation by Jewish landlords and merchants which first created black resentment toward
Jews—not Judaism. The white man is irrelevant to blacks, except as
an oppressive force. Blacks want to be in his place, yes, but not in
order to terrorize and lynch and starve him. They want to be in
his place because that is where a decent life can be had.

But our vision is not merely of a society in which all black men
have enough to buy the good things of life. When we urge that
black money go into black pockets, we mean the communal pocket.
We want to see money go back into the community and used to
benefit it. We want to see the cooperative concept applied in business and banking. We want to see black ghetto residents demand
that an exploiting store keeper sell them, at minimal cost, a building
or a shop that they will own and improve cooperatively; they can
back their demand with a rent strike, or a boycott, and a community
so unified behind them that no one else will move into the building
or buy at the store. The society we seek to build among black people,

then, is not a capitalist one. It is a society in which the spirit of community and humanistic love prevail. The word love is suspect; black expectations of what it might produce have been betrayed too often. But those were expectations of a response from the white community, which failed us. The love we seek to encourage is within the black community, the only American community where men call each other "brother" when they meet. We can build a community of love only where we have the ability and power to do so: among blacks.

As for white America, perhaps it can stop crying out against "black supremacy," "black nationalism," "racism in reverse," and begin facing reality. The reality is that this nation, from top to bottom, is racist; that racism is not primarily a problem of "human relations" but of an exploitation maintained—either actively or through silence—by the society as a whole. Camus and Sartre have asked, can a man condemn himself? Can whites, particularly liberal whites, condemn themselves? Can they stop blaming us, and blame their own system? Are they capable of the shame which might become a revolutionary emotion?

We have found that they usually cannot condemn themselves, and so we have done it. But the rebuilding of this society, if at all possible, is basically the responsibility of whites—not blacks. We won't fight to save the present society, in Vietnam or anywhere else. We are just going to work, in the way *we* see fit, and on goals *we* define, not for civil rights but for all our human rights.

The preceding essay tells what Stokely Carmichael says black Americans (or at least SNCC circa 1966) want. This one examines the problem from another perspective, the grass roots.

Using the techniques of participant observation and the focused interview, sociologist Joyce Ladner spent three months during the spring of 1966 studying the effects of the changed ideology on Mississippi Negroes. This is her report.

13

Joyce Ladner

WHAT "BLACK POWER" MEANS TO NEGROES IN MISSISSIPPI

For three months during the summer of last year, I conducted a study aimed at finding out how Mississippi Negroes who endorsed "black power" interpreted this new concept. I learned that even those civil-rights activists who welcomed the concept attached curiously different meanings to it. My research also helped me understand why the black-power slogan proved so welcome to these activists—and why its acceptance was accompanied by the expulsion of whites from positions of leadership. Finally, my investigation provided some hints on the usefulness of the black-power slogan in helping Mississippi Negroes achieve their goals.

The black-power concept that emerged during the past year created fierce controversy, not only among white liberals but among Negro activists and conservatives. Most of the nation's top civil-rights leaders denounced the slogan—or vigorously embraced it. Instead of "black power," Martin Luther King, Jr. advocated the

From *Trans-Action* Magazine, 5 (November 1967), 7–15. Copyright © 1967 by Washington University, St. Louis, Mo.

acquisition of "power for all people." The N.A.A.C.P.'s Roy Wilkins, in condemning the slogan, used such terms as "anti-white power . . . a reverse Hitler . . . a reverse Ku Klux Klan and . . . can only mean black death." On the other hand, Stokely Carmichael, former head of SNCC, was the chief advocate of the slogan, which he defined as "the ability of black people to politically get together and organize themselves so that they can speak from a position of strength rather than a position of weakness." CORE's Floyd McKissick agreed.

But though Negro civil-rights leaders were divided about black power, the slogan was welcomed by many disenchanted Negroes living in Northern ghettos. These Negroes tended to view black power as a tangible goal that, when acquired, would lift them from their inferior positions in the social structure. Still, despite the positive identification that Negroes in the Northern ghettos had with the rhetoric of black power, SNCC and CORE made no massive attempts to involve these Negroes in black-power programs.

But what about the South? How did Negroes in Mississippi, and civil-rights organizations in Mississippi, interpret the new slogan? This was what I wanted to find out.

I used two methods of study. The first was *participant-observation*—in informal, small meetings of civil-rights activists; in civil-rights rallies; and in protest demonstrations, including the historic Meredith march. The second was the *focused interview*. I chose to interview 30 Negroes who, I had found, were in favor of black power. All were friends or acquaintances of mine, and all had had long experience in Southern civil-rights work. They represented about two-thirds of the black-power leaders in the state. (My personal involvement with the civil-rights movement helped provide the rapport needed to acquire the observational data, as well as the interview data.)

Among other things, I learned that many Negro activists in Mississippi had immediately embraced the black-power slogan—because of the already widely-held belief that power *was* an effective tool for obtaining demands from the ruling elite in Mississippi. Since 1960, civil-rights organizations have been playing a major role in involving Mississippi Negroes in the fight for equality. As a result, these Negroes became more and more dissatisfied with their impoverished, powerless positions in the social structure. The 1960 census reports that the median family income for Mississippi Negroes (who constitute 42.3 percent of Mississippi's population) was $1168, as opposed to $3565 for whites. Until fewer than five years ago, only 6 percent of the eligible Negroes were registered to vote. Today, the traditional all-white primary still exists—in almost the same form as it did 25 years ago. Since many of the efforts Mississippi Negroes made to change the social structure—through integration—were futile, they began to reconceptualize their fight for equality from a different perspective, one designed to acquire long-sought goals through building bases of power.

The black-power concept was, then, successfully communicated to Mississippi Negroes because of the failure of integration. But it was also communicated to them by the shooting of James Meredith on his march through Mississippi. This act of violence made Negro activists feel justified in calling for "audacious black power." For only with black power, they contended, would black people be able to prevent events like the shooting.

Locals and Cosmopolitans

But there were varying degrees of acceptance of the slogan among Mississippi Negroes. Some, of course, did not accept the slogan at all—those who were never part of the civil-rights movement. Despite the fact that Mississippi has been one of the centers of civil-rights activity in the United States for the past six or seven years, no more than half the Negro population (I would surmise) has ever been actively involved in the movement. In such areas as Sunflower County, a very high percentage of Negroes have participated; but in many other areas, like Laurel, only a small percentage of the Negroes have taken part.

As for those Negroes active in the movement, they can be broadly classified into two groups. The first: the traditional, moderate, N.A.A.C.P.-style activists, who boast of having been "freedom fighters" before the "new movement" came into existence. They include ministers; small-businessmen; professionals; a sizable following of middle-class people; and a small number of the rank and file. Frequently the white ruling elite calls these activists the "responsible" leaders. The primary activities of this group include selling N.A.A.C.P. memberships; initiating legal action against segregation and discriminatory practices; negotiating with the ruling elite; and conducting limited boycotts and voter-registration campaigns.

The second group of activists are the less economically advantaged. Although a small number were once members of the N.A.A.C.P., most of them joined the movement only since 1960. They are readily identified with such organizations as the Freedom Democratic Party, CORE, SNCC, the Delta Ministry, and the Southern Christian Leadership Conference. Members of this group include plantation workers, students, the average lower-class Negro, and a small number of ministers, professionals, and businessmen. More militant than the first group, these activists conduct mass marches, large-scale boycotts, sit-ins, dramatic voter-registration campaigns, and so forth.

Members of the traditional organizations, in sum, are still committed to working for integration. It is the militants who are oriented toward a black-power ideology, who consider integration irrelevant to what they see as the major task at hand—uniting black people to build black institutions. I suspect that a larger number of activists identify with traditional organizations like the N.A.A.C.P. than with the more militant ones.

The 30 black-power advocates I interviewed were, of course, the militant activists. Even so, I found that even these 30 could be further classified—into categories that Robert K. Merton has called *local* and *cosmopolitan:*

> The localite largely confines his interest to this [town of Rovere] community. Devoting little thought or energy to the Great Society he is preoccupied with local problems, to the virtual exclusion of the national and international scene. He is, strictly speaking, parochial.
>
> Contrariwise with the cosmopolitan type. He has some interest in Rovere and must of course maintain a minimum of relations within the community since he, too, exerts influence there. But he is also oriented significantly to the world outside Rovere and regards himself as an integral part of that world. . . . The cosmopolitan is ecumenical.

In this paper, I shall use "local" to refer to those long-term residents of Mississippi—usually uneducated, unskilled adults—whose strong commitment to civil-rights activity stemmed primarily from their desire to produce massive changes in the "home-front," the area they call home.

I shall use "cosmopolitan" to refer to the urbane, educated, highly skilled young civil-rights activists who are usually newcomers to Mississippi. Because they went to the state to work in the civil-rights movement only temporarily, their identification with the area tends to be weak.

The Movement's Philosophers

One-third of my respondents, I found, hold the cosmopolitan view. The majority are Negro men, but there are a small group of Negro women and a very small group of white sympathizers. The mean age is about 23 or 24. About half are from the North; the remainder are from Mississippi and other Southern states. Most of the cosmo-politans are formally educated and many have come from middle-class Northern families and gone to the better universities. They are widely read and widely traveled. They are also artistic: Writers, painters, photographers, musicians, and the like are often found in the cosmopolitan group. Their general orientation toward life is an intellectual one. They are associated with SNCC, the Freedom Dem-ocratic Party, and CORE. Although a few are actively engaged in organizing black people in the various counties, much of their work in the state is centered on philosophical discussions, writing, and so forth. All of the cosmopolitans have had wide associations with white people. Some grew up and attended school with whites; others had contact with whites in the civil-rights movement. The cosmo-politans maintain that black people in American society must re-define the term "black" and all that it symbolizes, and that black pride and dignity must be implanted in all Negro Americans. The cosmopolitan position embraces the belief that the plight of Negro Americans is comparable to neocolonialized "colored peoples" of the world.

The cosmopolitans' participation in the Southern civil-rights scene, by and large, dates back to 1960 and the beginning of the student movement in the South. Their present ideology has to be viewed in the framework of the history of their involvement in the movement, with special emphasis on the negative experiences they encountered.

Some six years ago, black Americans began to seek their long-desired civil rights with a new sense of urgency. The N.A.A.C.P.'s painstaking effort to obtain legal, theoretical rights for Negroes was challenged. Groups of Negro college students in the South decided to fight the gradualism that had become traditional and to substitute radical action aimed at bringing about rapid social change. These students began their drive for equal rights with lunch-counter dem-onstrations. After much immediate success, they spread their drive to the political arena. Their only hope for the future, they felt, lay in the ballot. Much to their disappointment, acquiring political power was not so easy as integrating lunch counters. The students met their strongest resistance from whites in full possession of the sought-after political power. To deal with this resistance, the Federal Gov-ernment passed two civil-rights laws: public accommodation and voting rights. But the Government did little to implement these laws. Still, in the early 1960s, student civil-rights workers had an almost unrelenting faith in the Federal Government and believed that changes in the laws would rapidly pave the way for sweeping changes in the social structure. This was the era when students were much involved in hard-core organizing. They paid little attention to abstract philosophizing. Instead they occupied themselves with such pressing problems as the mass arrests of Negroes in Greenwood, Miss.

As time went on, the cosmopolitans became more and more discouraged about their organizing efforts. They began to seriously question the feasibility of their strategies and tactics. By the end of 1964, after the historic Mississippi Summer Project, the cosmopolitans began to feel that their organizational methods were just not effective. For roughly a year and a half, they groped and searched for more effective strategies. Frequently they felt frustrated; sometimes they despaired. A number of them returned to the North and got well-paying jobs or went to graduate and professional schools. Others were alienated from some of the basic values of American society. Some students developed a strong interest in Africa and began to look to various African states as possible havens. Still others, after deciding that they had accomplished all that was possible through organizations such as SNCC, associated themselves with radical leftist groups.

It was during the tail end of this six-year period that two position papers were written by the cosmopolitans. One was by a group that insisted that Negroes expel whites from leadership roles in civil-rights organizations, and that Negroes develop "black consciousness" and "black nationalism." "Black consciousness" refers to a set of ideas and behavior patterns affirming the beauty of blackness and dispelling any negative images that black people may have incorporated about blackness. "Black nationalism" is a kind of patriotic devotion to the development of the Negro's own political, economic, and social institutions. Black nationalism is *not* a racist ideology with separatist overtones, however, but simply a move toward independence from the dominant group, the whites. This paper states:

> If we are to proceed toward true liberation, we must cut ourselves off from white people. We must form our own institutions, credit unions, co-ops, political parties, write our own histories. . . . SNCC, by allowing whites to remain in the organization, can have its efforts subverted. . . . Indigenous leadership cannot be built with whites in the positions they now hold. They [whites] can participate on a voluntary basis . . . but in no way can they participate on a policy-making level.

In response, one white civil-rights worker—Pat McGauley—wrote a paper acceding to the demands of the black-consciousness group:

The time has indeed come for blacks and whites in the movement to separate; however, it must always be kept in mind that the final goal of the revolution we are all working for is a multi-racial society.

The cosmopolitans I interviewed conceived of black power in highly philosophical terms—as an ideology that would unite black people as never before. To most of them, black power was intricately bound up with black consciousness. To a long-time SNCC worker, black consciousness was:

> an awareness of oneself as a removed nation of black people who are capable of running and developing their own governments and who have pride in their blackness to the extent that they won't sell out. . . . To the extent that he can say, "I'm no longer ashamed of my blackness." The individual redefines the society's rules in terms of his own being. There is a new kind of awakening of the individual, a new kind of realization of self, a type of security, and a type of self-confidence.

Another cosmopolitan equated black consciousness with community loyalty:

> Black consciousness is not the question but rather [the question is] from which community one comes from. If you know that, you can identify with black people anywhere in the world then. That is all that is necessary.

These young people firmly believe that even the term "black" has to be redefined. To one of them, "Black has never had any favorable expression in the English language." To another, "American society has characterized black as the symbol for strength, evil, potency and malignancy. . . . People are afraid of the night, of blackness."

Most cosmopolitans feel that black people must acquire black consciousness before they can successfully develop the tools and techniques for acquiring black power. As one of them put it:

> Black consciousness is the developmental stage of black power. Black power will be incomplete without black consciousness. Black consciousness is basically the search for identity; or working out one's own identity. . . . There must be a long process of learning and unlearning in between and a period of self-questing.

In short, by developing black consciousness, a Negro can appreciate his blackness and thus develop a kind of community loyalty to other colored peoples of the world.

Most of the cosmopolitans felt that the redefinition of blackness must take place in the black community *on the black man's terms.* When such a redefinition has taken place, black men who feel psychologically castrated because of their blackness will be able to compete with whites as psychological equals. ("Psychologically castrated" is a popular term among cosmopolitans, and refers to Negroes whose beliefs and behavior have become so warped by the values of white American society that they have come to regard themselves as inferior.)

Heroes of the Black Revolution

Cosmopolitans are familiar with the works of Marcus Garvey, Malcolm X, Franz Fanon, Kwame Nkrumah, and other revolutionary nationalists. Some can quote passages from their works. To the cosmopolitans, Marcus Garvey (1887–1940), who tried to instill racial pride in Negroes, was a pioneer of black nationalism and black consciousness in America. The greatest impact on the cosmopolitans, however, comes from the contemporary Malcolm X, whose philosophy—toward the latter period of his life—reflected a revolutionary spirit and a total dissatisfaction with the plight of Negroes in this country. One of the cosmopolitans had this to say about Malcolm X:

> Malcolm was very much together. . . . He was a man who knew what he was doing and would have eventually showed everyone what he was capable of doing. . . . Malcolm had history behind him and was with the cat on the block.

To another:

> Malcolm X . . . was able to relate to people and to the press. The press is your right arm. . . . In order to be a real militant, you have to use the man [press] and that is what Malcolm did. They [the press] didn't create Malcolm. . . . The press was attuned to Malcolm. . . . Malcolm was not attuned to the press.

Some cosmopolitans call themselves students of Malcolm X and express the hope that another such leader will soon emerge.

Another symbolic leader is the late Algerian revolutionary, Franz Fanon, whose *The Wretched of the Earth* has become a veritable Bible to the cosmopolitans. Fanon tried to justify the use of violence by the oppressed against the oppressor, and to relate the neocolonialization of the black man in Algeria to the plight of colored peoples everywhere. Similarly, the cosmopolitans have great admiration for Stokely Carmichael, one of their associates, whose philosophy is highlighted in this passage:

> The colonies of the United States—and this includes the black ghettos within its borders, north and south—must be liberated. For a century

this nation has been like an octopus of exploitation, its tentacles stretching from Mississippi and Harlem to South America, the Middle East, southern Africa, and Vietnam; the form of exploitation varies from area to area but the essential result has been the same—a powerful few have been maintained and enriched at the expense of the poor and voiceless colored masses. This pattern must be broken. As its grip loosens here and there around the world, the hopes of black Americans become more realistic. For racism to die, a totally different America must be born.

Embodied within the philosophy of the cosmopolitans is an essential proposition that American society is inherently racist, that the majority of white Americans harbor prejudice against black people. Few make any distinction between whites—for example, the white Southerner as opposed to the Northern liberal. Whites are considered symbolic of the black man's oppression, and therefore one should not differentiate between sympathetic whites and unsympathetic whites. The conclusion of the cosmopolitans is that any sweeping structural changes in American society can come about only through the black man's taking an aggressive role in organizing his political, economic, and social institutions. The black man must control his destiny.

The Practical Orientation

I have categorized the remaining two-thirds of my 30 respondents as locals. (Of what significance these ratios are, by the way, I am not sure.) The locals are almost as committed to solving the pressing problems of inadequate income, education, housing, and second-class citizenship *practically* as the cosmopolitans are committed to solving them *philosophically*. Most of the locals are life-long residents of their communities or other Mississippi communities. Most of them, like the cosmopolitans, have been drawn into the movement only since 1960. Unlike the generally youthful cosmopolitans, the age range of the locals is from young adult to elderly. Many locals are indigenous leaders in their communities and in state-wide organizations. Whereas cosmopolitans tend to be middle-class, locals are members of the lower-class black communities and they range from plantation workers to a few who have acquired modest homes and a somewhat comfortable style of life. Many are leaders in the Mississippi Freedom Democratic Party, which in 1964 challenged the legality of the all-white Mississippi delegation to the national Democratic convention and in 1965 challenged the constitutionality of the elected white Representatives to serve in the U.S. House of Representatives. (Both challenges were based upon the fact that Negroes did not participate in the election of the delegates and Representatives.)

Although most of the locals are native Mississippians who have always been victimized by segregation and discrimination, I have also placed a number of middle-class students in this category— because of their very practical orientation to black power. The backgrounds of these students are somewhat similar to those of the cosmopolitans, except that the majority come from the South and are perhaps from lower-status families than the cosmopolitans are. These students are deeply involved in attempts to organize black-power programs.

Because of segregation and discrimination, the locals are largely uneducated; they subsist on a totally inadequate income; and they are denied the privileges of first-class citizenship. They have had a lot of experience with the usual forms of harassment and intimidation from local whites. Their entire existence can be perceived in terms of their constant groping for a better way of life. Because of many factors—like their low level of income and education and their Southern, rural, small-town mentality (which to some extent prevents one from acquiring an intellectualized world view)—the definition they have given to black power is a very practical one.

The black-power locals can be considered militants to much the same degree as the cosmopolitans, but on a different level. In essence, the nature and kind of activities in which they are willing to participate (voter registration, running for political office, boycotts, etc.) are indeed militant and are not surpassed by the nature and kind to which the cosmopolitans orient themselves. Indeed, in some cases the locals are deeply involved in realizing black-power programs: In certain counties, women have organized leathercraft and dress-making cooperatives. And in Senator Eastland's home county of Sunflower, an unsuccessful effort was even made to elect an all-black slate of public officials.

The great difference between cosmopolitans and locals is that the locals are committed to concrete economic and political programs, while the cosmopolitans—to varying degrees—endorse such programs but actually have made little effort to realize them.

Most locals perceived black power as a more effective, alternate method of organizing and acquiring those rights they had been seeking. In the past they had been committed to integration. Power had not originally been considered important in and of itself, for it was hoped that America would voluntarily give Negroes civil rights. Therefore the locals sought coalition politics—they aligned themselves with Northern labor groups, liberals, national church groups, and so forth. During their several years of involvement, they—like the cosmopolitans—suffered many defeats. For example, many were involved with the Mississippi Summer Project, which brought hundreds of Northerners into the state in 1964. At that time the locals were convinced that such a program would bring about the wide structural changes they desired. But, to their disappointment, once the volunteers returned to the North the old patterns of segregation and discrimination returned. Some of the locals had gone to the Democratic Convention in Atlantic City, N.J., in 1964 hoping to unseat the all-white slate of delegates from Mississippi. When this failed, they invested further moral and physical resources into challenging the legality of the all-white slate of Mississippi Representatives in the U.S. House. Another set-back came when a large contingent pitched their tents on the White House lawn in a last-ditch effort to obtain poverty funds to aid in building adequate housing. All were sharecroppers, evicted because their participation in voter-registration programs was contrary to the desires of their plantation landlords. These evicted sharecroppers later set up residence in the buildings of the inactive Air Force base in Greenville, Miss. They were deeply depressed when officials of the Air Force ordered military police to remove them. One of the leaders of this group remarked, "If the United States Government cares so little about its citizens that it will not allow them to live in its abandoned buildings rather than in unheated tents [this occurred during winter], then that government can't be for real."

I submit that the events outlined above, among many others, caused a large number of the locals—like the cosmopolitans—to pause and question the effectiveness of their traditional organizational tactics and goals. Indeed, many even came to seriously question the Federal Government's sincerity about alleviating the problems of the Negro. A number of the participants in these events stopped being active in the movement. Others began to express strong anti-white sentiments.

The Attractions of Black Power

Black power was embraced by many of the locals from the very beginning, and they began to reconceptualize their activities within the new framework. To the locals, black power was defined in various ways, some of which follow:

> Voter registration is black power. Power is invested in the ballot and that's why the white man worked like hell to keep you away from it. . . . We were even taught that it was not right to register [to

vote]. The civil-rights movement in this state started around the issue of voting—we shouldn't forget that.

Black power is political power held by Negroes. It means political control in places where they comprise a majority. . . . Black power is legitimate because any time people are in a majority, they should be able to decide what will and will not happen to them.

Black power was further viewed as a means of combining Negroes into a bond of solidarity. It was seen as a rallying cry, a symbol of identification, and a very concrete tool for action. Many said that former slogans and concepts such as "Freedom Now" were ambiguous. One could easily ask, "Freedom for what and from what?" One local said:

First we wanted Freedom Now. I ran around for six years trying to get my freedom. I really didn't know what it was.

Black power, they felt, was more concrete, for it had as its central thesis the acquisition of power. (Actually, the locals have also defined black power in various ways, and to some the slogan is as ambiguous as "Freedom Now.") The locals felt that Negroes would be able to acquire certain rights only through the control of their economic and political institutions, which—in some cases—also involves the eventual control of the black community. One black-power advocate put it succinctly when he said:

Black power means controlling the Negro community. It means that if the Negro community doesn't want white cops coming in, they can't come in. It means political, economic, and social control.

Asked how this control could be obtained, he replied:

We will have to start putting our money together to organize cooperatives, and other kinds of businesses. We can get political power by putting Negroes into public offices. . . . We will have to tell them to vote only for Negro candidates.

To others, control over the black community was not the goal, but rather a *share* in the existing power:

All we're saying to the white man is we want some power. Black power is just plain power. . . . It just means that Negroes are tired of being without power and want to share in it.

Thus, we can observe that there are several variations of the concept, all revolving around a central theme: the acquisition of power by Negroes for their own use, both offensively and defensively.

Despite the obvious practical orientation of the locals, there can also be found traces of black consciousness and black nationalism in their thought patterns. Most have never read Garvey, Fanon, Malcolm X, and other nationalists, but they tend to readily identify with the content of speeches made by Stokely Carmichael bearing the message of black nationalism. They are prone to agree with the cosmopolitans who speak to them about ridding themselves of their "oppressors." When the chairman of the Mississippi Freedom Democratic Party speaks of overthrowing neo-colonialism in Mississippi, shouts of "Amen!" can be heard from the audience. There is also a tendency in this group to oppose the current war in Vietnam on the grounds that America should first concentrate on liberating Negroes within the United States' borders. The locals also believe that the war is indeed an unjust one. Perhaps the following statement is typical:

> Black men have been stripped of everything. If it takes black power to do something about this, let us have it. Black power has got the country moving and white people don't like it. We marched into Dominica, we marched into Vietnam. Now if we [black people] can conquer this country, we will conquer the world.

There is a growing feeling among both locals and cosmopolitans of kinship with the colored peoples of the world, including the Vietnamese. To engage in warfare against other colored people is regarded as a contradiction of this bond of solidarity.

For both the Mississippi cosmopolitans and locals, then, it was mainly frustration that drew them to the concept of black power.

Why Whites Were Expelled

The black-power slogan should be viewed in the perspective of the overall civil-rights movement, one of the most popular social movements in the history of this country. Now, there are some scholars who maintain that, by viewing a particular social movement over a period of time, one can discern a typical sequence: the movement's crystallization of social unrest; its phase of active agitation and proselytism; its organized phase; and the achievement of its objectives. The civil-rights movement, with much success, achieved each of these phases—except the final one, the achievement of objectives. Despite the great amount of effort and resources expended by black people and their allies to obtain civil rights, there was a disproportionate lack of gains. Indeed, in much of Mississippi and the South, conditions have barely changed from 10 or even 20 years ago. Many black people are still earning their livelihood from sharecropping and tenant farming; many household heads are still unable to earn more than $500 a year; many black children are still deprived of adequate education because of the lack of facilities and adequately trained teachers. To date, only 42.1 percent of Negroes of voting age are registered as opposed to 78.9 percent of whites. We still hear of lynchings and other forms of violence of which Negroes are the victims.

The black-power thrust is thus an inevitable outgrowth of the disillusionment that black people have experienced in their intense efforts to become integrated into the mainstream of American society. Thwarted by traditional formulas and organizational restrictions, some Mississippi Negroes have responded to the black-power concept in a sometimes semirational, emotionally charged manner— because it seemed the only available resource with which they could confront white American society.

How was the black-power concept related to the expulsion of whites from leadership positions in the movement? The fact is that the alienation and disaffection found throughout the entire black-power group also resulted from strained interpersonal relations with white civil-rights workers. During the past two years, there has been a growing belief among black people in Mississippi that white civil-rights workers should go into the *white* communities of that state to work. Only then, they contended, could the "inherent racism" in American society, with particular reference to the "Southern racist," begin to be dealt with. Even the seriousness of white civil-rights workers was questioned. Many Negroes felt that a sizable number of them had come South mainly to resolve their very personal emotional difficulties, and not to help impoverished black Mississippians. Rather, they were considered rebellious youth who wanted only to act out their rebellion in the most unconventional ways. Stokely Carmichael stated:

> Too many young, middle-class Americans, like some sort of Pepsi generation, have wanted to come alive through the black community; they've wanted to be where the action was—and the action has been in the black community. . . .
> It's important to note that those white people who feel alienated from white society and run into the black society are incapable of confronting the white society with its racism where it really does exist.

Much strain also resulted from the inability of many black civil-rights activists—skilled organizers but lacking the formal education and other technical skills white workers possessed—to deal with the increased bureaucratization of the civil-rights movement (writing proposals for foundation grants, for example). Black activists, in addition, constantly complained about the focus of the mass media on white "all-American" volunteers who had come South to work in the movement. The media never paid attention to the thousands of black people who frequently took far greater risks. These factors played a major role in destroying the bond of solidarity that had once existed between whites and blacks in the movement. Before the emergence of the black-power concept, it is true, many young black civil-rights workers had cast white civil-rights workers in the same category as all other white people. The new slogan was, to some extent, a form of justification for their own prejudice against whites.

In terms of practical considerations, however, urging the white volunteers to leave the black communities has had negative effects. SNCC and CORE, which at one time directed most of the grass-roots organizing, have always depended upon the economic and volunteer resources of liberal white individuals and groups. These resources are scarce nowadays.

On another level, there have been positive results from removing whites from black communities. Black activists—all cosmopolitans and some locals—contend that, now that the whites have gone, they feel more self-confident and capable of running their own programs. They tend to view the earlier period of the movement, when whites played active roles in executing the programs, as having been a necessary phase; but they maintain that the time has arrived when black people must launch and execute their own programs.

Cosmopolitans vs. Locals

Clearly, the long-range aims of the locals and cosmopolitans are basically the same. Unlike Negroes in such traditional organizations as the N.A.A.C.P., locals and cosmopolitans have turned away from integration. Both groups want to unite black people and build political, economic, and social institutions that will render a certain amount of control to the black community. For some time, however, the two groups have been operating on different levels. The cosmopolitans focus on developing black consciousness among black people, which they consider a necessary step to developing black power; the locals concentrate on solving the immediate problems resulting from segregation and discrimination.

While it may seem that the locals are more prudent and realistic than the cosmopolitans, it should be said that there are many positive features to black nationalism and black consciousness. It *is* important to establish a positive black identity in a great many sectors of the black communities, both North and South, rural and urban, lower and middle class. Indeed, it is both important and legitimate to teach black people (or any other ethnic minority) about their history, placing special emphasis upon the positive contributions of other black people. Thus black consciousness has the potential to create unity and solidarity among black people and to give them hope and self-confidence. Perhaps it fulfills certain needs in black people that society, on the whole, cannot. Martin Luther King has made the following statement about black consciousness:

> One must not overlook the positive value in calling the Negro to a new sense of manhood, to a deep feeling of racial pride and to an audacious appreciation of his heritage. The Negro must be grasped by a new realization of his dignity and worth. He must stand up amid a system that still oppresses him and develop an unassailable and majestic sense of his own value. *He must no longer be ashamed of being black.* (Emphasis mine.)

Moreover, the task of getting blacks to act *as blacks, by* themselves and *for* themselves, is necessary for developing black consciousness, or psychological equality. Thus one is led to the conclusion that black consciousness does *necessarily* call for the expulsion of whites from leadership roles in the black communities.

The locals, on the other hand, have adopted concrete strategies that, in reality, involve the same kind of techniques that existed in the integration era. Specifically, when they refer to developing black-power programs, they speak of registering to vote, running for political office, and building independent political parties. As for the economic situation, they have begun to concentrate on building cooperatives and small businesses, and on almost-exclusively patronizing black merchants in an effort to "keep the money in the black community." If we turn back two years, however, we find that the same strategies, though somewhat modified, were being used then. In the past, the locals concentrated on registering large numbers of black people to vote, in an effort to be able to have a voice in the decision-making apparatus. The emphasis is now on registering to vote so that the Negro can have control over his community and eventual control over his political destiny. Cooperatives were organized at least a year before the black-power concept emerged, but —ever since emphasis was put on economic control—there has been an expansion and intensification in certain sectors of this area. At present, cooperatives are still operating on a small-scale, though, considering the masses of people whose lives could be immensely improved by cooperatives.

The differences in the emphasis on priorities of achieving black power between locals and cosmopolitans can be viewed as complementary rather than oppositional, because each level of emphasis is vital for the achievement of their goals. This is becoming increasingly true since, within the last year, black-power advocates have taken a far more aggressive and militant stance toward the realization of such aims. Locals who a year ago might have questioned the importance and feasibility of "Black Liberation" schools, which teach black history and culture, are less likely to do so now. This is an indication that there is a trend toward unity between the groups. Because of the strong emphasis among some sectors of the black-power movement on drawing the parallels of the plight of black Americans with that of the inhabitants of the Third World, locals are quite likely to become more cosmopolitan through time.

Through the development of such unity, there is a great possibility that black-power advocates in Mississippi will again turn to creative, large-scale organizing that would incorporate the major emphases of each group: black consciousness and immediate gains.

The Future of Black Power

The key question, of course, is, what are the prospects for Mississippi Negroes' developing black-power institutions in the near future? Clearly, this will depend to a great extent upon the number of organizers in the field, on adequate economic resources, and on commitments from major civil-rights organizations to the Mississippi scene. Certainly the presence of a local charismatic leader also would aid in the development of pervasive black-power institutions. Indeed, a black-power "prophet" whose task was to keep the message before all the advocates would give them immeasurable support and strength for their undertakings.

Where black-power institutions have a good chance of developing at present are in the small number of Mississippi counties where there are strong black-power organizations with large Negro voting populations. Since the cosmopolitans are reentering the field and beginning to organize (and some of the most skilled organizers are in this group), the prospects—here at least—seem favorable. On the other hand, it seems highly doubtful at this point that the needed resources can be obtained from the traditional sources (Northern students, white liberals, church and labor organizations). So these resources (inadequate as they may be) may have to be obtained from the black community. CORE and SNCC have already begun to establish financial bases in the black communities throughout the country. Should this tactic fail, perhaps there will be a revaluation of the strategies employed in the acquisition of black power.

Here Christopher Lasch describes the demise of the old civil rights movement and the lack of a unified and coherent program to replace it, particularly in the northern ghetto areas. Firmly convinced that the creation of black consciousness and nationalism are necessary, Lasch feels that "romantic anarchism . . . and a tendency to substitute rhetoric for political analysis and gestures for political action" are self-defeating.

The author develops his thesis as he reviews and comments upon several recent books, including Stokely Carmichael and Charles V. Hamilton's Black Power, *Nathan Wright's* Black Power and Urban Unrest, *and Harold Cruse's* The Crisis of the Negro Intellectual.

14

Christopher Lasch

THE TROUBLE WITH BLACK POWER

Whatever else "Black Power" means, the slogan itself indicates that the movement for racial equality has entered a new phase. Even those who argue that the change is largely rhetorical or that Black Power merely complements the struggle for "civil rights" would presumably not deny that "Black Power" articulates, at the very least, a new sense of urgency, if not a sense of impending crisis. Together with last summer's riots, it challenges the belief, until recently widespread, that the United States is making substantial progress toward racial justice and that it is only a matter of time and further effort before the color line is effectively obliterated.

Now even the opponents of Black Power issue warnings of apocalypse. "We shall overcome" no longer expresses the spirit of the struggle. Race war seems a more likely prospect. The Negro movement itself is splitting along racial lines. In the form in which it existed until 1963 or 1964, the civil rights movement is dead: this

From *The New York Review of Books,* February 29, 1968, pp. 4–13. Copyright © 1968 the New York Review. Reprinted by permission.

is not a conjecture but a historical fact. Whether the movement can be revived in some other form, or whether it will give way to something completely different, remains to be seen. Meanwhile time seems to be working on the side of an imminent disaster.

What has changed? Why did the civil rights movement, which seemed so confident and successful at the time of the Washington march in 1963, falter until now it seems to have reached the point of collapse? Why has "Black Power" displaced "freedom" as the rallying-point of Negro militancy?

There are several reasons for this change. The most obvious is that the apparent victories of the civil rights coalition have not brought about any discernible changes in the lives of most Negroes, at least not in the North. Virtually all the recent books and articles on Black Power acknowledge this failure or insist on it, depending on the point of view. Charles E. Fager's *White Reflections on Black Power*, for example, analyzes in detail the Civil Rights Act of 1964— the major legislative achievement of the civil rights coalition—and shows how the act has been systematically subverted in the South, title by title, and how, in the North, many of its provisions (such as voting safeguards and desegregation of public accommodations) were irrelevant to begin with. The inadequacy of civil rights legislation is not difficult to grasp. Even the most superficial accounts of the summer's riots see the connection between hopes raised by civil rights agitation and the Negroes' disappointing realization that this agitation, whatever its apparent successes, has nevertheless failed to relieve the tangible miseries of ghetto life.

Not only have the civil rights laws proved to be intrinsically weaker and more limited in their application than they seemed at the time they were passed, but the unexpectedly bitter resistance to civil rights, particularly in the North, has made it difficult to implement even these limited gains, let alone to win new struggles for open housing, an end to de facto segregation, and equal employment. Northern segregationists may not be strong enough to elect Mrs. Hicks mayor of Boston, but they can delay open housing indefinitely, it would seem, in Milwaukee as well as in every other Northern city—even those which have nominally adopted open housing. Everywhere in the North civil rights agitation, instead of breaking down barriers as expected, has met a wall of resistance. If anything, Negroes have made more gains in the South than in the North. The strategy of the civil rights movement, resting implicitly on the premise that the North was more enlightened than the South, was unprepared for the resistance it has encountered in the North.

The shifting focus of the struggle from the South to the North thus has contributed both to the weakening of the civil rights movement and to the emergence of Black Power. The implications of this change of scene go beyond what is immediately evident—that federal troops, for instance, appear on the side of the Negroes in Little Rock, whereas in Detroit they are the enemy. The civil rights movement in the South was the product of a set of conditions which is not likely to be repeated in the North: federal efforts to "reconstruct" the South; the tendency of Northern liberals to express their distaste for American society vicariously by attacking racism in the South, rather than by confronting racism at home; the revival of Southern liberalism. Moreover, the civil rights movement, in its Southern phase, rested on the indigenous Negro subculture which has grown up since the Civil War under the peculiar conditions of Southern segregation—a culture separate and unequal but semi-autonomous and therefore capable of giving its own distinctive character to the movement for legal and political equality.

E. Franklin Frazier once wrote that the Negro's "primary struggle" in America "has been to acquire a culture"—customs, values, and forms of expression which, transmitted from generation to generation, provide a people with a sense of its own integrity and collective identity. Under slavery, African forms of social organization, family life, religion, language, and even art disintegrated, leaving the slave neither an African nor an American but a man suspended, as Kenneth Stampp has said, "between two cultures," unable to participate in either. After the Civil War, Southern Negroes gradually developed institutions of their own, derived from American sources but adapted to their own needs, and therefore capable of giving the Negro community the beginnings at least of cohesiveness and collective self-discipline. The Negro church managed to impose strict standards of sexual morality, thereby making possible the emergence of stable families over which the father—not the mother, as under slavery—presided.

Stable families, in turn, furnished the continuity between generations without which Negroes could not even have begun their slow and painful self-advancement—the accumulation of talent, skills, and leadership which by the 1950s had progressed to the point where Southern Negroes, together with their liberal allies, could launch an attack against segregation. The prominence of the Negro church in their struggle showed the degree to which the civil rights movement was rooted in the peculiar conditions of Negro life in the South—conditions which had made the church the central institution of the Negro subculture. Even radicals like Charles M. Sherrod of SNCC who condemned the passivity of the Negro church realized that "no one working in the South can expect to 'beat the box' if he assumes . . . that one does not need the church as it exists."

The breakdown of the Southern Negro subculture in the North has recreated one of the conditions that existed under slavery, that of dangling between two cultures. Unlike other rural people who have migrated over the last hundred and forty years to the cities of the North, Southern Negroes have not been able to transplant their rural way of life even with modifications. The church decays; the family reverts to the matricentric pattern. The schools, which are segregated but at the same time controlled by white people, hold up middle-class norms to which black children are expected to conform; if they fail they are written off as "unteachable." Meanwhile the mass media flood the ghetto with images of affluence, which Negroes absorb without absorbing the ethic of disciplined self-denial and postponement of gratification that has traditionally been a central component of the materialist ethic.

In the South, the Negro church implanted an ethic of patience, suffering, and endurance. As in many peasant or precapitalist societies, this kind of religion proved surprisingly conducive—once endurance was divorced from passive resignation—to effective political action. But the ethic of endurance, which is generally found among oppressed peoples in backward societies, cannot survive exposure to modern materialism. It gives way to an ethic of accumulation. Or, if real opportunities for accumulation do not exist, it gives way to hedonism, opportunism, cynicism, violence, and self-hatred—the characteristics of what Oscar Lewis calls the culture of poverty. Lewis writes:

> The culture of poverty is a relatively thin culture. . . . It does not provide much support or long-range satisfaction and its encouragement of mistrust tends to magnify helplessness and isolation. Indeed, the poverty of culture is one of the crucial aspects of the culture of poverty.

These observations rest on Lewis's studies of the ghettos of Mexico City and of the Puerto Rican ghettos of San Juan and New York, where the breakdown of traditional peasant cultures has created a distinctive type of culture which comes close to being no culture at all. Something of the same thing has happened to the Negro in the North; and this helps to explain what Frazier meant when he said that the Negro's primary struggle in America had been "to acquire a culture."

This analysis in turn makes it possible to see why nationalist

sects like the Nation of Islam, which have never made much head-
way in the South, find the Northern ghetto a fertile soil; while the
civil rights movement, on the other hand, has become progressively
weaker as the focus of the Negroes' struggle shifts from the South
to the North. The civil rights movement does not address itself to
the question of how Negroes are to acquire a culture, or to the
consequences of their failure to do so. It addresses itself to legal
inequalities. In so far as it implies a cultural program of any kind,
the civil rights strategy proposes to integrate Negroes into the culture which already surrounds them.

Now the real objection to this is not the one so often given by
the advocates of Black Power—that Negroes have nothing to gain
from integrating into a culture dominated by materialist values.
Since most Negroes have already absorbed those values, this is a
frivolous argument—especially so since it seems to imply that there
is something virtuous and ennobling about poverty. What the assimilationist argument does overlook is that the civil rights movement
owes its own existence, in part, to the rise of a Negro subculture
in the South, and that the absence of a comparable culture in the
ghetto changes the whole character of the Negro problem in the
North. American history seems to show that a group cannot achieve
"integration"—that is, equality—without first developing institutions
which express and create a sense of its own distinctiveness. That is
why black nationalism, which attempts to fill the cultural vacuum
of the ghetto, has had a continuing attraction for Negroes, and why,
even during the period of its eclipse in the Thirties, Forties, and
Fifties, nationalism won converts among the most despised and degraded elements of the Negro community in spite of the low repute
in which it was held by Negro leaders.

Nationalist sects like the Black Muslims, the Black Jews, and the
Moorish Temple Science movement speak to the wretchedness of
the ghetto, particularly to the wretchedness of the ghetto male, in
a way that the civil rights movement does not. Thus while the free
and easy sexual life of the ghetto may excite the envy of outsiders,
the Black Muslims correctly see it as a disrupting influence and
preach a strict, "puritanical" sexual ethic. In a society in which
women dominate the family and the church, the Muslims stress the
role of the male as provider and protector. "Protect your women!"
strikes at the heart of the humiliation of the Negro male. Similarly,
the Muslims attack the hedonism of the ghetto. "Stop wasting your
money!" says Elijah Muhammad. ". . . Stop spending money for
tobacco, dope, cigarettes, whiskey, fine clothes, fine automobiles, ex-

pensive rugs and carpets, idleness, sport and gambling. . . . If you must have a car, buy the low-priced car." Those who see in the Black Muslims no more than "the hate that hate produced" mistake the character of this movement, which joins to the mythology of racial glorification a practical program of moral rehabilitation. As Lawrence L. Tyler has noted (*Phylon*, Spring 1966), the Muslim style of life is "both mystical and practical," and it is the combination of the two that "has definitely provided an escape from degradation for lower-class Negroes." If anyone doubts this, he should consider the Muslims' well-documented success in redeeming, where others have failed, drug pushers, addicts, pimps, criminals of every type, the dregs of the slums. In subjecting them to a harsh, uncompromising, and admittedly authoritarian discipline, the Black Muslims and other sects have organized people who have not been organized by non-violence, which presupposes an existing self-respect and a sense of community, or by any other form of Negro politics or religion.

Black Power represents, among other things, a revival of Negro-American nationalism and therefore cannot be regarded simply as a response to recent events. Black Power has secularized the separatist impulse which has usually (though not always) manifested itself in religious forms. Without necessarily abandoning the myth of the Negroes as a chosen people, the new-style nationalists have secularized this myth by identifying the American Negroes—whom many of them continue to regard as in some sense Negroes of the diaspora —not with "the Asian Black Nation and the tribe of Shabazz," as in Black Muslim theology, but with the contemporary struggle against colonialism in the Third World. Where earlier nationalist movements, both secular and religious, envisioned physical separation from America and reunion with Islam or with Africa, many of the younger nationalists propose to fight it out here in America, by revolutionary means if necessary, and to establish—what? a black America? an America in which black people can survive as a separate "nation"? an integrated America?

Here the new-style nationalism begins to reveal underlying ambiguities which make one wonder whether it can properly be called nationalist at all. Older varieties of black nationalism—Garveyism, DuBois's Pan-Africanism, the Nation of Islam—whatever their own ambiguities, consistently sought escape from America, either to Africa, to some part of America which might be set aside for black people, or to some other part of the world. The new-style nationalists, however, view their movement as a revolution against American "colonialism" and thereby embark on a line of analysis which leads to conclusions that are not always consistent with the premise that American Negroes constitute a "nation."

Clearly, the rhetoric of Black Power owes more to Frantz Fanon and to Che Guevara than it owes to Marcus Garvey or DuBois, let alone to Elijah Muhammad. Last August, Stokely Carmichael presented himself to the congress of the Organization of Latin American Solidarity in Havana as a conscious revolutionary. Claiming to speak for the black people of the United States, he is reported to have said:

> We greet you as comrades because it becomes increasingly clear to us each day that we share with you a common struggle; we have a common enemy. Our enemy is white Western imperialist society; our struggle is to overthrow the system which feeds itself and expands itself through the economic and cultural exploitation of non-white, non-Western peoples. We speak with you, comrades, because we wish to make clear that we understand that our destinies are inter-twined.

The advocates of Black Power, it should be noted, do not have a monopoly on this type of rhetoric or on the political analysis, or lack of it, which it implies. The New Left in general more and more identifies itself with Castro, Guevara, Régis Debray, and Ho Chi Minh; many of the new radicals speak of "guerrilla warfare" against "colonialism" at home; and in fact they see the black militants, as the black militants see themselves, as the revolutionary vanguard of violent social change. The congruence of the rhetoric of Black Power with the ideology of the more demented sections of the white Left suggests that Black Power is more than a revival of Negro-American nationalism, just as it is more than a response to the collapse of the civil rights movement in the North. Black Power is itself, in part, a manifestation of the New Left. It shares with the white Left not only the language of romantic anarchism but several other features as well, none of them (it must be said) conducive to its success—a pronounced distrust of people over thirty, a sense of powerlessness and despair, for which the revolutionary rhetoric serves to compensate, and a tendency to substitute rhetoric for political analysis and defiant gestures for political action. Even as they seek to disentangle themselves from the white Left, of which they are understandably contemptuous, black militants continue to share some of its worst features, the very tendencies that may indeed be destroying what strength the New Left, during its brief career, has managed to accumulate. The more these tendencies come to dominate Black Power itself, the gloomier, presumably, will be the outlook for its future.

Because Black Power has many sources, it abounds in contradictions. On the one hand Black Power derives from a tradition of Negro separatism, self-discipline, and self-help, advocating traditional "nationalist" measures ranging from cooperative businesses to proposals for complete separation. On the other hand, some of the spokesmen for Black Power contemplate guerrilla warfare against American "colonialism." In general, CORE is closer to the first position, SNCC to the second. But the ambiguity of Black Power derives from the fact that both positions frequently coexist—as in *Black Power*, the new book by Stokely Carmichael and Charles V. Hamilton, chairman of the political science department at Roosevelt University.

This book is disappointing, first of all because it makes so few concrete proposals for action, and these seem hardly revolutionary in nature: black control of black schools, black-owned businesses, and the like. Carmichael and Hamilton talk vaguely of a "major reorientation of the society" and of "the necessarily total revamping of the society" (expressions they use interchangeably) as the "central goal" of Black Power, and they urge black people not to enter coalitions with groups not similarly committed to sweeping change. But they never explain why their program demands such changes, or indeed why it would be likely to bring them about.

In order to deal with this question, one would have to discuss the relation of the ghetto to the rest of American society. To what extent does American society *depend* on the ghetto? It is undoubtedly true, as the advocates of Black Power maintain, that there is no immediate prospect that the ghettos will disappear. But it is still not clear whether the ghettos in their present state of inferiority and dependence are in some sense necessary for the functioning of American society—that is, whether powerful interests have a stake in perpetuating them—or whether they persist because American society can get along so well without black people that there is no motive either to integrate them by getting rid of the ghettos or to allow the ghettos to govern themselves. In other words, what interests have a stake in maintaining the present state of affairs? Does the welfare of General Motors depend on keeping the ghetto in a state of dependence? Would self-determination for the ghetto threaten General Motors? Carmichael and Hamilton urge black people to force white merchants out of the ghetto and to replace them with black businesses, but it is not clear why this program, aimed at businesses which themselves occupy a marginal place in American corporate capitalism, would demand or lead to a "total revamping of the society."

On this point the critics of Black Power raise what appears to be a telling objection, which can be met only by clarifying the Black Power position beyond anything Carmichael and Hamilton have done here. In a recent article in *Dissent* ("The Pathos of Black Power," January–February 1967), Paul Feldman writes:

> A separatist black economy—unless it were to be no more than a carbon copy of the poverty that already prevails—would need black steel, black automobiles, black refrigerators. And for that, Negroes would have to take control of General Motors and US Steel: hardly an immediate prospect, and utter fantasy as long as Carmichael proposes to "go it alone."

But a related criticism of Black Power, that it merely proposes to substitute for white storekeepers black storekeepers who would then continue to exploit the ghetto in the same ways, seems to me to miss the point, since advocates of Black Power propose to replace white businesses with black *cooperatives*. In this respect Black Power does challenge capitalism, at least in principle; but the question remains whether a program aimed at small businessmen effectively confronts capitalism at any very sensitive point.

Still, small businessmen, whatever their importance outside, are a sensitive issue in the ghetto and getting rid of them might do wonders for Negro morale. Not only that, but Negro cooperatives would help to reduce the flow of capital out of the ghetto, contributing thereby, if only modestly, to the accumulation of capital as well as providing employment. A "separatist black economy" is not really what Black Power seems to point to, any more than it points to exploitive Negro shopkeepers in place of white ones. "In the end," Feldman writes, "the militant-sounding proposals for a build-it-yourself black economy (a black economy, alas, without capital) remind one of . . . precisely those white moderates who preach self-help to the Negroes." But Black Power envisions (or seems to envision) *collective* self-help, which is not the same thing as individualist petty capitalism on the one hand, or, on the other hand, a separate black economy.

Black Power proposes, or seems to propose, that Negroes do for themselves what other ethnic groups, faced with somewhat similar conditions, have done—advance themselves not as individuals but as groups conscious of their own special interests and identity. The Irish advanced themselves by making politics their own special business, the Italians by making a business of crime. In both cases, the regular avenues of individual self-advancement were effectively closed, forcing ethnic minorities to improvise extra-legal institutions —the political machine in the one case, crime syndicates in the other. These were defined as illegitimate and resisted by the rest of society, but they were finally absorbed after protracted struggles. Those who urge Negroes to advance themselves through the regular channels of personal mobility ignore the experience of earlier minorities in America, the relevance of which is obscured both by the tendency to view the history of immigration as a triumph of assimilation and by the individualism which persistently blinds Americans to the importance of collective action, and therefore to most of history.

Carmichael and Hamilton mention the parallel with other ethnic groups, but only in passing, and without noticing that this analogy undermines the analogy with colonial people which they draw at the beginning of the book and wherever else their militant rhetoric appears to demand it. They observe, correctly, that on the evidence of ethnic voting "the American pot has not melted," politically at least, and they recognize that "traditionally, each new ethnic group in this society has found the route to social and political viability through the organization of its own institutions." But they do not explain how this analysis of the Negro's situation squares with the argument that "black people in this country form a colony and it is not in the interest of the colonial power to liberate them."

Quite apart from this inconsistency, the ethnic parallel, whether or not it finally proves useful, needs to be systematically explored. Did the struggles of other minorities contribute to a "major reorientation of the society"? Not if a "major reorientation" is equivalent to the "complete revision" of American institutions, which is the precondition, according to Carmichael and Hamilton, of black liberation. Perhaps the analogy is therefore misleading and should be abandoned. On the other hand, it may be that the special institutions created by other nationalities in America—like Tammany and the Mafia—do in fact represent "major reorientations," even though they fall somewhat short of a "total revamping" or "complete revision" of society. Perhaps it is confusing to think of "major reorientations" as synonymous with "complete revisions," particularly when the nature of the changes proposed remains so indeterminate. In that case it is the colonial analogy that should be dropped, as contributing to the confusion.

Black Power contains many other examples of sloppy analysis and the failure to pursue any line of reasoning through to its consequences. Basic questions are left in doubt. Is the Negro issue a class issue, a race issue, or a "national" (ethnic) issue? Treating it as a class issue—as the authors appear to do when they write that the "only coalition which seems acceptable to us," in the long run, is "a coalition of poor blacks and poor whites"—further weakens the ethnic analogy and blurs the concept of black people as a "nation" —the essential premise, one would think, of "Black Power."

Paul Feldman seems to me on the wrong track when he accuses SNCC of resorting to "what is primarily a racial rather than an economic approach." On the contrary, the advocates of Black Power tend, if anything, toward a class analysis, derived from popularized Marxism or from Castroism, which considers the American Negro as an exploited proletarian. Thus Carmichael and Hamilton try to sustain their analogy of the Negroes as a "colonial" people by arguing that the Negro communities "export" cheap labor. This may be true of the South, where Negroes do represent cheap labor (although mechanization is changing the situation even in the South) and where racism, accordingly, is functionally necessary as a way of maintaining class exploitation. Here the Negroes might be mobilized behind a program of class action designed to change society in fundamental ways.* In the North, however, the essential feature of the Negro's situation is precisely his dispensability, which is increasingly evident in the growing unemployment of Negro men, particularly young men. As Bayard Rustin has pointed out, ghetto Negroes do not constitute an exploited proletariat. They should be regarded not as a working class but as a lower class or *lumpenproletariat*.

> The distinction [he writes] is important. The working class is employed. It has a relation to the production of goods and services; much of it is organized in unions. It enjoys a measure of cohesion, discipline and stability lacking in the lower class. The latter is unemployed or marginally employed. It is relatively unorganized, incohesive, unstable. It contains the petty criminal and antisocial elements. Above all, unlike the working class, it lacks the sense of a stake in society. When the slum proletariat is black, its alienation is even greater.

It is precisely these conditions, however, that make Black Power more relevant to the ghetto than "civil rights," if Black Power is understood as a form of ethnic solidarity which addresses itself to the instability and to the "antisocial" elements of ghetto life, and

---

* This does not mean, however, that Southern Negroes will be receptive to the rhetoric of alienation, which depicts Negroes as a revolutionary vanguard. On the contrary, the Northern radicals at the Conference for New Politics failed to stir the delegates from the Mississippi Freedom Democratic Party with their "easy talk about violence and guerrilla warfare," as Feldman notes in an unpublished report on the conference. The rhetoric of alienation addresses itself not to the actual class situation of the Southern Negro sharecropper or tenant but to the rootlessness and despair of the Northern Negro.

tries to organize and "socialize" those elements around a program of collective self-help. The potential usefulness of black nationalism, in other words, lies in its ability to organize groups which neither the church, the unions, the political parties, nor the social workers have been able to organize. Rustin's analysis, while it effectively refutes the idea that the Negro lower class can become a revolutionary political force in any conventional sense, does not necessarily lead one to reject Black Power altogether, as he does, or to endorse "coalitions." Actually it can be used as an argument *against* coalitions, on the grounds that a marginal lower class has no interests in common with, say, the labor movement. If the Negroes are a lower class as opposed to a working class, it is hard to see, theoretically, why the labor movement is "foremost among [the Negroes'] political allies," as Paul Feldman believes. Theory aside, experience does not bear out this contention.

Concerning the revolutionary potential of Black Power, however, Rustin seems to me absolutely right. "From the revolutionist point of view," he says, "the question is not whether steps could be taken to strengthen organization among the *lumpenproletariat* but whether that group could be a central agent of social transformation. Generally, the answer has been no." But these observations, again, do not necessarily lead to the conclusion that Black Power has no validity. Rather they suggest the need to divorce Black Power as a program of collective self-advancement from the revolutionary rhetoric of the New Left, while at the same time they remind us that other ethnic minorities, faced with somewhat similar conditions, created new institutions that had important (though not revolutionary) social consequences. Negro-Americans cannot be considered a "nation" and a revolutionary *class* at the same time.

Nathan Wright's *Black Power and Urban Unrest* shares with the Carmichael-Hamilton book a tendency to ignore important theoretical questions or to discuss them without sufficient awareness of their implications. Nevertheless, the two books seem to have quite different conceptions of Black Power. As chairman of the Newark conference on Black Power last July, Dr. Wright, an Episcopal clergyman, appeared in the public eye as a militant. But Black Power seems to mean to him little more than the control by Negroes of civil rights organizations like SNCC and CORE (of which he is a long-time member). He does not appear to quarrel with the previous *aims* of those organizations. That is, he does not advocate black separatism, but "desegregation," which he insists should be distinguished from integration. Integration, Wright argues, has come to imply assimilation, which undermines Negro self-respect, thwarts the black man's struggle for "responsible selfhood," and perpetuates his dependence on whites. "Desegregation," on the other hand—"the universal goal," according to Wright, of "all other rising ethnic groups" in America—means that Negroes should have access to the same facilities and the same opportunities as everyone else, without forfeiting their identity as Negroes.

As an abstract proposition, this distinction is reasonably clear, but it is hard to see how it applies to concrete issues like housing and schools. How can "desegregation" in housing be distinguished from "integration"? If "desegregated" housing means anything, it means the disappearance of ethnic neighborhoods (something, incidentally, which has not yet happened in the case of other minorities) and the assimilation of Negroes into white neighborhoods. Similarly, the schools are in any case already "desegregated," in the sense that they try to inculcate black children with white norms and judge them by white standards of achievement.

Some people, Dr. Wright among them, propose to solve this problem by getting more Negroes on school boards. At one point Wright urges Negroes to band together "to seek executive positions in corporations, bishoprics, deanships of cathedrals, superintendencies of schools, and high-management positions in banks, stores, investment houses, legal firms, civic and government agencies, and factories." This is, of course, exactly what many Negroes are doing already, but there is little reason to think that the trickle of middle-class Negroes into executive positions, where they are used as window-dressing, will lead to "a radically new power balance," as Dr. Wright insists. Like Carmichael and Hamilton, he occasionally makes a parallel between Negroes and other ethnic groups, but he does not draw the proper conclusion from their history. Other ethnic groups achieved a larger share of power not by penetrating established institutions but by improvising their own institutions, which gave them political, economic, and cultural leverage as groups. They could not have achieved this leverage as upwardly mobile individuals. Irish Catholics did not win power by getting to be heads of corporations, infiltrating the Republican party, or becoming respectable leaders of municipal reform; they won power by creating the urban political machine.

Dr. Wright further confuses matters by criticizing Negro leaders for not advocating "social equality." He remarks that

> no major civil rights leader, even today, espouses as a major plank in his platform social equality, at the very heart of which is the matter of intermarriage. Yet economic survival and advancement, as well as a

sense of pride, depend in no small degree upon relationships of a blood and legal variety.

These observations seem to me to reveal a misunderstanding of the way in which intermarriage, historically, always tends to erode a sense of ethnic allegiance—which is why it has always been opposed by those wishing to preserve a sense of nationality, including most advocates of Black Power. Nor is the rate of intermarriage a reliable indication of a group's attainment of power, as Dr. Wright's remarks seem to imply. Intermarriage represents the intellectual's longed-for emancipation from what he regards as narrow ethnic prejudices, but the cultural emancipation of intellectuals, which often turns out to be illusory anyway, has nothing to do with the distribution of power in society. As an important social goal, intermarriage is utterly irrelevant.

By repudiating their white supporters, the advocates of Black Power have sent a moral shock through the liberal community, which two white veterans of the civil rights movement in different ways record. Charles E. Fager, a Northern radical and the younger of the two, has adjusted to the trauma of Black Power, and now defends it not only as an appropriate strategy for black people but as a strategy which makes clearer than before the kind of measures white radicals should take toward reorganizing their own communities. Fred Powledge, a Southerner and free-lance journalist who was formerly a reporter for *The New York Times,* sympathetically observed the civil rights movement in the South at first hand. He deplores the rise of black separatism, which he is convinced "will not work."

By separatism Powledge means "the construction of parallel societies, black and white." This is "impossible," he thinks, because "black institutions, built alongside existing white ones, would be poverty-stricken by comparison." Moreover, separatist "demagogues" would have to use violence "as an organizing tool" in order to keep the black community in line; and if that happened, "the white majority would respond with near-genocide." Integration, on the other hand, does not necessarily mean assimilation. In fact Powledge thinks that it is "essential" for the civil rights movement to "stamp out the idea, held so long by so many white liberals who did not even know that they held it, that integration consists of turning 'them' white."

Powledge's position resembles Nathan Wright's. Both writers advocate integration or desegregation—that is, equal rights and equal opportunities—while opposing assimilation on the one hand and black separatism on the other. If Black Power means that Negroes should not straighten their hair in order to win illusory acceptance by whites, then both Powledge and Wright support it. Nor does Powledge deny that, within the civil rights movement, Negroes should "run the show." When he urges whites to restrict themselves to contributing their special skills to a movement led largely by Negroes, he agrees not only with Wright, but with Carmichael and Hamilton, who believe that white people are most effective in "supportive" roles. Since neither Wright nor Carmichael and Hamilton advocate the conception of black separatism which Powledge attacks, one begins to wonder whether the whole controversy about Black Power doesn't boil down to a dispute about certain words. Everybody, it seems, supports Black Power and, at the same time, favors "integration."

But as Stokely Carmichael pointed out in an interview in *The Militant* (May 23, 1966), "You can *integrate communities,* but you *assimilate individuals.*" Until black people become a community, in Carmichael's view, efforts to integrate them necessarily imply assimilation. Here is the irreducible difference between the integrationist and Black Power positions. Fager's book helps to clarify the debate. Without indulging in the liberal-baiting that so often accompanies discussions of Black Power, he challenges integrationists to demonstrate why "integration" does not work out in practice to mean assimilation, whereby a few middle-class Negroes are provisionally admitted to white society, leaving the others behind in the ghetto as unassimilable. According to Fager, this is certainly the way things have worked out so far. If more money were spent on education and welfare programs, he argues, the rate of mobility could be speeded up, but it is unlikely that the ghettos could be completely eradicated—not for a long time, anyway, and in the meantime more assimilation at the top will merely add to the hatreds and frustrations at the bottom of Negro society.

Whereas Bayard Rustin and others argue that Negroes cannot hope to win equality except in coalition with other groups, Fager believes, as do other advocates of Black Power, that at the present time the black community is not cohesive enough to enter into coalitions without being swallowed up. As a white radical who until recently worked in the civil rights coalition, he is left with the question of where next to turn his energies. He tries to show that Black Power demands of white liberals a parallel strategy, based on the premise that the "liberal community," like the Negro community, "does not control the institutions around and through which its life is organized and controlled." Each of these communities must therefore develop "an economic base which it can control, which can support the community substantially, and which can confront other power groups as equals." Young radicals should "go back to school" and acquire the skills necessary to run parallel and competing institutions which will free the "liberal community" from its dependence on established structures; while the older radicals should "figure out how to withdraw their money and abilities as much as possible from status quo institutions and rechannel the *bulk* of them into the development and support of independent-base institutions."

Unfortunately these suggestions are exceedingly vague, although they are not much more vague than the strategy of Black Power itself. Fager's effort to translate Black Power into its white equivalent unintentionally reveals the poverty of Black Power as a political strategy. For while a program of collective self-help seems closer than civil rights solutions to the psychological and even to the economic needs of the ghetto, the advocates of Black Power have not been able to explain what such a program means in practice or what kind of strategy would be necessary to achieve it. This is probably why they spend so much time talking not about politics but about therapy. By detaching Black Power from its context—the psychic and spiritual malaise of the ghetto, which Black Power, like other versions of black nationalism, is designed to cure—Fager makes clear what we had already begun to suspect, that Black Power not only contains no political ideas that are applicable elsewhere, it contains very few political ideas at all. As a program of spiritual regeneration, it offers hope to people whom the civil rights movement ignores or does not touch; though, even here, Black Power may prove to be less successful than the religious versions of black nationalism, since it can appeal neither to the mystic brotherhood nor to the authoritarian discipline of the Black Muslims. As a political program, Black Power does not explain how Negro cooperatives are to come into being or what they will use for money, how the ghettos are to control and pay for their own schools, or why, even if these programs were successful, they would lead to sweeping changes in American society as a whole.

Are the proponents of Black Power capable of formulating a workable strategy? Are they even interested in formulating a strategy? Although Black Power does address itself to certain problems of the ghetto which other approaches ignore, one cannot even say with confidence that the emergence of Black Power is a hopeful sign, which, if nothing else, will teach black people to stop hating their own blackness. If it merely teaches them to hate whiteness instead, it will contribute to the nihilistic emotions building up in the ghetto, and thus help to bring about the race war which spokesmen for Black Power, until recently at least, claimed they were trying to prevent. In so far as Black Power represents an effort to discipline the anger of the ghettos and to direct this anger toward radical action, it works against the resentment and despair of the ghetto, which may never-theless overwhelm it. But Black Power is not only an attack on this despair, it is also, in part, its product, and reflects forces which it cannot control.

In the last few months, we have seen more and more vivid exam-ples of the way in which Black Power has come to be associated with mindless violence—as in the recent disturbances at San Francisco State College—and with a "revolutionary" rhetoric that conceals a growing uncertainty of purpose. It becomes increasingly clear that many of the intellectuals who talk of Black Power do not understand the difference between riots and revolution, and that they have no program capable of controlling the growing violence of the ghetto. It is also becoming clear that in fact they have not only given up the effort to control violence or even to understand it, but are themselves making a cult of violence, and by doing so are abdicating leadership of their own movement. Meanwhile white radicals, who supposedly know better but are just as foolish and patronizing about Black Power as they were about civil rights, applaud from the sidelines or, as at San Francisco State, join the destruction, without perceiving that it is radicalism itself that is being destroyed.

The nihilistic tendencies latent in Black Power have been identi-fied and analyzed not only by the advocates of "liberal" coalitions. The most penetrating study of these tendencies is to be found in Harold Cruse's *The Crisis of the Negro Intellectual*, which is also an analysis of integration and a defense of black nationalism. Cruse is a radical, but his book gives no comfort to the "radicalism" currently fashionable. It deals with real issues, not leftist fantasies. Cruse under-stands that radicals need clarity more than they need revolutionary purity, and he refuses to be taken in by loud exclamations of mili-tancy which conceal an essential flabbiness of purpose. At a time when Negro intellectuals are expected to show their devotion to the cause by acting out a ritual and expatiatory return to the dress and manners of their "people"—when intellectuals of all nationalities are held to be the very symbol of futility, and when even a respected journalist like Andrew Kopkind can write that "the responsibility of the intellectual is the same as that of the street organizer, the draft resister, the Digger: to talk *to* people, not *about* them"—Cruse feels no need to apologize for the intellectual's work, which is to clarify

issues. It is because Negro intellectuals have almost uniformly failed
in this work that he judges them, at his angriest and most impatient,
a "colossal fraud"—a judgment that applies without much modification to white intellectuals, now as in the recent past.

The Crisis of the Negro Intellectual is a history of the Negro Left
since the First World War. When all the manifestoes and polemics
of the Sixties are forgotten, this book will survive as a monument of
historical analysis—a notable contribution to the understanding of
the American past, but more than that, a vindication of historical
analysis as the best way, maybe the only way, of gaining a clear
understanding of social issues.

As a historian, an intellectual, a Negro, and, above all, perhaps,
as a man who came of political age in the 1940s, Cruse sees more
clearly than the young black nationalists of the Sixties how easily
Negro radicals—integrationists and nationalists alike—become "dis-
oriented prisoners of white leftists, no matter how militant they
sound." Instead of devising strategies appropriate to the special situation of American Negroes, they import ideologies which have no
relevance to that situation and which subordinate the needs of American Negroes to an abstract model of revolutionary change. Marxism
is such a model, and a considerable portion of Cruse's book elaborates
and documents the thesis that American Marxism has disastrously
misled Negro intellectuals over a period of fifty years.

But the ideology of guerrilla warfare, which in some Black Power
circles has replaced Marxism as the current mode, equally ignores
American realities. According to Cruse,

> The black ghettoes are in dire need of new organizations or parties of
> a political nature, yet it is a fact that most of the leading young na-
> tionalist spokesmen are apolitical. . . . The black ghettoes are in even
> more dire need of every possible kind of economic and self-help or-
> ganization, and a buyers and consumers council, but the most militant
> young nationalists openly ridicule such efforts as reformist and a waste
> of time. For them politics and economics are most unrevolutionary.
> What they do consider revolutionary are Watts-type uprisings—which
> lead nowhere.

Black Power—with or without the guerrilla rhetoric—is a "strategic retreat." "It proposes to change, not the white world outside,
but the black world inside, by reforming it into something else politically or economically." The Muslims, Cruse points out, have "already
achieved this in a limited way, substituting religion for politics"; and
Malcolm X (whom the advocates of Black Power now list as one of
their patron saints) quit the Black Muslims precisely because "this
type of Black Power lacked a dynamic, was static and aloof to the
broad struggle." By emphasizing "Psychological Warfare" as "Phase

1" of Black Power, as one of the new nationalists puts it, the advocates of Black Power have placed themselves "almost in the lap of the Nation of Islam." Moreover, they have reversed the proper order of priorities, according to Cruse, for "psychological equality" must be the product, not the precondition, of cultural regeneration and political power.

He thinks that integrationists, on the other hand, while they may have addressed themselves to the "broad struggle," conceive of the struggle in the wrong terms. They waste their strength fighting prejudice, when they ought to be organizing the ghetto so that it could exert more influence, say, over the use of anti-poverty funds. Instead of trying to change the Constitution in order to make it "reflect the social reality of America as a nation of nations, or a nation of ethnic groups," even advocates of violence like Robert Williams propose merely to "implement" the Constitution, with, in Williams's words, "justice and equality for all people." Cruse accuses integrationists of being taken in by the dominant mythology of American individualism and of failing to see the importance of collective action along ethnic lines, or—even worse—of mistakenly conceiving collective action in class terms which are irrelevant to the Negro's situation in America.

Cruse himself is a Marxist—that is, a historical materialist. But he opposes the obstinate effort to impose on the Negro problem a class analysis which sees Negroes as an oppressed proletariat. He thinks this obscures, among other things, the nature of the Negro middle class and the role it plays in American life. Actually "middle class" is a misnomer, because this class is not a real bourgeoisie. The most important thing about it is that "Negro businessmen must depend on the Negro group for their support," which according to Cruse means two things: Negro businessmen are more closely tied to the Negro nation than to their white middle-class counterparts, no matter how hard they may struggle against this identification; and they occupy a marginal position in American capitalism as a whole, since black capitalism can only function in limited areas—personal services to the Negro community, such as barbershops, insurance companies, etc.—which white capitalism does not choose to enter.

Because of its marginal position, the black bourgeoisie does not have the resources to support Negro institutions—a theater, for instance—which might help to give the Negro community some consciousness of itself. Negro intellectuals thus depend on white intellectuals—or white foundations—as much as Negro maids depend on white housewives, even though the intellectual world, according to Cruse, is the only realm in which genuine integration has taken place or is likely to take place. Even there, Negroes have been forced to compete at a disadvantage. They have had to regard their white counterparts not only as colleagues but as patrons. Hence the dominance of Jews in the Negro-Jewish coalition that has been characteristic of American Marxist movements.

The effort to explain how this coalition emerged and what it did to Negro radicalism occupies the better part of *The Crisis of the Negro Intellectual.* The history of the Negro intellectual from the 1920s to the present necessarily becomes a history of American Marxism as well. Cruse begins with the "Harlem renaissance," when Marcus Garvey's version of black nationalism was only one of many signs of cultural and political awakening among American Negroes, and he shows, step by step, how Negro intellectuals retreated from these promising beginnings and began to preach culturally sterile and politically futile doctrines of proletarian uplift. Thus in the Twenties and Thirties Negro intellectuals lent themselves to the Communists' efforts to convince Moscow that American Negroes could become the spearhead of a proletarian revolution. A delegation of Negro Communists in Moscow claimed in 1922 that "in five years we will have the American revolution"—just as Stokely Carmichael now carries a similar message to Havana. "I listened to the American delegates deliberately telling lies about conditions in America," wrote the poet Claude McKay, "and I was disgusted."

Thirty-eight years later Harold Cruse found himself in a somewhat similar position in Castro's Cuba, where he had gone with LeRoi Jones and other Americans "to 'see for ourselves' what it was all about." "The ideology of a new revolutionary wave in the world at large had lifted us out of the anonymity of the lonely struggle in the United States to the glorified rank of visiting dignitaries. . . . Nothing in our American experience had ever been as arduous and exhausting as this journey. Our reward was the prize of revolutionary protocol that favored those victims of capitalism away from home." But in the midst of this "ideological enchantment," none of the delegates bothered to ask: *"What did it all mean and how did it relate to the Negro in America?"*

The new-wave Negro militants, like their forerunners of the 1930s, "have taken on a radical veneer without radical substance" and have formulated "no comprehensive radical philosophy to replace either the liberalism they denounce or the radicalism of the past that bred them." In a chapter on "The Intellectuals and Force and Violence"— in some ways the most important chapter in the book—Cruse examines a notable instance of the prevailing confusion among Negro radicals (shared by white radicals): the cult of "armed self-defense" as a form of revolutionary action. Robert Williams, an officer of the NAACP, raised the issue of self-defense in Monroe, North Carolina, in 1959, when he armed his followers against the Ku Klux Klan. In the uproar following the NAACP's suspension of Williams and his deification by the new black Left, basic questions went unanswered. For one thing, violence in the South, where it is directed against the Klan, has been strategically different from violence in the North, where it has been directed against the National Guard. For another, the issue of armed self-defense does not touch the deep-rooted conditions that have to be changed if the Negro's position is to be changed. Violence, Cruse argues, becomes a meaningful strategy only in so far as American institutions resist radical change and resist it violently. Since the Negro movement has not yet even formulated a program for radical change, violence is tactically premature; and, in any case, "the *main* front of tactics must always be organizational and institutional."

Neither the black Left nor the white Left, however, understands that an American revolution (even if it were imminent, which it isn't) "would have very little in common with the foreign revolutions they have read about." Lacking a theory, lacking any understanding of history, confusing violent protest with radicalism, black radicals persist in yet another mistake—the equation of pro-blackness with hatred of whites. Violent hatred fills the vacuum left by the lack of an ideology and a program. Long before the new radicals came on the scene, Cruse writes, "this had been one of the Negro intellectual's most severe 'hang-ups' "—one that in our own time threatens to become the driving force of the Negro movement. "This situation results from a psychology that is rooted in the Negro's symbiotic 'blood-ties' to the white Anglo-Saxon. It is the culmination of that racial drama of love and hate between slave and master, bound together in the purgatory of plantations." The self-advancement of the Negro community, however, cannot rest on ambivalent hatreds. "All race hate is self-defeating in the long run because it distorts the critical faculties."

The complexity and richness of *The Crisis of the Negro Intellectual* is difficult to convey in a review. The book documents not only the failure of Negro radicalism but the failure of American radicalism in general, which lives off imported ideologies and myths of imminent revolution in which Negroes have always been assigned a leading part. Reading this book today, in the wake of such disasters as the Conference for New Politics, one realizes how little has changed, and how, in spite of its determination to avoid the mistakes of the radicals of the Thirties and Forties, the New Left remains trapped in the rhetoric and postures of its predecessors. The Left today should be concerned not only with the long-range problem of creating new institutions of popular democracy (a subject to which it has given very little thought) but with the immediate problem of saving what remains of liberalism—free speech, safeguards against arbitrary authority, separation of powers—without which further democratic experiments of any kind will come to an end.

The Left should take seriously the possibility which it rhetorically proclaims—that the crisis of American colonialism abroad, together with the failure of welfare programs to improve conditions in the ghetto, will generate a demand for thoroughgoing repression which, if it succeeded, would seal the fate of liberals and radicals alike. But instead of confronting the present crisis, the Left still babbles of revolution and looks to the Negroes, as before, to deliver the country from its capitalist oppressors. "We are just a little tail on the end of a very powerful black panther," says one of the delegates to the Conference for New Politics. "And I want to be on that tail—if they'll let me." In the next breath he urges white radicals to "trust the blacks the way you trust children."

In this atmosphere, Harold Cruse's book, quite apart from its intrinsic and enduring merits, might do much immediate good. It might help to recall American radicals to their senses (those that ever had any). Perhaps it is too late even for intelligent radicals to accomplish anything. *The Crisis of the Negro Intellectual* exposes the mistakes of the past at a time when the accumulated weight of those mistakes has become so crushing that it may be too late to profit from the lesson. Crises overlap crises. The defeat of liberal colonialism in Vietnam coincides with the defeat of liberalism in the ghetto, and the deterioration of the ghetto coincides with the deterioration of the city as a whole: the flight of industry and jobs from the city, the withdrawal of the middle class, the decay of public transportation and schools, the decay of public facilities in general, the pollution of the water, the pollution of the air.

In the 1930s an alarming crisis stirred enlightened conservatives like Franklin Roosevelt to measures which palliated the immediate effects of the crisis and thereby averted a general breakdown of the system. By throwing its support at a decisive moment behind the CIO, the New Deal made possible the organization of elements which, unorganized, threatened to become an immensely violent and disruptive force. One might imagine that the still graver crisis of the Sixties might lead conservatives to consider a similar approach to the more moderate black nationalists. Indeed some gestures have recently been made in this direction. But given the total lack of national political leadership at the present time, and given the decay of the city, the kind of "solution" which will seem increasingly attractive to many Americans is a solution that would merely carry existing historical trends to their logical culmination: abandon the cities completely, put up walls around them, and use them as Negro reservations. This could even be done under the cloak of Black Power—"self-determination for the ghetto." On their reservations, black people would be encouraged to cultivate their native handicrafts, songs, dances, and festivals. Tourists would go there, bringing in a little loose change. In American history there are precedents for such "solutions."

Not only have things reached the point where any program of radical reform may be inadequate, it is still not clear whether even Cruse's version of black nationalism, as it stands, points the way to such a program. That the book itself offers no program is not an objection—although the objection applies, it seems to me, to Carmichael and Hamilton's *Black Power* which claims to present "a political framework and ideology which represents the last reasonable opportunity for this society to work out its racial problems short of prolonged destructive guerrilla warfare." Cruse does not pretend to offer a "political framework"; his book attempts to clarify underlying issues. The question is whether his analysis clarifies those issues or obscures them.

That it clears up a great deal of confusion should already be evident. Certain questions, however, remain. One concerns the slippery concept of "nationalism," which may not be the best idea around which to organize a movement of Negro liberation. Cruse does not seem to me to confront the possibility that black nationalism, which he realizes has always been flawed by its "romantic and escapist" tendencies, may be *inherently* romantic and escapist—now looking wistfully back to Africa, now indulging in fantasies of global revolution. The analysis of American Negroes as an ethnic group should properly include a study of the role of other nationalist ideologies, like Zionism or Irish-American nationalism, in order to discover whether they played any important part in the successful efforts of those communities to organize themselves. From what I have been able to learn, Irish-American nationalism focused almost exclusively on Ireland and contributed nothing important to the political successes of the Irish in America. (See Thomas N. Brown, *Irish-American Nationalism.*) A study of other ethnic nationalisms might show the same thing. It is possible, in other words, that nationalist movements in America, even when they cease to be merely fraternal and convivial and actually involve themselves in the revolutionary politics of the homeland (as was true of some Irish-American movements), have had no practical bearing on ethnic group politics in America itself. In that case, nationalism may not serve Negroes as a particularly useful guide to political action, although it is clear that the Negroes' situation demands some sort of action along ethnic lines.

Even as a means of cultural regeneration, nationalism may be too narrowly based to achieve what Cruse wants it to achieve. Black nationalist movements in the United States are largely movements of young men—of all groups, the one least able to develop values that can be passed on to the next generation. According to C. Eric Lincoln's study of the Black Muslims, "up to 80 per cent of a typical congregation is between the ages of seventeen and thirty-five"; moreover, "the Muslim temples attract many more men than women, and men assume the full management of temple affairs." Frazier remarks, in another connection, "Young males, it will be readily agreed, are poor bearers of the cultural heritage of a people." Of course there is no reason, in theory, why black nationalism should remain a young man's movement. The chief exponents of Negro-American nationalism or of a point of view that could be called nationalist—Booker T. Washington, Garvey, and DuBois (when he was not swinging to the opposite pole of integration)—were themselves men of years and experience.

But historically the nationalist ideology has owed much of its appeal to the need of the young Negro male to escape from the stifling embrace of the feminine-centered family and church. The assertion of masculinity so obviously underlies the present manifestations of black nationalism that it is difficult, at times, to distinguish nationalist movements from neighborhood gangs. It is easy to see why black nationalism might be associated with riots, especially as nationalism becomes increasingly secularized and loses its capacity to instill inner discipline; but can it produce a culture capable of unifying the black community around values distinct from and superior to those of American society as a whole?

There is the further problem of what Cruse means by "culture." Sometimes he uses the word in its broad sense, sometimes narrowly, as when he asks Negro intellectuals to follow the lead of C. Wright Mills by formulating a theory of "cultural radicalism." In modern society, Cruse argues, "mass cultural communications is a basic industry," and "only the blind cannot see that whoever controls the cultural apparatus . . . also controls the destiny of the United States and everything in it." This statement is open to a number of objections; but quite apart from that, it is not clear what it has to do with what Frazier called the Negro's "primary struggle"—to acquire a "culture" much more basic than the kind of culture Mills and Cruse, in this passage, have in mind. How are Negroes to get control of the "cultural apparatus" until they have solved their more immediate difficulties? And how would their efforts to control the culture industry differ from the efforts of Lorraine Hansberry and Sydney Poitier, whom Cruse criticizes on the grounds that their personal triumphs on

Broadway and in Hollywood did nothing to advance Negro "culture"?

These questions aside, Cruse leaves no doubt of the validity of his main thesis: that intellectuals must play a central role in movements for radical change, that this role should consist of formulating "a new political philosophy," and that in twentieth-century American history they have failed in this work. They must now address themselves to a more systematic analysis of American society than they have attempted before, building on the social theory of the nineteenth century but scrapping those parts that no longer apply. This analysis will have to explain, among other things, how the situation of the Negro in America relates to the rest of American history—a problem on which Cruse has now made an impressive assault, without however solving the dilemma posed by W. E. B. DuBois: "There faces the American Negro . . . an intricate and subtle problem of combining into one object two difficult sets of facts"—he is both a Negro and an American at the same time. The failure to grasp this point, according to Cruse, has prevented both integrationists and nationalists from "synthesizing composite trends." The pendulum swings back and forth between nationalism and integrationism, but as with so many discussions among American intellectuals, the discussion never seems to progress to a higher level of analysis. Today, riots, armed self-defense, conflicts over control of ghetto schools, efforts of CORE to move Negroes into cooperative communities in the South, and other uncoordinated actions, signify a reawakening of something that can loosely be called nationalism; but they express not a new synthesis but varying degrees of disenchantment with integration. The advocates of Black Power have so far failed to show why their brand of nationalism comes any closer than its predecessors to providing a long-range strategy not for escaping from America but for changing it. The dilemma remains: more than ever it needs to become the object of critical analysis.

In the meantime, will events wait for analysis? Immediate crises confront us, and there is no time, it seems, for long-range solutions, no time for reflection. Should we all take to the streets, then, as Andrew Kopkind recommends? In critical times militancy may appear to be the only authentic politics. But the very gravity of the crisis makes it all the more imperative that radicals try to formulate at least a provisional theory which will serve them as a guide to tactics in the immediate future as well as to long-range questions of strategy. Without such a perspective, militancy will carry the day by default; then, quickly exhausting itself, it will give way to another cycle of disillusionment, cynicism, and hopelessness.

This essay begins with the author's now-famous "recipe for violence" ("Promise a lot; deliver a little. . .") concerning piecemeal programming to solve the racial situation.

Offering several theoretical explanations for recent rebellious behavior on the part of blacks, Wildavsky goes on to discuss ways of altering the structure that maintains two societies in this country. He suggests that even radically new policies regarding incomes, education, and community power will take time to make significant differences. In the meantime, says Wildavsky, white Americans will have to come to grips with a new reality: "The old truth may have been that blacks were invisible men for whites. The new truth [to blacks] is that whites are invisible because they all look alike."

15

Aaron Wildavsky

BLACK REBELLION AND
WHITE REACTION

Liberals have been moaning those empty-head blues. They feel bad. They know the sky is about to fall in. But they can't think of anything to do. Having been too sanguine and too self-righteous about their part in the civil rights movement, they are too easily prey to despair when their contribution is rejected by those they presumed to help. Torn between a nagging guilt and a secret desire to turn on their black tormentors, white liberals have become spectators watching with frozen horror as their integrationist ideals and favorite public programs disintegrate amidst violent black rebellion. How did this maddening situation come about? What can be done about it?

From Aaron Wildavsky, "The Empty-Head Blues: Black Rebellion and White Reaction," *The Public Interest*, 11 (Spring 1968), 3–16. © 1968 by National Affairs, Inc.

How to Enrage Whites Without Helping Blacks

A recipe for violence: Promise a lot; deliver a little. Lead people to believe they will be much better off, but let there be no dramatic improvement. Try a variety of small programs, each interesting but marginal in impact and severely underfinanced. Avoid any attempted solution remotely comparable in size to the dimensions of the problem you are trying to solve. Have middle-class civil servants hire upper-class student radicals to use lower-class Negroes as a battering ram against the existing local political systems; then complain that people are going around disrupting things and chastize local politicians for not cooperating with those out to do them in. Get some poor people involved in local decision-making, only to discover that there is not enough at stake to be worth bothering about. Feel guilty about what has happened to black people; tell them you are surprised they have not revolted before; express shock and dismay when they follow your advice. Go in for a little force, just enough to anger, not enough to discourage. Feel guilty again; say you are surprised that worse has not happened. Alternate with a little suppression. Mix well, apply a match, and run. . . .

The dilemma of liberal politicians is exquisite. Now they play only "minus-sum" games in which every player leaves the contest worse off than when he entered. The first rule is to get yourself hooked on purely symbolic issues. This guarantees that if you fail to get your policy adopted you are revealed as impotent and useless to the deprived. If you win your policy objective, you are even worse off because it is soon clear that nothing has changed. A typical game played under this rule is called "Civilian Police Review Board." The objective is to force a racist response from the voters who are fearful of their safety on subways and in the streets. The game begins with a publicity campaign focusing on fascist police, various atrocities, and other lurid events. The police and their friends counter with an equally illuminating defense: nothing is wrong that a little get-tough campaign would not cure. The game ends with a ballot in which white voters are asked to choose between their friendly neighborhood policeman and the specter of black violence. The usual result is that the whites vote for the police and defeat the review board. If a review board is created, however, it soon becomes apparent that a few judgments against policemen have no effect on the critical problem of securing adequate protection for Negroes. But the game is a perfect loser: everyone's feelings are exacerbated and the conflict continues at a new height of hostility.

There are many similar games. In Milwaukee, for example, wave after wave of Negro demonstrators cry out for a fair housing ordinance. The certain result is that whites are made furious. The sad thing is that, if the punitive marches succeed in their immediate goal, only a handful of Negroes at most will be helped. Or consider the drive to achieve school integration by bussing children to different parts of the city. If such integration is accompanied by huge efforts to create equality of educational achievement among black and white, all praise is due. But if black children continue to read poorly, race hatred may well increase. Black radicals will then be certain to condemn the liberal integrationists who have again left them and their children holding an empty bag.

The liberal politician is damned if he does and damned if he doesn't. He breaks his back to get two historic civil rights acts passed only to find himself accused of coming in too little and too late. The rat control bill is a perfect example of the classic bind. When Congress originally failed to pass the bill, it was made into a bitter example of inhumanity. Yet it can safely be said that had the bill sailed through Congress it would also have joined the list of those liberal measures that are not good enough to do the job. Too little and too late. How much all this is like Groucho Marx's famous crack that any country club willing to have him as a member wasn't exclusive enough for him to join.

We have learned some hard lessons. Every time we try to deal with problems of race we end up with symbolic gestures that infuriate everyone and please no one. Why? The American dilemma is a compound of racism suffused with class differences. Since America appears to be richer in economic resources than in brotherly love, it would be natural to tackle economic problems first. Few of us expect a quick solution to the lesser problems posed by large class differences among white people. None is surprised that upper-class whites do not integrate with their lower-class racial cohorts. Yet we persist in following policies that attack racism before economic equality has begun to be established. The result is that neither poverty nor racism is diminished.

Disheartened by the magnitude of the change required in racial behavior, unwilling to recognize the full extent of the resources required to improve economic conditions, we are tempted to try a lot of small programs that create an illusion of activity, ferment, and change. But nothing much happens. Confusion is rampant because it looks to some (mostly white) like so much is being done, and to others (mostly black) that nothing is happening. Hence the rival accusations of black ingratitude and white indifference. It is apparent that we should abandon symbolic policies that anger whites and do not help blacks and should concentrate instead on programs that will materially increase the well-being of poor people in the United States. Programs should be large rather than small, and provide tangible benefits to many citizens, not symbolic rewards for a few.

Income and Education

The most compelling need is for a fast and vast job program designed to virtually end unemployment among Negroes. The best alternative would be a superheated economy in which jobs searched for people and employers served their own interests by training any available man. Inflation would be a problem, but one of much lesser magnitude than present dilemmas. The next best alternative would be large government subsidies to finance decent jobs with futures, again leaving training to employers and motivation to indigenous groups and the near-universal desire for legitimate gain. Nothing else is possible until we end high rates of unemployment.

But any program designed to improve the longer-range prospects of the disadvantaged would also have to involve a fundamental change in elementary education. There are many things we do not know about improving education. But we do know that the child who reads well can do most anything, and the child who cannot is lost. If you are fourteen and cannot read, you know there is no future for you in ordinary American life. Following the principle of "bottleneck" planning (i.e., concentrating every effort on the most critical resources), one might abolish all subjects in the curriculum except reading and a little mathematics. Every six months there would be examinations in reading, and teachers whose classes fell behind would be held to account. Principals would be promoted on the basis of the accomplishment of their students in reading. Although family conditions may overwhelm all other factors in ability to learn, as the Coleman report suggests, this is a conclusion to which we should be driven only after making the absolute maximum effort to get every child to read.

Would these employment, income, and education policies stop black rebellions? * That is bound to be the question. Alas, it is a

---

* One has to be careful not to commit semantic aggression. The word "riot" is too aimless to apply to a phenomenon that is national in scope and that is clearly directed at expressing rage against the conditions of life of black people. To use "revolt," however, would suggest far more leadership, organization, and concerted action than appears to have been the case. So we are left with "rebellion," an appropriate word to designate violence by people who wish to express their hostility toward prevailing conditions but who are not yet organized to attack the larger society.

mean-spirited question because it deflects attention from human needs. But it will raise itself insistently, so we had better attend to it, especially if (as I believe) rebellions are bound to increase for a time. Let us assess the adequacy of these remedies by evaluating them in the context of theories of racial rebellion.

Reward and Blackmail Theories

We are everywhere confronted with exceedingly primitive notions of the causes of racial disturbances. According to one popular model, rebellions are caused by giving rewards to the people who engage in these activities. The reward theory posits ever-increasing violence in response to the hope of getting ever-increasing rewards. This vulgarized version of learning theory (Christians call it sinning to abound in grace) suggests that outbursts will continue so long as Negroes are rewarded by governmental policies designed to improve their conditions. Would it be true, then, that the less that is done for Negroes, the less the probability of racial rebellion? What will we do when at all future moments we will be looking back at past rebellions, passing through present rebellions, and anticipating future rebellions?

Another currently held model suggests that white people help black people only because black people rebel. Blackmail is an appropriate designation for this theory. Rebellions by blacks cause whites to provide rewards; these rewards presumably lead to a reduction in hostility. But, on this theory, a decrease in hostility inevitably leads to a lesser willingness by whites to give rewards to blacks. Hence there will be more riots.

Obviously, if one begins by assuming a connection between riots and rewards, one can only conclude that riots cause rewards or rewards cause riots. Disaster is predicted if help is given and doom if it is not. Perhaps a slightly more complex analysis would be helpful.

The Theory of Relative Deprivation

America is a country to which people who were worse off have come to be better off. And so it has proved to be for most of us. But not for Negroes. Not in slavery and not afterward. The southern system of slavery so effectively cut off Negroes from former home, family, and culture that comparisons with the past which sustained so many others against the initial adversity of life in America became meaningless. Being better off than in slavery hardly recommends itself to anyone as a criterion of judgment. For better or worse, black men

have been born anew in America. Negroes can only compare their
positions to their recent past or to others in America. They have evi-
dently chosen to be Americans if they can. That is our common hope.
But it can also be our despair because it is so difficult to satisfy people whose standard of comparison is the richest segment of the richest nation on earth.

Imagine that our fondest dreams were realized: we had secured
virtually full employment and higher income for Negroes as well as
other Americans. There would certainly be an improvement in the
Negro condition. But there would also be an increase in "relative
deprivation." The higher starting point for other Americans would
guarantee that result. The arithmetic is as follows:

Assume that Negroes make $4,000 a year and that other Americans
they compare themselves with make $10,000 a year. If whites in-
creased their income 5 per cent a year, Negroes would have to gain
an incredible 15 per cent a year in order to gain equality of income
in ten years. If we take the more reasonable assumption about the
best that could happen—a 10 per cent increase per year for Negroes
and a 5 per cent for others—the absolute difference in income would
actually continue to increase for the first decade! So, if rebellions
are caused in part by relative deprivation—by resentment at inequality—there will be more rebellions.

Now take education. The most optimistic assumption about education would be that the gap between whites and blacks would narrow dramatically in ten or twenty years and not sooner. While the
quality of education might improve significantly and quickly if we
are very lucky, the benefits would take time to manifest themselves.
Moreover, higher educational achievement, while desirable in itself,
would likely lead to still higher aspirations. Ergo: things will get
worse before they get better.

Job, income, and education policies may be necessary to stop
rebellions in the future but they will not suffice to halt them now.
Before accepting this melancholy conclusion as the final sentence on
our racial crimes, let us see if a closer look at black rebellion will
not suggest to us additional remedies.

The Anger-Plus-Opportunity Theory

The most straightforward explanation of riotous behavior is that
the violence is a combination of anger and opportunity. That whites
have long despised Negroes is no secret. That Negroes suffer numerous indignities on account of their color is all too evident. When

extraordinary levels of unemployment (running as high as 30 per cent for black youth) are added to these daily causes of resentment, it is no wonder that many Negroes feel enraged. But it is one thing to feel mad and angry and another to feel safe enough to act out those feelings. The relative lack of black violence in the South may be partly attributed to the well-founded fear by Negroes that severe retribution will be visited upon them. Just as soon as Negro strength increased sufficiently in Northern cities and whites became troubled about brutal retaliation, it became safer for Negroes to act on violent feelings. The faint stirrings of white conscience may have had the paradoxical effect of legitimizing black violence without simultaneously leading to actions that dramatically alleviated oppressive conditions.*

To the degree that this overly simple theory is correct, it also helps explain the essential perversity of the racial situation. The theory implies that one way of mitigating violence would be to reduce the pattern of injustice that gives rise to feelings of rage. So far, so good. But recognition of the problem and mobilizing political support to begin to act require widespread dissemination of information on just how bad things were and continue to be. The message to Negroes is that they have been and are being treated badly. There cannot help but be the suggestion that Negroes are justified in taking strong actions to improve their position. There are bound to be white people whose guilt disarms them when faced with destructive acts. Thus the laudatory efforts to reduce the desire of Negroes to act violently actually increases their opportunities for using force without the corresponding expectation of severe punishment. The two sides of the desire-plus-opportunities theory of racial violence are not in balance; attempts to reduce the desire have the exasperating effect of increasing the opportunity.

Black violence has reduced support for measures designed to help Negroes. Yet the polar opposite tactic—nonviolent pressure—is impossible to maintain. The emphasis of the civil rights movement on nonviolence was unnatural. It reassured whites and helped get bills on voting rights passed in Congress. But it left no place for self-defense. Where was all that black rage to go? Instead of a normal stress on self-defense, therefore, many Negro activists have shifted from turning the other cheek to abusing the man. One extreme has simply been substituted for another.

* Support for this hypothesis comes from a study of anti-white violence in Africa, which shows that there was little bloodshed in countries that engaged either in consistent repression or gave independence to the black majority; violence did occur when whites vacillated.

In such a situation it is easy for black men to succumb to a politics of outrage in which violent rhetoric provides a substitute for remedial action. Caught between rage and impotence, held responsible by no mass following of their own, Negro spokesmen compete in ragging the white man. Negroes can't help enjoying the fun, but we should be as clear as they are that the whole act is directed toward "Whitey." If whom a man loves can be determined by whom he can't resist talking to, then Whitey has captured all the affection these people have. No doubt this perverse form of Uncle Tomism will eventually be exposed by Negroes who want leaders to pay attention to them. In the meantime, we risk the consequences of a rhetoric of violence that angers whites without aiding blacks.

I conclude that all of us in America will need an acute sense of humor to survive the next decade. There will be rebellion if we do the best we know how. There will be even more violence if we do not. Almost harder to bear will be the incredible provocations— mixtures of arrogance, slander, paranoia, and duplicity. There are spectacular fantasies among black people about the deaths of Kennedy and Malcolm X right next to saccharine remarks about law and order from whites who have long practiced violence against Negroes. The one truth which white liberals are supposed to avow is that they do not know, have never known, and will never know anything about black people. Yet one would suppose that if two groups have contact, each would have an equal chance of failing to know the other. The old truth may have been that blacks were invisible men for whites. The new truth is that whites are invisible because they all look alike.

The language of "black power" should not, however, be dismissed without serious consideration. The fact that it means so many different things to different men does not prevent our observing that the slogan strikes a responsive chord among black men. At a minimum, black power signifies a widespread concern for a political dimension that has been conspicuously missing from previous theories of racial conflict.

The Identity and Legitimacy Theory

It will add to our understanding if we decide which features of the black rebellions we want to explain. The extensive looting, for example, does not appear especially deserving of explanation. There is looting all over the world when riots occur. That is why martial law is so often declared in the wake of natural disasters. When the police appear uncertain or absent, the urge to loot is apparently more than most of us can resist. Nor do we need to spend an excessive amount of time on the snipers. Virtually every society has small groups with an urge to disrupt its activities. The interesting question is why the mass of citizens in the ghettos did not react against the snipers and the incendiaries who put the torch to their neighborhoods.

The beginning of wisdom about black rebellion is that we are dealing with a problem in social control, with feelings widespread in an entire community, and not with just a few wild men. An entire community has become disaffected. That is not to say Negroes share common views on public policy. Indeed, they can hardly agree on anything. But they will not turn in one of their own to the white man. They will not defend what they have against the violence of their own people, not necessarily because they have nothing to lose, but because they do not have enough of the one thing that they would otherwise risk losing—participation in a common American life.

The great question raised by black rebellion is: Who will call himself an American? That has been the modal drama of life in America. Loyalist and patriot, patrician and plebian, slave and freeman, Southern man and Northern man, employer and worker, ethnic and Wasp, all have shattered the quiet of our vast continent with their wars. Today's rebellion is part of this struggle to forge a worthy American identity for black men. Black rebellion presents a crisis of legitimacy—a questioning of "white" authority. Hence the incessant demands for new power relationships. The immediate problems posed by black rebellion are, therefore, political, and require a political response.

Political Solutions

The most obvious political need is for mechanisms to reduce the blatant conflicts between Negroes and police with the police being the most visible and oppressive manifestation of governmental authority. Increasing the number of Negro policemen (and firemen) might help by blurring the purely racial nature of the encounters. The measures necessary to accomplish this end—allowing entry to people with minor police records, changing various requirements for health and examinations—are within our grasp. There are also various proposals for altering the role of policemen by putting them more in the role of helpers, and by sensitizing them to the problems of life among the severely deprived. It is difficult to quarrel with such humane measures. Yet they do not quite go to the heart of the matter. For policemen do have certain evident law-enforcement functions that may be blurred but not hidden. The rest of us manage to get along with police, not through mutual good will, but by avoiding contact with them unless we make a specific request for help. Not love but distance is the answer. A substantial increase in employment and rise in income will reduce the opportunity and need for crime. (Even the dope addict with a higher income is likely to be able to make arrangements that will keep him clear of the police.) Relationships with police could also be markedly improved by following Jacobus ten Broek's proposal to abolish the law of the poor. One reason that we have "two nations" in America is that there is literally a separate law for poor people. The difficulty is not merely that poor people receive less justice, but also that laws about sexual conduct, home finance, drug addiction, and dozens of other matters apply severely to them but laxly to other Americans. Hiring more Negro policemen will not be successful unless the frequency of unhappy contacts between them and the citizenry is sharply reduced.

Even were all this accomplished, however, it would not meet the profound Negro demand for autonomy, for control of some portion of their lives, for the self-esteem that comes from being powerful. If we cast aside the cynicism that tells us no man is truly master of his fate, we can recognize insistent political demands that may be accommodated or crushed but cannot be ignored. For present purposes we can dispense with a lot of research and simply assume that the best way to feel in control is to exercise control. Can this be done at all? Can it be done without generating the violence that will bring about the retribution that ends our hopes?

The usual American response to difficult political problems has been to disperse and fragment them into smaller conflicts that take place in different localities and times. Problems of church and state and education have been handled in just this way. Applying this procedure to racial problems in the past, however, has meant victory for racism or at least the status quo. Deprived of opportunities to exert influence at state and local levels because of official racism or lack of effective political resources, Negroes had no alternative except to look to the national government. This choice of a favored site for conflict was always opportunistic. Calhoun's doctrine of the concurrent majority meant control for regional racists. States rights and local autonomy were doctrines for keeping the Negro and the poor in their places. Now the old men are justified who say that if you live long enough everything comes full circle. Black nationalists, having little hope of a large voice in national and state politics, are talking about local autonomy. They demand a voice and a veto over policies affecting neighborhoods in which black people are in the majority. Bringing government closer to the people is a slogan that is no longer the exclusive property of conservatives. The pursuit of group interest by racial blacks thus creates opportunities for unusual political coalitions.

The Heller proposals for block grants to states, much of which would be distributed to cities, provide a strong basis for agreement. Local government would be strengthened. Negroes would find it more worthwhile to make demands on city governments. Cities would have the resources to grant some of these demands. The formation of neighborhood corporations or governments would be the next step. Run by elected councils within specified geographical boundaries, the corporations would provide a forum for airing grievances and working out common demands. In order to avoid complete focus on demands, and to provide experience in self-government, the neighborhood corporations would also negotiate with the city government to take over certain limited functions. Education has long been considered a neighborhood function and there are already moves toward further decentralization. If health and housing inspections are serious sources of grievances, cities may be willing to let neighborhood corporations hire and guide local people to do the job. Part of the energies within the neighborhood would thus be devoted to resolving disagreements among the local people about how they should run their own affairs.

We should be clear about what we are doing. The neighborhood corporation involves a return to earlier patterns of local rule that were regarded as offensive to principles of good government. The movement from the spoils system to neutral competence through civil service will, for a time, be reversed. What were previously despised as the worst attributes of boss rule and ethnic depravity— favoritism, trading of jobs for favors, winking at abuses when perpetrated by one's own kind, tolerance of local mores regarded by some as corrupt—will be reinstituted. Political practices worked out to accommodate the needs of lower-class immigrants, arrangements abandoned when they conflicted with rising professionalism and economic status, may understandably be preferred by underprivileged black people. The uneven development of all our people makes it difficult to pursue national practices. And Negroes, too, will have to reconcile themselves to the fact that programs which permit greater autonomy for urban Negroes may leave rural Negroes at the mercy of hostile state and local governments.

Today the black ghettoes resemble nothing so much as newly

emerging nations faced with extraordinary demands and few resources. There is the same ambivalence toward "foreign" aid: you
must have it and yet you hate the giver because of your dependence
on him. Highly educated and skilled people (black as well as white)
are deeply resented because of the well-founded fear that they will
"take over." The greater the disparity between aims and accomplishments, the greater the demagoguery and destructive fantasy life. Yet
underneath the pounding rhetoric there are men and women who are
learning the skills of leadership. They must be given a chance to
learn—that is, to make mistakes. They must have an opportunity to
generate growth in human resources in their own communities. Otherwise, they will lack the pride and security to re-enter American life
on conditions of mutual interest, respect, and allegiance.

We need to be reminded, however, that without a drastic decrease
in unemployment no other programs will be meaningful. It will prove
extraordinarily difficult to abolish the law of the poor because so
many people will be dependent on governmental assistance that the
tax burden will generate additional demands for obnoxious restrictions. When so many men cannot make a living now, educational
improvement will seem hopelessly long-range. Community action
programs suffer the most because of the utter futility of finding local
measures to create vast employment. Expectations are raised that no
local or state political system can meet. Ordinary politics are discredited. Each generation of community leaders is rejected as soon
as it becomes part of an "Establishment" that cannot deliver.

Income, education, and power are mutually supportive. They are
the bastions of legitimacy in our political system. Better education
will enable Negroes to receive higher income and to gain the communications skills necessary to carry on political activity. The exercise
of governmental power will strengthen the sense of mastery that
makes the long road of education seem worthwhile. Political power
also creates jobs. Good jobs at decent pay provide additional resources for education and political activity.

Political Support

What about the political feasibility of the economic and political
programs advocated here? Will the President and Congress agree to
spend the $5 or $10 billion a year that a job program will cost? Will
mayors and city councils agree to share limited powers with neighborhood corporations? Will a policy of suppression appear more
attractive as well as less expensive? There is an old story that goes,

"Harry, how's your wife?" "Compared to what?" he replies. The political desirability of these programs depends in part on how they compare with what we have been doing. Take the sad plight of our mayors.

Mayors in the United States are in an incredible position. The only things they can do, such as providing better recreation facilities, improving housing inspection, and the like are strictly marginal improvements. They lack the money and the power to do more. Yet they are held responsible for every evil. Rebellions appears to occur at random, afflicting cities whose mayors try hard to do the right thing and cities whose mayors are indifferent or hostile. What incentives will mayors have to do what good they can do? Since they cannot possibly do enough, the do-nothing mayor appears no worse off than the better mayors. (A major possibility is that mayors will learn to concentrate on the one area in which they might do well and reap credit from some segments of the population—suppression of rebellions.) Therefore, working with neighborhood corporations, invigorated by fresh infusions of federal funds, should prove attractive to mayors who despair of their present situation.

Politicians in the Democratic party are frantically pursuing ways of handling racial problems that will not end in disaster for everyone concerned. Buffeted between the hostility of blue-collar workers to civil rights legislation and the inability to satisfy radical Negroes no matter what, the politicians fear their party will be split on racial grounds. They foresee waves of repression and a permanent estrangement between black and white in America. But consider what a new orientation would have to offer to Democratic party politicians. They would not try to bid for the support of racial radicals, white or black. The Democrats would turn down both mass suppression and mass violence, avoiding especially symbolic issues that embitter whites and do not help blacks. The politicians would espouse primarily policies promising immediate and substantial improvement of the economic condition of poor people. Decent jobs at good pay come first. Next, there should be the most powerful education program that can be devised to enable the presently disadvantaged to participate as equals in the market place and the political arena. These policies should be presented at face value as measures for making good the promise of American life. These policies are consonant with the traditions of the Democratic party, and they need not divide the races. The poor need help. We are a rich nation. We can and should give that help.

No doubt a party promoting these income policies might lose an election or two. But when it did get into power it would have goals worth achieving. The difficulty with existing policies is that even when properly pursued they do not help enough people immediately in direct ways. The usual mode of alleviating difficult problems by incremental attack along diverse fronts does not work because there is no solid base on which to rest these efforts. We will never know what long-run contributions anti-poverty programs can make if we continue to insist that secondary programs substitute for primary ones, that supporting programs be adopted in place of the basic efforts they are intended to assist.

Democratic divisions over these issues also provide extraordinary opportunities for Republicans to recover from decades of declining support. The danger is that an anti-Negro stance will appear to offer hope of detaching white voters from the Democratic party. The resistance of these voters to conservative economic policies would be submerged under a tide of racial anger. There is another stance, however, that would be productive at the polls and fit comfortably with Republican principles. A massive employment program could be expected to win over some Negroes and poor whites while not alienating existing Republican support. Such a program would hold out greater long-run hope of alleviating rebellious conditions than would suppression. Republicans would presumably not support federal subsidies for radical community action. But a program that stressed local autonomy through neighborhood governments should prove attractive to conservatives. Indeed, Republicans are much less weighed down than are Democrats with commitments to existing welfare and education policies that Negroes find so disagreeable.

A Response to Rebellion

There will be rebellions; that much we can take for granted. The question is not whether these things will happen but how Americans will choose to react. It is easy to win tactical victories—disperse mobs brutally—and lose strategic battles. In the midst of consummate gall and endless effrontery, there is considerable danger of committing strategic suicide. What we do should depend on what we want. The prevailing confusion makes it advisable to take the risk of restating the obvious.

Just as Lincoln put preservation of the Union above all else in his times, so should we put construction of a multi-racial nation as our major objective. Our goal is that we all consider ourselves Americans who pay allegiance to the same political symbols and participate as citizens in the same national life. In pursuit of this goal, we must reaffirm our dedication to integration of the races for all who wish it.

Wholly white or black communities can be one mode of participation in a common life. But integration is the preferred way of life for those who believe that there must be a single nation in America. A surface integration, however, must not be pursued at the expense of equality of achievement among black and white, for then integration will become a barrier to the creation of a joint American identity.

If we do not wish white and black men to live as citizens in the same country, we will have no difficulty in finding policies appropriate to that end. We can continue what we are doing. Better still, we can let violence feed on violence. The early riots have largely been aimless affairs in which destruction has been visited by Negroes on their own neighborhoods. Mass repressions visited indiscriminately upon black people can give them new reasons for race hatred and further violence. White people can be turned into proto-blacks—people who fear destruction because of their color. The difference between the races is that whites possess more abundant means of committing mayhem.

Americans who wish to hold open the possibility of emerging as a single people should not engage in mass repression. The surest way for black bigots to get a following is for white racists to create it. We want to open and not to foreclose the possibilities of being American together. There will be riots, and they will have to be put down. But our aim should be to separate the actively violent from the rest of the black community. Force should be limited, specific, and controlled.

Capitulation to lawless behavior would be bad. The hunger for humiliation shown by the New Left can only succeed in demeaning everyone. The black man's dignity cannot be won by the white man's degradation; the bread of humiliation will feed few people. The most destructive elements will simply be encouraged to raise the level of abuse. White anger will rise. Acting out the ritual frenzy of hatred will close all doors.

Our program should be neither suppression nor capitulation, but affirmation of common possibilities in a civil society. Without promising what no man can deliver—an end to the rebellions that are the consequences of our past failures—we can try to do what we now see to be right and just: A massive employment program, a concerted effort to improve educational achievement, and then support for a process of self-generating growth in the urban ghettos.

"Power is not the white man's birthright." So wrote Martin Luther King shortly before his untimely death. The problem, as he saw it, was to find ways for black Americans to get and use power in the economic and political arenas.

In the following essay, taken from his last book, the late Dr. King discusses old and new techniques. He notes a common thread in that both concern the development of a cohesive spirit to strengthen group pride and communal action to realize more effectively the goals of his people.

16

Martin Luther King, Jr.

WHERE DO WE GO FROM HERE?

When a people are mired in oppression, they realize deliverance only when they have accumulated the power to enforce change. The powerful never lose opportunity—they remain available to them. The powerless, on the other hand, never experience opportunity—it is always arriving at a later time.

The nettlesome task of Negroes today is to discover how to organize our strength into compelling power so that government cannot elude our demands. We must develop, from strength, a situation in which the Government finds it wise and prudent to collaborate with us. It would be the height of naiveté to wait passively until the Administration had somehow been infused with such blessings of goodwill that it implored us for our programs.

We must frankly acknowledge that in past years our creativity and imagination were not employed in learning how to develop

Abridgment of (Chapter V) "Where Are We Going?" from *Where Do We Go from Here: Chaos or Community?* by Martin Luther King, Jr. Copyright © 1967 by Martin Luther King, Jr. By permission of Harper & Row, Publishers, and Hodder and Stoughton Limited.

power. We found a method in nonviolent protest that worked, and we employed it enthusiastically. We did not have leisure to probe for a deeper understanding of its laws and lines of development. Although our actions were bold and crowned with successes, they were substantially improvised and spontaneous. They attained the goals set for them but carried the blemishes of our inexperience.

This is where the civil-rights movement stands today. Now we must take the next major step of examining the levers of power which Negroes must grasp to influence the course of events.

In our society power sources can always finally be traced to ideological, economic and political forces.

In the area of *ideology*, despite the impact of the works of a few Negro writers on a limited number of white intellectuals, all too few Negro thinkers have exerted an influence on the main currents of American thought. Nevertheless, Negroes have illuminated imperfections in the democratic structure that were formerly only dimly perceived, and have forced a concerned re-examination of the true meaning of American democracy. As a consequence of the vigorous Negro protest, the whole nation has for a decade probed more searchingly the essential nature of democracy, both economic and political. By taking to the streets and there giving practical lessons in democracy and its defaults, Negroes have decisively influenced white thought.

Lacking sufficient access to television, publications and broad forums, Negroes have had to write their most persuasive essays with the blunt pen of marching ranks. The many white political leaders and well-meaning friends who ask Negro leadership to leave the streets may not realize that they are asking us effectively to silence ourselves. More white people learned more about the shame of America, and finally faced some aspects of it, during the years of non-violent protest than during the century before. Non-violent direct action will continue to be a significant source of power until it is made irrelevant by the presence of justice.

The *economic* highway to power has few entry lanes for Negroes. Nothing so vividly reveals the crushing impact of discrimination and the heritage of exclusion as the limited dimensions of Negro business in the most powerful economy in the world. America's industrial production is half of the world's total, and within it the production of Negro business is so small that it can scarcely be measured on any definable scale.

Yet in relation to the Negro community the value of Negro business should not be underestimated. In the internal life of the Negro society it provides a degree of stability. Despite formidable obstacles it has developed a corps of men of competence and organizational discipline who constitute a talented leadership reserve, who furnish inspiration and who are a resource for the development of programs and planning. They are a strength among the weak though they are weak among the mighty.

There exist two other areas, however, where Negroes can exert substantial influence on the broader economy. As employes and consumers, Negro numbers and their strategic disposition endow them with a certain bargaining strength.

Within the ranks of organized labor there are nearly two million Negroes, and they are concentrated in key industries. In the truck transportation, steel, auto and food industries, which are the backbone of the nation's economic life, Negroes make up nearly 20 per cent of the organized work force, although they are only 10 per cent of the general population. This potential strength is magnified further by the fact of their unity with millions of white workers in these occupations. As co-workers there is a basic community of interest that transcends many of the ugly divisive elements of traditional prejudice. There are undeniably points of friction, for example, in certain housing and education questions. But the severity of the abrasions is minimized by the more commanding need for cohesion in union organizations.

The union record in relation to Negro workers is exceedingly uneven, but potential for influencing union decisions still exists. In many of the larger unions the white leadership contains some men of ideals and many more who are pragmatists. Both groups find they are benefited by a constructive relationship to their Negro membership. For those compelling reasons, Negroes, who are almost wholly a working people, cannot be casual toward the union movement. This is true even though some unions remain incontestably hostile.

In days to come, organized labor will increase its importance in the destinies of Negroes. Negroes pressed into the proliferating service occupations—traditionally unorganized and with low wages and long hours—need union protection, and the union movement needs their membership to maintain its relative strength in the whole society. On this new frontier Negroes may well become the pioneers that they were in the early organizing days of the thirties.

To play our role fully as Negroes we will also have to strive for enhanced representation and influence in the labor movement. Our young people need to think of union careers as earnestly as they do of business careers and professions. They could do worse than emulate A. Philip Randolph, who rose to the executive council of the A.F.L.-C.I.O. and became a symbol of the courage, compassion and integrity of an enlightened labor leader.

Indeed, the question may be asked why we have produced only

one Randolph in nearly half a century. Discrimination is not the whole answer. We allowed ourselves to accept middle-class prejudices against the labor movement. Yet this is one of those fields in which higher education is not a requirement for high office. In shunning it, we have lost an opportunity. Let us try to regain it now, at a time when the joint forces of Negroes and labor may be facing a historic task of social reform.

The other economic lever available to the Negro is as a consumer. The Southern Christian Leadership Council has pioneered in developing mass boycott movements in a frontal attack on discrimination. In Birmingham it was not the marching alone that brought about integration of public facilities in 1963. The downtown business establishments suffered for weeks under our almost unbelievably effective boycott. The significant percentage of their sales that vanished, the 98 per cent of their Negro customers who stayed home, educated them forcefully to the dignity of the Negro as a consumer.

Later we crystallized our experiences in Birmingham and elsewhere and developed a department in S.C.L.C. called Operation Breadbasket. This has as its primary aim the securing of more and better jobs for the Negro people. It calls on the Negro community to support those businesses that will give a fair share of jobs to Negroes and to withdraw its support from those businesses that have discriminatory policies.

Operation Breadbasket is carried out mainly by clergymen. First, a team of ministers calls on the management of a business in the community to request basic facts on the company's total number of employes, the number of Negro employes, the departments or job classifications in which all employes are located, and the salary ranges for each category. The team then returns to the steering committee to evaluate the data and to make a recommendation concerning the number of new and upgraded jobs that should be requested. Then the team transmits the request to the management to hire or upgrade a specified number of "qualifiable" Negroes within a reasonable period of time. If negotiations on this request break down, the step of real power and pressure is taken: a massive call for economic withdrawal from the company's product and accompanying demonstrations is necessary.

At present S.C.L.C. has Operation Breadbasket functioning in some 12 cities, and the results have been remarkable. In Atlanta, for instance, the Negroes' earning power has been increased by more than $20-million annually over the past three years through a carefully disciplined program of selective buying and negotiations by the

Negro ministers. During the last eight months in Chicago, Operation Breadbasket successfully completed negotiations with three major industries: milk, soft drinks and chain grocery stores. Four of the companies involved concluded reasonable agreements only after short "don't buy" campaigns. Seven other companies were able to make the requested changes across the conference table, without necessitating a boycott. Two other companies, after providing their employment information to the ministers, were sent letters of commendation for their healthy equal-employment practices. The net results add up to approximately 800 new and upgraded jobs for Negro employes, worth a little over $7-million in new annual income for Negro families. In Chicago we have recently added a new dimension to Operation Breadbasket. Along with requesting new job opportunities, we are now requesting that businesses with stores in the ghetto deposit the income for those establishments in Negro-owned banks, and that Negro-owned products be placed on the counters of all their stores. In this way we seek to stop the drain of resources out of the ghetto with nothing remaining there for its rehabilitation.

The final major area of untapped power for the Negro is in the *political* arena. Higher Negro birth rates and increasing Negro migration, along with the exodus of the white population to the suburbs, are producing fast-gathering Negro majorities in the large cities. This changing composition of the cities has political significance. Particularly in the North, the large cities substantially determine the political destiny of the state. These states, in turn, hold the dominating electoral votes in Presidential contests. The future of the Democratic party, which rests so heavily on its coalition of urban minorities, cannot be assessed without taking into account which way the Negro vote turns. The wistful hopes of the Republican party for large-city influence will also be decided not in the board rooms of great corporations but in the teeming ghettos.

The growing Negro vote in the South is another source of power. As it weakens and enfeebles the Dixiecrats, by concentrating its blows against them, it undermines the Congressional coalition of Southern reactionaries and their Northern Republican colleagues. That coalition, which has always exercised a disproportionate power in Congress by controlling its major committees, will lose its ability to frustrate measures of social advancement and to impose its perverted definition of democracy on the political thought of the nation.

The Negro vote at present is only a partially realized strength. It can still be doubled in the South. In the North even where Ne-

groes are registered in equal proportion to whites, they do not vote
in the same proportions. Assailed by a sense of futility, Negroes
resist participating in empty ritual. However, when the Negro citizen
learns that united and organized pressure can achieve measurable
results, he will make his influence felt. Out of this consciousness the
political power of the aroused minority will be enhanced and consolidated.

We have many assets to facilitate organization. Negroes are almost instinctively cohesive. We band together readily, and against
white hostility we have an intense and wholesome loyalty to each
other. We are acutely conscious of the need, and sharply sensitive
to the importance, of defending our own. Solidarity is a reality in
Negro life, as it always has been among the oppressed.

On the other hand, Negroes are capable of becoming competi-
tive, carping and, in an expression of self-hate, suspicious and in-
tolerant of each other. A glaring weakness in Negro life is lack of
sufficient mutual confidence and trust.

Negro leaders suffer from this interplay of solidarity and divisive-
ness, being either exalted excessively or grossly abused. Some of these
leaders suffer from an aloofness and absence of faith in their people.
The white Establishment is skilled in flattering and cultivating
emerging leaders. It presses its own image on them and finally, from
imitation of manners, dress and style of living, a deeper strain of
corruption develops. This kind of Negro leader acquires the white
man's contempt for the ordinary Negro. He is often more at home
with the middle-class white than he is among his own people. His
language changes, his location changes, his income changes, and
ultimately he changes from the representative of the Negro to the
white man into the white man's representative to the Negro. The
tragedy is that too often he does not recognize what has happened
to him.

I learned a lesson many years ago from a report of two men who
flew to Atlanta to confer with a Negro civil rights leader at the
airport. Before they could begin to talk, the porter sweeping the
floor drew the local leader aside to talk about a matter that troubled
him. After 15 minutes had passed, one of the visitors said bitterly
to his companion, "I am just too busy for this kind of nonsense. I
haven't come a thousand miles to sit and wait while he talks to a
porter."

The other replied, "When the day comes that he stops having
time to talk to a porter, on that day I will not have the time to
come one mile to see him."

We need organizations that are permeated with mutual trust, incorruptibility and militancy. Without this spirit we may have numbers but they will add up to zero. We need organizations that are responsible, efficient and alert. We lack experience because ours is a history of disorganization. But we will prevail because our need for progress is stronger than the ignorance forced upon us. If we realize how indispensable is responsible militant organization to our struggle, we will create it as we managed to create underground railroads, protest groups, self-help societies and the churches that have always been our refuge, our source of hope and our source of action.

Negroes have been slow to organize because they have been traditionally manipulated. The political powers take advantage of three major weaknesses: the manner in which our political leaders emerge; our failure so far to achieve effective political alliances; and the Negro's general reluctance to participate fully in political life.

The majority of Negro political leaders do not ascend to prominence on the shoulders of mass support. Although genuinely popular leaders are now emerging, most are still selected by white leadership, elevated to position, supplied with resources and inevitably subjected to white control. The mass of Negroes nurtures a healthy suspicion toward this manufactured leader, who spends little time in persuading them that he embodies personal integrity, commitment and ability and offers few programs and less service. Tragically, he is in too many respects not a fighter for a new life but a figurehead of the old one. Hence, very few Negro political leaders are impressive or illustrious to their constituents. They enjoy only limited loyalty and qualified support.

This relationship in turn hampers the Negro leader in bargaining with genuine strength and independent firmness with white party leaders. The whites are all too well aware of his impotence and his remoteness from his constituents, and they deal with him as a powerless subordinate. He is accorded a measure of dignity and personal respect but not political power.

The Negro politician therefore finds himself in a vacuum. He has no base in either direction on which to build influence and attain leverage.

In two national polls among Negroes to name their most respected leaders, out of the highest 15, only a single political figure, Congressman Adam Clayton Powell, was included and he was in the lower half of both lists. This is in marked contrast to polls in which white people choose their most popular leaders; political personalities are always high on the lists and are represented in goodly numbers. There is no Negro political personality evoking affection, respect and emulation to correspond to John F. Kennedy, Eleanor Roosevelt, Herbert Lehman, Earl Warren and Adlai Stevenson, to name but a few.

The circumstances in which Congressman Powell emerged into leadership and the experiences of his career are unique. It would not shed light on the larger picture to attempt to study the very individual factors that apply to him. It is fair to say no other Negro political leader is similar, either in the strengths he possesses, the power he attained or the errors he has committed.

And so we shall have to create leaders who embody virtues we can respect, who have moral and ethical principles we can applaud with an enthusiasm that enables us to rally support for them based on confidence and trust. We will have to demand high standards and give consistent, loyal support to those who merit it. We will have to be a reliable constituency for those who prove themselves to be committed political warriors in our behalf. When our movement has partisan political personalities whose unity with their people is unshakable and whose independence is genuine, they will be treated in white political councils with the respect those who embody such power deserve.

In addition to the development of genuinely independent and representative political leaders, we shall have to master the art of political alliances. Negroes should be natural allies of many white reform and independent political groups, yet they are more commonly organized by old-line machine politicians. We will have to learn to refuse crumbs from the big-city machines and steadfastly demand a fair share of the loaf. When the machine politicians demur, we must be prepared to act in unity and throw our support to such independent parties or reform wings of the major parties as are prepared to take our demands seriously and fight for them vigorously.

The art of alliance politics is more complex and more intricate than it is generally pictured. It is easy to put exciting combinations on paper. It evokes happy memories to recall that our victories in the past decade were won with a broad coalition of organizations representing a wide variety of interests. But we deceive ourselves if we envision the same combination backing structural changes in the society. It did not come together for such a program and will not reassemble for it.

A true alliance is based upon some self-interest of each component group and a common interest into which they merge. For an alliance to have permanence and loyal commitment from its various elements, each of them must have a goal from which it benefits and none must have an outlook in basic conflict with the others.

If we employ the principle of selectivity along these lines, we will find millions of allies who in serving themselves also support us, and on such sound foundations unity and mutual trust and tangible accomplishment will flourish.

In the changing conditions of the South, we will find alliances increasingly instrumental in political progress. For a number of years there were *de facto* alliances in some states in which Negroes voted for the same candidate as whites because he had shifted from a racist to a moderate position, even though he did not articulate an appeal for Negro votes. In recent years the transformation has accelerated, and many white candidates have entered alliances publicly. As they perceived that the Negro vote was becoming a substantial and permanent factor, they could not remain aloof from it. More and more, competition will develop among white political forces for such a significant bloc of votes, and a monolithic white unity based on racism will no longer be possible.

Racism is a tenacious evil, but it is not immutable. Millions of underprivileged whites are in the process of considering the contradiction between segregation and economic progress. White supremacy can feed their egos but not their stomachs. They will not go hungry or forgo the affluent society to remain racially ascendant.

Governors Wallace and Maddox, whose credentials as racists are impeccable, understand this, and for that reason they present themselves as liberal populists as well. Temporarily they can carry water on both shoulders, but the ground is becoming unsteady beneath their feet. Each of them was faced in the primary last year with a new breed of white Southerner who for the first time in history met with Negro organizations to solicit support and championed economic reform without racial demagogy. These new figures won significant numbers of white votes, insufficient for victory but sufficient to point the future directions of the South.

It is true that the Negro vote has not transformed the North; but the fact that Northern alliances and political action generally have been poorly executed is no reason to predict that the negative experiences will be automatically extended in the North or duplicated in the South. The Northern Negro has never used direct action on a mass scale for reforms, and anyone who predicted 10 years ago that the Southern Negro would also neglect it would have dramatically been proved in error.

Everything Negroes need will not like magic materialize from the use of the ballot. Yet as a lever of power, if it is given studious attention and employed with the creativity we have proved through our protest activities we possess, it will help to achieve many far-reaching changes during our lifetimes.

The final reason for our dearth of political strength, particularly in the North, arises from the grip of an old tradition on many individual Negroes. They tend to hold themselves aloof from politics as a serious concern. They sense that they are manipulated, and their defense is a cynical disinterest. To safeguard themselves on this front from the exploitation that torments them in so many areas, they shut the door to political activity and retreat into the dark shadows of passivity. Their sense of futility is deep, and in terms of their bitter experiences it is justified. They cannot perceive political action as a source of power. It will take patient and persistent effort to eradicate this mood, but the new consciousness of strength developed in a decade of stirring agitation can be utilized to channel constructive Negro activity into political life and eliminate the stagnation produced by an outdated and defensive paralysis.

In the future we must become intensive political activists. We must be guided in this direction because we need political strength, more desperately than any other group in American society. Most of us are too poor to have adequate economic power, and many of us are too rejected by the culture to be part of any tradition of power. Necessity will draw us toward the power inherent in the creative uses of politics.

Negroes nurture a persisting myth that the Jews of America attained social mobility and status solely because they had money. It is unwise to ignore the error for many reasons. In a negative sense it encourages anti-Semitism and overestimates money as a value. In a positive sense the full truth reveals a useful lesson.

Jews progressed because they possessed a tradition of education combined with social and political action. The Jewish family enthroned education and sacrificed to get it. The result was far more than abstract learning. Uniting social action with educational competence, Jews became enormously effective in political life. Those Jews who became lawyers, businessmen, writers, entertainers, union leaders and medical men did not vanish into the pursuits of their trade exclusively. They lived an active life in political circles, learning the techniques and arts of politics.

Nor was it only the rich who were involved in social and political action. Millions of Jews for half a century remained relatively poor, but they were far from passive in social and political areas. They lived in homes in which politics was a household word. They were deeply involved in radical parties, liberal parties and conservative parties—they formed many of them. Very few Jews sank into despair and escapism even when discrimination assailed the spirit and corroded initiative. Their life raft in the sea of discouragement was social action.

Without overlooking the towering differences between the Negro and Jewish experiences, the lesson of Jewish mass involvement in social and political action and education is worthy of emulation. Negroes have already started on this road in creating the protest movement, but this is only a beginning. We must involve everyone we can reach, even those with inadequate education, and together acquire political sophistication by discussion, practice and reading.

The many thousands of Negroes who have already found intellectual growth and spiritual fulfillment on this path know its creative possibilities. They are not among the legions of the lost, they are not crushed by the weight of centuries. Most heartening, among the young the spirit of challenge and determination for change is becoming an unquenchable force.

But the scope of struggle is still too narrow and too restricted. We must turn more of our energies and focus our creativity on the useful things that translate into power. We in this generation must do the work and in doing it stimulate our children to learn and acquire higher levels of skill and technique.

It must become a crusade so vital that civil rights organizers do not repeatedly have to make personal calls to summon support. There must be a climate of social pressure in the Negro community that scorns the Negro who will not pick up his citizenship rights and add his strength enthusiastically and voluntarily to the accumulation of power for himself and his people. The past years have blown fresh winds through ghetto stagnation, but we are on the threshold of a significant change that demands a hundredfold acceleration. By 1970 ten of our larger cities will have Negro majorities if present trends continue. We can shrug off this opportunity or use it for a new vitality to deepen and enrich our family and community life.

We must utilize the community action groups and training centers now proliferating in some slum areas to create not merely an electorate, but a conscious, alert, and informed people who know their direction and whose collective wisdom and vitality commands respect. The slave heritage can be cast into the dim past by our consciousness of our strengths and a resolute determination to use them in our daily experiences.

Power is not the white man's birthright; it will not be legislated for us and delivered in neat government packages. It is a social force any group can utilize by accumulating its elements in a planned, deliberate campaign to organize it under its own control.

SUGGESTED READINGS

Barbour, Floyd, editor. *The Black Power Protest*. Boston: Porter Sargent, 1968.
A collection of recent papers explaining the need for Negroes to become "black" and to unite.

Carmichael, Stokely, and Charles V. Hamilton. *Black Power: The Politics of Liberation in America*. New York: Vintage, 1967.
This book spells out the ideology of the Black Power Movement and discusses its political implications for black and white Americans.

Hayden, Tom. *Rebellion in Newark: Official Violence and Ghetto Response*. New York: Random House, 1967.
A personal view of what happened during the riots in Newark in 1967.

Killian, Lewis M. *The Impossible Revolution? Black Power and the American Dream*. New York: Random House, 1968.
A sociological analysis and critique of the Black Power Movement and an assessment of its prospects for success.

King, Martin Luther, Jr. *Where Do We Go from Here? Chaos or Community*, New York: Harper & Row, 1967.
The last book written by Dr. King.

Report of the National Advisory Commission on Civil Disorders. New York: Bantam Books, 1968.
Perhaps the most important social document to be published in this century, this report examines the causes and consequences of discrimination and disorder.

Wright, Nathan, Jr. *Black Power and Urban Unrest*. New York: Hawthorn, 1967.
The case for Black Power is offered by the organizers of the famous Newark Conference.

"Negroes" Nevermore

. . . we learned that America simply couldn't *be* color-blind. It would have to *become* color-blind and it would only *become* color-blind when we gave up our color. The white man, who presumably has no color, would have to give up only his prejudices. We would have to give up our identities. Thus, we would usher in the Great Day with an act of complete self-denial and self-abasement.

JAMES FARMER

At the end of the last essay in the previous section Martin Luther King commented on what black Americans could learn from the experience of Jews. Here Erik Erikson begins with a comment on Jewish identity to illustrate the meaning of a communal culture, or what Freud once referred to as the "consciousness of inner identity."

As Erikson sees it, the Negro American has long regarded himself in terms of a "surrendered identity," an identity of "negative recognition." Other writers, including some black critics, have a different conception. Erikson is well aware that his is a view from the outside. Indeed, he poses the question: "Do we (and can we) know enough about the relationship of positive and negative elements within the Negro personality and within the Negro community?" The answer is not given. However, Erikson does discuss the spectrum of "identities" that appear to be competing for the commitment of black Americans today.

17

Erik H. Erikson

THE CONCEPT OF IDENTITY
IN RACE RELATIONS

The following notes represent an expansion of the remarks on the
concept of identity which I was asked to make in November 1964 at
the meeting of the committee gathered to plan the issues of *Dædalus*
devoted to the Negro American. Shortly after that meeting, I un-
dertook a trip abroad in order to interview the surviving witnesses
and to study the remaining documents of what seemed, when the
study was first planned, a long-past episode in a faraway country,
namely, one of Gandhi's nonviolent campaigns. I am now returning
to my fragmentary contribution to this symposium for the very reason that the concept or at least the term identity seems not only to
have pervaded the literature on the Negro revolution in this country, but also to have come to represent in India (and in other

From Erik H. Erikson, "The Concept of Identity in Race Relations: Notes and
Queries," in Talcott Parsons and Kenneth Clark, eds., *The Negro American,*
Boston: Houghton Mifflin, 227–253. Reprinted with permission of *Dædalus,*
Journal of the American Academy of Arts and Sciences, Boston, Mass. Winter
1966, "The Negro American."

countries) something in the psychological core of the revolution of
the colored races and nations who seek inner as well as outer emancipation from colonial rule and from the remnants of colonial patterns of thought. When, for example, Nehru said (as I have been
told) that "Gandhi gave India an identity," he obviously put the
term into the center of that development of a nonviolent technique,
both religious and political, by which Gandhi strove to enhance a
unique unity among Indians while insisting on their complete autonomy within the British Empire. But what did Nehru mean?

R. P. Warren, in his *Who Speaks for the Negro?* reacts to the
first (but by no means last) mention of the word by one of his in-
formants with the exclamation:

> I seize the word *identity*. It is a key word. You hear it over and over
> again. On this word will focus, around this word will coagulate, a dozen
> issues, shifting, shading into each other. Alienated from the world to
> which he is born and from the country of which he is a citizen, yet
> surrounded by the successful values of that world, and country, how
> can the Negro define himself? [1]

Usually, the term is used without explanation as if it were obvious
what it means; and, indeed, faddish as the word has become, it has
also come to mean to many something both profound and unfathom-
able.

Social scientists sometimes attempt to make it more concrete.
However, if they do not quickly equate it with the strangely pat
question "Who am I?" they make such words as "identity crisis,"
"self-identity," or "sexual identity" fit whatever they are investigat-
ing. For the sake of logical or experimental maneuverability (and in
order to keep in good academic company) they try to treat these
terms as matters of social roles, personal traits, or conscious self-
images, shunning the less manageable and the less obscure (and
often more sinister) implications of the concept. Its use has, in fact,
become so indiscriminate that the other day a German reviewer (of
a new edition of my first book in which I first used the term in the
context of psychoanalytic ego theory) called the concept the pet
subject of the *amerikanische Popularpsychologie*. As we might say
in American popular psychology: that does it. I return to the subject because (in spite of slogan-like misuse and lip service) it does
seem to speak to the condition of many serious observers at this
juncture of history. I will try to explain some of its dimensions and
relate them to what can only be approximate illustrations from race-
relations. I will claim no further status for this effort than "notes
and queries" [2] within a symposium, that is, in a context in which
what will be referred to here as a *revolution of awareness* can be

seen against the background of what Gandhi called the "four-fold ruin" wrought by political and economic as well as cultural and spiritual degradation; for surely, power, or at least the power to choose, is vitally related to identity. In this context, I shall emphasize rather than minimize the alternatives and controversies, the ambiguities and ambivalences concerning various aspects of the identity issue.

Individual and Communal

At a time when the term identity refers, more often than not, to a more or less desperate quest, or even (as in the case of the Negro American) to something mostly negative or absent ("invisible," "inaudible," "unnamed"), it may be well to introduce the subject with quotations from two men who asserted strongly what identity feels like when you become aware of it. My two witnesses are the bearded and patriarchal founding fathers of the kind of psychology on which this writer's thinking on identity is based. As a *subjective sense* of an *invigorating sameness* and *continuity*, what I would call a sense of identity seems to me best described by William James in a letter to his wife. "A man's character," he wrote, "is discernible in the mental or moral attitude in which, when it came upon him, he felt himself most deeply and intensely active and alive. At such moments there is a voice inside which speaks and says: '*This* is the real me!'" Such experience always includes

> An element of active tension, of holding my own, as it were, and trusting outward things to perform their part so as to make it a full harmony, but without any *guaranty* that they will. Make it a guaranty—and the attitude immediately becomes to my consciousness stagnant and stingless. Take away the guaranty, and I feel (provided I am *uberhaupt* in vigorous condition) a sort of deep enthusiastic bliss, of bitter willingness to do and suffer anything . . . and which, although it is a mere mood or emotion to which I can give no form in words, authenticates itself to me as the deepest principle of all active and theoretic determination which I possess. . . .[3]

James uses the word "character," but I am taking the liberty of claiming that he describes what today we would call a sense of identity, and that he does so in a way which can in principle be experienced by any man. To him it is both mental and moral (the last a word also often swallowed up by ours); and he experiences it as something that "comes upon you" as a re-cognition, almost as a surprise rather than as something strenuously "quested" after. It is an active tension (rather than a paralyzing question)—a tension which,

furthermore, must create a challenge "without guaranty" rather than
one dissipated in a clamor for certainty. But let us remember in
passing that James was in his thirties when he wrote this, that he
had faced and articulated an "identity crisis" of honest and desperate
depth, and that he became *the* Psychologist-Philosopher of American
Pragmatism only after having attempted to integrate other cultural,
philosophic, and professional identity elements.[4]

One can study in James' life history the emergence of a "self-
made" identity in a new and expansive civilization. But for a statement of that unity of *personal and cultural* identity which is rooted
in an ancient people's fate we turn to Sigmund Freud. In an address
to the Society of B'nai B'rith in Vienna in 1926 he said:

> What bound me to Jewry was (I am ashamed to admit) neither faith
> nor national pride, for I have always been an unbeliever and was
> brought up without any religion though not without a respect for what
> are called the "ethical" standards of human civilization.
>
> Whenever I felt an inclination to national enthusiasm I strove to
> suppress it as being harmful and wrong, alarmed by the warning
> examples of the peoples among whom we Jews live. But plenty of other
> things remained over to make the attraction of Jewry and Jews ir-
> resistible—many obscure emotional forces, which were the more
> powerful the less they could be expressed in words, as well as a clear
> consciousness of inner identity, the safe privacy of a common mental
> construction. And beyond this there was a perception that it was to
> my Jewish nature alone that I owed two characteristics that had become
> indispensable to me in the difficult course of my life. Because I was a
> Jew I found myself free from many prejudices which restricted others
> in the use of their intellect; and as a Jew I was prepared to join the
> Opposition and to do without agreement with the "compact majority." [5]

No translation ever does justice to the grandiose choice of words in
Freud's German original. "Obscure emotional forces" are *"dunkle
Gefuehlsmaechte"*; the "safe privacy of a common mental construction" is *"die Heimlichkeit der inneren Konstruktion"*—not just "mental," then, and certainly not "private," but a deep communality
known only to those who share in it.

This quotation takes on new meaning in the context for which
this is written, for *this* "consciousness of inner identity" includes a
sense of bitter pride preserved by a dispersed and often despised
people throughout a long history of alternating persecution and re-
establishment. It is anchored in a particular (here intellectual) gift
which had victoriously emerged from the suppression of other opportunities. At the same time, it should not be overlooked (for we
will need to refer back to it later) that this *positive identity* is seen
against the background of a *negative* counterpart in all "the peoples among whom we Jews live," namely, "prejudices which re-

strict others in the use of their intellect." Identity here is one aspect of the struggle for ethnic survival: one person's or group's identity may be relative to another's; and identity awareness may have to do with matters of an *inner emancipation* from a more dominant identity, such as the "compact majority." An exquisite triumph is suggested in the claim that the same historical development which restricted the prejudiced in the free use of their intellect made those discriminated against freer and sturdier in intellectual matters.

These two statements (and the life-histories behind them) serve to establish a first dimension of identity which immediately helps to explain why it is so tenacious and yet so hard to grasp: for here we deal with something which can be experienced as "identical" *in the core of the individual* and yet also identical *in the core of a communal culture,* and which is, in fact, the identity of those two identities.

But we can also see that this is a matter of *growth,* both personal and communal. For a mature psychosocial identity presupposes a community of people whose traditional values become significant to the growing person even as his growth and his gifts assume relevance for them. Mere "roles" which can be "played" interchangeably are not sufficient; only an integration of roles which foster individual vitality within a vital trend in the existing or developing social order can support identities. (We may speak, then, of a *complementarity* of an *inner synthesis* in the individual and of *role integration* in his group.)

In all their poetic spontaneity these two statements prove to be the product of trained minds and therefore exemplify the main dimensions of a positive sense of identity almost systematically: from here one could proceed in a number of directions. But since these utterances are taken not from theoretical works, but from special communications (a letter to his wife from a man who married late; an address to his "brothers" by an observer long isolated in his field), it would seem most fitting now to quote corresponding voices among Negroes. But the mere contemplation of the task reveals two difficulties. The corresponding statements of Negro authors are couched in terms so negative that they at first suggest an absence of identity or the prevalence of what we will call *negative* identity elements. From Du Bois' famous passage (quoted in Myrdal's introduction to *Dark Ghetto*) [6] on the *inaudible* Negro, we would be led to Baldwin's and Ellison's very titles suggesting *invisibility, namelessness, facelessness.* But I would not approach these themes as a mere plaintive expression of the Negro American's sense of "nobody-ness," a social role which, God knows, was his heritage. Rather, I would tend to interpret the desperate and yet determined pre-occupation with invisibility on the part of these creative men as a demand to be heard and seen, recognized and faced as *individuals with a choice* rather than as men marked by what is all too superficially visible, namely, their color (and by the stereotypes which go with it). In a haunting way they defend an existing but in some ways voiceless identity against the stereotypes which hide it. They are involved in a battle to reconquer for their people, but first of all (as writers must) for themselves, what Vann Woodward calls a "surrendered identity." I like this term because it does not assume total absence as many contemporary writings do, something to be searched for and found, to be granted or given, to be created or fabricated, but something to be liberated. This will be emphasized in this paper because I consider it to be an actuality, and thus the only bridge from past to future.

I almost quoted Ellison as saying that his writing was indeed an attempt to transcend "as the blues transcended the painful conditions with which they deal." But I stopped myself; and now I have quoted him to show up a second difficulty. Except for extraordinary moments of lucidity, all self-images and images of otherness (and, yes, even the blues) change their connotation kaleidoscopically before our eyes and in our discussions; and no writer of today can escape this. To have something to hold on to, we all use stereotypes temporarily endowed with ideological connotations which are a measure of Negro or white distance from the thoughtless accommodation to the postslavery period from which we are all emerging. What before was a more unconscious mixture of guilt and fear on the white side, and a mixture of hate and fear on the other, is now being replaced by the more conscious and yet not always more practical sentiments of remorse and mistrust. We have, at the moment, no choice but to live with those stereotypes and these affects: confrontation will disprove some of them, history dissolve others. In the meantime, it may be helpful to bring some concepts to bear on this problem so that the kaleidoscope may reveal patterns as well as bewildering changes.

Conscious and Unconscious

A "sense of identity" obviously has conscious aspects, such as the experience of an increased unity of the physical and mental, moral and sensual selves, and of a oneness in the way one experiences oneself and the way others seem to experience us. But this process *can* also be visible to others, for he who "knows where he is going and who is going with him" demonstrates an unmistakable, if not always easily definable, unity and radiance of appearance, physiognomic as well as postural. And yet, just when a person, to all appearances, seems to "find himself," he can also be said to be "losing himself" in new tasks and affiliations. He transcends identity-consciousness; and this is surely so in the early days of any revolution and was so in the case of the young of the Negro revolution who found themselves and, in fact, found their generation in the very decision to lose themselves (as well as all guaranty) in the intensity of the struggle. Here identity-consciousness is absorbed in actuality. There are vivid and moving descriptions of this state (none more so than in Howard Zinn's account of the early days of SNCC).[7] Afterwards, no doubt, these at first anonymous heroes faced redoubled self-consciousness, a kind of double-take on the stage of history. Conversely, Negroes who must now prove themselves in the sober light of a more integrated day cannot escape a self-consciousness which is apt to interfere with the happiness of finding or losing oneself: there are and there will be the martyrs of self-chosen or accidentally aggravated identity-consciousness, who must sacrifice the innocent unity of living to a revolutionary awareness.

But the core of that inner unification called identity is at best (as we psychoanalysts would say) *pre-conscious,* that is, accessible only to musings at moments of special awareness or to the revelatory experiences of intuitive writers. Mostly it is *unconscious* and even repressed, and hereby related to all those unconscious conflicts to which only psychoanalysis has found a methodical access. Thus the concept not only is difficult to work with; it also arouses deep-seated "resistances," which must be pointed out not in the hope of doing away with them (for they are an intricate and insurmountable part of the problem of human awareness), but in order to get acquainted with a shadow which will always follow us.

"Resistance" is a term from psychoanalytic treatment proper. There it indicates a "technical" problem met with in the therapeutic attempt to induce an individual to recognize the nature (or sometimes the very fact) of his illness, to describe his thoughts freely, and to accept the interpretations given to him. But the term has also been used in a wider sense in order to characterize a general resistance to psychoanalytic insights or, indeed, to "psychic reality" itself. However, the widespread acceptance of psychoanalysis (or of what Freud is understood to have said or is reported to have said) and the freer commission of sexual and verbal acts, the omission of which is now considered to be a symptom of repression, have not done away with a more fundamental aspect of "resistance," for it concerns the relation of man's awareness to his need for a free will, and thus something in the core of man's identity. This resistance can come to awareness in vague discomfort, often the more gnawing as it contradicts our professed interest in enlightenment:

1. If unconscious determinants should, indeed, prove operative

in our very sense of self and in the very pathos of our values, does this not carry the matter of determination to a point where free will and moral choice would seem to be illusory?

2. If a man's individual identity is said to be linked to communal identities, are we not faced with another crypto-Marxism which makes man's very sense of destiny a blind function of the dialectics of history?

3. And if such unconscious determinants could, indeed, be demonstrated, is such awareness good for us?

Philosophers, no doubt, have answers to these questions, which recur in the reactions of the best-trained students when faced somewhat more systematically with insights which they otherwise devour eagerly in a non-systematic mixture of paperbacks.[8] But it must be clear that nobody can escape these questions which are really only part of a wider trend in the scrutiny of human motivation ranging from Darwin's discovery of our evolutionary animal ancestry and Marx's uncovery of class-bound behavior, to Freud's systematic exploration of the unconscious. The preoccupation with identity, therefore, may be seen not only as a symptom of "alienation," but also as a corrective trend in psychosocial evolution. It may be for this reason that revolutionary writers and writers from national and ethnic minority groups (like the Irish expatriots or our Negro and Jewish writers) have become the artistic spokesmen and prophets of identity confusion. Artistic creation, as pointed out, goes beyond complaint and exposure; it includes the moral decision that a certain painful identity-consciousness may have to be tolerated in order to provide the conscience of man with a critique of conditions, with the insight and with the conceptions necessary to heal himself of what most deeply divides and threatens him, namely, his division into what we will call *pseudo-species*.

In this new literature, pre-conscious processes are faced and unconscious ones symbolized in a way which often resembles the process of psycho-analysis; but the "case" is transcended by human revolt, the inner realignment by intense contact with historical actuality. And, in the end, are these writers not proclaiming also an essential superiority of identity-in-torment over those identities which feel as safe and remote as a suburban home?

What is at stake here is nothing less than the realization of the fact and the obligation of man's specieshood. Great religious leaders have attempted to break through the resistances against this awareness, but their churches have tended to join rather than shun the development which we have in mind here, namely, man's deepseated conviction that some providence has made his tribe and race or class, caste, or religion "naturally" superior to others. This seems to be part of a psychosocial evolution by which he has developed into *pseudo-species*. This fact is, of course, rooted in tribal psychology and based on all the evolutionary changes which brought about man. Among these is his prolonged childhood during which the newborn, "naturally" born to be the most "generalist" animal of all and adaptable to widely differing environments, becomes specialized as a member of a human group with its complex interplay of an "inner world" and an ethological environment. He becomes indoctrinated, then, with the conviction that his "species" alone was planned by an all-wise deity, created in a special cosmic event, and appointed by history to guard the only genuine version of humanity under the leadership of elect élites and leaders. "Pseudo" suggests pseudologia, a form of lying with at least transitory conviction; and, indeed, man's very progress has swept him along in a combination of developments in which it seems hard to bring to bear what rationality and humanity he can muster against illusions and prejudices no longer deserving of the name mythology. I mean, of course, that dangerous combination of technological specialization (including weaponry), moral righteousness, and what we may call the *territoriality of identity,* all of which make *hominem hominis lupum* far exceeding anything typical for wolves among wolves. For man is not only apt to lose all sense of species, but also to turn on another subgroup with a ferocity generally alien to the "social" animal world and, of course, with an increasingly sophistication in all three—lethal weaponry, moral hypocrisy, and identity-panic. Sophistication, in fact, seems to escalate the problem just at the time when (and this would seem to be no coincidence) a more universal, a more inclusive human identity seems forcefully suggested by the very need for survival. National-socialist Germany is the most flagrant and all too recent manifestation of the murderous mass-pseudologia which can befall a modern nation.

While we all carry with us trends and tendencies which anchor our identities in some pseudo-species, we also feel in our bones that the Second World War has robbed such self-indulgence of all innocence, and that any threat of a third one would lead man's adaptative genius to its own defeat. But those who see what the "compact majority" continues to deny and to dissimulate must also attempt to understand that for man to realize his specieshood and to exchange a wider identity for his pseudo-species, means not only the creation of a new and shared technological universe, but also the out-growing of prejudices which have been essential to all (or almost all) identities in the past. For each *positive identity* is also defined by *negative* images (as we saw even in Freud's reference to the intellectual components of his identity), and we must now discuss the unpleasant fact that our god-given identities often live off the degradation of others.

Positive and Negative

As I restudied Freud's address, I remember a remark made recently by a warm-hearted and influential American Jew: "Some instinctive sense tells every Jewish mother that she must make her child study, that his intelligence is his pass to the future. Why does a Negro mother not care? Why does she not have the same instinctive sense?" This was a rhetorical question, of course; he wanted to know which of many possible answers I would give first. I suggested that, given American Negro history, the equivalent "instinctive sense" may have told the majority of Negro mothers to keep their children, and especially the gifted and the questioning ones, away from futile and dangerous competition, that is, for survival's sake to keep them in their place even if that place is defined by an indifferent and hateful "compact majority."

That the man said "mothers" immediately marks one of the problems we face in approaching Negro identity. The Jewish mothers he had in mind would expect to be backed up by their husbands or, in fact, to act in their behalf; the Negro mothers would not. Negro mothers are apt to cultivate the "surrendered identity" forced on Negro men for generations. This, so the literature would suggest, has reduced the Negro to a reflection of the "negative" recognition which surrounded him like an endless recess of distorting mirrors. How his positive identity has been undermined systematically—first under the unspeakable system of slavery in North America and then by the system of enslavement perpetuated in the rural South and the urban North—has been extensively, carefully, and devastatingly documented.

Here the concept of a negative identity may help to clarify three related complications:

1. Every person's psychosocial identity contains a hierarchy of positive *and* negative elements, the latter resulting from the fact that the growing human being, throughout his childhood, is presented with evil prototypes as well as with ideal ones (by reward and punishment, by parental example, and by the community's typology as revealed in wit and gossip, in tale and story). These are, of course, culturally related: in the background which gives prominence to intellectual achievement, some such negative roles as the Schlemihl will not be wanting. The human being, in fact, is warned *not* to become what he often had no intention of becoming so that he can learn to anticipate what he must avoid. Thus, the positive

identity (far from being a static constellation of traits or roles) is always in conflict with that past which is to be lived down and by that potential future which is to be prevented.

2. The individual belonging to an oppressed and exploited minority, which is aware of the dominant cultural ideals but prevented from emulating them, is apt to fuse the negative images held up to him by the dominant majority with his own negative identity. The reasons for this exploitability (and temptation to exploit) lie in man's very evolution and development as pseudo-species. There is ample evidence of "inferiority" feelings and of morbid self-hate in all minority groups; and, no doubt, the righteously and fiendishly efficient way in which the Negro slave in America was forced into and kept in conditions preventing in most the incentive for independent ambition now continues to exert itself as a widespread and deep-seated inhibition to utilize equality even where it is "granted." Again, the literature abounds in descriptions of how the Negro, instead, found escape into musical or spiritual worlds or expressed his rebellion in compromises of behavior now viewed as mocking caricatures, such as obstinate meekness, exaggerated childlikeness, or superficial submissiveness. And yet, is "the Negro" not often all too summarily and all too exclusively discussed in such a way that his negative identity is defined *only* in terms of his defensive adjustments to the dominant white majority? Do we (and can we) know enough about the relationship of positive and negative elements *within* the Negro personality and *within* the Negro community? This alone would reveal how negative is negative and how positive, positive.

3. As yet least understood, however, is the fact that the oppressor has a vested interest in the negative identity of the oppressed because that negative identity is a projection of his own unconscious negative identity—a projection which, up to a point, makes him feel superior but also, in a brittle way, whole. The discussion of the pseudo-species may have clarified some of this. But a number of questions remain. One comes to wonder, for example, about the ways in which a majority, suddenly aware of a vital split in itself over the fact that it has caused a near-fatal split in a minority, may, in its sudden zeal to regain its moral position and to face the facts squarely, inadvertently tend to *confirm* the minority's negative image of itself and this in the very act of dwelling exclusively and even self-indulgently upon the majority's sins. A clinician may be forgiven for questioning the curative values of an excessive dose of moral zeal. I find, for example, even the designation "culturally deprived" somewhat ironic (although I admire much of the work done under this banner) because I am especially aware of the fact that the middle-class culture, of which the slum children are de-

prived, deprives some of the white children of experiences which might prevent much neurotic maladjustment. There is, in fact, an exquisite poetic justice in the historical fact that many white young people who feel deeply deprived *because* of their family's "culture" find an identity and a solidarity in living and working with those who are said to be deprived for lack of such culture. Such confrontation may lead to new mutual insights; and I have not, in my lifetime, heard anything approaching the immediacy of common human experience revealed in stories from today's South (and from yesterday's India).

In this connection we may also ask a question concerning the measurements used in diagnosing the Negro American's condition; and diagnosis, it must be remembered, defines the prognosis, and this not least because it contributes to the patient's self-awareness and attitude toward his suffering.

Our fellow panelist Thomas Pettigrew, in his admirable compilation *A Profile of the Negro American*, employs identity terms only in passing. He offers a wealth of solid and all the more shocking evidence of the disuse of the Negro American's intelligence and of the disorganization of his family life. If I choose from the examples reported by Pettigrew one of the most questionable and even amusing, it is in order to clarify the place of single testable *traits* in the whole *configuration* of an individual's development and of his people's history.

Pettigrew, following Burton and Whiting, discusses the problem that

> [Boys] from fatherless homes must painfully achieve a *masculine self-image* late in their childhood after having established an original self-image on the basis of the only parental model they have had—their mother. Several studies point to the applicability of this *sex-identity problem* to lower-class Negro males.

He reports that

> Two objective test assessments of widely different groups—Alabama jail prisoners and Wisconsin working-class veterans with tuberculosis —found that Negro males scored higher than white males on a *measure of femininity*. . . . This measure is a part of the Minnesota Multiphasic Inventory (MMPI), a well-known psychological instrument that requires the respondent to judge the applicability to himself of over five hundred simple statements. Thus, Negroes in these samples generally agreed more often with such "feminine" choices as, "*I would like to be a singer*" and "I think that *I feel more intensely* than most people do." [9]

Pettigrew wisely puts "feminine" in quotation marks. We will assume that the M.M.P.I. is an "objective test assessment for widely different groups" including Alabama jail prisoners and patients on a tubercular ward, and that incidental test blemishes in the end all come-out-in-the-wash of statistics so that the over-all conclusions may point to significant differences between Negroes and whites and between indices of femininity and of masculinity. That such assessment singles out as "feminine" the wish to be a singer and "feeling more intensely than most people do," may be a negligible detail. And yet, this detail suggests that the choice of test items and the generalizations drawn from them may say at least as much about the test and the testers as about the subjects tested. To "want to be a singer" or "to feel intensely" seems to be something only a man with feminine traits would acknowledge in that majority of respondents on whom the test was first developed and standardized. But why, one wonders, should a lower-class Negro locked up in jail or in a tuberculosis ward not admit to a wish to be a man like Paul Robeson or Harry Belafonte, and also that he feels more intensely (if, indeed, he knows what this means) than the chilly business-like whites around him? To be a singer and to feel intensely may be facets of a masculine ideal gladly admitted if you grew up in Alabama (or, for that matter, in Napoli), whereas it would be a blemish to be denied in a majority having adjusted to other masculine ideals. In fact, in Alabama and in Naples an emphasis on artistic self-expression and intense feeling may be close to the core of your positive identity—so close that the loss or devaluation of such emphasis by way of "integration" may make you a drifter on the murky sea of adjustable "roles." In the case of the compact white majority, the denial of "intense feelings" may, in turn, be part of a white identity problem which contributes to the prejudiced rejection of the Negro's potential or periodical intensity. Tests harboring similar distinctions may be offering "objective" evidence of racial differences, but may also be symptomatic of them. If this is totally overlooked, and this is my main point, the test will only emphasize, and the tester will only report, and the reader of the report (white or Negro) will only perceive the distance between the Negro's "disintegrated" self-imagery and what is assumed to be the white's "integrated" one.

As Pettigrew (in another connection) says starkly, putting himself in the shoes of a Negro child to be tested:

> After all, an intelligence test is a middle-class white man's instrument; it is a device whites use to prove their capacities and get ahead in the white world. Achieving a high test score does not have the same meaning for a lower-status Negro child, and it may even carry a definite connotation of personal threat. In this sense, scoring low on intelligence measures may for some talented Negro children be a rational response to perceived danger.[10]

The whole *test-event* thus itself underlies a certain historical and social relativity to be clarified in each case in terms of the actual identity configuration. By the same token, it is by no means certain that the individual undergoing such a procedure will be the same person when he escapes the predicament of the test procedure and joins, say, his peers on the playground or on a street corner. Thus, a "profile" of the Negro American made up of different methods under different conditions may offer decisively different configurations of "traits." This does not make one procedure wrong and the other right, but it makes both (and more) essential in the establishment of criteria for an existing identity configuration. On the other hand, it is all too often taken for granted that the *investigator* (and his identity conflicts) invisibly blends into his method even when he is a representative of a highly (and maybe defensively) verbal subgroup of whites and is perceived as such by subjects who are near-illiterate or come from an illiterate background.

In this connection, I would like to refer to Kenneth Clark's moving characterization of the sexual life of the "marginal young people in the ghetto." As a responsible father-figure, he knows he must not condone what he nevertheless must also defend against deadly stereotypes.

> Illegitimacy in the ghetto cannot be understood or dealt with in terms of punitive hostility, as in the suggestion that unwed mothers be denied welfare if illegitimacy is repeated. Such approaches obscure, with empty and at times hypocritical moralizing, the desperate yearning of the young for acceptance and identity, the need to be meaningful to someone else even for a moment without implication of a pledge of undying fealty and foreverness. . . . To expose oneself further to the chances of failure in a sustained and faithful relationship is too large to risk. The *intrinsic value* of the relationship is the only value because there can be no other.[11]

This places a legal or moral item into its "actual" context—a context which always also reveals something about those who would judge and stereotype rather than understand: for is not the *intrinsic value of the relationship* exactly that item (hard to define, hard to test, and legally irrelevant) which may be lost in some more fortunate youths who suffer under a bewildering and driving pluralism of values?[12]

Past and Future

Turning now to the new young Negroes: "My God," a Negro woman student exclaimed the other day in a small meeting, "what

am I supposed to be integrated *out of?* I laugh like my grandmother—and I would rather die than not laugh like that." There
was a silence in which you could hear the stereotypes click; for
even laughter had now joined those aspects of Negro culture and
Negro personality which have become suspect as the marks of submission and fatalism, delusion and escape. But the young girl did
not give in with some such mechanical apology as "by which I do
not mean, of course . . ." and the silence was pregnant with that
immediacy of joint experience which characterizes moments when
an identity conflict becomes palpable. It was followed by laughter
—embarrassed, amused, defiant.

To me, the young woman had expressed one of the anxieties
attending a rapid reconstitution of identity elements: "supposed to"
reflects a sense of losing the active, the choosing role which is of the
essence in a sense of identity as a continuity of the living past and
the anticipated future. I have indicated that single items of behavior or imagery can change their quality within new identity
configurations; and yet these same indices once represented an integration as well as an integrity of Negro life—"such as it was," to be
sure, but the only existing inner integration for which the Negro is
now "supposed to" exchange an unsure outer integration. Desegregation, compensation, balance, re-conciliation—do they all sometimes
seem to save the Negro at the cost of an absorption which he is
not sure will leave much of himself left? Thus the "revolution"
poses an "identity crisis" in more than one way; the Negro writer's
"complicated assertions and denials of identity" (to use Ellison's
words) have simpler antecedents, not less tragic for their simplicity.

For identity development has its time, or rather two kinds of
time: a *developmental stage* in the life of the individual, and a
period in history. There is, then, also a complementarity of life-
history and history. Unless provoked prematurely and disastrously
(and the biographies of sensitive Negro writers as well as direct
observations of Negro children attest to such tragic prematurity)
psychosocial identity is not feasible before the beginning, even as
it is not dispensable after the end of *adolescence,* when the body,
now fully grown, grows together into an individual appearance;
when sexuality, matured, seeks partners in sensual play and, sooner
or later, in parenthood; when the mind, fully developed, can begin
to envisage a career for the individual within a historical perspective—all idiosyncratic developments which must fuse with each
other in a new sense of sameness and continuity. But the increasing
irreversibility of all choices (whether all too open or foreclosed)
leads to what we call the *identity* crisis which here does not mean a
fatal turn but rather (as in drama and in medicine) an *inescapable*

turning point for better *or* for worse. "Better" here means a conflu-
ence of the constructive energies of individual and society, which
contributed to physical grace, sexual spontaneity, mental alertness,
emotional directness, and social "actualness." "Worse" means prolonged *identity confusion* in the young individual. Here it must be
emphasized—for this is the point at which the psychosexual theories of psychoanalysis fuse with the psychosocial ones—that identity formation is decisive for the integration of sexuality (whether
the cultural trend is toward repression or expression) and for the
constructive use of aggression. But the crisis of youth is also the
crisis of a generation and of the ideological soundness of its society.
(There is also a complementarity of identity and ideology). The
crisis is least marked and least "noisy" in that segment of youth
which in a given era is able to invest its fidelity [13] in an ideological
trend associated with a new technical and economic expansion,
(such as mercantilism, colonialism, industrialization). For here new
types and roles of competence emerge. Today this includes the
young people in all countries and in all classes who can fit into and
take active charge of technical and scientific development, learning
thereby to identify with a lifestyle of testing, inventing, and producing. Youth which is eager for such experience but unable to find
access to it will feel estranged from society, upset in its sexuality, and
unable to apply its aggression constructively. It may be that today
much of Negro Youth as well as an artistic-humanistic section of
White Youth feel disadvantaged and, therefore, come to develop a
certain solidarity in regard to "the crisis" or "the revolution": for
young people in privileged middle-class homes as well as in underprivileged Negro homes may miss that sameness and continuity
throughout development which makes a grandmother's warmth and
a fervent aspiration part of an identical world. One may go further
and say that this whole segment of American youth is attempting
to develop its own ideology and its own rites of confirmation by following the official call to the external frontiers of the American way
of life (Peace Corps), by going to the internal ones (deep South),
or by attempting in colleges (California) to fill an obvious void in
the traditional balance of the American way of life—a void caused
by a dearth of that realism, solidarity, and ideology which welds together a functioning radical opposition.

We will come back to this point. Here we may suggest that
identity also contains a complementarity of past and future both in
the individual and in society: it links the actuality of a living past
with that of a promising future. This formulation excludes, I hope,
any romanticizing of the past or any salesmanship in the creation of
future "postures."

In regard to "the revolution" and its gains, one can only postulate that the unblinking realism and ruthless de-masking of much of the present literature supports a new sense of toughness in the "face of reality." It fits this spirit that Pettigrew's "Profile," for example, fails to list such at any rate untestable items as (in alphabetical order) companionability, humor, motherhood, music, sensuality, spirituality, sports, and so forth. They all are suspect, I know, as traits of an accommodation romanticized by whites. But this makes presently available "profiles" really the correction of caricatures, rather than attempts at even a sketch of a portrait. But can a new or renewed identity emerge from corrected caricatures? One thinks of all those who are unable to derive identity gains from the "acceptance of reality" at its worst (as the writers do and the researchers) and to whom a debunking of all older configurations *may* become a further *confirmation* [14] of worthlessness and helplessness.

It is in this context also that I must question the fact that in many an index the Negro father appears *only* under the heading of "absence." Again, the relationship between family disintegration, father-absence, and all kinds of social and psychiatric pathology is overwhelming. "Father absence" does belong in every index and in the agenda of national concern. But as the *only* item related to fatherhood *or* motherhood does it not do grave injustice to the presence of many, many mothers, and at least some of the fathers? Whatever the historical, sociological, or legal interpretation of the Negro mother's (and grandmother's) saving presence in the whole half-circle of plantation culture from Venezuela through the Caribbean into our South, is it an item to be omitted from the agenda of the traditional Negro identity? Can Negro culture afford to have the "strong mother" stereotyped as a liability? For a person's (and a people's) identity begins in the rituals of infancy, when mothers make it clear with many pre-literate means that to be born is good and that a child (let the bad world call it colored or list it as illegitimate) is deserving of warmth. As I pointed out in the *Dædalus* issue on Youth, these mothers have put an indelible mark on "Negro Culture" and what they accomplished should be one of the proudest chapters in cultural history.

The systematic exploitation of the Negro male as a domestic animal and the denial to him of the status of responsible fatherhood are, on the other hand, two of the most shameful chapters in the history of this Christian nation. For an imbalance of mother-and-father presence is never good, and becomes increasingly bad as the child grows older; for then the trust in the world established in infancy may be all the more disappointed. Under urban and industrial conditions it may, indeed, become the gravest factor in personality disorganization. But, again, the "disorganization" of the Negro family must not be measured solely by its distance from the white or Negro middle-class family with its one-family housing and legal and religious legitimizations. Disintegration must be measured and understood also as a distortion of the *traditional* if often unofficial *Negro family pattern*. The traditional wisdom of the mothers will be needed as will the help of the Negro men who (in spite of such circumstances) actually did become fathers in the full sense.

In the meantime, the problem of the function of both parents, each strong in his or her way, and both benignly present in the home when needed most is a problem facing the family in any industrial society on a universal scale. The whole great society must develop ways to provide equality of opportunity in employment and yet also differential ways of permitting mothers and fathers to attend to their duties toward their children. The maternal-paternal dimension may well also serve to clarify the fact that each stage of development needs its own optimum environment, and that to find a balance between maternal and paternal strength means to assign to each a period of dominance in the children's life. The mother's period is the earliest and, therefore, the most basic. There is a deep relation between the first "identity" experienced in the early sensual and sensory exchanges with the mother(s) —the first re-cognition—and that final integration in adolescence when all earlier identifications are assembled and the young person meets his society and his historical era.

Total and Whole

In his book *Who Speaks for the Negro?* R. P. Warren records another exclamation by a young woman student:

> The auditorium had been packed—mostly Negroes, but with a scattering of white people. A young girl with pale skin, dressed like any coed anywhere, in the clothes for a public occasion, is on the rostrum. She is leaning forward a little on her high heels, speaking with a peculiar vibrance in a strange irregular rhythm, out of some inner excitement, some furious, taut èlan, saying: "—and I tell you I have discovered a great truth. I have discovered a great joy. I have discovered that I am black. I am black! You out there—oh, yes, you may have black faces, but your hearts are white, your minds are white, you have been whitewashed!"

Warren reports a white woman's reaction to this outburst and surmises that if this woman at that moment heard any words in her head, they were most likely the echo of the words of Malcolm X: "White devils!" And if she saw any face, it must have been the long face of Malcolm X grinning with sardonic certitude.

I think we understand this fear. She has witnessed what I will call a "totalistic" re-arrangement of images which is, indeed, basic to some of the ideological movements of modern history. By totalism I mean an inner regrouping of imagery, almost a *negative conversion*, by which erstwhile negative identity elements become totally dominant, making out of erstwhile positive elements a combination to be excluded totally.[15] This, however, can happen in a transitory way in many young people of all colors and classes who rebel and join, wander off or isolate themselves; it can subside with the developmental storm or lead to an unexpected commitment. Depending on historical and social conditions, the process has its malignant potentials, as exemplified in "confirmed" pervert-delinquent or bizarre-extremist states of mind and forms of behavior.

The chill which this process can give us in its political implications refers back to our sense of historical shock when post-Versailles German youth, once so sensitive to foreign critique, but then on the rebound from a love of Kultur which promised no realistic identity, fell for the Nazi transvaluation of civilized values. The transitory Nazi identity, based on a *totalism* marked by the radical *exclusion* of foreign otherness, failed to integrate historically given identity elements, reaching instead for a pseudologic perversion of history. Obviously both radical segregationism, in its recourse to an adjusted Bible, and Black Muslimism are the counterparts of such a phenomenon in this country. In the person of Malcolm X the *specific rage* which is aroused wherever identity development loses the promise of a traditionally assured wholeness, was demonstrated theatrically. Such latent rage (by no means always unjustified) is easily exploited by fanatic and psychopathic leaders: it can explode in the arbitrary destructiveness of mobs; and it can in a more repressed form serve the efficient violence of organized machines of destruction. Yet, the Black Muslims, too, were able to call on some of the best potentials of the individuals who felt "included."

This country as a whole, however, is not hospitable to such totalistic turns, and the inability or, indeed, unwillingness of youth in revolt to come to systematic ideological conclusions is in itself an important historical fact. The temporary degeneration of the Free Speech Movement in California into a revolt of dirty words was probably representative of the intrusion of an impotent totalism into a promising radicalism. This reluctance to be regimented in the service of a political ideology, however, can make the latent violence in our disadvantaged youth that much more destructive to personal unity and, sporadically, to "law and order." But note also, that the rate of crime and of delinquency in some Southern counties was reported to have dropped sharply when the Negro population became involved in social protest.

The alternative to an exclusive totalism is the wholeness of a *more inclusive identity*. This leads to another question: If the Negro American wants to "find" that wider identity which will permit him to be self-certain as a Negro (or a descendant of Negroes) *and* integrated as an American, what joint *historical actuality* can he count on? For we must know that when all the *objective realities* are classified and investigated, and all the studies assessed, the question remains: what are the *historical actualities* with which we can work?

Returning once more to the individual, I can now register a certain impatience with the faddish equation of the term identity with the question "Who am I?" This question nobody would ask himself except in a more or less transient morbid state, in a creative self-confrontation, or in an adolescent state sometimes combining both; wherefore on occasion I find myself asking a student who claims that he is in an "identity-crisis," whether he is complaining or boasting. For most, the pertinent question really is "What do I want to make of myself—and—what do I have to work with?" Here, the awareness of inner motivations is, at best, useful in keeping the future from being swamped by infantile wishes and adolescent defenses. Beyond that, only a restored or better trained sense of historical actuality can lead to a deployment of those energies which both activate and are activated by potential developments. How potential developments become historical fact is demonstrated by the way in which "culturally deprived" Negro children meet a sudden historical demand with surprising dignity and fortitude. In an unpublished manuscript, Robert Coles, who has made significant contributions to this problem, presents psychiatric data which (according to our theories) would have predicted for a lone Negro boy an inevitable and excusable failure in his task of personifying (with one other child) the desegregation of a whole school. But he did stand up to it unforgettably—and he is on his way.

In all parts of the world the struggle now is for anticipatory and *more inclusive identities*: what has been a driving force in revolutions and reformations, in the founding of churches and in the building of empires has become a contemporaneous world-wide competition. Revolutionary doctrines promise the new identity of peasant-and-worker to the youth of countries which must overcome their tribal, feudal, or colonial past; new nations attempt to absorb regions; new markets, nations; and world space is extended to include outer space as the proper locale for a universal technological identity.

At this point, we are beyond the question (and Gandhi did much to teach this to the British) of how a remorseful or scared colonialist may dispense corrective welfare in order to appease the need for a wider identity. The problem is rather how he includes himself in the wider pattern. For a more inclusive identity is a development by which two groups who previously had come to depend on each other's negative identities (by living in a traditional situation of mutual enmity or in a symbiotic accommodation to one-sided exploitation) join their identities in such a way that new potentials are activated in both.

Exclusive and Inclusive

What wider identities are competing for the Negro American's commitment? Some, it seems, are too wide to be "actual," some too narrow. As too wide I would characterize the identity of a "human being" bestowed, according to a strange modern habit of a latter-day humanistic narcissism, by humans to humans (patients, women, Negroes, and so on). While this at times represents genuine transcendence of the pseudo-species mentality, it often also implies that the speaker, having undergone some revelatory hardships, is in a position to grant membership in humanity to others. But it also tends to take all specificity out of "human" relations; for man meets man always in categories (be they adult and child, man and woman, employer and employee, leader and follower, majority and minority) and "human inter-relations" can truly be only the expression of divided function and the concrete overcoming of the specific ambivalence inherent in them. I would not be surprised to find that our Negro colleagues and friends often sense a residue of species-wide colonialism in our vague humanity. In contrast, the concrete work on the achievement of minimum rights for the *Negro American citizen* has created moments of the most intense sharing of the human condition.

Probably the most inclusive and the most absorbing identity potential in the world today is that of *technical skill*. This is what Lenin meant when he advocated that first of all the mushik be put on a tractor. True, he meant: as a preparation for the identity of a class-conscious proletarian. But it has come to mean more today, namely, the participation in an area of activity and experience which (for better or for worse) verifies modern man as a worker and planner. It is one thing to exclude oneself from such verification because one has proven oneself gifted in other respects and able to draw on the traditional verification provided by Humanism or the Enlightenment—at least sufficiently so that alienation from the present, too, adds up to some reasonably comfortable "human identity." It is quite another to be excluded from it by literacy requirements which prevent the proof that one is mechanically gifted or the use of the gift after such proof is given. Israel, a small country with a genius for renewing identities, has shown (for example, in the use of its army as an educational institution) that illiteracy can be corrected in the process of putting people where they feel they are needed and are needed.

The *"African identity"* is a strong contender for a wider identity, as Harold Isaacs has shown. It offers a highly actual setting for the solidarity of black skin color, and probably also provides the American Negro with an equivalent of what all other Americans could boast about or disavow: an (if ever so remote) homeland. However, the American Negro's mode of separation from Africa robbed him of the identity element *"immigrant."* There seems to be a question also whether to Africans a Negro American is more black or more American, and whether the Negro American, in actual contacts with Africans, wants to be more American or more Negro. The Black Muslims, at any rate, seem to have called themselves at first Asiatics, to emphasize the wider mystical unity of Muslimism.

The great *middle class* as the provider of an identity of consumers (for whom, indeed, Pettigrew's prescription of "dollars and dignity" seems to be most fitting) has been discussed in its limitations by many, but by none more eloquently than by the President in his Howard University speech. The middle-class identity (a class pre-occupied with matters of real estate and of consumption, of status and of posture) will include more and more of the highly gifted and the fortunate, but, if it does not yield to the wider identity of the Negro American, it obviously creates new barriers between these few and the mass of Negroes, whose distance from white competition is thereby only increased. "Work and dignity" may be a more apt slogan, provided that work dignifies by providing a "living" dollar as well as a challenge to competence, for without both "opportunity" is slavery perpetuated.

But here as everywhere the question of the Negro American's identity imperceptibly shades into the question of what *the* American wants to make of himself in the technology of the future. In this sense, the greatest gain all around (and one now to be consolidated) may be what the doctors at Howard University have discussed as *pro-social action* on the part of Negroes. I mean the fact that their protest, pervaded by nonviolent spirit and yet clearly defying local law and custom, has been accepted by much of the nation as American, and that the President himself would echo the slogan "we shall overcome," thus helping to align "pro-social" action with American action. The judiciary and legislative levels, too, have attempted to absorb "the revolution" on a grand scale. But absorption can be defensive and merely adjustive, or it can be adaptive and creative; this must as yet be seen.

In the meantime, the success of pro-social action should not altogether obscure an *anti-social* identity element revelantly recounted in the autobiographies of Negro Americans. I mean the tragic sacrifice of youth designated as delinquent and criminal. They, no doubt, often defended whatever identity elements were available to them by revolting in the only way open to them—a way of vicious danger, and yet often of self-respect and solidarity. Like the outcast heroes of the American frontier, some anti-social types among the Negroes are not expendable from the history of their people—not yet.

Our genuinely humanist youth, however, will continue to extend a *religious identity element* into race-relations: for future over-all issues of identity will include the balance within man of technological strivings and ethical and ultimate concerns. I believe (but you must not tell them for they suspect such words) that the emergence of those youths who stepped from utter anonymity right into our national affairs does contain a new and *wider religious element* embracing nothing less than the promise of a mankind freer of the attitudes of a pseudo-species: that utopia of universality proclaimed as the most worthy goal by all world religions and yet always entombed in new empires of dogma which turned into or allied themselves with new pseudo-species. The churches, too, have come to the insight that earthy prejudices—fanatical or outspoken, hiding in indifference, or latent and repressed—feed into that deadly combination which now makes man "the lethal factor" in the universe, for as pointed out it ties limitless technical ambition (including the supremacy of weapons of annihilation) and the hypocrisy of outworn moralistic dogma to the territoriality of mutually exclusive identities. The counter force, *nonviolence*, may always be a compelling and creative actuality only at critical moments, and only for "the salt of the earth." But Gandhi took the first steps toward a world-wide application to politics of principles once purely religious.

As far as the world-wide frontier of *post-colonial* and *colored identities* is concerned, it is hard to predict their fate in the clash of new national interests in Africa and Asia. As of now, however, one cannot ignore the possible implications of American action in Vietnam for a world-wide identification of colored people with the naked heroism of the Vietcong revolutionaries. The very demand that North Vietnam give in (and even if it were nearly on her own terms) to a super-organized assault by a superfluity of lethal weapons may simply be too reminiscent of the function of firepower in colonial expansion in general; of police power in particular; and of a certain (implicitly contemptuous) attitude which assumes that "natives" will give in to pressures to which the master-races would consider themselves impervious (*vide* the British in the Blitz). It must be obvious that differences of opinion in this country in regard to American military involvement in Asia are not merely a matter of the faulty reading of facts or of lack of moral stamina on one side or the other, but also of a massive identity conflict. Intrinsic to the dominant political-technological nucleus of an American identity is the expectation that such power as can now be unleashed can be used to advantage in limited employment, and has built-in safeguards against an unthinkable conflagration. But there will be urgent voices abroad and sincere protest at home expressing the perplexity of those who perceive only one active moral frontier of equality and of peace extending from the center of the daily life of America to the peripheries of its foreign concerns. Here the Negro American shares the fate of a new and wider American dilemma.

I have now listed a few of the emerging "wider" identity elements in order to introduce queries which other members of the symposium are better equipped to answer. Such listing can only lead to one tentative impression, namely, that none of these alternatives offers to the American Negro a nucleus for a total realignment, and that all of them must find their place in a new constellation, the nucleus of which is already clearly suggested by the two words Negro and American.

As used in the foregoing, the term identity has betrayed its clinical origin in the study of individual disturbances and of social ills. But even where applied to the assessment of a social problem it remains clinical in methodology, that is, it can be used only to focus the thinking of a "staff." For the consideration of identity problems calls for the "taking of history," the localization and the diagnostic assessment of disintegration, the testing of intact resources, the approximate prognosis, and the weighing of possible action—each based on specialties of approach and often of temperament. In addition to all this, a certain intuitive insight based on experience *and* on conviction is indispensable in the assessment of *verifiable reality* and of *modifiable actuality*. On the way some theory may help; but a concept should be retained only as long as it brings some preliminary order into otherwise baffling phenomena.[16]

NOTES

1 Robert Penn Warren, *Who Speaks for the Negro?* (New York, 1965), p. 17.
2 These notes are a counterpart to the "Memorandum on Identity and Negro Youth," *Journal of Social Issues,* Vol. 20, No. 4 (October 1964).
3 Henry James (ed.), *The Letters of William James,* Vol. 1 (Boston, 1920), p. 199.
4 See my introduction to G. B. Blaine and C. C. McArthur (eds.), *Emotional Problems of the Student* (New York, 1961).
5 Sigmund Freud, "Address to the Society of B'nai B'rith," in *The Standard Edition* (London, 1959), p. 273.
6 Kenneth B. Clark, *Dark Ghetto* (New York, 1965).
7 Howard Zinn, *SNCC, The New Abolitionists* (Boston, 1964).
8 Not all doubt or discomfort regarding the conception of identity is to be seen as "resistance" by any means. Powerful methodological quandaries are inescapable. I would also share the reluctance to accept psychosocial identity as "all there is" to human identity. Psychosocial phenomena, however, are part of that engagement in a period of the life cycle and in a given historical era without which an unfolding of human potentials (including an eventual transcendence) seems unthinkable.
9 Thomas F. Pettigrew, *A Profile of the Negro American* (Princeton, N.J., 1964), p. 19. (Italics added.)
10 *Ibid.,* p. 115.
11 Kenneth B. Clark, *op. cit.,* p. 73. (Italics added.)
12 Under the tense conditions of a sudden awareness of facts long suppressed and distorted, new stereotypes are apt to enter the imagery of the most thoughtful. In *Crisis in Black and White,* C. E. Silberman discusses S. M. Elkin's basic book *Slavery* and, half-quoting and half-editorializing, uses the stereotype "childlike" as a common denominator of Negro personality and the transient regressions of inmates in concentration camps. Along with truly childish qualities, such as silliness, we find fawning, servile, dishonest, mendacious, egotistic, and thievish activities all summed up under "this childlike behavior" (p. 76). Here childlike replaces childish or regressed, as feminine often replaces effeminate, which is both misleading and destructive of the image of the genuine article.
13 See Erik H. Erikson, "Youth: Fidelity and Diversity," *Youth: Change and Challenge* (New York, 1963), pp. 1–23.
14 Erik H. Erikson and Kai T. Erikson, "The Confirmation of the Delinquent," in Hendrik M. Ruitenbeek (ed.), *The Condition of Modern Man in Society* (New York, 1962).
15 See Robert J. Lifton, *Thought Reform and the Psychology of Totalism* (New York, 1961).
16 Attempts at transverting clinical concepts into quantifiable items subject to experimental verification are always undertaken at the risk of the experimenter.

Psychiatrist Alvin Poussaint discusses the extent to which Negroes have played and internalized the roles prescribed by white racists. Explaining what has often been called the "pathology of the ghetto," the author suggests that many a black person has said to himself, "Yes, I am inferior and I hate myself for it."

The civil rights movement began to alter that image of self-hatred. The most recent thrust for black consciousness has changed it further. Poussaint says that true equality will come about when, like Jewish-, Irish-, and Chinese-Americans, Afro-Americans have pride in themselves and in their own subculture and have learned to use their communal strength to exercise power over their own destinies.

18

Alvin F. Poussaint

THE SELF-IMAGE OF THE NEGRO AMERICAN

Most psychiatrists and psychologists would agree that the Negro American suffers from a marred self-image, of varying degree, which critically affects his entire psychological being. It is also a well-documented fact that this negative self-concept leads to self-destructive attitudes and behavior that hinder the Negro's struggle toward full equality in American life.[1] Civil rights leaders have long been aware of the need to build a positive sense of identity in the Negro masses. Today, however, there are widening schisms among these leaders as to how this can best be accomplished.

For the past decades civil rights groups have vigorously pursued the ideal that the integration of Negroes into "all phases of American life" combined with the teaching of a bit of "Negro History" would solve most of the Negro's identity problems. Exceptions have been the Black Muslims and other nationalist groups who have insisted upon separation of the races as the ultimate solution to the

From Alvin F. Poussaint, "The Negro American: His Self-Image and Integration," *Journal of the National Medical Association,* 58 (1966), 419–423.

racial problem. In recent years, however, some of these same civil rights groups have begun to lose faith in the virtues of integration. A few militants have described integration as "a subterfuge for white supremacy," i.e., as always involving only a token number of Negroes integrated into "white institutions on the white man's terms." They believe that integration as presently conceived and practiced in America will lead eventually to a greater crisis in identity for the mass of American Negroes, especially the poor, unless there are counter-measures. Therefore, some have advocated "black consciousness" and different forms of racial solidarity as the way to the Negro's eventual psychological salvation and dignity.

Before we attempt to explore in detail some of the above ideas and approaches, it is necessary to review briefly the historical factors that have led to the Negro's chronic identity crisis.

Historical Background

To understand the Negro's self-image, self-concept, and "Who am I?" problems we must go back to the time of the birth and creation of the "American Negro." Over 300 years ago black men, women, and children were extracted from their native Africa, stripped bare both psychologically and physically, and placed in an alien white land. They were to occupy the most degraded of human conditions: that of a slave, a piece of property, a non-person. For inhumane economic reasons, the Negro family was broken up and scattered from auction block to auction block all over America. The Negro male was completely emasculated, and the Negro woman systematically exploited and vilely degraded. The plantation system implanted a subservience and dependency in the psyche of the Negro that made him forever dependent upon the good will and paternalism of the white man.

By 1863, when slavery was abolished, the Negro had been stripped of his culture and left with this heritage: an oppressed black man in a hostile white man's world. In the late 1800's and early 1900's the systematized racist and sometimes psychotic propaganda of the white man, haranguing about the inferiority of the Negro, increased in intensity. He was disenfranchised, terrorized, mutilated and lynched. The Negro became every unacceptable, pernicious idea and impulse that the white man's psyche wished to project, i.e., the black man was animal with a violence to murder, ravaging sexual impulses, etc. The intensity of the white man's psychological need that the Negro be shaped in the image of this projected mental sickness was such as to inspire the whole system of organized discrimination, segregation and exclusion of Negroes from society.

In the resulting color caste system, white people made certain that any wares they allotted to the Negro were inferior. The Caucasian American socialized the black man to internalize and believe all of the many vile things he said about him. They encouraged and rewarded behavior and attitudes in Negroes that substantiated their indicting stereotypes. Black men were happy-go-lucky, lazy, stupid, irresponsible, etc. Our mass media disseminated these images with vigor on radio, in movies, etc., and like unrelenting electric shocks conditioned the mind of the Negro to say, "Yes, I am inferior."

Not only have black men been taught that blackness is evil and Negroes "no-good," they have, in addition, been continually brainwashed that only "white is right." It was the light-skinned Negroes with straight hair who were allowed to elevate themselves in America. Of course, the white people suggested, and Negroes came to believe, that such Negroes were better because they had much "white blood." And there are still cliques of light-skinned Negroes in our communities who reject their darker brothers. Black men were taught to despise their kinky hair, broad nose, and thick lips. Our "black" magazines pushed the straightening of hair and bleaching cream as major weapons in the Negro's fight for social acceptability and psychological comfort.

Current Situation

The most tragic, yet predictable, part of all this is that the Negro has come to form his self-image and self-concept on the basis of what white racists have prescribed. Therefore, black men and women learn quickly to hate themselves and each other because they are Negroes. And, paradoxically, some black men tend to distrust and hate each other more than their white oppressor.[1,2] There is abundant evidence that racism has left almost irreparable scars on the psyche of Afro-Americans that burden them with an unrelenting, painful anxiety that drives the psyche to reach out for a sense of identity and self-esteem.[1,2,3]

Although the Negro's self-concept is determined in part by factors associated with poverty and low economic class status, being a Negro has many implications for the ego development of black people that are not inherent in lower-class membership. The black child develops in a color caste system and inevitably acquires the negative self-esteem that is the natural outcome of membership in the lowest stratum of such a system. Through contacts with institutionalized symbols of caste inferiority such as segregated schools, neighborhoods, etc., and more indirect negative indicators such as the reactions of his own family, he gradually becomes aware of the social and psychological implications of racial membership. He may see himself as an object of scorn and disparagement, unwanted by the white high caste society, and as a being unworthy of love and affection. Since there are few counterforces to this negative evaluation of himself, he develops conscious or unconscious feelings of inferiority, self-doubt, and self-hatred.

From that point in early life when the Negro child learns self-hatred, it molds and shapes his entire personality and interaction with his environment. In the earliest drawings, stories, and dreams of Negro children there appear many wishes to be white and a rejection of their own color. They usually prefer white dolls and white friends, frequently identify themselves as white, and show a reluctance to admit that they are Negro.[1,2,3] Studies have shown that Negro youngsters assign less desirable roles and human traits to Negro dolls.[2,3] One study reported that Negro children in their drawings tend to show Negroes as small, incomplete people and whites as strong and powerful.[4]

In Mississippi or any northern city ghetto, one has only to visit Head Start schools with three to five year olds to see that these children already suffer damaged self-esteem. You hear the children shouting at each other in anger, "Black pig," "Dirty nigger," etc. Much of this negative self-image is passed to them directly by parents who themselves have been conditioned by racism to hate their blackness. And thus, a vicious circle is perpetuated from generation to generation.

Sometimes this self-hatred can be quite subtle. Some black people may retreat into their own world and actually be more afraid of success than they are of failure because too often failure has come to be what they know and expect. It is all too frequent that Negroes with ability, intelligence and talent do not aspire to higher levels because they fear the responsibility that will be needed to handle success. Many Afro-Americans tend to have lower aspirations and shy away from competition, particularly with white people. One study showed that even when Negroes were given objective evidence of their equal intellectual ability in an interracial situation they typically continued to feel inadequate and react submissively.[5]

The Negro community's high rate of crimes of violence, illegitimacy, and broken homes can be traced in part to the Negro's learned self-hatred as well as to poverty. Black crime rates are particularly elevated for crimes involving aggression, such as assault and homicide, and these acts are usually committed against other Negroes, and for escapist deviations such as gambling, drug addiction and alcoholism.[2] Many Negroes are caught up in a vicious circle of self-destructive behavior as if to say to the world, "Yes, I am inferior and I hate myself for it."

Discussion

Many of the civil rights gains in the past decade and especially in the 1960's have done, one can surmise, a great deal to modify the negative self-concept of the Negro. The civil rights movement itself has brought a new sense of dignity and respect to those blacks most severely deprived by poverty and oppression in the rural south and northern ghetto. One factor that may have been important in the movement that helped to improve the self-image of the masses of Negroes was that black men were leading the struggle, and not white men. This fact in itself probably made Negroes, through the process of identification, take a pride in their group and feel less helpless knowing that they could bring about positive change in their environment. The feeling that one can have "control" over social forces is crucial to one's feelings of ego-strength and self-esteem. Thus, the movement brought to the Negro a new sense of power in a country dominated by a resistant white majority. Beyond this achievement, however, civil rights leaders tended to see total integration of the black and white races as the final step in destroying the Negro's negative self-image.

In stark contrast to this position, and not without a salutary influence on the Negro's self-image, was that of the Black Muslims. This was the one major Negro group that called for separation of the races and black supremacy as an alternative approach to the black man's problems of identity and self-esteem. Observers generally agree that the Muslims were quite effective in rehabilitating many anti-social and criminal types by fostering in them a positive self-image and pride in their blackness.[6,7] The significant fact is that the Muslims were able to alleviate much of the individual Negro's self-hatred without holding up or espousing integration or "full acceptance" of the black man into American white society.

Now we see slowly emerging in segments of the civil rights movement a disenchantment with the social and psychological consequences of integration. This disenchantment is due at least in part to the fact that integration has moved at a snail's pace and has been marked by white resistance and tokenism. The Negro has found himself in the uncomfortable position of asking and demanding the white man to let him in his schools, restaurants, theatres, etc., even though he knew the white man did not want him. In the south and north, many Afro-Americans resented the indignity of being in the eternal position of "begging for acceptance" into the white man's institutions. And it was further demoralizing to the mass of Negroes that the recent civil rights laws did not effectively change this pattern. It became apparent that integration was not to be integration in a real sense at all, particularly in the schools. Negro parents in the south never speak of sending their children to the "integrated school"; they say, "My child is going to the *white* school." No white children are "integrated" into Negro schools. Since integration is only a one-way street that Negroes travel to a white institution, then inherent in the situation itself is the implied inferiority of the black man.

Parents who fear psychological harm to their children are not anxious to send them to "integrated" schools. Some of the college-aged young people in the movement state frankly that they find this type of integration personally degrading and do not want to go to any school where they have to be "accepted by Southern white racists."

Since the Negro numbers at any white school are token, particular hardships are created for them because they are placed in a school with children who are generally the products of white racists' homes. The black child must withstand abundant psychological abuse in this situation as well as be an "experimental laboratory" for bigoted whites "to learn to live with Nigras." Since all children want to belong, the Negro must become an expert at "being liked and accepted." If such a child's self-esteem grows in such a situation it is not from a greater comfortness in being Negro but more likely because of his own conditioned belief that "white is right," or because he is successfully being a true martyr or pioneer.

Assimilation by definition always takes place according to the larger societal (white) model of culture and behavior, and thus the Negro must give up much of his black identity and subculture to be comfortably integrated. Many Negroes who seek complete assimilation become preoccupied with "proving" themselves to white people and trying to show them that "we are just like all other human beings," that is, that they are really *not* Negro.

Many Afro-Americans expend a great deal of internal energy trying to seek "individual freedom" in a white man's world. But it is a vain effort because "personal acceptability" has to be repeatedly proven to each new white group. The Negro group's vigorous pursuit of middle-class status symbols is frequently an overdetermined attempt to demonstrate to the white man, as well as to themselves, that they can be successful, worthwhile human beings. White America, however, has lumped all Negroes together in one collective image and hence, for no Negro can there be "individual freedom" unless there is "group freedom," which means undoing racial self-hatred. The Negro too often aspires to and gets entangled in the perverse situation where he feels that the most flattering compliment his white friends can pay him is: "You don't act like all the other Negroes," or "You don't seem Negro to me."

Many Negroes, including segments of the civil rights movement and nationalists, are beginning to fear that this type of "token integration" may augment the identity problems of the Negro. Little has been done to study the changes in self-concept of Negro children who attend "desegregated" schools in the south. Clearly, much more research has to be done in this field. But we do know that such integration as has existed in the north has not substantially helped to solve the Negro's identity problems.[3] In any event, there is a growing sense of racial solidarity and pride in Negroes both in the north and south. Afro-Americans are beginning to feel that it is through their strength as a group that they will win human dignity and power.

"Black consciousness," including the call for "black power," movement supporters argue that as long as Negroes are powerless politically and do not have their own sense of pride and worth as black men, they are psychological beggars in a white man's house. As has been pointed out, there are many negative implications of "token integration" for the Negro. On the other hand, would all-black institutions provide Negroes with a more stable, positive sense of identity and self-esteem?

It is known that such groups as the Black Muslims have frequently had many positive and constructive effects on the black community.[6,7] This group has brought greater self-reliance and dignity to the Negro community. They have also instilled pride and esteem in Negroes by emphasizing Negro history and achievements. "Black consciousness" programs can build Negro self-confidence by calling upon the black man to think and do for himself. They may also provide the stimulus for more independent thought and grass-roots problem-solving and the development of community leadership. Such programs seem to have the potential for undoing much of the Negro's learned self-hatred that leads to self-destructive behavior. Finally, such groups could constructively channel Negro frustrations and anger that lead to destructive violence and riots.

The question must be raised, however, whether such "all black" programs will in some way lead to more identity and self-esteem problems for the Negro since such groups would always exist within the pervading dominant white culture. There is some chance for such negative effects to develop, but if Negroes are truly *equals* in the larger society, a black subculture could exist much in the same way that America has subcultures of other national and racial groups such as the Jews, Irish, Chinese, etc. It is also clear that despite the drive for racial integration this is being vigorously resisted by the white population and we can expect to have isolated, predominantly black communities for a long time to come.

Since the Negro's self-concept problems cannot be solved through token integration, it is important that black men turn to the development of their own communities as an alternative and supplementary approach for building the Afro-American's self-image and esteem. Unfortunately, the white man cannot give Negroes "black consciousness," Negro Americans must give it to each other. This means that black people must undo the centuries of brain-washing by the white man, and substitute in its stead a positive self-image and positive concepts of oneself—and that self happens to be the black, dispossessed, disenchanted, and particularly poverty-stricken Negro.

Summary

The Negro suffers from many problems of identity and negative self-image because of the racism, discrimination, and segregation in American life. The civil rights movement has generated some changes, but integration as presently practiced does not seem to offer the mass of Negroes a solution to problems of negative self-concept. It has been suggested in this paper that token integration into "white institutions" may lead to greater identity crises for Afro-Americans. "Black consciousness" movements appear to be able to contribute a great deal to the Negroes' sense of identity and self-esteem, and could mobilize the black community for positive political and social action. The development of "black consciousness" could serve as an alternative and supplementary approach to the building of the Negroes' self-image along with the present drive toward complete racial integration.

NOTES

1 W. C. Kvaraceus *et al.*, *Negro Self-Concept: Implications for School and Citizenship.* McGraw-Hill, New York, 1965.
2 T. F. Pettigrew, *A Profile of the Negro American.* Van Nostrand, Princeton, 1964.

3 M. M. Grossack, *Mental Health and Segregation.* Springer, New York, 1965.
4 R. Coles, "When I Draw the Lord He'll be a Real Big Man," *The Atlantic,* May, 1966, p. 69.
5 I. Katz and L. Benjamin, "Effects of White Authoritarianism in Biracial Work Groups," *J. Abnormal and Soc. Psych.,* 61:448, 1960.
6 C. E. Lincoln, *The Black Muslims in America.* Beacon Press, Boston, 1961.
7 A. Haley, *The Autobiography of Malcolm X.* Grove Press, New York, 1965.

"There has never been a Negro born in America who has not been crippled and marred by the great lie of racial inferiority." Beginning with this statement, C. Eric Lincoln discusses the negative results of caste constriction imposed on black Americans and explains how those now engaged in the revolution are "involved . . . in changing the social structure of America."

To Lincoln the most significant result of the recent and continuing protest movement is that all black Americans are learning to accept themselves. That is the meaning of "mood ebony."

19

C. Eric Lincoln

MOOD EBONY:
THE ACCEPTANCE OF BEING BLACK

What is my disease?
Tell me.
Who can name my crime?
Is it only that I am black
And not white? [1]

A quarter of a century ago W. E. B. Du Bois, then teaching sociology at Atlanta University, complained bitterly about the white man's unwillingness to recognize the Negro genius. Commenting on the rewriting of history to fit the Negro image that had been conjured out of the white man's guilt over long centuries of black slavery, Du Bois declared:

> The whole attitude of the world was changed to fit this new economic reorganization. Black Africa, which had been a revered example to

From C. Eric Lincoln, *My Face Is Black*, Boston: Beacon Press, 1964, pp. 72–90. Reprinted by permission of the Beacon Press, copyright © 1964 by C. Eric Lincoln.

ancient Greece and the recognized contender with imperial Rome, became a thing beneath the contempt of Modern Europe and America. All history, all science was changed to fit this new condition. Africa had no history. Wherever there was history in Africa or civilization, it was of white origin; and the fact that it was civilization proved that it was white. If black Pharaohs sat on the throne of Egypt, they were not really black men but dark white men. Ethiopia, land of blacks, was described as a land of whites. If miracles of art appeared on the West Coast these were imported from artless Portugal. If Zymbabwe, with mines and irrigation appeared in the East, it was wholly Asiatic. If at any time, anywhere there was evidence in Africa of the human soul and the same striving of spirit and the same build of body found elsewhere in the world, it was all due to something non-African and not to the inherent genius of the Negro race.[2]

There has never been a Negro born in America who has not been crippled and maimed by the great lie of racial inferiority. That such is the case is patent at first consideration, but the subtle ramifications of the obvious fact are more difficult to perceive, even by Negroes themselves. Many Negroes are sufficiently accommodated to the racial *rapprochement* as to be superficially oblivious of its more serious detriments. A small number of others have by popular acclaim or professional attainment managed to escape to a limited degree the consummate detrition of personality and human worth which is the inevitable accompaniment of being a Negro in America. But there is no escape for the masses, and even for those who feel themselves emancipated there is the lurking fear of someday finding their emancipation to be a dream that has been shattered with a single word or gesture.

The self-hatred engendered by the caste constrictions is intense. In the lower classes it is expressed as displaced aggression upon other Negroes. In the middle and upper classes it is projected outward as hatred for Caucasians (especially Jews) and lower-class Negroes. In his study of the psychology of the Negro, Bertram P. Karon[3] finds that the lower-class Negro, in order to control his anger and resentment, "engages in various sorts of compensatory behavior: flashy dressing, denial of Negro attributes, narcosis (alcohol), . . . gambling, and explosive spending." Though emotionality is somewhat improved in the middle and upper classes, Karon observes that

> nearly all of that is cancelled out by the pressure for status. . . . They drive themselves harder, and refuse the compensatory activities of the lower class. They are vulnerable to depressed self-esteem, and have a harder time with the control of anger. . . . Their guilt over hatred of other Negroes, plus a fear of retaliation, leads to a "success phobia."

They also overshoot the mark of conformity to the white ideals . . . [and] their feelings of worthlessness may take the form of an unconscious identification with feces. . . .

In an independent analysis cited in Kardiner and Ovesey's classic study of the destructive effects of segregation on the Negro personality,[4] the following conclusions were drawn:

a summary of ratings of intellectual status . . . indicates that all the subjects are assayed as average or better. However, 92% of the group give evidence of reduced efficiency and incomplete utilization of potential capacity.

Profound anxiety is hypothesized in all the records. Life is viewed as dangerous, hostile, and assaultive. They feel small and inferior; and they have a persistent fear of mutilation and destruction.

Another universal trait in this group is their inability to give free rein to their assertive and aggressive drives and destructive impulses. These impulses are a source of conflict and disability; and they are not accepted complacently. The subjects are tense and strained and they sit uncertainly on the lid of a turbulent and explosively simmering cauldron of hostility. They expend great energy in containing and controlling aggression. Yet, always, it remains a problem to them.

The control of his aggressive tendencies and the accommodation to the white man's persistent image of what the Negro is or ought to be amount to the same thing. The Negro has been bottled up like some high explosive for generations. The present concern seems variously to be to de-fuse him by discrediting his leaders; de-activate him by controlled detonation, such as the march on Washington; or render him *implosive* rather than *explosive* by suffocating his organizations with well-meaning moderates. There does not appear to be anywhere any serious general intention of accepting him as a person without qualifications which ultimately reflect the racial prejudices we claim to have forgotten.

The myth-makers have done their work well. Self-hatred has scarred the Negro personality like some corrosive acid. No sane man can marvel that this is so, because for all his life in America the Negro has been hated for being black and he has learned from his haters to hate himself. Harold Isaacs, a Jewish scholar whose empathy for the Negro's emotional struggle has the peculiar keenness and perception common to some Jews who have been able to extrapolate the sufferings of their own people, writes poignantly of "reaching back to take the hand of that . . . lonely [Negro] child and hear again his cry of pain and anger at being taken for "*cannibal, evil, black African* . . ." Being of "cannibal, evil, and black African" descent, the Negro aspirant's hopes for acceptance and meaningful participation in this society were precluded before ever he saw the light of day. Far more devastating was the fact that he could not hope, and nowhere in his hated ancestry could he find an image to make his ideal. His only reference was the white man, and white America alternately greeted his bumbling efforts to be a black white man with benign tolerance or with outright derision, or else ignored him altogether. "I am prepared to say," Isaacs writes,

> that the systematic debasement, and self-debasement of the Negro in this white world has . . . been underpinned by the image the Negro child has gotten of the naked, savage, uncivilized African. . . . It is the picture of his contemporaneous ancestor which for generation after generation, has stared out at every Negro child who did get to school from nearly the first book he held in his hands. At a given moment of great and fearful and wondering interest he turned the pages of the geography text from which he was to learn the nature and shape of the world, and there . . . was the portrait of his origins, the picture of himself, the reason (as the text often inferred or flatly said) for his lowly backwardness and dim prospects.[5]

"The Picture" is a universal experience in the life of Negro Americans. It is the picture of a black savage with a bone through his nose, hoops in his ears and discs in his lips. There are feathers around his knees, and circulets around his ankles. His teeth are filed to points, and his face is horribly marked with tribal scars. His countenance sags under the weight of ignorance and stupidity. And he is black, black, *black!* This is the representation of the black race—the people who have "contributed nothing" to civilization.

We need not here dignify such nonsense with a digression for the purpose of rebuttal. It will suffice to say that those who need it may have it for themselves. What is significant is that a hundred years of solid Negro achievement under the most harrowing circumstances is a persistent *de facto* rebuttal, and the contemporary black revolution argues forcefully for a reassessment of history.

America claims surprise and disbelief at the depth of the revolution which is wracking our cities and threatening the carefully institutionalized values and taboos which have given us our characteristic image as a two-caste democracy. There is of course an obvious paradox inherent in the existence of a democratic caste system, but we have lived with it so long that to be called now to reexamine its postulates seems rude beyond forgiveness. The tragedy is that we do not really recognize what the revolution is about or what is at stake in it. We keep asking the Negro leaders, "What do 'your people' want now?" "When will they be satisfied?" The leaders can no more say what the people want than America can give it to them in a civil rights bill. What the people want is to some degree ineffable. It defies articulation in terms of objectives that can be enumerated or specified. Some have called it "dignity," but no nation can bestow dignity upon its citizens. Men can only dignify themselves. That is part of what the revolution is about—the denial of the "Big Lie"; the repudiation of "The Picture"; the challenges of a spurious history. The Negro leaders talk about jobs, and housing, and better schools and voting rights. Yes. All this too. These are the minimum objectives; and despite the long, long, century of denial, they are the things America can give most easily. It is so much harder to relinquish an idea than a thing or a privilege.

Columbia University Professor Daniel Bell, writing in the *New York Times* magazine,[6] is—like many other Americans—baffled by the proliferation of Negro leaders and the multiplicity of objectives they seem to be pursuing. "There are," Professor Bell insists, "two preconditions for successful political bargaining in the American system":

> One is that the Negro community has to choose its political spokesmen in a responsible way (in the way the farm groups have done); the other is that the Negro community has to specify its priorities and demands so that we know what to bargain about. In short there has to be a consensus about the ends desired—and such a consensus is not simply a list of slogans.

Obviously Professor Bell is confused as to the nature of the revolution. Or perhaps he is not convinced that there is one. The kids in the streets of Cambridge, Maryland and St. Augustine, Florida are not fighting to raise the price of ham a few cents. *They are involved and their lives are involved in changing the social structure of America!* There *is* a revolution going on, call it by another name or not; and while the goals and objectives are not always finely delineated or articulated with clarity and consistency, they are, or they will be discovered to be, goals of ultimate value rather than such immediate values as jobs and housing. The college students who risk their lives in voter registration efforts in Mississippi or in the picket lines in Tuscaloosa know that they are engaging in something of greater breadth and depth than a simple campaign to persuade the white man to let some Negroes vote, or eat at a public lunch counter. Their young white allies know it too. They have not come south to risk their lives for the sake of an integrated hamburger, but because they see that beyond the hamburger and beyond the ballot box their country is in trouble. It is right and just that the Negro should have his hamburger and his ballot, but the critical issue is how to change the basic presuppositions responsible for their being withheld in the first place.

It is probable that Professor Bell speaks for a growing number of white people (and not a few middle-class Negroes) when he complains about the proliferation of Negro leaders of questionable ability and about what seems to be a sharp increase in "militancy." The professor illustrates his own impatience with a quote from another writer in the *New York Times* who said that, "Almost every week a new civil rights organization is born . . . and another man or woman is acclaimed as a civil rights leader . . . Experience, education and social standing are not necessary for this leadership. What is necessary is the ability to articulate the desperate feelings of the impatient members of the community." Doubtless, it would be reassuring if all of the protest leaders could be chosen by ballot, and if only well-bred, educated men and women with "social standing" could qualify as candidates for leadership. It would be pleasant too if, once these "leaders" were chosen, they could sit down with their counterparts in the white community and negotiate the end of racial discrimination in America. But too many "well-bred, educated" Negroes are too busy trying to maintain precisely that image to be found where the action is—on the picket lines, and the "well-bred, educated" whites sit silently by on their suburban patios where no Negroes are—yet. The bombing and the head-smashing isn't being done by the "best" white people, and the "best" Negroes would rather not offend anyone lest they jeopardize the tenuous approbation they have laboriously earned for behaving themselves.

For the first time in recent history the Negro is choosing his own leaders. When his primary concern was to accommodate to the prevailing order, the white man chose the Negro's leaders and imposed them upon the black community. From time to time, various enterprising individuals with a sense of mission (or a scent of money) have represented themselves as "leaders" and have so presented themselves to the White Establishment with varying degrees of success. In fact, the would-be leadership of the tortured black caste has run the gamut from the brilliant intellectuals like Du Bois to the latest Johnny-come-lately with nothing more than his "militance" to recommend him. But the people have not followed all who presumed to lead. In his plea for a new phase in Negro leadership, Professor Bell articulates the concern among careful students of social change that the protest movement is heading for an explosion. He also articulates the anxiety of leaders like Whitney Young, who work within the established consensus, that too many distractions obscure the main issues with which we shall ultimately have to deal.

From another perspective the proliferation of leadership is an unmistakable sign of the revolutionary spirit which is energizing the Negro masses. As the volcano bubbles and seethes, new leaders will continue to be spewed up. The vast majority of them will be, in the words of the poet, "like snow upon the desert's dusty face, lighting a little hour or two" before passing on into obscurity. But out of this process will come the leadership that is truly representative of the people, and ultimately this is the leadership with which America must make its peace. Perhaps that leadership is already on the scene: it may be a man with a methodical plan, such as Whitney Young; or a man with a dream, such as Martin Luther King; or an apostle of nonviolence, such as James Farmer; or a flaming radical, such as Malcolm X, or a black apostle, such as Elijah Muhammad. The point is that whoever leads the Negro people from this point on will be someone that they themselves have chosen. This will be a good thing. They may, of course, make mistakes, as other people looking for quick and easy solutions to complex problems of social change have made mistakes. Indeed, there is no guarantee that they may not follow a man on a white horse (or more likely, a black horse!) a long way down the wrong road. There is ample precedent in history.

One of the most significant achievements to come out of the whole Negro protest is that in striving for the white man's acceptance, the black man has learned to accept himself. In a society oriented completely to the white man's value construct, this is an accomplishment of no little moment. The Negro's self-acceptance is far from being universal, of course, but it is clearly illustrated in the new ideas he has about himself—and his new behavior, while not characteristic, is indicative of a trend. The *mood ebony,* this new feeling about himself that is expressed in the acceptance—even the glorification—of being black in a white man's world, has challenged the Negro before, but never so deeply or at a level that is both emotional and intellectual. When Marcus Garvey, that Africanesque little Jamaican, came screaming out of the Caribbean after the First World War, his doctrine of black nationalism was an emotional panacea for the black masses of America who were shaken and confused by the white man's summary rejection of their notion that the world they had fought to make safe for democracy somehow included them. In the midst of the unprecedented wave of lynchings and race riots that signaled America's return to normalcy, Garvey's constant reminder that Negroes were persons of value did more than he was ever given credit for to relieve the mass frustrations of a shocked and disappointed people. In *The Negro World,* the propaganda organ for his movement,

> Garvey proudly recalled for his followers, though not always with complete accuracy, the stirring heroism of such leaders of American slave rebellions as Denmark Vesey, Gabriel Prosser, and Nat Turner. The struggles of Zulu and Hottentot warriors against European rule, the histories of Moorish and Ethiopian empires, and the intrepid exploits of Toussaint L'Ouverture against the French in Haiti were not neglected in the effort to make Negroes conscious and proud of their racial heritage.[7]

At the height of his movement, Garvey had possibly two or three million Negroes enrolled in his Universal Negro Improvement Association. "Up, you mighty race!" he thundered. "You can accomplish what you will." The Negro masses were impressed. They wanted desperately to believe in Marcus Garvey's reconstruction of the Negro past, and his grand dream for the black man's future. They wanted to be black men because they were rejected by white men. And they bought a dream in Africa because, in the American Dream, they always woke up screaming.

The Negro intelligentsia wanted no part of Garvey's black nationalism and no share in his dream of redemption in Africa. Africa was still a nightmare to them, a land of ignorance, savagery, and above all, *blackness.* "Blackness" not merely as a skin color, but as a philosophy, a way of life. Blackness was the antithesis of whiteness, and whiteness was synonymous with culture—culture, progress and acceptance. *Acceptance.* Surely the white man would accept them some day if they learned carefully to duplicate his behavior, his manners, his morals and his ideals. In his revealing study entitled *The New World of Negro Americans,*[8] Harold Isaacs of the Massachusetts Institute of Technology probes the hidden recesses of some well-known Negro personalities "who have crashed through the 'big gate' from the Negro world into the larger white world beyond." Without exception their attitudes toward Africa are either negative or very carefully guarded. Here are some samples of responses made to Isaacs on questions about Africa:

> As a child I remember my mother and father talking about African classmates they had at college, they were brown, Moroccans—not black.
> My interest in Africa came late and is still limited, not only limited, but I have numerous inadequacies on this. When I was working on my lectures and writings, I had to work very hard at it. I have great diffi-

culties in sustaining my interest and retaining knowledge about Africa or any part of it.

I suppose I shared the general vague picture Americans had, and I suppose still have: a place by our standards backward, uncivilized . . . I have no sense of any tie between me and Africa.

I had an aunt who . . . when kids got out of hand would say: "You little black Africans" or "you little fuzzy headed Africans!" She herself was quite light.

The worst thing anyone could say to you in addition to calling you "black nigger" was "black African."

Garvey's movement was foredoomed to failure. In the first place his back-to-Africa plans were neither conceived soundly, planned with thoroughness nor executed effectively. Further, the task Garvey set for himself far exceeded his personal abilities and those of his officers. He was a man born out of time. Arrayed against him were the European colonial powers, the American government and the Black Establishment with its white allies. Despite Garvey's success in enrolling millions in this movement, Negroes did not want to live in Africa, and the Africans, who were themselves subdued by the insidious philosophies of colonialism, were not anxious to welcome them there. But the crucial point is that the American Negro considered his heritage and his destiny to be no less American than that of any American white man. They wanted to live in the land for which they had toiled, fought and died. Marcus Garvey's greatest contribution to those who followed him was a new sense of self-esteem, however tentative. Never before Garvey, since Negroes had been free in America, did they dare examine the possibility of accepting themselves and their antecedents at face value. It is true that the limited success of Garveyism was to large degree an emotional reaction against the racial atrocities which swept America following World War I. But it is no less true that he planted the seed for the *mood ebony* through which contemporary Negroes express their disdain for what to them is the delusive ideal of whiteness.

In the 1920's and 1930's the "Negro Renaissance" rediscovered African culture, and Negro art and literature began to explore African themes. But the "talented tenth" (as the Negro intellectuals called themselves), were not *identifying* with blackness. They were simply willing to discuss it in a detached, disinterested way. Only since the emergence of self-governing African states have the Negro intellectuals felt secure enough to risk some degree of identification.

The *mood ebony* is not so much an identification with Africa as it is the abatement of the yearning after whiteness in America, and the rejection of the traditional order of values which, because they cannot be attained with reasonable effort, are productive of increasing anxiety and frustration. It expresses itself as a rejection of integration (sometimes as an insistence on separation). It does not necessarily imply a hatred for the white man, but it does imply a negation of the symbols of his culture, his power and his status. The tendency is, as it was expressed by a Harlem minister, to "let the white man go *his* way—but get him out of *my* way—and fast." But then it is easy to hate what you negate. The Negro has had a long and painful experience of that fact.

The best-known exponents of the *mood ebony* are the Black Muslims of Elijah Muhammad, the inevitable heirs of the Garvey movement. Muhammad does not view his movement as being either "social" or "racial," but as a religion. "My word," he insists, "is divine. And this is what distinguishes it from all other attempts to set the black man in the place Allah has willed him to be." We need not argue the "divine" nature of his mission to be moved to admit that the Muslim Messenger has been an important force in pushing the Negro masses toward a sense of adequacy. The preoccupation of the Black Muslim with his personal and racial image is well known, as is his firm belief that his history and his destiny transcend this brief moment of power which the white man has abused so badly. "We can afford to wait," says Muhammad. "We were here long before the blue-eyed devils were brought to civilization; we will be here for countless generations after they are gone."

Muhammad's avowed millenarianism can be deceptive if it is thought to be generally representative of the Negro masses. *They* cannot wait. They *won't* wait. It has come suddenly to the Negro that if he is going to be saved, he is going to have to save himself. For a hundred years he looked to the heroic institutions of a democratic society to take note of his peculiar condition—a condition not of his making, but one incident to the making of America. For a hundred years his unshakable confidence in The Church, his inalienable confidence in The Law, and his unsophisticated confidence in the social morality of The White Man gave him patience to endure the lash, the rope, the ghetto, the depersonalization of abject discrimination and segregation.[9] Suddenly it was evident that in the mid-twentieth century, here on the threshold of the space age and the precipice of eternity, neither The Church, The Law, nor The White Man had yet effected his release from social bondage and did not seem impressed with an urgency to do so. The whole world was in radical metamorphosis. Undemocratic institutions all over the world were being abandoned. Only in South Africa, Portuguese Angola and the United

States did the white man maintain a studied obliviousness to the black man's plea for freedom.

"Work and pray; live on hay. You'll have a pie in the sky when you die." This, the Negro complains bitterly, is his lot. As for the white man's law, many Negroes have come to feel that it was made by white men for the benefit of white men. So they contest it in the streets. One wit has remarked of the law that "Between white men it mediates. Between black men it speculates. And between whites and blacks it deviates." If this were a concept widely held, we would soon be living in chaos.

In the Muslim community the lamp of resentment with its flame of black hatred is carefully tended against the Day of Armageddon— the final confrontation between the forces of good and those of evil, when the non-white races of the world will inundate and (annihilate) the despised whites. Theirs is the hate that hate produced, or so the Black Muslims believe. For if the white man does not hate the black man, then why has he degraded him for so long? "You cannot tell me you love me," says Elijah Muhammad, "when you are giving me hell night and day. If I were to believe that, I would be sicker than you are." The discovery of "the truth about the white man," i.e., his demonic state, his hatred of the Negro, and his perversion of Christianity to support a racist philosophy, is the central fact that makes the Black Muslim movement a popular expression of America's bitterest and most disillusioned Negroes.

The Black Muslims have existed since 1930, but ten years after World War II they suddenly became news. They became news because the ferment in the black ghetto began to produce a rumbling that threatened the racial facade which has so long obscured democracy. The Black Muslims did not produce the rumblings, but they, like the students in the picket lines with bandages on their heads, are the symbols of racial unrest which could explode into a kind of civil violence that would make the infamous Red Summer of 1919 pale by comparison. We are fortunate that instead of civil violence we have had civil disobedience, and although there has been blood, the determined march for civil rights has not yet become bloody.

The Black Muslims are a part of the Negro's all-out struggle for freedom. They represent the extreme radical wing of the Negro's spectrum of protest. But they do not want integration. They want separation. They want no part of anything associated with the white man. The Muslims want a completely separate economy in a separate territory under the hegemony of black men. They want separation because they question the white man's ability to adjust to an integrated society, or even to a pluralistic one. They do not accept non-violence as an effective principle of negotiation.[10]

The Negro masses have not flocked to join Muhammad's Nation of Islam as they did Marcus Garvey's Universal Negro Improvement Association. Compared to the millions Garvey claimed, Muhammad's seventy or eighty mosques scattered about the country are not numerically impressive. Times have changed. Perhaps Garvey's defeat and deportation is still too vivid in the mind of the race. More likely is the resistance of the contemporary Negro to the idea of "going anywhere," for any reason. He does not want a separate state. The thought of emigrating to Africa seems ridiculous to him. *He is going to stay in America and still be black without apology for his blackness!* There is new pride in being black, and it is this aspect of Muslim philosophy that is impressive far beyond the numbers of men and women who confess the faith that is Elijah Muhammad's interpretation of Islam. And this, not the number of his followers, is the power of the Muslim leader. His black-suited followers, with their exaggerated formality yet a certain sureness, do not defer to the white man. They are polite to everybody. but they do not defer. And yet they came, for the most part, from the class which survives on deference. The Muslims appear to thrive. Their houses are neat and clean. Their children are not delinquents. They are seldom before the white man's courts except when in contest with the white man himself. Their own explanation is "knowledge"—knowledge about themselves and knowledge of "the truth about the white man." The Negro masses are impressed, and they accept Muhammad's "truth" without necessarily accepting his hatred. There is no compelling drive for integration among the masses, but there is a compulsion to be free—to be free in spite of being black.

If Elijah Muhammad is its Messenger, then James Baldwin, whether or not he accepts the role, is the uncontested philosopher for the *mood ebony*, and Malcolm X is its chief political spokesman. Among them, these three men have an interesting potential for assuming the leadership of America's black masses. Despite his intellectualism, Baldwin does not write for or about intellectuals. His descriptions and his message are visceral, and the images he conjures are the realities which are universal in the black man's experience. Baldwin says of Malcolm X:

> When Malcolm talks or one of the Muslims talks, they articulate for all the Negro people who hear them; who listen to them. They articulate their suffering, the suffering which has been in this country so long denied. That's Malcolm's great authority over his audiences. He corroborates their reality; he tells them that they really exist.[11]

Baldwin could well have been speaking of himself. Certainly he lacks Malcolm's vindictiveness (or, if he has it, its presence is carefully muted by the engaging language through which he communicates himself). And Baldwin, like Malcolm, has a cultivated honesty which can be quite literally disarming.

New York City abounds with black nationalist cults, but with no unified program to promote together the philosophies they separately espouse. In addition to the Black Muslims, there are the Muslim Brotherhood; the United African Nationalist Movement; the Universal African Nationalist Movement; the Cultural Association for Women of African Heritage; The World Federation of African People, Inc.; the Yoruba Temple of New Oyo, and perhaps two dozen others of greater or lesser importance.[12] The *mood ebony* is not black nationalism with an African orientation as is true of most organized nationalist groups. As one Negro businessman put it, it is not so much a desire to identify with Africa as it is a determination to enjoy ham hocks and turnip greens here in America without caring whether or not the white man is watching, and not giving a damn if he is.

NOTES

1 *Poems in Protest*, an unpublished manuscript by C. Eric Lincoln.
2 W. E. B. Du Bois, *Black Folk Then and Now* (New York: Holt, Rinehart & Winston, Inc., 1939).
3 Bertram P. Karon, *The Negro Personality* (New York: Springer Publishing Co., Inc., 1958).
4 Abram Kardiner and Lionel Ovesey, *The Mark of Oppression* (New York: W. W. Norton & Company, Inc., 1951), pp. 325–326.
5 Harold Isaacs, *The American Negro and Africa: Some Notes.* Read before the Second Annual Conference, The American Society of African Culture, New York, June 28, 1959.
6 Daniel Bell, "Plea for a 'New Phase in Negro Leadership,'" *The New York Times*, May 31, 1964.
7 Edmund David Cronon, *Black Moses* (Madison: The University of Wisconsin Press, 1955), p. 47.
8 Harold Isaacs, *The New World of Negro Americans* (New York: The John Day Co., 1963).
9 *See* C. Eric Lincoln, "The Black Muslims and Christian Conscience," *Concern*, Sept. 5, 1963.
10 *See* C. Eric Lincoln, *The Black Muslims in America* (Boston: Beacon Press, 1961).
11 "A Conversation with James Baldwin," *Freedomways*, Summer, 1963.
12 *See Freedomways*, Fall, 1961, and Summer, 1963.

One of the most perplexing problems these days is what to call those Americans whose ancestors came from Africa. Here Lerone Bennett traces the history of a controversy that has been going on for four hundred years.

Bennett suggests that what was most crucial in each of the periods he cites was what the various labels meant to those who used them. Throughout the various phases there have always been those who objected to the most popular term, "Negroes." Benjamin Lee Whorf may have put his finger on why. Bennett quotes him as writing: "We say that we speak as we think. In fact we tend to think as we speak."

20

' **Lerone Bennett, Jr.**

WHAT'S IN A NAME?

"When I use a word," Humpty Dumpty said in a rather scornful tone, "it means just what I choose it to mean—neither more nor less."
"The question is," said Alice, "whether you can make words mean so many different things."
"The question is," said Humpty Dumpty, "which is to be master—that's all."
     —Lewis Carroll, *Through the Looking Glass*

More concretely, within the context of the racial looking glass, the question is whether one can make the word "Negro" mean so many different things or whether one should abandon it and use the words "black" or "Afro-American."

This question is at the root of a bitter national controversy over the proper designation for *identifiable* Americans of African descent. (More than 40 million "white" Americans, according to some scholars, have African ancestors.) A large and vocal group is pressing an aggressive campaign for the use of the word "Afro-American" as the only historically accurate and humanly significant designation of this

From *Ebony*, 23 (November 1967), 46–52, 54.

large and pivotal portion of the American population. This group charges that the word "Negro" is an inaccurate epithet which perpetuates the master-slave mentality in the minds of both black and white Americans. An equally large, but not so vocal, group says the word "Negro" is as accurate and as euphonious as the words "black" and "Afro-American." This group is scornful of the premises of the advocates of change. A Negro by any other name, they say, would be as black and as beautiful—and as segregated. The times, they add, are too crucial for Negroes to dissipate their energy in fratricidal strife over names. But the pro-black contingent contends, with Humpty Dumpty, that names are of the essence of the game of power and control. And they maintain that a change in name will short-circuit the stereotyped thinking patterns that undergird the system of racism in America. To make things even more complicated, a third group, composed primarily of Black Power advocates, has adopted a new vocabulary in which the word "black" is reserved for "black brothers and sisters who are emancipating themselves," and the word "Negro" is used contemptuously for Negroes "who are still in Whitey's bag and who still think of themselves and speak of themselves as Negroes."

This controversy, which rages with religious intensity from the street corners of Harlem to the campuses of Southern colleges, has alienated old friends, split national organizations and disrupted national conventions. It was discussed with gravity at a meeting of the National Advisory Commission on Civil Disorders, and it is a matter of grave concern to prominent Negro leaders who have been heckled and publicly denounced for using the word "Negro."

Within the last year, several organizations have gone on record in opposition to continued use of the word. At the Racism in Education Conference of the American Federation of Teachers, the delegates unanimously endorsed a resolution which called on all educators, persons, and organizations to abandon the "slavery-imposed name "Negro" for the terms "African-American" or "Afro-American." A similar resolution was unanimously adopted at the National Conference on Black Power. But the Black Power conferees compounded the problem by insisting upon the substitution of the word "Black" for the word "Negro." There was additional ferment during this same period on the local level where militant groups passed a variety of pro-Black and pro-Afro-American resolutions and peppered newspapers and magazines with angry and, in some cases, abusive letters.

Some pro-*Negro* advocates charged indignantly that "the whole black issue was raised by a handful of intellectuals, none of whom are black, except for their beards." But it was obvious that the controversy touched deep emotions in the black community where many segments, particularly the young, are engaged in an agonizing search for self-identity and self-determination. Pressures from these groups and from black professionals gave the movement an edge that isolated nationalists, working alone, had never been able to forge. And it was in response to the growing edge of blackness that several organizations, some of them composed of black professionals, changed their letterheads to indicate the new vision they have of themselves and of their relation to Africa and America. The Negro Teachers Association of New York City, for example, became the African-American Teachers Association. More significantly, in terms of mass impact, the New York Amsterdam News, one of the largest black newspapers, announced that it would no longer use the word "Negro." The newspaper, which now identifies Americans of African descent as Afro-Americans, reports a favorable response to the change. Dick Edwards, the assistant managing editor, says letters are running nine to one in favor of Afro-American. "We like the word," he says. "We use it because we are descendants of Africans and because we are Americans." He added: "There is a cringing from the word 'Negro,' especially by the young, because of the oppression into which we were born and because that name was imposed on us. There seems to be violent objection to the term among young people, who link the word 'Negro' with Uncle Tom. They seldom use the word 'Negro.' They use 'Black' and 'African.' Some of them even object to the word 'Afro-American,' preferring the term 'Afram.' "

Is the name game real?

Will it last?

Are there substantial grounds for the violent opposition to the word "Negro"?

To answer these questions and to relate them to the whole bubbling controversy, one must go back 400 years. For Americans of African descent have been arguing about names ever since they were forcibly transported from Africa by Europeans who arbitrarily branded them "Blackamoors," "Moors," "negers," and "negros." The English word "Negro" is a derivative of the Spanish and Portuguese word *negro*, which means black. The Portuguese and Spanish, who were pioneers in the African Slave Trade, used this adjective to designate the African men and women whom they captured and transported to the slave mart of the New World. Within a short time, the Portuguese word *negro* (no capital) became the English noun-adjective "negro." This word, which was not capitalized at first, fused not only humanity, nationality and place of origin but also certain white judgments about the inherent and irredeemable inferiority of the persons so designated. The word also referred to certain Jim Crow places, i.e., the "negro pew" in Christian churches.

The reaction of the first Americans of African descent to the word "Negro" has never been adequately studied. But it appears from an examination of surviving documents that literate black people resisted the word with cunning and tenacity. The first black immigrants seem to have preferred the word "African." In surviving documents, they referred to themselves as "blacks," "blackes," and "Africans." And the first institutions organized by Americans of African descent were designated "African," viz., "The Free African Society," "the African Methodist Episcopal Church," "the African Baptist Church." The preamble of the Free African Society, which was founded in Philadelphia in 1787, began: "We, the Free Africans and their descendants of the City of Philadelphia in the State of Pennsylvania or elsewhere. . . ."

The tentative efforts of Americans of African descent to define themselves in African terms were reversed suddenly and dramatically in the first two decades of the 19th century. When the American Colonization Society organized a movement to send free Africans "back" to Africa, the colored community reacted by abandoning the word African in favor of the words "coloured" and/or "free persons of colour." In 1835, the fifth annual convention of the colored people of America passed a resolution which recommended "as far as possible, to our people to abandon use of the word 'coloured,' when either speaking or writing concerning themselves; and especially to remove the title of African from their institutions, the marbles of churches, and etc. . . ." Philadelphia leaders later recommended use of the term "Oppressed Americans." This advice was scorned by militant colored leaders. "Oppressed Americans!" snorted Samuel Cornish, "who are they? Nonsense brethren!! You are COLORED AMERICANS. The Indians are RED AMERICANS, and the white people are WHITE AMERICANS *and you are as good as they, and they are no better than you.*"

The "oppressed Americans" were routed by the "colored Americans," and the term "colored" became the dominant word in the colored community for the rest of the nineteenth century. There were, to be sure, dissents. Frederick Douglass, the leading colored public figure, used the word "Negro" occasionally; and some eccentrics experimented with terms like "Anglo-African." For reasons that were probably connected with the tendency of "the free people of color" to withdraw from the great masses of freedmen, there was a sharp reaction to the word "colored" in the Civil War and Reconstruction periods. For a short spell, the term "Negro" occupied roughly the same place in Negro life as the words "black" and "Afro-American" occupy today. In other words, it was a term of militancy, self-consciously used by black men defiantly asserting their pride of race. We are told, for example, that Blanche Kelso Bruce, the first black man to serve a full term in the U. S. Senate, refused to use the word "colored," saying: "I am a Negro, and proud of my race." Bruce's example was not followed by all Reconstruction leaders. In the North Carolina constitutional convention of 1868, James Walker Hood, one of 15 black delegates, denied that "there was a Negro on the floor of the Convention." Outraged and insulted, he insisted "that the word *Negro* had no significance as to color, but could only be used in a reproachful or degrading sense, and he further declared that no man on that floor knew where the term originated, since it was not found in ancient history, inspired or profane." In the South Carolina constitutional convention of the same year, T. J. Coghlan, a radical white Southerner, offered a resolution which urged that steps be taken to "expunge forever from the vocabulary of South Carolina, the epithets, 'nigger,' 'negro,' and 'yankee' . . . and to punish this insult by fine and imprisonment."

In periods of reaction and extreme stress, black people usually turn inward. They begin to redefine themselves and they begin to argue seriously about names. The post-Reconstruction period, one of the whitest times in American history, was an archetypal expression of this process. The word "coloured" still retained a commanding position in this period, but men like Frederick Douglass and Booker T. Washington used the word "Negro" freely. There were also articulate exponents of the Afro-American theme, as evidenced by the founding, in 1899, of the National Afro-American League, and the Baltimore Afro-American newspaper, established in 1892. Toward the end of the century, the word "Negro" began to supplant the words "colored" and "Afro-American." It was during this period that the first national *Negro* organizations (the American Negro Academy in 1897 and the National Negro Business League in 1900) were founded. The founding of the National Association for the Advancement of *Colored* People in 1909 marked, it seems, the disappearing peak of the colored movement. By 1919, the *Negro Year Book* could report: "There is an increasing use of the word 'Negro' and a decreasing use of the words 'colored' and 'Afro-American' to designate us as a people. The result is that the word 'Negro' is, more and more, acquiring a dignity that it did not have in the past." During this same period, there was an aggressive campaign for capitalization of the word "Negro." This campaign, which was led by the NAACP, peaked in 1930 when the New York Times announced that it would print the word "Negro" with a capital letter. In an editorial (March 7, 1930), the newspaper said:

"In our 'style book' 'Negro' is now added to the list of words to be capitalized. It is not merely a typographical change; it is an act in recognition of racial self-respect for those who have been for generations in 'the lower case.' "

Although the word "Negro" became a generally acceptable designation in the 1930s, there was strong opposition from militant radicals like Adam Clayton Powell, who continued to use the word "black," and from militant nationalists like Elijah Muhammad, who continued to speak of "so-called Negroes." This opposition, inchoate and unorganized, was sharpened in the '50s and '60s by the rhetorical artistry of Malcolm X and the emergence of the Black Power movement. But Malcolm X and the Black Power movement were reflections of a general crisis of identity which is similar in tone and urgency to the crises of the 19th century and the first decades of the 20th.

It appears, from this short historical sketch, that the word "Negro" has been a generally acceptable term in the black or, if you prefer, the Negro community for a relatively short time. It appears also that there has been continuous and sustained opposition to the term. Contemporary critics of the word "Negro" say Booker T. Washington was primarily responsible for the campaign in which the word "Negro" supplanted the words "black," "colored," and "Afro-American." There is truth in this—the *Negro Year Book* and the Negro Business League were Washington projects—but it is not the whole truth. The movement for adoption of the word "Negro" was also given a strong impetus by militant radicals like W. E. B. Du Bois, who was one of the founders of the American Negro Academy, and militant nationalists like Marcus Garvey, who used the word "Negro" consistently and named his organization the Universal Negro Improvement Association. As a matter of fact, the classic argument in favor of the word "Negro" was articulated by W. E. B. Du Bois in a reply to a pro-African letter. Since this exchange, which appeared in *The Crisis* in March, 1928, capsules the main issues in the controversy, we are printing it in some detail.

THE NAME "NEGRO"

South Bend, Indiana

Dear Sir:

I am only a high school student in my sophomore year, and have not the understanding of you college educated men. It seems to me that since THE CRISIS is the Official Organ of the National Association for the Advancement of Colored People which stand for equality for all Americans, why would it designate, and segregate us as "Negroes," and not as Americans."

The most piercing thing that hurts me in this February CRISIS, which forced me to write, was the notice that called the natives of Africa, "Negroes," instead of calling them "Africans," or "natives." The word, "Negro," or "nigger," is a white man's word to make us feel inferior. I hope to be a worker for my race, that is why I wrote this letter. I hope that by the time I become a man, that this word, "Negro," will be abolished.

Roland A. Barton

My dear Roland:

Do not at the outset of your career make the all too common error of mistaking names for things. Names are only conventional signs for identifying things. Things are the reality that counts. If a thing is despised, either because of ignorance or because it is despicable, you will not alter matters by changing its name. If men despise Negroes, they will not despise them less if Negroes are called "colored" or "Afro-Americans."

Moreover, you cannot change the name of a thing at will. Names are not merely matters of thought and reason; they are growths and habits. As long as the majority of men mean black or brown folk when they say "Negro," so long will Negro be the name of folks brown and black. And neither anger nor wailing nor tears can or will change the name until the name-habit changes.

But why seek to change the name? "Negro" is a fine word. Etymologically and phonetically it is much better and more logical than "African" or "colored" or any of the various hyphenated circumlocutions. Of course, it is not "historically" accurate. No name ever was historically accurate: neither "English," "French," "German," "White," "Jew," "Nordic" nor "Anglo-Saxon." They were all at first nicknames, misnomers, accidents, grown eventually to conventional habits and achieving accuracy because, and simply because, wide and continued usage rendered them accurate. In this sense "Negro" is quite as accurate, quite as old and quite as definite as any name of any great group of people.

Suppose now we could change the name. Suppose we arose tomorrow morning and lo! instead of being "Negroes," all the world called us "Cheiropolidi"—do you really think this would make a vast and momentous difference to you and to me? Would the Negro problem be suddenly and eternally settled? Would you be any less ashamed of being descended from a black man, or would your schoolmates feel any less superior to you? The feeling of inferiority is in you, not in any name. The name merely evokes what is already there. Exorcise the hateful complex and no name can ever make you hang your head.

Your real work, my dear young man, does not lie with names. It is not a matter of changing them, losing them, or forgetting them. Names are nothing but little guideposts along the Way. The Way would be there and just as hard and just as long if there were no guideposts,—

but not quite as easily followed! Your real work as a Negro lies in two directions: *First*, to let the world know what there is fine and genuine about the Negro race. And *secondly*, to see that there is nothing about that race which is worth contempt; your contempt, my contempt; or the contempt of the wide, wide world.

Get this then, Roland, and get it straight even if it pierces your soul: a Negro by any other name would be just as black and just as white; just as ashamed of himself and just as shamed by others, as today. It is not the name—it's the Thing that counts. Come on, Kid, let's go get the Thing!

W. E. B. Du Bois

Du Bois' argument is, as usual, persuasive. But, in the eyes of the pro-black contingent, it is hardly conclusive. Critics of this famous exchange say Du Bois' premises are dubious, to say the least. For example: He starts out with the correct premise that names are *objectively* unimportant. In other words, there is no necessary connection between the name and the thing. From this premise, which is objectively true, he draws a very different conclusion: that names are unimportant *to people*. Keith Baird, the coordinator of the Afro-American History and Cultural Center of the New York City Board of Education, and other opponents of the word "Negro" point out that modern linguistic scholarship is virtually unanimous in its findings that names and words determine, to a great extent, what we see and what we feel. They are also critical of Du Bois' assertion that "wide and continued usage" can make an inaccurate word accurate. As for the eloquent conclusion, critics say that Du Bois evaded the issue. Nobody doubts that the Thing is important, at least on certain levels. But the whole point of racism in America is the determination to deny human status to certain people—millionaires as well as world-famous scholars like Du Bois—who have won the Thing but lack a certain Name.

Du Bois was too honest and too brilliant to be content with the eloquent but evasive 1928 statement. As late as 1958, he was still wrestling with the issue of terminology. Moreover, his works (*The Souls of Black Folk, The Gifts of Black Folk, Black Folk: Then and Now, Black Reconstruction*) testify to a certain ambivalence about the word "Negro."

For all that, Du Bois stated the problem with lucidity and power, and his words are echoed by some contemporary intellectuals. Dr. Jeanne Spurlock, a prominent psychiatrist who has been active in the freedom movement, does not believe that a change in name will change the way Negroes experience themselves and the way others experience them. "The word 'Negro'," she says, "means different things to different people, depending on so many things in their individual backgrounds." Some *individuals,* she added, may have a need, depending on their individual backgrounds, to reject the term. She has no objections to these individuals using the words "black" or "Afro-American," if the words help them to achieve a sense of identity and internal organization. Dr. Spurlock says she prefers the word "Negro," if ethnic designations are necessary. "I'm not offended by the word," she says. "I feel comfortable about being a Negro, about being black."

A similar comment came from Dr. Benjamin Quarles, professor of history at Morgan College. "One's estimation of himself," he says, "takes many forms. There are levels of sophistication on which you voice your protest and make clear your identity. For some people, the best way they can make clear their identity is by denying the word 'Negro' which traditionally, they say, is a slave-oriented name. Other people may prefer what they would consider more sophisticated techniques of projecting their identity. But, nevertheless, you have to grant that it may be necessary for certain individuals to avoid the name 'Negro.' I wouldn't quarrel with them. Nevertheless, I would not myself stop using the word 'Negro,' because I see nothing wrong with it. Words change in their context. We have many words historically that once were terms of denigration. For instance, the Friends were sometimes called Quakers in derision. Instead of dodging the word, they adopted it and made it a term of great respect and meaning. I believe you will begin to see the same evolution of the word 'Negro' as Americans of African descent move into their rightful place in American society."

The to-each-his-own approach is rejected by opponents of the word "Negro." They say that all black people are affected in the deepest reaches of their being by the collective label. And they contend that the quest for the right name is the most sophisticated level of finding and projecting one's identity. Perhaps the most articulate exponent of this view is Keith Baird, the young Afro-American expert of the New York City Board of Education. According to Baird, "The continuing depressed economic and social status of the African people in America, enforced and maintained by the dominant European-originated Americans, is symbolized and instrumentally promoted by the continuing use of the déclassé designation 'Negro.' " Baird adds: "The militant efforts being made by Americans of African descent require attention in respect of every fact or factor which confers the status of humanity on the individual—the right and power to obtain and enjoy the physical necessities of life as well as the psychological. Positive and enhancing self-regard is a psychological necessity of life, and the name borne by an individual or group can be an effective vehicle and symbol of group or individual self-regard."

Baird cites an impressive array of scholars, including Benjamin Lee Whorf, in support of his contention that language tends to pre-structure thinking and acting. "We say," he adds, "that we speak as we think. In fact, we tend to think as we speak." The meaning of a word, or expression, he continues, "is what it does, that is, the effect which it produces in its hearers. . . . A name can determine the na-ture of the response given to it by virtue of the associations which its use conjures up." Baird does not claim that the adoption of the word "Afro-American" will *solve* the American race problem. He does be-lieve, however, that it will make a significant difference in the internal economies of black and white Americans. "The very act and fact of changing the designation," he says, "will cause the individual to be redesignated to be reconsidered, not only in terms of his past and his present but hopefully in terms of his future." He adds: "Designation has an important bearing on destiny."

Baird objects to the word "Negro" on two grounds: (1) The word "Negro" is a slave-oriented epithet which was imposed on Americans of African descent by slavemasters. "The word came into use," Baird says, "in connection with the enslavement of the African in the New World. The use of the word became connected with what Earl Conrad has so well called the 'Negro-Concept,' that grotesque conception of the African which has been shaped in the mind of the European and forced with Procrustean cruelty on the person and personality of the black American."

(2) The word "Negro" is not geographically or culturally specific. "Historically, he says, "human groups have been named according to the land from which they originated. . . . The unwillingness of the dominant group to recognize the humanity of the African is evidenced by the fact that when it is necessary or desired to identify Americans in terms of the land of their origin, terms such as Italian-American, Polish-American, Spanish-American, Jewish-American (referring back to the ancient kingdom and culture of Judaea), etc., are employed. In the American mind there is no connection of the black American with 'land, history and culture'—factors which proclaim the humanity of an individual." Baird denies that the English word "Negro" is a synonym for black. He says: " 'Negro' does not mean simply 'black' which would be the simple, direct opposite of 'white.' We talk about a 'white man' or a 'white Cadillac'; we may talk, as many unfortunately do, of a 'Ne-gro man,' but never of a 'Negro Cadillac.' "

Baird believes the word "Afro-American" will soon supplant the word "Negro." He does not object to the term "black," which, he says, lacks the historical and cultural precision of the word "Afro-American." He is supported in this view by Richard Moore, Harlem book store owner and author of *The Name "Negro"—Its Origin and Evil Use*. Moore says the word "Negro" is so "saturated with filth," so "polluted" with the white man's stereotypes, that "there is nothing to be done but to get rid of it." He prefers the word "Afro-American" because of its "correctness, exactness, even elegance." He believes adoption of the word will force "these prejudiced European-Americans" to reevaluate black people in terms of their history and culture. "Black," Moore said, "is a loose color designation which is not connected with land, history and culture. While I recognize it as a step forward in getting rid of the term 'Negro,' I think it is necessary to take the next step."

To take the next step, whatever that step might be, millions of Americans of African descent are going to have to search their souls and their internal maps. At the request of EBONY Magazine, Ossie Davis, the playwright-actor, searched his soul and came up with the following passionately eloquent statement:

> *I am a Negro. I am clean, black and I smile a lot. Whenever I want something—to get a job in motion pictures, for instance, or on television or to get a play produced on Broadway, whenever I need a political favor—I go to white folks. White folks have money. I do not. White folks have power. I do not. All of my needs—financial, artistic, social, my need for freedom—I must depend on white folks to supply. That is what is meant by being a Negro.*
>
> *Malcolm X used to be a Negro, but he stopped. He no longer depended upon white folks to supply his needs—psychologically or sociologically—to give him money or lead his fight for freedom or to protect him from his enemies or to tell him what to do. Malcolm X did not hate white folks, nor did he love them. Most of all, he did not need them to tell him who he was. Above all, he was determined to make it on his own. That was why Malcolm was no longer a Negro. Malcolm was a man, a black man! A black man means not to accept the system as Negroes do but to fight hell out of the system as Malcolm did. It can be dangerous. Malcolm was killed for it. Nevertheless, I like Malcolm much better than I like myself.*

In this statement, Ossie Davis, who is considered a *black* man by the leaders of the pro-black movement, adds a new and personal dimension to the controversy which will be settled finally by the internal movement of Americans of African descent. And in the course of that movement, on one level or another, every "Negro" and/or "black" and/or "Afro-American" is going to have to choose a name in the process of choosing his being.

Who are you?

What is your name?

In the following pages Richard B. Moore documents the long tradition of identification with Africa and its peoples by a long list of black Americans from slavery days to the present. Moore predicts that consciousness of Africa will continue to grow in the years to come, especially "as it is more fully realized that rationally no conflict really or properly exists between vital interest in African peoples and deep and active devotion to the issue of human rights and equal citizenship status here in the U.S.A."

21

Richard B. Moore

AFRICA CONSCIOUS HARLEM

Consciousness of Africa, if not coeval, certainly existed very early in the development of the Afroamerican community in Harlem. This consciousness grew almost as rapidly as the community itself expanded. From the few occupants of two houses on 134th Street west of Fifth Avenue in 1900, this unique community had grown by 1920 into a city within the City of New York. Embracing many thousands, this Harlem enclave then reached from 127th Street on the south to 145th Street on the north and from Fifth to Eighth Avenues. Now some 300,000 people of African descent reach down below 110th Street and up into the Washington Heights area, spread almost from the East to the Hudson Rivers.

Harlem's main thoroughfare in 1920 was 135th Street between Lenox and Seventh Avenues, with an almost solid block of houses and stores on its north side owned by St. Philip's Protestant Episco-

From John Henrik Clarke (ed.), *Harlem: A Community in Transition*, New York: Citadel Press, 1964, pp. 77–96. Reprinted by arrangement with Citadel Press, Inc.

pal Church. In one of these stores, number 135 to be exact, sharing space with the weekly *New York News,* George Young conducted the first Afroamerican book shop in Harlem. A pullman porter who had made good use of his travels through the country to assemble a fine collection of Africana and Afroamericana, Young also endeavored to supply such literature to his people.

In Young's Book Exchange, known then as *The Mecca of Literature Pertaining to Colored People,* there was to be seen what would seem to many, even today, an astonishing array of material treating of Africa and her dispersed descendants. In this small establishment during 1921, a visitor would have seen several copies of the compact book by Dr. W. E. B. Du Bois, which bore the all too current title *The Negro,* though this was chiefly devoted to Africa. Alongside would be seen *From Superman to Man* by J. A. Rogers, which exposed racism and pointed to the ancient history and culture of the African peoples.

On the shelves at Young's there reposed histories written by Afroamericans such as George W. Williams, *History of the Negro Race in America.* These generally followed the pattern set by William Wells Brown in *The Black Man, His Antecedents, His Genius, and His Achievements* and *The Rising Son,* which began with an account of the African background. *A Social History of the American Negro* by Prof. Benjamin Brawley of Howard University, then just published, also included an entire chapter on Liberia.

Books by African authors included the older *Letters of Ignatius Sancho* and the *Life of Olaudah Equiano* or *Gustavus Vassa.* Beside these were more recent treatises: Duse Mohamed, *In the Land of the Pharaohs;* Sol. T. Plaatje, *Native Life in South Africa;* Casely Hayford, *Ethiopia Unbound, Gold Coast Native Institutions,* and *The Truth About the West African Land Question;* Dr. James Africanus B. Horton, *West African Countries and Peoples* and *A Vindication of the African Race;* John Mensah Sarbah, *Fanti Customary Laws;* Bishop Samuel Adjai Crowther, *Journal of an Expedition Up the Niger and Tshadda Rivers.*

Numerous books by European and Euroamerican authors included important references to Africans by Abolitionists such as Granville Sharp, Thomas Clarkson, Wilson Armistead, Abbe Gregoire, Anthony Benezet, Mrs. Lydia Maria Child, and Charles Sumner. Beside these were accounts of explorers, travelers, missionaries, and investigators—Mungo Park, Livingstone, Moffat, Bruce, Speke, Baker du Chaillu, Reclus, Barth, Schweinfurth, Caillie, Du Bois, Burton, Crawford, Talbot, Ellis, Cardinall, Duff Macdonald, Bleek and Lloyd, Pitt-Rivers.

Specially emphasized were Frobenius, *Voice of Africa;* Ratzel, *History of Mankind;* Mary Kingsley, *West African Studies;* Flora L. Shaw (Lady Lugard), *A Tropical Dependency;* Dennett, *At the Back of the Black Man's Mind;* Morel, *Red Rubber* and *The Black Man's Burden.* George Young's signed personal copy of this last, purchased from his widow, is still among the highly prized books in my collection. As a special indulgence to those who evinced great interest, Young would exhibit such rare, old, large tomes as Ludolph's *History of Ethiopia* and Ogilby's *Africa.*

Expressing the consciousness of Africa already existing among Afroamericans, there were revealing volumes like *The African Abroad* by Prof. William H. Ferris, and *Negro Culture in West Africa* by George W. Ellis which recorded the alphabet and script invented by a genius of the Vai-speaking peoples. There, too, was the masterful work of the Haitian scholar Anténor Firmin, *De l'égalité des races humaines,* which marshalled evidence of early African culture and its significant contribution to Europe and the world in a crushing refutation of the racist theories of inequality propounded by Gobineau.

Though written in 1886, the challenging book *Liberia: The Americo-African Republic* by T. McCants Stewart urged Afroamericans to "put their own ships upon the sea. . . . We must have our own vessels carrying our African workers, our civilization, and our wares back to the 'Fatherland,' and bringing back its riches." This exhortation concluded with the confident vision of a great "Americo-African Republic," extending "into the Soudan, throughout the Niger and into the Congo; and under a mighty African ruler, there will arise a stable and powerful Government of Africans, for Africans, and by Africans, which shall be an inestimable blessing to all mankind."

Likewise far-visioned were the writings of Alexander Crummell: *The Future of Africa* and *Africa and America.* This last contained his classic essay on *The Relations and Duties of Free Colored Men in America to Africa,* originally published in 1861. This dedicated thinker affirmed "a natural call upon the children of Africa in foreign lands, to come and participate in the opening treasures of the land of their fathers."

Further indicative of this consciousness of African provenience and common heritage were typical writings by scholars native to the African motherland, the Caribbean areas, and the American mainland. Pointed to with particular pride by George Young would be such books as the *History of the Yorubas* by Rev. Samuel Johnson, *Glimpses of the Ages* by Theophilus E. Samuel Scholes, *The Lone Star of Liberia* by F. A. Durham, and especially *African Life and Customs* and *Christianity, Islam and the Negro Race* by Edward Wilmot Blyden.

That this consciousness of Africa was active and widespread was perhaps significantly shown in the reprinting and distribution by George Young in 1920 of *The Aims and Methods of a Liberal Education for Africans,* the Inaugural Address delivered by Edward Wilmot Blyden, LL.D., President of Liberia College, January 5, 1881. Nor was this interest in Africa a new thing. For despite ruthless repression under the chattel slave system, the transplanted Africans could never be reduced to total cultural blankness.

Early Ties to Africa

Consciousness of their ancestral homeland has thus been historically evident from the first arrivals when some of these Africans, brought as slaves into the Americas, killed themselves believing that they would thereby return to Africa. Awareness of their heritage of culture and dignity continued during the colonial period and the early days of this republic. The name *African* was then preferred and used instead of the slave-masters' degrading epithet "negro." Witness thus The Free African Society, founded in Philadelphia in 1817 by Richard Allen and Absalom Jones. This was the forerunner of the African Protestant Episcopal Church of St. Thomas and also of the African Methodist Episcopal Church. Note also the African Lodge of Prince Hall Masons in Boston; the African Methodist Episcopal Zion Church, African Society for Mutual Aid, African Grove Playhouse in New York; and many so named throughout the country.

As early as 1788 an organized body of Afroamericans in Newport, R. I., which included Paul Cuffee who was soon to make history in this respect, wrote to the Free African Society of Philadelphia proposing a plan for emigration to Africa. In 1811 Paul Cuffee sailed in his own ship to Sierra Leone to investigate the feasibility of founding a settlement there. In 1815 at his own expense amounting to some $4,000, Captain Paul Cuffee, consummating twenty years of thought and effort, sailed forth again to Sierra Leone, this time commanding the good ship *Traveler* with 38 Afroamerican emigrants aboard, which included several whom he had boldly rescued from slavery along the Atlantic seaboard.

Paul Cuffee's achievement gave impetus to the founding of the American Colonization Society in 1817. But this body was dominated by slaveholders with the object of getting rid of free Afroamericans whose very presence and example encouraged the slaves to seek freedom. Hence the American Colonization Society was powerfully opposed by free-spirited Afroamericans and their Abolitionist allies.

Nevertheless, several Afroamerican leaders took advantage of the operation of the American Colonization Society to foster self-government in Africa through the founding of Liberia. Outstanding among these were Daniel Coker, Elijah Johnson, Lott Cary, Colin Teague, John B. Russwurm, Hilary Teague, and Joseph Jenkins Roberts who was elected first president of Liberia in 1848. By this time the population of Liberia included some 3,000 persons of African descent who had emigrated from the United States of America and the Caribbean.

The distinguished Afroamerican scholar, Rev. Alexander Crummell, after graduating from Cambridge University in 1853, spent 20 years teaching and laboring in Africa. Commissioned by a convention of Afroamericans held in Chatham, Canada West, in 1858, Martin R. Delany led an expedition into what is now Nigeria and published his *Official Report of the Niger Valley Exploring Party* in 1861. This mission had even signed a treaty with African rulers at Abeokuta which authorized a projected settlement, but this project lapsed after the outbreak of the Civil War in the U.S.A. The other commissioner of this expedition, Professor Robert Campbell, published his report in *A Pilgrimage to My Motherland*.

After the Civil War and Reconstruction, interest was revived in African settlement as a great exodus began from the south, due to the wholesale massacre of some 40,000 Afroamericans by such terrorist organizations as the Ku Klux Klan. This reign of terror reached monstrous proportions after the withdrawal of federal troops from the south. A new movement for migration to Africa was fostered jointly by Afroamerican Baptists and Methodists; Bishop H. M. Turner played a leading part in this endeavor. Organizations were established in several states, notably the Liberian Exodus and Joint Stock Company in North Carolina and the Freedmen's Emigration Aid Society in South Carolina. This last acquired the ship *Azor* for $7,000 and this ship actually carried 274 emigrants to Africa on one of its trips, despite the efforts of prejudiced European Americans to impose outrageous costs and to hinder its operation. The *Azor* was soon stolen and sold in Liverpool; the attempts to recover it failed when the U.S. Circuit Court refused even to entertain the suit brought to this end.

About 1881 a descendant of Paul Cuffee, Captain Harry Dean, sailed to Africa commanding his ship the *Pedro Gorino* with the object "to rehabilitate Africa and found an Ethiopian Empire as the world has never seen." Another expedition took 197 emigrants from Savannah, Georgia to Liberia. "Chief Sam" of Kansas launched a movement to sail ships and build a state in Africa but this movement failed to achieve its goals.

Role of Speakers and Press

This tradition was known in Harlem and interest in Africa was constantly stimulated by the generally well-informed outdoor speakers of the twenties. Free lance advocates such as William Bridges, Strathcona R. Williams, Alexander Rahming, Edgar M. Grey, Arthur Reid, and the Basuto "Prince" Mokete M. Manoede held forth constantly on African history and stressed unity with the African people.

Militant socialists like Chandler Owen, A. Philip Randolph, Rev. George Frazier Miller, Grace P. Campbell, Anna Brown, Elizabeth Hendrickson, Frank Poree, Otto Huiswoud, W. A. Domingo, Tom Potter, Frank D. Crosswaith, Rudolph Smith, Herman S. Whaley, John Patterson, Victor C. Gaspar, Ramsay, Ross D. Brown, and the writer of this account—all steadily emphasized the liberation of the oppressed African and other colonial peoples as a vital aim of their world view. Above all Hubert H. Harrison gave forth from his encyclopedic store, a wealth of knowledge of African history and culture which brought this consciousness to a very great height.

A vigorous press which circulated widely in Harlem also intensified this consciousness of Africa. Notable among these journals were *The Amsterdam News* while edited by Cyril V. Briggs, the *Crisis* magazine under Dr. Du Bois, the *Challenge* of William Bridges, the radical *Messenger* magazine projected by Chandler Owen and A. Philip Randolph, the *African Times and Orient Review,* published by Duse Mahomed in London, imported by John E. Bruce, and distributed by this writer, the *Crusader* magazine edited by Cyril V. Briggs as the organ of the African Blood Brotherhood, the powerful *Voice* of the Liberty League of Afro-Americans then being led by Hubert H. Harrison. Later the *Emancipator* conducted chiefly by W. A. Domingo and this writer, warned against the weaknesses of the Garvey movement, while striving for an end to colonialist subjugation and all forms of oppression.

Vibrant echoes too had reached Harlem of the Pan African Conference, organized in London during 1900 by Henry Sylvester-Williams, a barrister-at-law born in Trinidad of African ancestry. This Conference elected as general chairman Bishop Alexander Walters of the African Methodist Episcopal Zion Church and Dr. W. E. B. Du Bois chairman of the Committee on Address to the World. Stimulating news had come also of the Second Pan African Conference organized by Dr. Du Bois and held in Paris early in 1919, following the significant though unsuccessful attempts made independently by William Monroe Trotter and Dr. Du Bois to present the case of the oppressed peoples of African descent before the Versailles Peace Conference in 1918.

Several distinguished visitors to Harlem contributed greatly to this ever growing consciousness of Africa, among them F. E. M. Hercules, a native of Trinidad and founder of an organization seeking to unify all the descendants of Africa everywhere. Dr. J. Edmeston Barnes, born in Barbados, came directly from London with a similar program calling also for the rejection of the disrespectful and denigrating name "Negro," which he condemned as "a bastard political colloquialism." Likewise, Albert Thorne of Barbados and Guiana projected the ideas of his African Colonial Enterprise which was designed to embrace all peoples of African origin.

Arrival of Marcus Garvey

Harlem had thus become considerably Africa conscious and this consciousness was soon to build the movement which was carried to great heights of mass emotion, widespread projection, and stupendous endeavor by the skillful propagandist and promoter, Marcus Garvey. When Garvey arrived from Jamaica in 1916, Harlem was emerging as the vanguard and focal point, "the cultural capital" of ten million Afroamericans and to some extent also of other peoples of African origin in the Western Hemisphere. The demand for labor, due to the first World War, rapidly augmented the growth of Harlem, as thousands poured in from the south, the Caribbean, and Central America.

Harlem then seethed with a great ferment, bitterly resenting oppression and discrimination, particularly the treatment meted out to its crack Fifteenth Regiment. Harlem reacted vigorously also against the brutal lynchings then growing throughout the country, and especially against the frightful wholesale massacre in East St. Louis in July 1917. Some 10,000 of Harlem's citizens marched down Fifth Avenue carrying placards in the Silent Protest Parade led by the National Association for the Advancement of Colored People. The hanging of 13 Afroamerican soldiers following the Houston affair, when they had retaliated against wanton attack by prejudiced southerners, stirred mounting anger, frustration, and despair.

Marcus Garvey saw the opportunity to harness this upsurge against oppression and to direct the existing consciousness of Africa into a specific organized movement under his leadership. Realizing the deep-seated if unconscious desire of the disinherited people of African origin for equal or similar status to that of others in every phase of human thought and endeavor, Garvey projected various means and enterprises which appealed to and afforded expression of this basic human desire.

After a poor initial meeting at St. Mark's Hall and some outdoor attempts, Marcus Garvey secured his first favorable public response when introduced by Hubert H. Harrison, leader of the Liberty League of Afro-Americans, at a huge meeting at Bethel A. M. E. Church. Following several abortive attempts, Garvey finally launched the reorganized New York Division of the Universal Negro Improvement Association and African Communities League. With the publication of the *Negro World* in January 1918, carrying sections in French and Spanish as well as in English, the movement spread through the United States and abroad.

The founder of the *Negro World* was astute enough to secure the editorial services of Professor William H. Ferris, graduate of Yale University and well versed in African lore, of the able and erudite Hubert H. Harrison, and of such skillful writers as W. A. Domingo, Eric Walrond, and Hudson C. Pryce. Duse Mohamed, the Sudanese Egyptian nationalist who had formerly employed Garvey in London, and from whom Garvey derived the slogan "Africa for the Africans," also worked for a time on the *Negro World*. Contributors like John E. Bruce (Grit), William Pickens, T. Thomas Fortune, Anselmo Jackson, and Hodge Kirnon presented various aspects of the ancient history, noteworthy achievements, and the current aspirations of people of African origin.

The convention held in August 1920 in Liberty Hall, Boston, the dramatic, colorful, and impressive parade, costumes, and pageantry, and the mammoth meeting at Madison Square Garden, established the Garvey movement as a powerful international force. Stirring hymns with African themes, especially the U.N.I.A. anthem composed by Rabbi Arnold J. Ford of Barbados, were rendered by choral groups and massed bands. Thousands joined the U.N.I.A., the African Legion, the Black Cross Nurses, and later the African Orthodox Church. Enthusiastic supporters poured their savings into the enterprise started by Garvey, the restaurants, hotel, grocery, millinery, tailoring and dressmaking establishment, publishing concern, and finally the Black Star Line, and the Negro Factories Corporation.

Estimate of Garvey

It is difficult and still perhaps somewhat hazardous to attempt an objective estimate of the Garvey movement, yet this is necessary if we are to learn from its lessons and to apply them wisely in our present endeavors. To the present writer it appears that the founder and leader of the U.N.I.A. demonstrated two powerful drives which were basically opposed to each other. One was clearly the progressive tendency which projected "the redemption of Africa" and the "Declaration of Rights of the Negro People of the World." The other was obviously reactionary in its Napoleonic urge for personal power and empire, with the inevitable accompaniment of racial exclusiveness and hostility. This latter tendency was evident when Garvey declared, on taking the title of Provisional President of Africa in 1920, "The signal honor of being Provisional President of Africa is mine. . . . It is like asking Napoleon to take the world."

Unfortunately, Marcus Garvey veered evermore toward the more extreme forms of empire building, unlimited individual control, and unrestrained racism. At length these destructive forces were allowed to overshadow and outweigh the constructive, pristine ideas of African nationalism, liberation, and independence. Stridently advocating "racial purity," Garvey came at length to agree openly with the worst enemies of the Afroamerican people—the white supremacist leaders of the Anglo-Saxon clubs and even of the murderous Ku Klux Klan —in declaring America to be "a white man's country."

Besides, the constant attacks which Marcus Garvey made upon people of both African and European ancestry, whom he derisively called "the hybrids of the Negro race," did not conduce to the unifying of all people of African descent, who, regardless of varying shades of color and other physical characteristics, were compelled to suffer similar oppression whether as colonial subjects or as oppressed minority groups. Likewise, Garvey's condemnation of the principal leaders and organizations who were striving for human rights and equal citizenship status for the Afroamerican minority group in this country, was bound to arouse opposition and internal strife.

Finally, the open condemnation of Liberian officials by Marcus Garvey, his severe reprisals against several of his chief associates, his poor choice of certain officers, and the inept conduct of the business enterprises which he controlled, left the movement wide open to the disastrous blows of those who began to fear its growing power. Following his conviction and imprisonment on February 8, 1925, upon a charge of using the mails to defraud in connection with the sale of Black Star Line stock, the Garvey movement split into wrangling factions, and despite efforts to revive it only a few splinter groups remained. Nevertheless, the Garvey movement did heighten and spread the consciousness of African origin and identity among the various peoples of African descent on a wider scale than ever before. This was its definite and positive contribution.

Harlem Literary Renaissance

Developing almost parallel with the Garvey movement was what has come to be known as the Harlem Literary Renaissance. A number of creative writers of poetry, fiction, essays, and criticism then emerged: Claude McKay, Langston Hughes, Countee Cullen, Jean Toomer, Eric Walrond, Rudolph Fisher, Wallace Thurman, Nella Larsen, Zora Neale Hurston, James Weldon Johnson, Jessie Fauset, Georgia Douglas Johnson, Lucian B. Watkins, Walter White, and others.

This literary movement was no Minerva sprung full-fledged from the head of Jove, for while its immediate inspiration lay in the surrounding social conditions, its roots, too, went back through earlier Afroamerican writers to the bards of ancient Africa. Alain Locke in his preface to *The New Negro* which proclaimed this movement in 1925, noted "the approach to maturity" and the role of *Crisis*, under the leadership of Dr. Du Bois, and *Opportunity*, edited by Charles S. Johnson, in fostering this movement by publishing many of the works of these budding authors. Locke further observed two constructive channels: "One is the advance-guard of the African peoples in their contact with Twentieth Century civilization; the other, the sense of a vision of rehabilitating the race in world esteem. . . ."

How these Harlem avant-garde writers felt, expressed, and stimulated consciousness of Africa may be observed in a few typical outpourings. In the sonnet *Africa* published in *Harlem Shadows*, the Caribbean-born poet Claude McKay extolled:

> The sun sought thy dim bed and brought forth light,
> The sciences were sucklings at thy breast;
> When all the world was young in pregnant night
> Thy slaves toiled at thy monumental best.
> Thou ancient treasure-land, thou modern prize,
> New peoples marvel at thy pyramids!

The rather pessimistic note on which this sonnet ended still persisted in *Outcast* when McKay lamented the ancestral motherland in a mood of wistful nostalgia:

> For the dim regions whence my fathers came
> My spirit, bondaged by the body, longs
> Words felt, but never heard, my lips would frame;
> Thy soul would sing forgotten jungle songs.

In *Enslaved* the poet broods over his people

> For weary centuries despised, oppressed,
> Enslaved and lynched, denied a human place

In the great life line of the Christian West;
And in the Black Land disinherited,
Robbed in the ancient country of its birth; . . .

At length this searing consciousness gave rise to that famous cry
of passionate revolt in *If We Must Die*—

What though before us lies the open grave?
Like men we'll face the murderous, cowardly pack,
Pressed to the wall, dying, but fighting back!

And in *Exhortation: Summer, 1919* Claude McKay turns toward
the future confidently with this clarion call:

From the deep primeval forests where the crouching
    leopard's lurking,
Lift your heavy-lidded eyes, Ethiopia! awake!

For the big earth groans in travail for the strong,
    new world in making—
O my brothers, dreaming for long centuries,
Wake from sleeping; to the East turn, turn your eyes!

Similarly, in *The Negro Speaks of Rivers* in his first published
volume *The Weary Blues*, Langston Hughes sang profoundly:

I've known rivers
I've known rivers ancient as the world and older
    than the flow of human blood in human veins.

My soul has grown deep like the rivers.

I bathed in the Euphrates when dawns were young.
I built my hut near the Congo and it lulled me to sleep.
I looked upon the Nile and raised pyramids above it. . . .

Langston Hughes further expressed his retrospective identification with Africa:

We should have a land of trees
Bowed down with chattering parrots
Brilliant as the day,
And not this land where birds are gray.

Again, in the poem *Georgia Dusk* included in *Cane*, Jean Toomer,
while etching the toilers in southern canefield and saw mill, recalls
the ancestors from the long-past life of dignity and freedom in Africa:

Meanwhile, the men, with vestiges of pomp,
    Race memories of king and caravan,
    High priests, an ostrich and a ju-ju man,
Go singing through the footpaths of the swamp.

Countee Cullen mused long and lyrically in the poem *Heritage* which is outstanding in the book *Color:*

What is Africa to me:
Copper sun or scarlet sea,
Jungle star or jungle track,
Strong bronzed men, or regal black
Women from whose loins I sprang
When the birds of Eden sang?
One three centuries removed
From the scenes his fathers loved,
Spicy grove, cinnamon tree,
What is Africa to me?

Plaintively pondering his "high-priced conversion" to Christianity and humility, the poet needs must transmute this experience in terms consonant with his deeper ancestral self:

Lord, I fashion dark gods, too,
Daring even to give You
Dark despairing features where,
Crowned with dark rebellious hair,
Patience wavers just so much as
Mortal grief compels, while touches
Quick and hot, of anger, rise
To smitten cheek and weary eyes.
Lord forgive me if my need
Sometimes shapes a human creed.

The sense of dignity and power derived from Africa led this poet to an anguished effort to restrain with reason from a premature revolt against intolerable oppression:

All day long and all night through,
One thing only must I do:
Quench my pride and cool my blood,
Lest I perish in the flood,
Lest a hidden ember set
Timber that I thought was wet
Burning like the dryest flax,
Melting like the merest wax,
Lest the grave restore its dead.
Not yet has my heart or head
In the least way realized
They and I are civilized.

Finally, Lucian B. Watkins looked with serene confidence to Africa exulting in his *Star of Ethiopia:*

Out in the Night thou art the sun
Toward which thy soul-charmed children run,

The faith-high height whereon they see
The glory of their Day To Be—
The peace at last when all is done.

Following the failure of the Garvey movement, consciousness of
Africa was bolstered in Harlem by the campaign of the American
Negro Labor Congress for the liberation of the colonial peoples of
Africa and Asia. Representing this body, the present writer went as a
delegate to the Congress Against Imperialism held in Brussels in 1927.
As the forerunner of the Asian-African Conference held at Bandung
in April 1955, the Brussels Congress was recalled and noted by President Sukarno of Indonesia in his opening address, "At that Conference many distinguished delegates who are present here today met
each other and found new strength in their fight for independence."

The Commission on the African Peoples of the World elected at
the Brussels Congress Against Imperialism included the brilliant
Senegalese leaders Lamine Senghor, who unfortunately died shortly
afterward in a French jail, and Garan Kouyatte who was shot by the
Nazis during their occupation of Paris in 1940. Other outstanding
members of this Commission were Mr. Makonnen of Ethiopia, J. T.
Gumede, vice president of the African National Congress of South
Africa, and J. A. La Guma, secretary of the South African Non-Euro-
pean Trade Union Federation. The writer of this present summary
served as secretary of the Commission.

The resolution prepared by the Commission and adopted by the
Brussels Congress Against Imperialism, called for the complete liberation of the African peoples, the restoration of their lands, and
several other measures including the establishment of a University at
Addis Ababa for the training of candidates for leadership in the trade
union, cultural, and liberation movements of the oppressed African
peoples.

Reaction to Mussolini's Aggression in Ethiopia

A new wave of consciousness spread through Harlem as the people
reacted strongly against Mussolini's fascist, military aggression against
Ethiopia in October 1935. Organizations were set up to mobilize support; the executive director of the International Council of Friends
of Ethiopia, Dr. Willis N. Huggins, was commissioned to deliver an
appeal on behalf of Ethiopia to the League of Nations in Geneva,
Switzerland. Arden Bryan, president of the Nationalist Negro Movement, sent petitions to the League and protests to the British Foreign
Office and the U. S. State Department against their failure to aid
Ethiopia.

When invading Italian airplanes monstrously rained down deadly
yperite gas on the Ethiopian people, huge protest meetings were or-
ganized. The Ethiopian Pacific Movement, from a gigantic rally at
Rockland Palace, forwarded protests and also sent telegrams to Asian,
African, Australian, Central and South American nations, appealing
for action in defense of Ethiopia. Several organizations joined in the
United Aid to Ethiopia with Rev. Wm. Lloyd Imes, chairman, Cyril
M. Philip, secretary, and Dr. P. M. H. Savory, treasurer.

The officers just named were sent as a delegation to seek to influence the First Congress of the International Peace Campaign, which
met at Brussels early in September 1936, to take action in support
of Ethiopia. The delegation interviewed Emperor Haile Selassie in
London and requested him to send a representative to cooperate in
the work here. Dr. Malaku E. Bayen, cousin and personal physician
to the Emperor, was appointed and was greeted with acclaim at a
great meeting at Rockland Palace. Meanwhile funds were raised and
medical supplies sent through the Medical Aid to Ethiopia, of which
body, Dr. Arnold W. Donawa was chairman and Dr. J. J. Jones,
secretary.

The Ethiopian World Federation, then organized in Harlem,
spread through the country, the Caribbean, and elsewhere. *The Voice
of Ethiopia* published news from the Ethiopian front and further
stimulated the campaign of resistance. J. A. Carrington and Dr.
R. C. Hunt published the pamphlet *Yperite and Ethiopia*, with the
full text of *Emperor Haile Selassie's Memorable and Immortal
Speech at Geneva*, along with pictures of victims of the horrible
yperite gas, so called because this gas was first used at Ypres in
France. Volunteers generally could not secure passports to go to
join in the military defense of Ethiopia, however the Afroamerican
aviator, Colonel John C. Robinson, known as the "Brown Condor,"
executed many heroic missions in that ravaged land. The *Pittsburgh
Courier*, then directed by Robert L. Vann, sent J. A. Rogers as a
war correspondent who on his return published the booklet *The
Real Facts of Ethiopia*.

After the Italian invaders were driven out of Ethiopia in 1941,
this intense fraternal consciousness in Harlem subsided into a residual sense of unity with all African peoples. But when Egypt was
invaded in October 1956 by Israel followed by Britain and France,
and ruthless massacre and destruction descended upon the people
of Port Said, Suez, Alexandria, and Cairo, Harlem reacted with a
rally organized by the Asian-African Drums and demonstrated its
solidarity with President Nasser and the stricken people of Egypt.
Harlem rejoiced when the note sent by Premier Khrushchev of the

Soviet Union, demanding that withdrawal of the invading forces begin with 24 hours, led to the timely evacuation of these aggressors.

Harlem Rallies to African Freedom

Consciousness of Africa mounted again as more and more African nations regained their independence. The inhuman atrocities of the French colonialists against the Algerian people, who were struggling valiantly for their independence, aroused widespread sympathy and fraternal support among the people of Harlem. Active consciousness reached its zenith when the Congo was betrayed and dismembered and its dedicated leaders, especially the Prime Minister Patrice Lumumba, were foully and brutally done to death. Harlem boiled with fierce resentment against the failure of the United Nations to support the government of the Congo Republic and to prevent the murder of its Prime Minister and other officials.

This white hot indignation among the people of Harlem gave rise to the outburst in the visitors' gallery of the United Nations on February 15, 1961. Reactionary forces loudly denounced this protest upsurge and pseudo-liberals like Max Lerner in his *New York Post* column presumed to lecture and to condemn the protesting Afroamerican people while excusing the Belgian and other colonialist seceders and murderers. An open letter, exposing Max Lerner's hypocritical and racist attack, was addressed by this writer to him and to the editor and owner of the *New York Post*. But this answer to Lerner's diatribe has never been published or even acknowledged by them.

Harlem remains today quite conscious of its African heritage and basic kinship. This consciousness is by no means limited to the various groups which call themselves "nationalists," and who are quite vocal but who actually contribute little or no substantial, direct support to the African liberation movements. *Yet such effective support is vitally needed at this very moment in the present critical and decisive struggle now being waged for the liberation of the peoples of Central and South Africa.*

The limits of this article preclude more detail here. It should be stated, however, that these "nationalist" groups are as yet unable to unite among themselves, due largely, it appears, to self-centered power drives and competition for leadership. The tendency persists among them, unfortunately, to oppose other organizations which have the largest following of the Afroamerican people and to condemn these leaders caustically and constantly. Obviously, this hinders rather than helps to achieve essential *united action* either in support of the African liberation movements or to further the struggle for civil liberties and human rights here in the U.S.A.

Returning to the main currents of Harlem life, it is fitting to recognize the chief intellectual forces which have heightened consciousness of Africa since the 1930's. Outstanding is the Schomburg Collection of literature on Africa and people of African descent, brought together during a lifetime by Arthur A. Schomburg and established as a special reference library by the New York Public Library. The development of this institution has been carried forward by Mrs. Catherine Latimer and by the present genial curator, Mrs. Jean Blackwell Hutson. The Countee Cullen Branch, under the supervision of Mrs. Dorothy R. Homer, displays and features books on Africa for general circulation. Stimulating study classes were led by Dr. Willis N. Huggins and of special note were the several profound and scholarly lecture series given by Prof. William Leo Hansberry.

Significant also has been the activity of the Association for the Study of Negro Life and History, founded by Dr. Carter G. Woodson. This dedicated scholar published many volumes treating of Africa, notably his own *The Negro in Our History*, with its opening chapter emphasizing our African heritage, and the *African Background Outlined*. Among other widely read books were those by Dr. W. E. B. Du Bois, *Black Folk Then and Now* and the *World and Africa;* the writings of J. A. Rogers, *World's Great Men of Color, Sex and Race,* and *Africa's Gift to America;* Dr. Willis N. Huggins and John G. Jackson, *Guide to African History* and *Introduction to African Civilizations:* George G. M. James, *Stolen Legacy,* J. G. de Graft-Johnson, *African Glory;* Jomo Kenyatta, *Facing Mount Kenya,* Elton Fax, *West African Vignettes;* the writings of George Padmore, concluding with *Pan-Africanism and Communism;* and those of Dr. Kwame Nkrumah, *Ghana* and *I Speak of Freedom.* Making their contribution have been the works of the English author Basil Davidson, *Old Africa Rediscovered* and *Black Mother,* as well as that of the German writer Janheinz Jahn, *Muntu: An Outline of Neo-African Culture.*

Quite encouraging is the fact that today, in the main stream of life and thought in Harlem, interest as well as identification with Africa grows apace. In homes, more books on African life and development are seen and read. This concurs with the increasing sale of African literature in Harlem bookshops; the trend in the Frederick Douglass Book Center has been markedly away from general fiction and toward the history and culture of peoples of African origin. Among fraternal societies and clubs, in church and school, library and lecture hall, more programs than ever before are being presented on various aspects of African life and liberation.

To mention a few indications: A program for African diplomats organized by Sudia Masoud, secretary of the African-Asian Drums, began at the Prince Hall Masons' Auditorium and concluded with a dinner at the Hotel Theresa. The Seventh Day Adventist Church presented several representatives of African states. The Afro-Arts Cultural Center, Simon Bly, Jr., Executive Director, in cooperation with Dr. Charles M. Schapp, Assistant Superintendent of District Schools, has conducted In-Service courses on Africa for teachers for several years. Along with its work to emphasize the names *African* and *Afroamerican* as fitting and honorable designations, the Committee to Present The Truth About The Name "Negro" has conducted and plans more lecture series on *The History and Culture of African Peoples.*

In Unity Lies Strength

Still more significant was the American Negro Leadership Conference held last November at Arden House in Harriman, New York. For this involved the principal Afroamerican organizations active or represented in Harlem and the country—the NAACP, CORE, Brotherhood of Sleeping Car Porters, National Council of Negro Women, National Urban League, the Southern Christian Leadership Conference, and the American Society For African Culture. It has been alleged that these leaders suddenly evinced a new interest in Africa, but even in that case this interest definitely reflects the rising consciousness of Africa among the vast majority of the members and supporters of these organizations.

In any case such expressed concern for the African peoples should be welcomed and encouraged by all who are sincerely devoted to African liberation. If any of these Afroamerican leaders exhibit wariness or weakness, then those who honestly and wholeheartedly seek to aid Africa should, in order to infuse greater clarity and strength, indicate what they consider these weaknesses to be. Thoughtful supporters of African unity and progress must, therefore, regret the ill-advised, intemperate, and harmful attack made in the article entitled *Negro Stooges Bid For Africans Challenged,* which stands out offensively in the January 1963 issue of *Voice of Africa.*

When the leaders in the American Negro Leadership Conference are challenged on the ground that "they had the audacity to make attempts to move ahead of the African nationalists in America," this statement admits motivation from selfish considerations on the part

of those who make this challenge. It is also obviously feared that these
Conference leaders might get ahead in securing diplomatic posts or
other prized considerations. Branding these Conference leaders as
"opportunists," after making such a charge, will be logically regarded
as an unconscious confession of competition in opportunism. Again,
to affirm that "these organizations represent American colonialism,
imperialism, and exploitation," is patently to go beyond the bounds
of truth.

Moreover, such a statement is destructive of unity and must offend
and repel the hundreds of thousands of members of the organizations
in this Conference who are rallying to the cause of African freedom
and progress. Thinking people, too, must pause to question the
strange self-praise projected in this article by self-styled "Ghana
patriots," who are not known to have given up their United States
citizenship or to have been accorded citizenship by the government
of Ghana. Likewise deplorable is the unwarranted use of the good
name of Osagyefo of Ghana in these derisive proceedings which tend
only to separate the Afroamerican leaders and people from the African statesmen and their peoples.

But utterly reprehensible is the disruptive campaign being waged
by George S. Schuyler and his accomplices in mind-twisting which
has rendered aid and comfort to the Belgian and other neo-colonial-
ist oppressors in the Congo Republic and to the Portuguese imperial-
ist butchers of the peoples of Angola and Mozambique.

Completely disproving the false and venomous general accusations
made by George S. Schuyler et al. in the *N. Y. Courier* against African
statesmen, of indifference and hostility against Afroamerican people,
was the reported reaction of African Foreign Ministers at the Conference of African States held in Addis Ababa, Ethiopia. *The New York
Times* of May 19th published their special correspondent's report that
the Foreign Minister of Nigeria rose "to denounce racial discrimination in South Africa and the United States." This report also states,
"American observers have been dismayed to hear Alabama linked
with South Africa in attacks on apartheid inside and outside the
conference hall," and further that "American correspondents approaching members of delegations frequently hear the question,
'What's the latest news from Birmingham?' "

The Ethiopian *Herald*, which is the official publication of the
Ministry of Information, is quoted as having commented:

> What happened in Birmingham last week shows the United States in
> its true light. To be black is still a crime. . . . The colored American
> must fight hard for freedom rather than waste time and much needed
> energy bellyaching about Communism. The United States version of
> "civilized apartheid" must be fought.

Acting on behalf of the 30 African nations assembled in this Conference at Addis Ababa, Prime Minister Milton Obote of Uganda sent a letter to President Kennedy of the U.S.A. which condemned the "most inhuman treatment" perpetrated upon Afroamericans at Birmingham, Alabama, and which further stated:

> Nothing is more paradoxical than that these events should take place in the United States at a time when that country is anxious to project its image before the world as the archetype of democracy and champion of freedom.

At a news conference held on May 23rd, as reported in the *New York Times*, Prime Minister Obote recognized that those "who had been doused with blasts of water from fire hoses in Birmingham were 'our kith and kin,'" and declared further that, the eyes of the world were "concentrated on events in Alabama and it is the duty of the free world, and more so of countries that hold themselves up as leaders of the free world, to see that all their citizens, regardless of color, are free."

It may be predicted confidently, despite the malicious efforts of a few venal slanderers, that consciousness of Africa will continue to grow in Harlem and among Afroamericans generally. An even more vigorous and healthy development of this consciousness will come when it is more fully realized that rationally no conflict really or properly exists between vital interest in our African heritage and the liberation of the African peoples and deep and active devotion to the cause of human rights and equal citizenship status here in the U.S.A. For the same social forces which spawned colonialist subjugation in Africa and other areas are the identical forces responsible for brutal enslavement and racist oppression in the Americas and elsewhere.

Freedom and the full development of the human personality, therefore, require independence for the African peoples as well as full citizenship rights with equal status and opportunity for the minority people of African descent wherever they now exist. The same inherent self-respect and will to be free, which led Paul Cuffee to wage a successful struggle for the vote and equal citizenship rights in Massachusetts, immediately after the American Revolution of 1776, also led this great pioneer leader to promote self-determination through migration and the development of Sierra Leone in Africa. An enlightened awareness of African lore and liberty is, and will continue to be, the inevitable expression of the indomitable will to self-knowledge, self-determination, self-realization, and self-development on parity with all mankind.

This essay was written by the Kenyan leader, Tom Mboya, several months before his assassination in Nairobi. Mboya expressed delight in the interest in Africa but argued that many American Negroes have distorted pictures of African societies and of African concepts of nationalism.

Mboya quotes W. E. B. DuBois, who argued that it should be possible for a man to be both a Negro and an American. According to the African observer, this is as it must be. Mboya saw himself as a black Kenyan; his "cousins" here, he felt, would have to come to terms with the fact that they are black Americans.

22

Tom Mboya

THE AMERICAN NEGRO CANNOT
LOOK TO AFRICA FOR AN ESCAPE

Black Americans today are more concerned with their relationship to Africa than at any point in recent memory. The emergence of this concern at the present time is a phenomenon of great significance and a source of increasing controversy and confusion. The *nature* of the relationship between Africans and black Americans therefore merits extensive dialogue between the two groups, in the hope that issues can be clarified, illusions dispelled, and a common understanding reached as to where our immediate objectives coincide and where they do not. Our struggle and goal are the same, and we need a common understanding on strategy so as not to cancel each other out.

It is precisely because communication and clarification are so important that I was deeply disturbed by an incident that occurred when I spoke in Harlem on March 18 [1969]. In my one-hour speech I explained the challenges of development in our new African nations.

I discussed the difficult period of post-independence through which we are now passing. The economic and social problems we face are complex, and it is very important that those who are interested in our development understand the formidable task that now confronts us. I found the audience in Harlem highly receptive to my remarks on this subject. At the end of my speech, however, in response to some people who had approached me before the meeting, I decided to comment on the proposal for a mass movement of black Americans back to Africa. I began by rejecting the proposal, but before I had a chance to elaborate I was noisily interrupted by two or three people, one of whom projected four or five eggs in my direction. His aim was as bad as his manners.

Needless to say, I found this a rather curious and crude way of impressing African leaders with the genuine desire of black Americans to identify with Africa. By their deliberate and planned activities, a handful of people succeeded in disrupting a very important opportunity for dialogue between an African leader and black people who feel the need for closer relations with our new nations. Africans involved in the serious task of nation-building can hardly be expected to look kindly upon the discourteous and self-indulgent activities of these few individuals. They may also be led to doubt that black Americans in general have any appreciation of, or desire to understand, the problems that we must cope with. Apart from this, the enemies of the black man's struggle were given yet another excuse to justify their continued efforts to disorganize and divide and weaken us.

We must, however, be careful not to dramatize or generalize this incident. Indeed, I have received many letters from black people disassociating themselves from it. The only significance that I now attach to the incident is that it may, by underlining certain confusions, help clarify the relationship between Africans and Afro-Americans. Thus the disrupters, who wanted to obstruct dialogue, may unwittingly have helped to foster it.

In a fundamental way, Africans and Afro-Americans today find themselves in remarkably similar political and economic situations. As I have already indicated, the new nations in Africa have passed through one stage—that of the movement to independence from colonial rule —and are now engaged in the post-independence stage of nation-building. The first stage was primarily *political,* our objective being to achieve the political goal of self-determination.

We suffered during our struggle for independence, but in many ways it was a simpler period than today. It was one of mass mobilization, dramatic demonstrations, and profound nationalist emotions. The present period is less dramatic. Fewer headlines are being made;

fewer heroes are emerging. Nationalist sentiment must remain powerful, but it can no longer be sustained by slogans and the excitement of independence. Rather, it must itself sustain the population during the long process of development. For development will not come immediately. It is a process that requires time, planning, sacrifice, and work. Colonialism could be abolished by proclamation, but the abolition of poverty requires the establishment of new institutions and the development of a modern technology and an enormously expanded educational system. We are engaged, therefore, in an economic and social revolution that must take us far beyond the condition we had achieved when we won our independence.

Our slogan during the independence struggle was "Uhuru Sasa," and I do not think it is a coincidence that its English translation, "Freedom Now," was the slogan for the civil rights movement in America. For the black American struggle in the nineteen-fifties and early sixties was very similar to our own. The objective of both was political liberty for black people. In America, black people demanded the abolition of Jim Crow segregation and the right to vote, and they won their fight through courageous and inspiring political protest. But like their African cousins who must meet the challenge of development, they now confront the more difficult task of achieving economic equality.

I have seen black ghettos in America. I have seen individuals living under degrading conditions. Black poverty is more outrageous in America than in my own country because it is surrounded by unparalleled wealth. Thus, for black America the problem of equality looms larger than the problem of development, but they are similar in that the achievement of both requires massive institutional changes.

The struggles of black people in Africa and America are related on more concrete levels. Let us not forget that the independence movement in Africa has had a great impact on the civil rights movement in America, besides giving it a slogan. In addition, this movement for independence has posed many important questions for white America in regard to the race problem in the United States. For example, James Baldwin has noted in *The Fire Next Time* that the 1954 Brown vs. Topeka Board of Education decision concerning school desegregation was largely motivated by "the competition of the cold war, and the fact that Africa was clearly liberating herself and therefore had, for political reasons, to be wooed by the descendants of her former masters." In its supporting brief in the Brown case, the Justice Department explained that "it is in the context of the present world struggle between freedom and [Communist] tyranny that the problem of racial discrimination must be viewed." In other words, the United States Government understood very well that it would have difficulty making friends in Africa so long as the black American remained subjugated. Africans are highly conscious of the plight of black America, and they will be suspicious of the intentions of American foreign policy until they are convinced that the goal of American domestic policy is social justice for all.

I believe, furthermore, that our independence movement has also influenced the thinking of black Americans toward Africa and toward themselves. I have returned to the United States many times since my first visit in 1956, and have observed a remarkable transformation in the black's attitude toward Africa. Thirteen years ago Africa was seen as a mere curiosity, a jungle country of primitive people. This is not surprising, since the image that *all* Americans had of Africa was created by sensational novels and Hollywood films that were far more indicative of American values than of actual life in Africa. Of course, there were some exceptions, like Dr. W. E. B. Du-Bois, but the majority of black Americans either were ashamed of their association with Africa or were entirely indifferent to her.

These attitudes changed rapidly as much of Africa gained independence. New states and leaders took their place in the world community. African flags flew high and the national anthems of the new nations were sung with dignity. Respected statesmen, scientists, and professional men became visible representatives of Africa, thereby destroying the stereotypes that had existed for so long. Many black Americans observed these phenomena at first with disbelief, but soon their shame in their African heritage was transformed into great pride, and they began to identify with Africa with great intensity. Indeed, it can be said that some of them became, in a sense, more African than the Africans.

It is important that this new identification be understood within its proper context. Most African leaders have emphasized the *universality* of the black man's struggle for freedom and equality. Thus, we see the gains made in Africa as representing battles won in a much bigger war that must continue until total victory is achieved. It is in this spirit that African states accept as their responsibility struggles that continue in parts of our continent not yet freed from colonialism and white racist domination. Thus, the new nations of Africa will not be entirely free until the black man is liberated in South Africa, Namibia, Rhodesia, Angola, and Mozambique.

The social movement of black people in the United States is also part of this universal struggle for equality and human dignity for all our people. We cannot survive as free nations if there is any part of the world in which people of African descent are degraded. This is the context in which African interest and aspirations extend beyond the borders of our individual nations and of our continent. This is also the basis of the long-standing collaboration between African nationalists and black leaders from other lands. The heroes of the black man's struggle include those who fought in Africa as well as in America. A. Philip Randolph and Jomo Kenyatta are universal black spokesmen, as were the late Malcolm X and Dr. Martin Luther King, Jr. Africa is the birthplace of the black man, but his home is the world. To us, this is the meaning of total independence. We refuse to think of being free in Africa but treated as inferiors the moment we step out of the continent.

In this decade the black man has made enormous progress, in Africa and elsewhere. It is our political decade. Particularly in America, the society has been forced to undergo a genuine social revolution in response to the black struggle. Special note must be taken of the role of young people in this cause. Their fearlessness, resourcefulness, and resolve must be recognized and encouraged. My only regret is that many of our leaders and people in Africa have not had the opportunity to visit the United States and thus do not fully appreciate the new mood of militancy and self-assurance that prevails there among black people.

African nationalism is, by its very nature, integrationist, in that its primary objective is to mold numerous tribes into a single political entity. Tribalism, in fact, was one of the major obstacles in the way of independence, and it remains a problem today, as can be seen in the Nigerian-Biafran conflict. The European colonial powers tried for a long time to build up tribal antagonisms in order to weaken nationalist opposition to their rule. Local energies that were channeled into tribal hostilities obviously could not be used to oppose colonialism, and if one tribe became hostile to the Europeans, the latter would befriend another tribe, foment tribal conflict, and then watch the fighting from the sidelines as "neutral" observers. This was the straightforward tactic of divide-and-rule.

This tactic is by no means unique either to Africa or to colonialism. In Northern Ireland, for example, conservative aristocrats have been able to maintain their power by playing on the religious hostilities between working-class Protestants and Catholics, and have thereby prevented the emergence of a broad-based opposition. A kind of religious tribalism is thus obstructing the formation of a unified and progressive political force there, and in the United States I would think that the same role is played by racial and ethnic tribalism.

Just as the African must reconcile the differences between his tribal and his national identity, so too must the black American realize to the fullest extent his potential as a black man and as an American. I find his task an extraordinarily difficult one, particularly because he has been part of an oppressed racial minority. His new assertiveness is important here. He has cast off the myth of racial inferiority, and he is demanding that he be treated with dignity. But the danger is that his racial pride may become a form of racialism that would be unfortunate not only from a moral point of view but also from a political one, in that he would be separated from potential allies. From the African point of view, the black man's struggle in America must assert the right of equal treatment and opportunity. I have not found a single African who believes in a black demand for a separate state or for equality through isolation.

The contradiction between black nationalism and American nationalism can lead to much confusion, particularly when black nationalists, in search of a national base that they cannot find at home, turn to Africa. There is the possibility that they want to identify with Africans on a purely racial basis—which is unrealistic since they are citizens of different nations. I think it is this confusion that has led some black Americans to try to impose upon the American political situation concepts and ideologies that grew out of the African experience with colonialism and imperialism. Thus, writers like Frantz Fanon have become popular in certain black American circles, even though these very writers would be the last to want their ideas exported to other continents. Fanon, for example, wrote that "the test cases of civil liberty whereby both whites and blacks in America try to drive back racial discrimination have very little in common in principles and objectives with the heroic fight of the Angolan people against the detestable Portuguese colonialism."

Fanon, who advocated the use of violence by the oppressed, is popular among some black Americans because of their tremendous frustration with the conditions under which they must live. The fact that these black Americans would turn to an African for guidance may be an indication of why some of them are now thinking of expatriating to Africa. I think the reason is, again, their frustration, as well as their inability or unwillingness to resolve the tension between their racial and national identities.

At this point I should deal with the specific question of the Kenya Government's attitude toward a motion tabled in our Parliament last year. Reference was made to this motion at the Harlem meeting. Some of the Afro-Americans who spoke to me were angry that our Govenment had rejected a motion calling for automatic citizenship for any black American who wished to come to settle in Kenya. The point here is a legal one. The fact is that even Africans coming from neighboring states cannot acquire automatic citizenship. The Constitution lays down the conditions that must be fulfilled by all persons who wish to become citizens. We could not discriminate in favor of any group without first having to amend the Constitution itself. The point must also be made that our Government has to retain the right to keep out undesirable individuals; i.e., people with criminal records, mental cases, or others whose presence would create problems for our new nation.

I know that those who meet the conditions will be able to acquire citizenship as easily as have many foreigners since Kenya's independence. Kenya has a large body of non-black and non-African citizens. At the time of independence we gave all persons of non-African origin two years to become citizens by registration, and more than 40,000 Asians as well as thousands of Europeans took advantage of this. Since December, 1965, when the two-year period ended, many more have become citizens through the Naturalization Act. This method is available to foreigners even today. What is more, we now have many more foreigners in Kenya who have come as businessmen, technicians, etc., since independence, and who enjoy protection under the law without actually being citizens.

Perhaps some of our critics do not realize that we, too, have the many problems confronting black people in America. We have our slums, our unemployed, and other social shortcomings. Our first responsibility must be to our own citizens. Emotional crusades cannot change this hard fact. It may help our American cousins to understand the mood in Kenya better if I quote from the manifesto of our party published in 1963, just before the general election leading to our independence:

"KANU will lead and inspire Kenya with a dynamic spirit of national unity toward a Democratic, African, Socialist society.

"Divisions of tribe or of party, of color, custom, caste, or community, of age or faith or region will be subordinate to the national effort.

"Far from accepting the inevitability of tribal and racial antagonisms, we believe these differences are a challenge and an opportunity for creating a nation united in its purpose, yet rich in the diversity of its people."

Perhaps the desire to return to Africa is so unrealistic because it is based upon despair. I do *not* mean by this that African states should refuse black Americans who wish to expatriate. On the contrary, those who want to make a home in Africa are free to do so. There are many opportunities in the new nations, particularly for trained and skilled persons. They could help us enormously during our period of development, and we welcome our American cousins to come and work among us.

What is unrealistic about the proposal is the ease with which some black Americans think that they can throw off their American culture and become African. For example, some think that to identify with Africa one should wear a shaggy beard or a piece of cloth on one's head or a cheap garment on one's body. I find here a complete misunderstanding of what African culture really means. An African walks barefoot or wears sandals made of old tires not because it is his culture but because he lives in poverty. We live in mud and wattle huts and buy cheap Hong Kong fabrics not because it is part of our culture but because these are conditions imposed on us today by poverty and by limitations in technical, educational, and other resources. White people have often confused the symbols of our poverty with our culture. I would hope that black people would not make the same error.

Our culture is something much deeper. It is the sum of our personality and our attitude toward life. The basic qualities that distinguish it are our extended family ties and the codes governing relations between old and young, our concept of mutual social responsibility and communal activities, our sense of humor, our belief in a supreme being, and our ceremonies for birth, marriage, and death. These things have a deep meaning for us, and they pervade our culture, regardless of tribe or clan. They are qualities that shape our lives, and they will influence the new institutions that we are now establishing. I think that they are things worth preserving, defending, and living for.

But I should point out that there is a great debate raging in Africa today over our culture. Certain customs and traditions are being challenged by our movement toward modernization. People are asking what should be preserved and what should be left behind. They argue about the place universities should have in the society. African intellectuals and governments demand the teaching of African history, and efforts are being made to provide new school syllabuses and to encourage African writers. Some fear the breakdown of the extended family, others the emergence of a new elite removed from the people. We even argue about the use of cosmetics, hair-straighteners, miniskirts, and national dress. Thus, black people who come to Africa will find many of their questions unanswered even by us.

Our new nations are in a transitional stage, and I think we can benefit greatly from contact with our American cousins. The African needs to understand and encourage the revolution of the black people in America, while the black people in America need to understand and encourage the effort of nation-building now taking place in Africa. Communication must be strengthened between us.

I have been impressed by new enterprises and economic and social institutions organized by black Americans. There is also a movement in the universities to establish programs in African studies. These are areas in which we could cooperate and promote our joint interests. Of course, I do not share the view of those who demand black studies and then insist that white students be barred from them. Such an attitude reflects a contradiction, and conflicts with our search for recognition and equality.

Freedom for both Africans and black Americans is not an act of withdrawal, but a major step in asserting the rights of black people and their place as equals among nations and peoples of the world. Freedom involves the full realization of our identities and potential. It is in this sense that the objective of the African must be the development of his nation and the preservation of his heritage. And the objective of the black American must be the achievement of full and unqualified equality within American society. The black American should look to Africa for guidance—and for a chance to give guidance—but not for escape. He must merge his blackness with his citizenship as an American, and the result will be dignity and liberation.

Black people in Africa and America have survived slavery, colonialism, and imperialism. Today we can survive change. We have been oppressed as a people, and have been divided to the point of taking roots in different cultures. But as we struggle to achieve our full liberation, these differences should become less important. If and when we are all free and equal men, perhaps even those racial distinctions that now divide our societies and that separate one nation from the other will disappear in the face of our common humanity.

In conclusion, I note a similarity between the positions of the black American and our own people. In both cases there is impatience to see a promise kept—on the one hand is the promise of civil rights legislation, and on the other, the promise of independence. There is a crisis of confidence. The danger in America, as in Africa, is that such impatience can lead to confusion of priorities and failure to recognize the goals of the movement. Effective unity and committed national leaders are needed more now than ever before. If these elements are absent, the enthusiasm of the young people and the tremendous sympathy and support of other groups may be lost in despair.

This, in my view, is the challenge before the black people and their leaders in America. The struggle calls for even greater resolution and dedication if they are to translate past victories into a pro-

gram of action for the more difficult task of achieving actual equality
—as against legal and constitutional proclamations.

Bayard Rustin has offered the best explanation I have yet read of
the origins of the "Back to Africa" movement among his people:

"There is a reason for this movement which has far less to do with
the Negro's relation to Africa than to America. The 'Back to Africa'
and separatist tendencies are always strongest at the very time when
the Negro is most intensely dissatisfied with his lot in America. It is
when the Negro has lost hope in America—and has lost his identity
as an American—that he seeks to re-establsh his identity and his roots
as an African.

"This period of despair has historically followed hard upon a
period of hope and of efforts to become integrated—on the basis of
full equality—into the economic, social, and political life of the
United States. The present separatist mood, as we know, has come
after a decade in which the Negro achieved enormous and unprecedented gains through the civil rights struggle, and it has coincided
with a right-wing reaction that has obstructed further measures
toward equality. The combination of progress, aroused hopes, frustration, and despair has caused many Negroes to withdraw into
separatism and to yearn for Africa."

Rustin goes on to observe that this syndrome has occurred three
times in the past: in the early eighteen-hundreds, when the African
Methodist Episcopal Church was formed; in the late nineteenth century, when Booker T. Washington became famous, and in the nine-
teen-twenties, during the heyday of Marcus Garvey.

I have accepted the opportunity to contribute this article, not as an
apology for the Harlem incident, but because of my genuine concern about the relations between Africa and the black people in
America. The achievement problems they face are of great interest
to us in more than one way. In the first place, they are our cousins
and we share together the black man's fate in the world. His complete liberation is our joint concern because, as I have said, black
people cannot be fully free if there remains any part of the globe
where a black man is denied his rights. Second, the complete emancipation of America's blacks will influence the country's policies in a
way that can only lead to a better understanding of and sympathy
for the cause of black people everywhere. And finally, a free and
vigorous black community in the United States can, within its own
organization, play a much more effective and practical role in helping African and other black nations meet some of their challenges of
development.

I have, since 1958, witnessed the true potential of the black American in this regard. People like Ralph Bunche, Jackie Robinson, Harry Belafonte, Sidney Poitier, Frank Montero, Bayard Rustin, and the heads of such Negro institutions as Howard University, Tuskegee Institute, and Morehouse, Morris Brown, and Spelman Colleges in Atlanta played a decisive part in my campaign for a students' airlift to the United States. This program helped to bring over 1,000 students from Kenya and other parts of East and Central Africa to study in America; today, many of these students are home, and are providing the backbone for our new public service.

A number of Afro-American leaders in church and community groups, like the Rev. James Robinson of New York, labor leaders like A. Philip Randolph and Maida Springer, and many black families across the United States, took part in this unique experiment in people-to-people international cooperation. And there were, of course, many white Americans, like the late Senator Robert F. Kennedy and his brother, Senator Edward Kennedy; Theodore Kheel, the attorney and mediator; the distinguished statesman, Averell Harriman; Dr. Buell Gallagher, the educator; I. W. Abel, the labor leader; and white institutions and families who contributed to it.

The point I am making, however, is that black people have the scope and capacity to join in the challenge of development in Africa as free citizens in America. We need them there. I am not afraid of an exodus of black people from America to Africa because I know there will be no such exodus. I am, rather, concerned that the emotion and effort needed to promote such a movement would lead to sterile debate and confusion when there is an urgent need for unity and decisive leadership.

The challenge of the black American was stated with great beauty by W. E. B. DuBois over a half a century ago:

"One ever feels this twoness—an American, a Negro; two souls, two thoughts, two unreconciled strivings; two warring ideals in one dark body, whose dogged strength alone keeps it from being torn asunder.

"The history of the American Negro is the history of this strife—this longing to attain self-conscious manhood, to merge his double self into a better and truer self. In this merging he wishes neither of the older selves to be lost. He would not Africanize America, for America has too much to teach the world and Africa. He would not bleach his Negro soul in a flood of white Americanism, for he knows that Negro blood has a message for the world. He simply wishes to make it possible for a man to be both a Negro and an American, without being cursed and spit upon by his fellows, without having the doors of Opportunity closed roughly in his face."

In this final selection, Robert Blauner first discusses the widespread contention that "American Negroes are white men with black skins," that they are a people devoid of a culture of their own. This, he points out, is patently false—and absurd.

There is such a thing as black culture: a dynamic way of life with roots in the quasi-communities of the ante-bellum period, the promises and failures of Emancipation, the southern heritage, and persistent relegation to a low rung on the status ladder.

Blauner, a white sociologist, does not try to describe black culture, but only to explain why it exists. The former task he leaves to black Americans themselves.

23

Robert Blauner

BLACK CULTURE: MYTH OR REALITY?

In their communities across the nation, Afro-Americans are discussing "black culture." The mystique of "soul" is only the most focused example of this trend in consciousness. What is and what should be the black man's attitude toward American society and American culture has become a central division in the Negro protest movement.[1] The spokesmen for black power celebrate black culture and Negro distinctiveness; the integrationists base their strategy and their appeal on the fundamental "American-ness" of the black man. There are nationalist leaders who see culture-building today as equal or more important than political organization. From Harlem to Watts there has been a proliferation of black theater, art, and literary groups; the recent ghetto riots (or revolts, as they are viewed from the nationalistic perspective) are the favored materials of these cultural endeavors. The spread of resistance to the draft and the Vietnam war seems to indicate an increasing tendency among blacks to reject certain basic

Source: Original for this volume.

values of American life. But as with so many of these apparent "tendencies," it is difficult to know whether this one portends an actual change in sentiment or instead reflects the new conditions that have lifted some of the past inhibitions against its expression.

The emergence of this cultural revitalization movement among American Negroes poses a number of dilemmas for the larger society. There are the problems of practice and policy for the institutions of education, welfare, politics, and their professional and administrative representatives. There is also an intellectual dilemma for the analysts of American society and its culture. The black culture movement flies in the face of certain basic assumptions upon which social scientists and liberal intellectuals have constructed the nation's official "enlightened" attitudes toward race relations and the Negro minority. The primary tenet is that Negroes—unlike other minority groups—have no ethnic culture because the elimination of African ancestral heritages brought about total acculturation. A second related assumption posits the distinctiveness of the ghetto subculture to *lower-class* conditions rather than to ethnic or national traditions. The middle-class character and mobility goals of most federal anti-poverty efforts follow from this tenet. The present essay is addressed to these contradictions. I attempt to make sense of today's cultural ferment in the black communities by questioning the standard sociological position on the ethnic character of Afro-Americans.

The view that Negroes lack any characteristics of a distinctive nationality, that they are only Americans and nothing else has become almost a dogma of liberal social science. Gunnar Myrdal and his great study *An American Dilemma* set the tone for the present outlook.[2] In this influential and otherwise voluminous work there is no chapter on Negro cultural orientations and only a very brief treatment of the black community. Furthermore, Myrdal's statement that the Negro is "an exaggerated American" and that his values are "pathological" elaborations on general American values has been widely quoted for a generation.[3] In the introduction to *The Peculiar Institution*, published in 1956, the historian Kenneth Stampp asserted that Negroes are "white men with black skins," even though his thorough scholarship raises troubling questions about this statement.[4] And as recently as 1963, Glazer and Moynihan took the Myrdal position when they wrote "the Negro is only an American and nothing else. He has no values and culture to guard and protect."[5]

It is misleading to give the impression that the standard position reflects only the vantage point of the white liberal sociologist. E. Franklin Frazier has been at least as influential as Myrdal in gaining acceptance for this outlook. Frazier entered the debate in an effort to counter the extremism of Melville Herskovits, who in his *Myth of the Negro Past* imputes African origins to many, if not most, Afro-American social and cultural patterns. Frazier's view was published as late as 1957 in the revised edition of his comprehensive work, *The Negro in the United States:*

> As a racial or cultural minority the Negro occupies a unique position. He has been in the United States longer than any other racial or cultural minority with the exception, of course, of the American Indian. Although the Negro is distinguished from other minorities by his physical characteristics, unlike other racial or cultural minorities the Negro is not distinguished by culture from the dominant group. Having completely lost his ancestral culture, he speaks the same language, practices the same religion, and accepts the same values and political ideals as the dominant group. Consequently, when one speaks of Negro culture in the United States, one can only refer to the folk culture of the rural Southern Negro or the traditional forms of behavior and values which have grown out of the Negro's social and mental isolation. Moreover, many of the elements of Negro culture which have grown out of his peculiar experience in America, such as music, have become a part of the general American culture.
>
> Since the institutions, the social stratification, and the culture of the Negro minority are essentially the same as those of the larger community, it is not strange that the Negro minority belongs among the assimilationist rather than the pluralist, secessionist or militant minorities. It is seldom that one finds Negroes who think of themselves as possessing a different culture from whites and that their peculiar culture should be preserved.[6]

When Negro sociologists present community studies of Southern towns and Northern ghettos, however, they describe distinctive institutions and unique ways of looking upon life and society that resemble the depiction of an ethnic culture.[7] Yet until recently the positive assertion of Negro culture has been confined to nationalist and political circles; it has not been defended through analysis and evidence in the academic field. *Urban Blues* by Charles Keil is an innovative book in this respect. Keil, a white anthropologist, uses the blues singer and his audience as the raw materials to outline the distinctive traits and ethos of Negro-American culture. He finds the core of this culture in the "soul" ideology. Soul may be related to the more archetypal "wisdom-through-suffering" theme, but as Keil pieces it together, it suggests that "Negroes have a dearly bought experiential wisdom, a 'perspective by incongruity,'" that provides black Americans a unique outlook on life that cannot be shared by whites.[8]

Keil's rich study, to which I shall return later, stimulated an incisive critical review by the sociologist Bennett Berger. In the context of general admiration for Keil's achievement, Berger attacks his major thesis at three pivotal points. First, he asserts that "soul" theorists like Keil in their romanticization of Negro life miss the key fact that "black culture" is at bottom only an American Negro version of lower-class culture. Second, because this culture has no future, analytical appreciation of it may be misplaced. Lower-class culture in America is no basis for the development of a national consciousness and ethnic solidarity. Since it will have no appeal to the socially mobile, it can only interfere with progress toward integration and equality. Third, this suggests for Berger that black cultural spokesmen are only confusing the intellectual atmosphere and obstructing the road to Negro progress and racial harmony. As intellectuals and political men, they have the obligation to clearly specify what in Negro culture is to be affirmed, so that we all can see whether anything solid or meaningful is involved. But, speaking so generally if not demagogically, they fail to do so.[9]

The various positions discussed, from Myrdal to Frazier to Berger, share in common the idea that Black Americans have no ethnic culture. The first formulation asserts that Negro culture is American culture; the second and more recent positions argue that Negro orientations are Southern-regional or lower-class. I suggest that this approach is based on a number of misconceptions about culture and ethnicity in modern American society. It reflects first a narrow usage of the culture concept, but more important, the mechanical application of the model of immigrant ethnic group assimilation to the deviant cultural process of the black man. Second, it is a response to the confusion and complexity of Afro-American culture which stems from its many contradictory sources as well as a refusal to credit the prime role of racism—and its residues, Negro political history—in that cultural process. Finally, it is based on a static, deterministic approach to cultural development, an approach which minimizes its open-ended quality and therefore underplays the role of consciousness and culture-building in affecting that development. Let us examine each of these issues in turn.

First Dimension: The Unique Cultural Process

There is a sociological plausibility to the argument that Negroes are only Americans with black skins. As Frazier stressed, the manner in which North American slavery developed—in contrast to Caribbean and South American slavery—eliminated the most central African traits, those elements of ethnicity which European and Asian immigrants brought to this country: language, dress, religions, and other traditional institutions, a conscious identification with an overseas homeland. Basic as is this critical difference, it misses the point in assuming that there is only one generic process—that model of European ethnic assimilation—through which nationality cultures and the dominant American ethos have interacted. What must be understood is the uniqueness of the Afro-American condition, an essential aspect of which has been a deviant cultural experience that to some degree is the reverse of those of the traditional ethnic minorities.

Howard Brotz has observed that the "no Negro culture" argument rests on the assumption that an ethnic group must possess three attributes—a distinctive language, a unique religion, and a national homeland.[10] This position is also tied to the anthropologist's classical concept of culture, a usage that is less and less applicable to the condition of any ethnic group in modernized mass society. This is the *holistic* view of culture, which points to the integrated way of life, that system of customs, institutions, beliefs, and values that fit together into some organic whole, perhaps dominated by a central ethos. This concept was of course developed from the study of primitive peoples. Yet it fairly well captures the unity of the social heritages that the various immigrant groups brought to America.[11] The parallel holistic cultures of the African peoples were destroyed in America because slaves from the diverse tribes, kingdoms, and linguistic groups were consciously separated so that language, religion, and national loyalties were lost. But ethnic cultures as organic, holistic ways of life did not last very long either for the immigrant nationalities. Today when we characterize Jews, Italians, or Greeks as ethnic groups, we are referring implicitly to a different notion of culture. This is the idea that the ethnic culture resides in a certain number of distinctive values, orientations to life and experience, and shared memories that co-exist within the framework of the general American life-style and allegiances. Most sociologists and laymen find little difficulty in calling American Jews an ethnic group despite the fact that in most of their institutional and cultural behavior, Jews are eminently American and middle-class. But there are also distinctive cultural orientations, a peculiarly ethnic style in humor, for example, that came from a common historical and social experience.

Let us look more closely at the model of ethnic group assimilation that dominates sociological thinking about national cultures. The holistic way of life was introduced at the outset of the immigrant group's entry, or, more accurately, early in the peak periods of its immigration. It soon gave way to the demands of the American environment and the competition of American ways of life. Typically, after one generation an ethnic culture developed that combined old country and American ways, that was more fragmented and full of normative and value conflicts than the traditional culture, and yet that still provided some round of life and center of community for the group. As time went on, the numbers of people in each group involved in the more traditional holistic culture declined, and the emerging ethnic-American culture tended to take on more and more characteristics of the larger society. Assimilation meant the modification or the giving up of certain ethnic institutions and culturally distinct values as the generations followed one another. Though life experience may have been incredibly subtle and complex, the sociological model that captures the immigrants' cultural experience is fairly simple. There are basically two variables—the traditional culture and the American values and conditions. The process tends to be a one-way, nonreversible one, from immigrant extra-national status to ethnic group to assimilation, though Herberg and others have noted a tendency to reassert ethnic identity in the third generation. The means that move this process forward are occupational mobility and the ethnic group's increasing contact with dominant institutions, especially education.

Very little of this fits the cultural experience of Afro-Americans. How a minority group enters the host society has fateful—if not permanent—consequences. The very manner in which Africans became Americans undermined traditional culture and social organization. The black man did not enter this country with a group identity as a Negro. As Singer has pointed out, blacks were first simply a social-legal category, rather than a group in sociological terms.[12] This group category could only be formed by the slave-making operation which vitiated the meaning and relevance of the traditional, specific African identities. Therefore the cultural process could not be one of movement from ethnic group to assimilation, since Negroes were not an ethnic group. What took place first was not acculturation but an incorporation into a legal status that did not permit the group autonomy, and the social and economic progress that accompanied assimilation for other minorities—a forced deculturation, a spurious but not genuine assimilation. But at the same time, beginning with slavery, the group- and culture-building process began among the black population, and the development of an ethnic group identity and distinctive culture has been going on ever since. But this cultural process is infinitely more complex than that of the immigrant ethnic groups. One reason is the general reversal in direction. But it is not a simple one-way process in the opposite direction, from "assimilation" to ethnic group. The black cultural experience more resembles an alternating current than it does a direct current. The movement toward ethnicity and distinctive consciousness has been paralleled by one of becoming more "American" in action and identity.* Sometimes these conflicting vectors characterize different time periods; sometimes they reflect different segments of the large and diversified black minority—but in addition, these contradictory cultural tendencies have taken place simultaneously and within the psyches and social orientations of the same individuals. Behind all this are the many and various historical and social conditions that have produced Afro-American culture. Black culture therefore cannot be understood in terms of the simplified two-variable model which is reasonably satisfactory for the ethnic groups.

Second Dimension:
The Many Sources of Negro American Culture

The present essay will not attempt to characterize the contents of black culture. As I see it, this is a difficult if not impossible job for a white social scientist in today's America. The job will be eventually done by the more appropriate workmen in this jurisdiction, the Negro intellectuals and sociologists. Furthermore, it is my estimate that black culture is at present too much in flux for a systematic schematization to have much value. My task rather is to make some broad generalizations about the conditions in American life that have and are presently giving rise to distinctive Afro-American cultural orientations. Central to my argument against the conventional position is the thesis that the *ghetto subculture involves both lower-class and ethnic characteristics.* Poverty is only one source of black culture, and as I shall attempt to prove, even the lower-class traits and institutions in Negro life have been modified by strictly ethnic values. Among the other sources of black culture are Africa, slavery, the South, Emancipation and Northern migration, and above all, *racism.* That racist oppression provides the basis for a more elaborate and more ethnic cultural response than does class exploitation and lower-class status is a central postulate of the present thesis.

Negro-American culture is an ethnic as well as a class culture because the history of black people *in the United States* has produced a residue of shared collective memories and frames of reference. It is because black Americans have undergone unique experiences in

* In his account of Harlem, Claude Brown emphasizes the cultural conflict between the traditional "down home" (Southern) older generation and their more modern, urban-oriented offspring.

America, experiences that no other national or racial minority or
lower-class group have shared, that a *distinctive* ethnic culture (in
contrast to a holistic culture) has evolved. Though this culture is
overwhelmingly the product of American experience, the first contributing source is still African. Herskovits probably exaggerated the
power of African continuities, but it seems plausible that some aes-
thetic and linguistic principles that underlie Negro-American music
and dialect (as well as possibly some movement patterns and religious orientations) have their origins in those peoples, tribes, and
kingdoms that furnished the slave trade. However, the importance
of African patterns for American Negro ethnicity was greatly reduced
by the fact that these orientations had to be transmitted largely on
the subliminal level rather than that of conscious awareness and
identification. Recently, of course, with the emergence of independent
African nations, a concern with this continent has become more
prominent in the cultural symbolism of the black community and
presumably also in the personal identities of many black men and
women. We can also assume that considerable ambivalence toward
the African "homeland" remains.[13] See Harold Isaacs, *The New World
of Negro Americans,* for an excellent treatment of attitudes toward
Africa.

The first great source of black culture in America is slavery. Here
under seriously restricting conditions, American Negroes began developing their own quasi-communities and their own codes of conduct.[14] Here certain prevailing patterns such as ecstatic religion,
mother-led families, antiwhite attitudes, and the yearning for freedom
and autonomy got their start. To slavery also more negative adaptations and character-types, for example, the submission, timidity, fear,
and manipulation embedded in the "Uncle Tom" orientation, owe
their origins. It is these kinds of cultural adaptations that many
nationalist leaders are trying to stamp out in their attacks on "the
slave mentality."

Related to slavery as a second great source of Negro ethnicity is
the subculture of the American South. Ralph Ellison and more recently Calvin Hernton [15] have pointed out how much of the black
man's attitudes and cultural styles reflect the patterns of this region.
Certain features of Negro religion, "soul food," and language are similar to poor white counterparts. But the black man also assimilated
some of the values and the style of the Southern ruling classes,
though he was not always in a position to emulate them. Ellison has
attributed the general aristocratic flavor of ghetto life-styles to this
origin, as well as the American Negro's apparent lack of passion for
business entrepreneurship. Still an unexplored area are the ways in

which Afro-Americans themselves have shaped (rather than only reflected) the subculture of the South: the black influence is probably
more profound than generally recognized.

A further source was Emancipation: the promises, the betrayals,
and the frustrations that followed upon release from servitude. There
may be much in Negro-American patterns that still reflects a "freedman's culture"; I refer to the great mobility, the moving about and
restlessness that characterizes the life patterns of an important minority (especially male) within this great minority group. This
mobility, the promise of the North, the attractions of industry, and
the push from a depleted Southland, set the stage for ghetto life in
the urban North. This is the source of black culture which is most
clearly tied to poverty and lower-class existence. And yet the Negro
ghetto is different from the ethnic ghettos of the Irish, Jews, or Chinese
because it comes out of a different history, that of slavery, Southern
jim crow, and a northern migration which only partly parallels a
transoceanic search for a better life. *It is also different in its cultural
impact because it exists in a racist society which strongly resists the
assimilation of black Americans.* For this reason the Negro ghettos
have served more as the setting for the flowering of a distinctive
ethnicity, whereas the immigrant ghettos were actually way-stations
in the process of acculturation and assimilation.[16]

The lower-class component. The black ghettos are overwhelmingly
made up of low-income people, and poverty is the first fact of life.
This has naturally encouraged the view that the ghetto subculture
is lower-class culture, or the "culture of poverty" to use Oscar Lewis'
now fashionable phrase. This interpretation is based on the liberal
assumption that Negro Americans lack distinctive ethnic or national
characteristics, and the social science discovery that lower-class groups
in America share somewhat deviant orientations and way of life that
we call a subculture. Since black Americans are overwhelmingly in
the low-income population, then whatever appears to be distinctive
in the ghetto culture must be due to class status rather than ethnicity.

In *Urban Blues*, the most exhaustive, serious treatment of Negro
American culture up to now, Keil does not deal explicitly with the
analytical problem of class and ethnic contributions. Working with
the blues as his chief material, he identifies the ideology and be-
haviors associated with "soul" as the keystones of that culture. Bennett Berger, on the other hand, in his interesting review, bases his
argument on the theory that ghetto culture is essentially lower-class
in character. I think Berger finds Keil's overplaced emphasis (from
my viewpoint) on "soul" very convenient to his position, since this

real and yet elusive cultural symbol of black America does contain
many of the values, orientations, and virtues that have been historically attributed to the poor and downtrodden. As Berger (drawing
from Keil) summarizes "soul," it has become the stereotype that
flatters the oppressed Negro lower class and thus can serve as a compensation, an ideological palliative for its discontents:

> . . . strong emotions and feelings, especially when shared with others;
> something pure, nonmachined; staying power and wisdom through
> suffering; telling it like it is, being what you are, and believing in
> what you do. The concept suggests further a tight intermingling of
> sex, love, and reciprocal responsiveness which constitute the pattern
> of Negro Dionysianism, manifest in the swing of the blues-jazz-gospel
> musical milieu and in the brilliant, moving, linguistic innovations
> which spring from it. The pattern emphasizes the erotic, the frenetic,
> and the ecstatic—a pattern which when made ideological constitutes
> a claim to emotional depth and authenticity. . . .[17]

As this capsule summary suggests, there are many themes in
ghetto life that can be identified in other lower-class groups, for
example, the Latin American poor described by Lewis or the immigrant ghettos of the Irish and the Poles. Some of these themes are a
present-oriented and expressive style of life, characterized by minimal
planning and organization. Religion is usually a more dominant value
and release than politics; crime, hustling, rackets, and other forms of
"deviance" are commonplace. Economic pressures strain the family,
and matriarchal trends are visible. Aggression and violence seem to
be more frequent than in middle-class neighborhoods. Expressive
personal releases that some sociologists label "immediate rather than
deferred gratifications"—sex, drinking, drugs, music—are emphasized
in the life organization of individuals. A sense of fatalism, even
apathy or quasi-paranoid outlooks, the "world is against me," per-
vades the streets, where the public life of the lower-class subculture
is set.

That the black ghetto shares these cultural traits with other lower-
class milieus and that these themes flow primarily from the condition
of poverty I do not doubt. But that is not the whole story. Even the
class characteristics gain an ethnic content and emphasis when people
with unique problems live under similar conditions and associate
primarily with one another for generations. The expressive style of
Negroes is more articulated and developed than that of lower-class
Poles, for example. Not only music but language, styles of dress, and
movement also are more consciously cultivated. The religion of Southern blacks has similar institutional origins as that of Southern whites,
but as Powdermaker observed in the 1930's, a Negro church service
is a totally different happening from a poor white one.[18]

Berger correctly observes that lower-class traits do not become institutionalized or legitimated.* But when class traits are modified and given ethnic content by a national group, they may become institutionalized, that is conscious, expected, and infused with value (which can be positive or negative). Black Americans have long infused value into their folk music; today Southern rural cuisine, modes of walking and talking, and even the alleged "supersexuality" of Afro-Americans are becoming symbols of group identity and cohesiveness. (The development of ethnic cultural values does not, of course, preclude ambivalence; the fact that many people may feel ambivalent toward these phenomena is no argument against their cultural reality. Just the contrary!) My argument can perhaps be best illustrated by the matriarchy controversy. Though some reactions to the "Moynihan report" may suggest otherwise, Negro people with whom I have discussed the matter are well aware that for centuries the mother has played a more dominant role in the black family and community than she does in the larger society. Unlike the situation with lower classes in which the matrifocal theme generally operates amid a value system that stresses patriarchy and therefore obscures the detection and confrontation of this trend, Negroes *expect* to see women playing independent and powerful roles. Since the matriarchy is a conscious and expected reality, it is talked about, joked about, defended against, debated pro and con, and more and more actively acted upon, for example in selecting the leadership of community antipoverty boards and other political groups. It is becoming more and more infused with negative value. This type of cultural ferment in the black communities is not characteristic of lower classes—nor even of organized working classes in America—it indicates a dynamic of self-definition through which an ethnic group is shaping its character.

The class and the ethnic factors in Negro-American culture are so intimately intermingled that they are very difficult to distinguish. The effort must be made, however, because the intellectual and social consequences of this apparently innocent distinction are considerable—as I shall suggest in my concluding section.

RACISM

Perhaps the critical reader might agree that slavery, emancipation, and the Southern heritage are a unique constellation that no other lower-class minority group shared. Yet, these great events are more than 100 years past, and the Southern element weakens with migration

---

* As many have pointed out, the organization of lower-class people into Christian, Marxist, or trade union associations leads toward middle-class socialization as much as the institutionalization of working-class values.

and the modernization of the region. There is still much in the Northern ghettos today that resembles the life conditions of the ethnic
immigrants. All this is true and it might shatter my argument except
for one fact. *A continuing racist social structure has served to consolidate rather than to erase the distinctive experience of the past.* There
is no other lower-class group in America's pluralistic society that has
met in the past or meets in the present the systematic barriers of
categorical exclusion, blockage, and discrimination based on race and
color. This has been such an omnipresent reality for Negroes that
just as the way in which each black individual has confronted the
patterns of exclusion and denigration remains a central theme of his
or her personal biography, the direct and indirect struggle against
racism is the core of the history of the Negro group in this country.
It is through this continuing struggle to surmount and change a racist
social system—a struggle which began at least with Emancipation,
and has stepped up to new levels each generation after periods of
decline up to the zenith of the present day—that black Americans
have created a *political history*. This political history is the core of
the emerging ethnic culture, and the clue to the contemporary revitalization movement which celebrates blackness.

Despite the clichés of the "Kerner Report," it is still difficult for
most whites to accept the unpleasant fact that America remains a
racist society. Such an awareness is also obscured by the fact that
more sophisticated, subtle, and indirect forms, which might better be
termed neoracism, tend to replace the traditional, open forms that
were most highly elaborated in the old South. By American racism, I
refer to two key characteristics of our social structure. First, that the
division based upon color is the single most important split within the
society, the body politic, and the national psyche.* Second, that
various processes and practices of exclusion, rejection, and subjection
based on color are built into the major public institutions (labor
market, education, politics, and law enforcement) with the effect of
maintaining special privileges, power, and values for the benefit of
the white majority.

Racism is not only a central though subterranean theme of American culture; its attitude toward black cultures has had from the beginning a profound impact on the course of Negro ethnicity. Initially
it alienated its slave population from African culture. A further manifestation of its destructive and exploitative character was the tendency
to appropriate and use for profit the cultural creations of Negro

---

* If race is a more important division in present-day American society than
that of class, this raises serious questions about the tendency to reduce Negro
American culture to lower-class culture.

Americans: jazz has been the classic example here, but the present day use of ghetto language is in the same vein.[19] And today's liberal ideologies deny the legitimacy, or even the existence, of these subcultural values that make up the black man's distinctive culture.

American racism has been the key reality that has encouraged the development of black culture. There are several related reasons for this. First, it blocked the participation of Negroes in the dominant culture so that unfilled needs for symbols, meaning, and value had to be met elsewhere. Though for many years southern-oriented Negroes named their sons after George Washington and other presidents, the founding fathers have become negative symbols for a Northern ghetto generation who are finding their heroes elsewhere. Second, Negroes have perceived the fact (as Hernton has recently made explicit [20] that racism is not American aberration, but an institution built into the society and its cultural values. In order to protect their selfhoods, black men had to at least partly distance themselves from this culture (if not reject it outright), as the possibilities for assimilation and acculturation in certain areas opened up. Thus again, counter-values and symbols were necessary. (Of course many blacks did not distance themselves and thereby suffered intense inner conflict.) Third, racism made inevitable and necessary group struggles to transform it as a social system and individual efforts to transcend its crippling effects on life, liberty, and the pursuit of opportunity. This century-long battle against racism has created a legacy—the political history of Negroes within the United States. This shared political history is the solid core, the hard-rock nonmystical aspect of Negro American culture.

A unique political history plays an essential role in the development and consolidation of ethnic groups, as well as nations.* For the Irish-American community in the late nineteenth and early twentieth century, Ireland's struggle against England and the heroes of this national movement were at the center of ethnic group values and concerns. As others have pointed out, the Jews may be the purest example of a group that has institutionalized its political history into a culture, ritual, and sacred values. The Old Testament depicts the political vicissitudes of the Jewish nation and the religious holidays memorialize this millennial struggle for liberation. Perhaps then the attempt of many black nationalist groups to memorialize the assas-

---

* Howard Brotz has noted that sects like the "Black Jews" and the "Black Muslims" attempt to attach themselves to a long and respectable political history as well as to unique religions because they understand how important for culture both these elements are. See his perceptive book, *The Black Jews of Harlem, op. cit.*, especially Chapter IV.

sination of Malcolm X as an "official" holiday can be understood as a similar recognition of the relation between political history and national culture.

The content of the Negro Americans' political history is beyond the scope of this essay. It is clear, however, that in the past decade, there has been a significant change in the intensity and nature of this history—a change which lies behind the present-day ferment and interest in black culture. In the past the Negro masses—like the lower orders of all colors and nations in most eras—were primarily passive politically, acted upon more than acting. After the 1954 Supreme Court decision (the last major turning point in American race relations that was initiated by an act of a "white" institution), blacks have become the primary active agents for change with respect to the nation's social structure. Since the mid-fifties Negroes have created the big news in domestic American history.*

But important as the decade is, it does not exhaust the contents of Negro political history that makes black culture a real sociological phenomenon rather than a group myth. Despite the fateful reciprocity of black and white in America (a theme that has been stressed in the essays of Baldwin and the fiction of Faulkner and W. M. Kelley),[21] Negroes share a consciousness of a common past (and a concomitant national or ethnic identification) to which white Americans simply are not privy. How could whites perceive, react, and relate to slavery, emancipation, to the South and its history of jim crow and lynching, to early twentieth-century race riots, and even to Montgomery and Watts in the same way as blacks? No matter how democratic our ideals and how sensitive our human capacities, we were on the other side sociologically and existentially.

The point I am laboring has been made most succinctly by a reflective blues singer, Al Hibbler. When Charles Keil asked him what it takes to make a soul singer, Hibbler listed three ingredients, "having been hurt by a woman," "being brought up in that old-time religion," and "knowing what that slavery shit is all about."[22] In a nutshell, this is the essence of the Negro's distinctive political history that lies behind the autonomy of his ethnic culture—since no white American can really know "what that slavery shit is all about." Hibbler, of course, was not referring only to the past.

The black man's unique social-political experience also lies beyond the other elements of Negro culture that have been recently

---

* Berger notes that moderate civil rights groups like the NAACP do not accept the notion of a distinctive Negro culture. By restricting black culture to the "soul" complex and ignoring political history, he misses the point that they have willy-nilly played a part, and an important one, in developing this culture.

stressed. The "soul" orientation can be discussed in its Dionysian aspects which emphasize its relation to poverty and lower-class status. But it can also be looked at as a philosophy of life or world view that places tragedy, suffering, and forbearance in a more central position than does the dominant American ethos. The construction of an orientation toward inner experience that clashes with the more external instrumental orientation of our industrial culture reflects as much the racism that has excluded Negroes from American life as it does lower-class status *per se*.

Another contribution of racism to Afro-American culture is the prominence of *survival* as a focal concern in the black community. The preoccupation with survival is worth examining because of its remarkable salience and because it seems once again simply to reflect the conditions of poverty and lower-class status. What do I mean by the "survival theme"? For one thing, it is very common for black people to express group pride through the argument that the white race would not have survived had we been subject to the past or present life conditions of American Negroes. This sense of tough resilience is one of the central themes in the blues and in the mystique of soul. In the ghetto there is consensus that the problem of every individual is "making it"; "How you makin' it, man," is a common form of greeting. Interviews I have conducted in the Negro community suggest that "making it with dignity" is central to a leading concept of manhood. Finally on the political level, black leaders are becoming concerned with the problem of group survival; a number of "Black Survival Conferences" have been convened on the West Coast.

Poverty and lower-class existence *per se* also make survival an inevitable and insistent preoccupation. But the Negro American's self-conscious concern with survival and "making it" only reflects in part alimentary and economic subsistence needs. When black people talk about surviving, they are even more pointedly referring to the problem of maintaining life, sanity, and dignity in a racist society. The backdrop of the "making it" imagery is the presence of the Klan, lynch mobs, ghetto police, and the closed, restricted white power and economic structures. "Making it" appears to be a response to poverty and blocked economic opportunities, but "making it with dignity" is the response of a suppressed national group with their distinctive ethnic (read human) values to defend. Here I refer to the more subtle pressures of white institutions to make Negroes "tom," smile to fit conventional stereotypes, or more commonly today, to the pressures to change in middle-class ways that acceptance and success seem to require. Rightly or wrongly, these constraints are interpreted as forms of racism. The survival fears of the black politicos (which incidentally are commonly met among ordinary people in the ghettos today) are not directed at economic poverty. Rightly or wrongly again, they fear that a racist plot to eliminate the black population is behind the birth control efforts aimed at Negro welfare clients, the Vietnam war and its draft policies, and even an alleged readying of concentration camps for ghetto rioters.

Racist social relations have different cultural consequences from class relations, and therefore black culture cannot be forced into the Procrustean bed of lower-class culture in the way that Marxists at one time and some liberal social scientists today want to reduce race relations to class relations. For several centuries in America, blacks have lived together in ways that are markedly different from those of the lower and working classes. This difference is largely because the manner in which Negroes have been compelled to relate to individual whites and to the larger society is so divergent from the typical relations of the lower classes to the middle classes or to that of the proletariat to a capitalist social order. Racism excludes a category of people from participation in society in a different way than does class hegemony and exploitation. Racism insults; it attempts to violate dignity and to degrade personalities in a much more pervasive and inclusive way than class exploitation—which in the U.S., at any rate, has typically not been generalized beyond the "point of production." Racist oppression attacks men and manhood more directly and thoroughly than does class oppression. For these reasons racist and class oppression—while intimately interacting—still have diverse consequences for group formation, for the salience of identities based on these groups and for individual and group modes of adaptation and resistance. Class exploitation does not *per se* stimulate ethnic and national cultures and liberation movements; colonialism and domestic racism do.

Oscar Lewis has recently noted that there is a complementary and conflicting relation between the culture of poverty and ethnic group cultures. The classical lower-class culture characterized by apathy, social disorganization, aggression, sexuality, and other themes, lacks strong ethnic as well as organized political traditions. When an ethnic culture is viable or when political working-class consciousness is cultivated (as Lewis believes has taken place among the Cuban poor), the culture of poverty with all its negative and problematic effects declines.[23] If Lewis is correct—and he makes sense to me—the black culture movement among American Negroes may represent the strengthening of ethnic consciousness, the ethnic cultural component, at the expense of lower-class culture. This strikes me as something that liberal social scientists and intellectuals would want to applaud and appreciate rather than meet with carping criticisms.

Third Dimension:
Culture-Building and Its Present-Day Role

The fact that Negroes possess an ethnic culture does not make them less American, though it conditions their relation to American life in distinctive ways. There is no question but that the society's prevailing standards have been a major if not an overwhelming influence on ways of life in the black community. Precisely because black men were stripped of their traditional culture, language, and institutions, they were more vulnerable than other groups to American values. But since Negroes could never share fully and participate as equals in that way of life, they assimilated American values from a unique perspective, that of the outsider. As many Negro writers have pointed out, the majority of black population never bought the big myths of America, no matter how much they desired their realization. Certainly Negro culture is American in that it accepts the desirability of money and the material accoutrements of affluence, probably even the suburban life-style. But there is a distinctive ethnic element in the awareness of the social costs of these goods, in the sensitivity to the hypocrisy in American public and private life, to the gap between the ideal and reality. This long-term awareness appears to be changing into a more outspoken and outright rejection of American middle-class values by at least a substantial (though unknown) number of young Negroes today.

There is a remarkable paradox here in the phenomenon of Negro Americans more actively rejecting the society and its values at the very time when that social order has begun to open its doors to their participation. To some degree and in some cases this may be a "defense mechanism," a protection against the anxieties of openness, competition, and new possibilities. But from another point of view, the paradox is resolved if we understand the peculiarities of the Negro cultural experience set forth in the first section of this essay. In contrast with the situation of the immigrant ethnics, the period of integration and potential assimilation for Negroes is coinciding with the upsurge of the group's sense of peoplehood and with the institutionalization of its culture, rather than with the decline of these phenomena. Negro Americans with mobility and integration chances are more profoundly torn than were the children of immigrants, the so-called marginal men.

One reason why the existence of a Negro American *ethnic* (as opposed to the lower-class ghetto) culture has been easily dismissed by social scientists and policy-makers may be a certain lack of form and unity in Afro-American life-styles. Its traditions, values, and patterns of social organizations may not be as firm as were those of the immigrant nationality groups, though today black music, language, and experience are more compelling in their power and influence than the residual counterparts of the European ethnic cultures. The black culture that has emerged has grown out of the soil of American life, and the time in which cultural evolution has been possible is relatively brief—perhaps a hundred years. In addition, our social structure does not easily provide the physical isolation and autonomy for groups to develop their own distinctive ways of life (only people like the Amish who have been able to isolate themselves in self-contained and economically sufficient rural pockets have shown quick results in ethnic development). On the one hand, America in its racist dimension excludes the black man and maintains the ghettoized communities that provide the groundwork for Negro ethnicity; with the other hand America in its inclusive, mass homogenizing dimension beckons black men and all others to identify with its material and ideal symbols and to participate in at least the middle levels of consumption and life-styles. This duality and the fact that Negro American culture has so many diverse sources also contributes to this lack of clarity and unity. Compared once again to the immigrant groups upon which sociological models of ethnic group assimilation were built, the Negro minority is extremely large and highly differentiated. At the high points of immigrant ethnicity, most of these groups were small, their members concentrated primarily in a few cities and socially in the lower classes. During the periods that black culture has been building up (including the present) the Negro minority continues to differentiate itself. The middle classes grow; new political and religious movements proliferate (e.g., the Muslims); the black population spreads out more evenly across the country—though predominantly now in the urban centers. The development of an ethnic culture moves on at an uneven pace. New values and styles are born and institutionalized in the Northern ghettos at the same time that Southern-originated values and styles lose their hold on many people. There is yet a final reason why Negro American culture has been relatively "invisible." Blacks have learned to respond to racist depreciation and opportunistic cultural appropriation by concealing many of their deeply held patterns from the white world. White America therefore has not been prepared to respond to any affirmation of black culture beyond the conventional and usually racist stereotypes. We are hearing so much about "soul" today because this old adaptation is dying as a new mood of pride motivates cultural spokesmen to celebrate rather than to deny black values.

The many ambiguities within Negro American cuture do not imply its nonexistence. Nor are the black radicals necessarily misguided or visionary in their efforts to strengthen and consolidate it. For it is precisely this deviant, paradoxical character of black culture that makes it especially critical for the group formation and personal identity needs of its bearers. The immigrant ethnic groups had a clear-cut and holistic traditional culture; this gave them an implicit strength and bargaining power in the game of assimilation and acculturation. They had something deep inside the group and individual to fall back upon in the event the American staircase became blocked or its climb too perilous. But the black man has faced the American colossus with an original culture that was shattered. And most important, racism is more profound in its destructive impact on personal identity than was the prejudice and discrimination leveled against the nonblack outlanders.

Of course, the present cultural ferment in the Negro community is not totally new. Well known is the Harlem renaissance of the 1920's which saw the emergence of a group of self-conscious black intellectuals and artists, along with a somewhat parallel nationalist development in the political field, that of the Garvey movement. This earlier cultural renaissance came after the post-World War I setbacks to racial democratization, just as today's cultural movement gains its power from the limited successes and possibilities of the civil rights movement—specifically the failure of integration to become a social-economic reality. But if culture-building feeds on "backlash," this does not mean it is a temporary will-of-the-wisp that will die out when integration finally hits its stride. The very successes and social legitimation of the civil rights experience of the last ten years is beginning to teach us what most blacks have probably always known—that racism is not a dying phenomenon in American life, confined largely to decadent Southern elites and their redneck allies. Unfortunately it is only on the way out in these more blatant forms. In various and subtle ways, racism and neoracism permeate the social institutions of society—North, South, West, and East. Thus the black culture movement is a reasonable response to the realities of a society and a people that—as they are at present organized in socio-economic and psychic structures—are not going to accept Negroes without imposing ceilings on their possibilities to reach "the heights of a man." The stronger that Negro ethnic culture becomes, the greater the possibility for black people to utilize *both* group power and individual mobility to take what they can and give what will be accepted from this basically racist society—a process that in time will contribute to the transformation of this society and its racism. For in American life, ethnic culture is identity, and there is no individual or group progress without a clear sense of who one is, where one came from, and where one is going.

The black consciousness and culture-building movements of today seem much more significant than the earlier Harlem development, though for a nonhistorian this can only be an impressionistic guess. Today's movement is more widespread; it is taking place in every major ghetto, not just New York. It encompasses large segments of the black bourgeoisie and working-class masses, rather than primarily marginal people and intellectuals. The appeal of black culture seems *especially* strong today to the occupationally and socially mobile, a group which in the past tended to resist ethnic identification.

Professor Berger, however, in the review referred to earlier, argues that the soul ideology cannot meet the needs of the upwardly mobile integrationist. It is, he asserts, a lower-class mystique, and they are moving into the middle classes. I think that Professor Berger is dead wrong on this point. Even in America, people cannot live by bread (or television) alone. The mobile young blacks of today seem to be seizing upon the soul concept (and the related black power ideal) because they provide bulwarks of identity and identification in the face of the very anxieties of mobility and assimilation into the cultural vacuum of American life. My recent research and interviewing of community organizers and young college students from low-income ghetto origins suggests that this is so. Certainly, as Berger suggests, there may be new pressures to conform to militant postures and nationalist identifications in order to avoid charges of selling or copping out. But the external pressure point is overemphasized when the need is so intrinsic. This may be why there is more active support for the black power radicals (as well as for the Muslims) from the mobile Negroes, rather than from the "stable" lower classes in the ghetto. This again seems to reflect a change. A generation ago middle-class Negroes reputedly rejected jazz, blues, gospel music, and all other signs of lower-class and Southern roots. Today I find that middle-class black youth keep their car radios tuned in to the soul music stations and switch them on automatically whether riding with whites or other Negroes.*

---

* The young and the youthful are of course at the forefront of the black culture and black power movements. If Claude Brown is correct, E. Franklin Frazier may have had much to do with this generational change in the outlook of the "black bourgeoisie." Brown mentions that Frazier's lectures and his

In the same review, Berger presents a criticism of the Negro cultural "radicals" that probably is representative of much white liberal and intellectual thinking on this matter. It is important to understand why he is presumptuous in his plaint that "once the radicals invoke the perspective and rhetoric of black culture, they place themselves under the intellectual obligation to concern themselves with clarifying precisely *what* patterns of Negro culture they are affirming, *what* sources of institutional support for these patterns they see in Negro social organization, and *how* these patterns may be expected to provide the bases of 'racial pride' and 'ethnic identity' sufficient to motivate the black masses to claim both their full rights as Americans *and* the nation's respect for their ethnicity." [24] First he is asking the black intelligentsia to do for their subculture what American social scientists have not adequately accomplished for the society as a whole. The concept of culture—as well-taught undergraduates should know—is very sticky and troubling. Much scholarly controversy and uncertainty surrounds its essential features. American culture, further, is a most vague and amorphous reality; it simply cannot be pinned down as neatly and conveyed to us as graphically as the ethnographer can capture the culture of a tribal people. This may be partly because we are all caught up in it; more probably it reflects the diversity, the contradictions, and even the weakness of meaning systems and of central patterns in American life. Finally as we have seen, Negro culture is an even more complex reality.

Berger has every right not to accept the key assumptions of the black power movement; we differ politically and I respect these differences. But he should at least be listening to what these men are saying, for one premise is most central to his pointed criticism of their "failings." As Carmichael reiterates and expresses personally in his dealings with the mass media, one of the essences of black power is self-definition. This means that Negroes select the time, place, and manner in which to reveal their plans and strategies outside their own group. Self-definition implies that whites no longer can demand that Negroes do this or that; they have an intellectual obligation to com-

---

Black Bourgeoisie had a great impact on his own thinking, and presumably those of other college students. Of course, there is a sense in which these mobile black youth did not have to be motivated to become different from their parents, since in America all young people are predisposed to reject their elders and break away from their life patterns. But in so clearly dissecting the group-denying and the self-negating hang-ups of their parents, Frazier also helped teach the young generation to identify with their own blackness and with the oppressed ghetto masses. Many of these middle-class college educated youth have taken on the task of attempting to organize politically, as well as to articulate self-consciously, the less conscious cultural values of the lower-class black man.

municate with us only if they choose to become part of our general intellectual community, and for many, the present mood is to choose otherwise. But Berger misses the boat when he implies that black intellectuals are not striving for whatever clarity and specificity that is possible in the present situation. Ralph Ellison has long been calling for such an approach to the Negro cultural experience; conferences where such issues are hammered out have been taking place all over the country recently. But this has become an in-group matter; most of these meetings have been closed to white people. Berger is probably right that such discussions and clarification are essential for the cultural and political dynamics of the Negro movement today; I suspect many black leaders agree with him thus far. But we are not going to hear what is happening until they are good and ready. His demand (and there are many who would voice similar ideas) is out of order because our long-used behind-the-scenes *cartes blanches* have expired for sociological voyeurs like Berger and myself.

The demand that Negro spokesmen give us the lowdown once and for all on black culture so that we can define our attitude toward it overlooks a reality that is more profound than the new nationalist definition on intergroup relations. It reflects a static approach to social and cultural reality. It assumes that Negro culture is *all there*, or all-determined, needing only to be fully detected so the chaff can be separated from the wheat. On the contrary, Negro culture—like all cultures, but even more so today—is *in process*, it is a dynamic, open-ended phenomenon, and that is why it is becoming such a central concern of the protest movement. On the basis of the culture that has already been built up out of the American experience of the until recently relatively dormant, silent folk masses, a more self-conscious and explicit national culture is in the process of development. This requires the synthesis of the orientations of the ghetto masses with the articulations of the intellectual and political leaders. The middle classes and the marginal people are playing a crucial part as enunciators and systematizers of this nascent culture. From this point of view, Berger and others cannot lightly dismiss the activities of such men as LeRoi Jones who affirm soul and other black mystiques. Whether or not their every statement is judicious and wise, these spokesmen have a historic hand at present in the development of black culture. They know "where it's at," and they are there where the action is, and they influence this cultural action process because Negro culture is not a finished, determined, or static thing.

The same is true for the notion of soul which Mr. Berger feels is becoming a stereotype. This does not tell us anything about its present or future significance. The cultural reality of an affirmed trait is not in its statistical or scientific reality but in what it does and accomplishes as a rallying point and symbol. As we have come to know unhappily in less ambiguous race relations situations, stereotypes have living effects whatever the scientist may do to deflate them. The fate, function, and thus reality of soul-like black power remains to be revealed in the practical course of events. What soul is and becomes is therefore in part a product of the conscious decisions and political-educational activities of the cultural leadership of the Negro community and even more of the response of its less articulate masses. Its fate will not be determined by white social analysts.

Whites are no longer calling the shots on these matters that most deeply affect black Americans. This is the great and historic gain of a decade of Negro protest, culminating in the black power mood— which from this viewpoint is not as total a departure from the previous civil rights activity as most people assume. And this applies also to the intellectual and social science community's grappling with such issues as Afro-American culture. Yet even while our academic theorizing is no longer as central as it once may have been, the Negro political and cultural movement still operates within these American conditions that we affect. For this reason, white social scientists have a responsibility to probe deeply into the assumptions and consequences of our characterizations of race relations in this country. This I believe justifies the present essay.

Postscript on Neo-Racism

The viewpoint that black culture is only a lower-class life-style and Negro Americans have no ethnic traditions to value and defend falls within a general perspective that I would call Neo-Racism. Superficially this argument seems to say that blacks are as American as whites and therefore, their cultural orientations reflect their social class position. But, as I have pointed out, this theory ignores the group-forming and culture-producing effects of racism and therefore, as an analytical position leads to the minimization of the reality of racial oppression. In addition, this position leads to an overconcern with the pathological features of the black community at the expense of its unique strengths and contributions, since the culture of poverty is generally (and correctly) seen in terms of the predominance of suffering and the destruction of choice and human possibility. If Negro culture is only lower-class culture, then the questionable assumption that *all* black people want integration, mobility, and assimilation (middle-class status) seems justifiable as a basis for institutional policy and it is not necessary to consult, to offer alternative choices, or to respect individual diversity. Furthermore, this position is historically tied to past patterns of negating or appropriating the cultural possessions and productions of black people. The racist pattern was to destroy culture, to steal it for profit or to view it contemptuously or with amusement. The neo-racist equivalents today are to deny that any Negro culture exists or to deny and desire these values which the black man creates and defends as his own. (Witness the pathetic need of many young and not-so-young liberal and radical "friends" of the Negro movement to feel that they, too, have "soul.") The denial of Negro ethnicity is the more serious form that white appropriation takes today. Through abstract and intellectual analysis, the social scientist attempts to undermine the claims of Negro Americans to a distinctive ethos and value-system. The very existence of our possibility to so influence the cultural process among Negroes is based on the original alienation of the black man from his African traditions. Because colored Americans could only use the English language to carry on their business, their politics and their intellectual life, their physical and moral communities became vulnerable to the penetration of white Americans in a way that other ethnic groups—insulated by exotic languages, religions, and other institutions—could escape. Thus, the original culture-stripping and the consequent appropriation of indigenous black culture laid open the Negro community to economic and political colonialism, to the contamination of group ideology by alien, pride-destroying perspectives, and to the participation of paternalistic whites in racial movements.

It is time for social scientists to insist that there are no exceptions to the anthropological law that all groups have a culture: if black Americans are an ethnic group then they possess an ethnic culture; and just as the Jews explain to the world what Jewish culture is and Italians define Italian-American culture, we will learn what Afro-American culture is from American blacks rather than from our own dogmas and fantasies.

NOTES

1 Bennett M. Berger, "Soul Searching," review of Charles Keil's *Urban Blues, Trans-Action,* June, 1967, p. 54.
2 Gunnar Myrdal, *An American Dilemma* (New York: Harper, 1944).
3 *Ibid.,* pp. 927–930.
4 Kenneth Stampp, *The Peculiar Institution* (New York: Random House, 1956), p. vii.
5 Nathan Glazer and Daniel Patrick Moynihan, *Beyond the Melting Pot* (Cam-

bridge, Mass.: M.I.T. Press and Harvard University Press, 1963), p. 53. Glazer, it is true, views Negroes as an ethnic group rather than simply a racial category. But for him the contents of black ethnicity are only common interests and social problem. His account of Negro New York ignores the existence of a collective ethos, community social structure, and group institutions.

6 E. Franklin Frazier, *The Negro in the United States,* rev. ed. (New York: Macmillan, 1957), pp. 680–681.

7 For example, Charles S. Johnson, *Shadow of the Plantation* (Chicago: University of Chicago Press, 1934); St. Clair Drake and Horace Cayton, *Black Metropolis* (New York: Harcourt, Brace, 1945); and Hylan Lewis, *Blackways of Kent* (Chapel Hill: University of North Carolina Press, 1955). The distinctive culture of Harlem is emphasized also in the writings of James Baldwin and Claude Brown, *Manchild in the Promised Land* (New York: Macmillan, 1965), though not in the scholarly study of Kenneth Clark, *Dark Ghetto* (New York: Harper & Row, 1965).

8 Charles Keil, *Urban Blues* (Chicago: University of Chicago Press, 1966), p. 170.

9 Berger, *op. cit.,* pp. 54–57.

10 Howard Brotz, *The Black Jews of Harlem* (New York: The Free Press of Glencoe, 1964), pp. 129–130.

11 One of the most comprehensive studies of the Eastern European heritage of American Jews was written explicitly from the anthropologist's view of culture. See Mark Zborowski and Elizabeth Herzog, *Life Is with People* (New York: International Universities Press, 1952), with an introduction by Margaret Mead.

12 L. Singer, "Ethno-genesis and Negro American's Today," *Social Research,* 29 (1962), 419–432.

13 See K. Stampp, *op. cit.,* for historical evidence on this point.

14 Interview with Ralph Ellison, in Robert Penn Warren, *Who Speaks for The Negro?* (New York: Random House, 1965), pp. 334–336. See also the stimulating and surprisingly neglected collection of essays by Calvin Hernton, *White Papers for White Americans* (New York: Doubleday, 1965).

15 See Harold Isaacs, *The New World of Negro Americans* (New York: The Viking Press, Compass Books Edition, 1964), Part III, pp. 105–322, for an excellent treatment of attitudes toward Africa.

16 Cf. Oscar Handlin, *The Uprooted* (New York: Little, Brown, 1951).

17 Berger, *op. cit.,* p. 56.

18 Hortense Powdermaker, *After Freedom* (New York: The Viking Press, 1939), pp. 259–260.

19 C. Hernton, *op. cit.*

20 A brilliant analysis of this process of cultural imperialism informs Harold Cruse's recent book, *The Crisis of the Negro Intellectual* (New York: William Morrow, 1967).

21 James Baldwin, *Notes of a Native Son* (Boston: Beacon Press, 1955); William M. Kelley, *A Different Drummer* (Garden City: Doubleday, 1962).

22 Keil, *op. cit.,* p. 152.

23 Oscar Lewis, *La Vida* (New York: Random House, 1967), p. xlvii–xlviii.

24 Berger, *op. cit.,* p. 54.

SUGGESTED READINGS

The Autobiography of Malcolm X. New York: Grove Press, 1965.
The life story of one of America's most charismatic black leaders.

Baldwin, James. *Nobody Knows My Name.* New York: Dial, 1961.
Essays on the problems of being black in white America.

Bone, Robert. *The Negro Novel in America.* New Haven: Yale University Press, 1965.
One of the best examinations of the various forms and functions of "Negro" novels.

Brotz, Howard. *The Black Jews of Harlem.* New York: The Free Press, 1964.
A study of a small sect of Harlem dwellers searching for their past. Of special note is the last chapter on "Negro Nationalism."

Cleaver, Eldridge. *Soul on Ice.* New York: McGraw-Hill, 1968.
Poignant essays on life and society by a gifted black writer.

Cronin, E. D. *Black Moses.* Madison: University of Wisconsin Press, 1957.
A biography of Marcus Garvey and commentary on his Universal Negro Improvement Association.

Duberman, Martin B. *In White America.* Boston: Houghton Mifflin, 1964.
A documentary play.

Du Bois, W. E. B. *The Souls of Black Folk.* Chicago, 1903.
The famous Negro leader offers penetrating insights into the marginality of Afro-Americans. The book is available in various paperback editions.

Essien-Udom, E. U. *Black Nationalism.* Chicago: University of Chicago Press, 1962.
An African's assessment of the "Black Muslim" movement and its appeal.

Hill, Herbert, editor. *Anger and Beyond.* New York: Harper & Row, 1966.
A collection of writings by and about black American writers. It includes essays by Robert Bone, Nat Hentoff, LeRoi Jones, and others.

Hughes, Langston, editor. *The Book of Negro Humor*. New York: Dodd, Mead, 1966.
A collection of "black" humor from minstrel days to the present.

Jones, LeRoi. *Blues People*. New York: William Morrow, 1963.
A sociology of music and of the people who make it.

Lincoln, C. Eric. *The Black Muslims in America*. Boston: Beacon Press, 1961.
The first major study of the movement and its program.

INDEX